Art and Intellect in the
Philosophy of Étienne Gilson

Eric Voegelin Institute Series in Political Philosophy

# Art and Intellect in the Philosophy of Étienne Gilson

Francesca Aran Murphy

University of Missouri Press
Columbia and London

Copyright © 2004 by
The Curators of the University of Missouri
University of Missouri Press, Columbia, Missouri 65201
Printed and bound in the United States of America
All rights reserved
5  4  3  2  1    08  07  06  05  04


Library of Congress Cataloging-in-Publication Data

Murphy, Francesca Aran.
    Art and intellect in the philosophy of Étienne Gilson /
Francesca Aran.
        p.    cm. — (Eric Voegelin Institute series in political
philosophy)
    Includes bibliographical references (p.    ) and index.
    ISBN 0-8262-1536-X (alk. paper)
    1. Gilson, Étienne, 1884–1978.  2. Philosophers—
France—Biography.  I. Title.  II. Series.
B2430.G474M87   2004
194—dc22
[B]                                                    2004047942


♾™ This paper meets the requirements of the American
National Standard for Permanence of Paper for Printed
Library Materials, Z39.48, 1984.

Designer: Stephanie Foley
Typesetter: Phoenix Type, Inc.
Printer and binder: The Maple-Vail Book Manufacturing Group
Typefaces: ITC Galliard and Snell Roundhand

Publication of this book has been assisted by a generous
contribution from the Eric Voegelin Institute.

*In memoriam*
David Levy

# Contents

# *Acknowledgments*

Tony Schmitz proofread this book, remedying errors on nearly every page: what can I say? I would particularly like to thank Fr. Joe Komanchak for stimulating conversations that helped me to deepen my knowledge of twentieth-century French theology, and of much else. I have been given much-needed encouragement by Dan Scuiry. Paul Molnar and Philip Rosemann exemplified the virtue of intellectual charity in their creative criticisms. When I fell ill in the middle of writing, Leila and Leslie McFarland, Pauline Jacobson, Fr. Richard Cropsey, and Lotte Gaberle behaved like angels. My mother never fails in her support of anything that I write; none of my literary endeavors would be possible without her. I could never have written a book about a man who devoted his vast intellectual energies to the defense of Christian philosophy without having known a great Christian philosopher, Dallas Willard. I am most grateful to all of these kind friends.

Clio is a Muse simply because she invents endlessly, and, as indeed she boasts in her franker moments, reinvents the past.

—Étienne Gilson, *Choir of Muses*

# Art and Intellect in the
# Philosophy of Étienne Gilson

# *Introduction*

## Time and Eternity

This is an "intellectual life" of Étienne Gilson. The "intellect" follows a thematic order, but lives are chronological. I have tried to give both chronology and thematicism their due, for certain intellectual themes shaped Gilson's life. The thematic currents all flow from one historical fact, the French modernist crisis. Gilson was an impressionable nineteen year old when the modernist crisis began in France. It was like being nineteen during the French Revolution, or like being a real-life Johnny Tremaine at the start of the American Revolution. One can hardly imagine a real Johnny Tremaine putting it all behind him when the War of American Independence concluded. This book tries to show how Gilson was marked throughout his life by his reactions to modernism.

If Gilson's reaction had been straightforward, it would have been easy to describe, but perhaps not worth describing. If a historian could play with counterfactuals, one would say that if, between 1903 and 1914, Gilson had been simply *for* the modernists, or if he had simply been *against* them, he would have made no contribution to twentieth-century philosophy. In fact, his response made for a serious internal conflict. Gilson was a devout and loyal French Catholic who felt a great sympathy with the modernists. So modernism worked in him like the grit in the oyster, producing a pearl.

There were four great issues at work in the French modernist crisis, each of which played out in Gilson's life and thought. The first—the political theme—is the most difficult to grasp for people who are not natives of France. It concerns the battle of many French Catholics against "social modernism," or political liberalism. Nearly all French Catholics resented the French Revolution; many do so to this day. In the minds of many of Gilson's contemporaries, both believers and their adversaries, monarchism went along with Catholic faith and republicanism was inimical to it. Opposition to everything that they imagined to have resulted from the Revolution, such as the emancipation of Jews, was ingrained in the French Catholic

1

mentality. Thus, they lined up against the Jewish Dreyfus: being anti-Dreyfus, and anti-Semitic, was a natural deduction from the monarchist creed.

In 1903 this conviction was repaid by the decision of a French republican government to expel all the religious orders from France. Thousands of nuns and priests were compelled to abandon the work of centuries and depart for Belgium, the Channel Islands, England, and Canada. If you can imagine the reaction of American Catholics to a decision of the U.S. Supreme Court to expel the religious orders from the United States, that could help to put you in the picture; but you would have to consider also that this Catholic versus secular tug-of-war for the heart of France had been going on since Voltaire, that secular schools were the temples of French republican culture, and that nearly all religious school teaching had been in the hands of priests and nuns.

Now ask, how would the American Catholic media and episcopate respond to vociferous American *critics* of the decision to expel the religious orders from the United States? And what if those critics did not happen to be Catholic or even believers in God? What happened in France, with the strong encouragement of the papacy, was that they welcomed with open arms the backing of atheist monarchists like Charles Maurras. To them, Maurras' atheism was far less significant than his pro-Catholic ideology, the result of his monarchism.

What was Gilson to make of this? Loyalty to the church and to friends was one of the deepest character traits of this fierce but humble man. He was not sufficiently pompous to imagine that one could stand outside or above the conflict, and the situation did not allow for noncombatants. Gilson trod the boards of French intellectual life for sixty years, and he waited until 1965, when he was eighty-one years old, to criticize the church in public. He revered priests. Every letter that Gilson wrote to lifelong priest friends opens, "Mon réverend Père." He said he considered priests as "sacred animals": for him, the curtain between lay and cleric symbolized the sanctity of the church. In 1902, Gilson no more wanted to see the church uprooted from France than to pull out his fingernails. He took no delight in the expulsion of the orders from France. Equally, Gilson detested Charles Maurras and his atheist monarchism. Gilson was a republican. He was a not a thoroughbred political animal; the philosopher racehorse is seldom much good at practical politics. Gilson was sure, however, that French Catholic monarchism was impractical and spiritually dangerous.

This assurance worked on him in an affective, emotional way. It made him take intellectual decisions on the existential level, before he began to turn them into unemotive prose. Gilson's great friend, Jacques Maritain—

a pro-monarchist until 1928—composed deliciously affective texts, which sprang from cold intellectual intuition of principles. By contrast, the elegant, lucid philosophy of Gilson's books emerged, not just from his heart, but from his viscera.

So that they could ally with the atheists who, like them, detested social modernism and who wrote pro-Catholic propaganda, French Catholic monarchists had to conceive of "nature" and "grace" as different worlds. How else should they find common ground with their nonbelieving allies? If both were right that political liberalism is wrong, then both must have achieved that insight on the "neutral" ground of *natural* political philosophy and ethics. As they saw it, the only difference was that the Catholics had grace as well. Gilson's rejection of this separation of nature and grace was visceral; his philosophical theology posed a direct alternative to it, one he claimed to find in Saint Thomas Aquinas.

Between 1903 and 1914, modernists like Alfred Loisy were brought to book for "fideism." Fido is a faithful dog, from the Latin "I believe," and *fideism* is literally "faith-ism." When they excommunicated Loisy as a fideist, the church authorities did so because they thought he was taking the rational substructure of philosophical argument away from doctrine, basing doctrine purely on *belief* stripped of reason. From time to time throughout his career, Gilson took delight in being called a fideist. The second theme generated by the modernist crisis is reason and faith, faith and reason. Which way round does it go?

Gilson was no irrationalist. He was a great debater, brilliantly skilled in reasoned argument. So why was he so determined to make faith and mystery the hinge on which reason turns? It was not because he rejected reason or philosophy, but because he felt that something was being forgotten when fideism was condemned during the modernist crisis, namely, the mystery of faith. Gilson considered that, if the *mystery* of faith had not already been swept under the carpet for decades by an excessively rationalist Thomism, men like Loisy would not have denied the use of reason within theology. Somewhat as the anti-Dreyfusard campaigning of Catholic ideologues created a republican counterreaction, so neo-Scholasticism got the comeback it deserved in irrationalist philosophies. The fact that Maurras fought and won a campaign to have the books of Gilson's intellectual father, Henri Bergson, set on the Index on the grounds that Bergsonism amounted to fideism did not endear the rationalist attitude to Gilson. In his second book, written before the First World War, about Thomas Aquinas, he insisted that the saint was first and foremost a theologian. Christian reason can no more be separated from faith, for Gilson, than nature from grace. This came to the fore in Gilson's defense of "Christian philosophy." For him, Christian philosophy is created neither by Christians who wander into philosophy by accident nor by philosophers whose Christianity is accidental to their thought, but by believers who think *by means of* their faith.

Many contemporary Christians would buy into "Gilson the fideist" a little too quickly for his liking. For those believers who have made a ghetto peace with nonbelief, revealed faith is without philosophical foundations. They give up the claim that revelation tells them what reality is like and say, "This is reality *for me,* a believer." Gilson, too, was a nonfoundationalist. He did not think we can intuit principles on which to build the house of reason and to which construction the rooftop of faith can be added. But he was a nonfoundational *realist.* He claimed that revealed faith stimulates better arguments for metaphysical and epistemological realism than any non-Christian philosophy can reach. Thus, the third theme of Gilson's life is realism. For Gilson, Thomas Aquinas was a great philosophical realist *because he was a theologian.*

The evangelical flaw in the "Christian fideist temperament" is not that it lacks the zest for a good argument—who could accuse Tertullian, Kierkegaard, or Stanley Hauerwas of that? The flaw in much Christian fideism is that it is inward looking. Many Christian fideists devote their evangelical talents, not to communicating the Gospel of Christ, but to arguing with other Christians, telling them to stop being so rationalist and foundationalist. Pascal is an exception, and Gilson is his heir. He was a ceaseless, dynamic apologist for Christian philosophy. He saw the public defense of Christianity as part of the territory of being a Catholic professor in a secular French university, much as any good chess player knows that the only way to win the game is not just to defend but to attack. Does that mean that Gilson put rational argument at the top of his priorities? Not precisely.

Gilson had an aesthetic perception that the rationalist presentation of Christian faith that detonated the modernist crisis was *ugly.* On the other hand, he sensed *beauty* in the philosophy of Bergson—in particular, a musical sort of beauty, a sense of existence and reality as being beautiful in the way that, for Gilson, the operas of Wagner are entrancing. Gilson allies the real to the beautiful, in whose face he saw mystery. Bergson thought that the lesson of his own philosophy was about how we know reality: he staked his claim on a "musical" perception of reality, as against the tone-deaf positivism of his day. But Gilson, a realist from the bones, heard Bergson say that reality itself is musical. He was not satisfied with his own presentations of what it means "to be" until he was able to articulate existence as a springing tempo.

The fourth issue is time and eternity. It entered the consciousness of early twentieth-century Catholicism through the historical study of scripture, the revelation of the eternal God. In 1900, Catholic Church authorities were suspicious of the historical study of scripture, thinking it dangerous because it seemed to undermine the *absolute* quality of scriptural revelation. When Loisy tried his hand at biblical criticism, he noticed a disparity between the Thomist conception of revelation, as timeless truth, and the slow emergence of religious ideas over time that he saw in Old and New Testament history. Because the two struck him as irreconcilable, and because an evolutionary history was the more attractive to him, Loisy rejected the Thomist conception of revelation. He felt that revelation is living and growing, like a root vegetable, whereas Thomism canned the temporality and the life out of it. Loisy wanted to "historicize" Christian doctrines, and so got himself condemned, in 1907, as a "historicist." He was looking for a livelier way of understanding God's revelation than as the transmission of timeless truths. But the way he expressed the idea that doctrines are alive and growing smelled to the authorities of relativism, making the words in scripture just relative to their time, not the revelation of the eternal God.

The question was serious for Gilson and planted a seed that took forty years to bear fruit, so difficult did he find it to create an analogy that balanced the claims of history and eternity. The aim of Gilson's musical, "existential Thomism" was to put across an idea of God's eternal being as active, a supernatural "fourth-dimension" of divine vitality. For the truth is that when Thomas is defining *revelation,* he says that revelation is expressed in timeless propositions, and when he is defining *faith,* he compares God's eternity to youthfulness and vigor.

It is not just the historical fact of the modernist crisis that creates the four themes of this book, but Gilson's reaction to that fact. If we want to know how modernism affected Gilson, we need to explain the various issues in the French modernist crisis, of course; but we must also recognize what Gilson thought and felt about those facts. One has to surrender oneself to time in order to allow it to reveal its goods, and in a sense, one must trust one's subject. The philosopher who most influenced Gilson was Bergson, and Gilson got it into his head that Bergson was an Aristotelian. Whether Bergson was or not, I do not attempt to say. All that matters for the purposes of this book is that Gilson believed that Bergson taught him to be a metaphysical realist. One will get "Aristotle" out of Bergson, not by reading him blind or through the filter of modern Bergson scholarship, but by reading him through Gilson's eyes. Gilson appears to have felt that, between 1905 and 1914, the church's reaction to the emergence of modernism was not especially well managed. I do not attempt to portray the controversy from every possible perspective—or perhaps I should say I *did* try, just as I tried to put down an objective description of the contents of Bergson's writings. Most of it had to come out. In order to get inside what formed Gilson's mind, one had to trust his own perspective, and that meant describing matters as he saw them. Ronald Knox or Jacques Maritain were made Catholics by their approval of the church's firm stand against relativism between 1900 and 1915. Gilson's life-line is very different, because, unlike them, he was *already* wholly Catholic and was disturbed by how the church treated the people it called modernists. Is it possible to use texts that Gilson composed up to sixty years after the event as genuine testimonies to what he experienced during the modernist crisis? I have come to trust such late documents, because they offer the best explanation of why he reconceived Thomism, presenting it as a theology whose truth is eternal and yet living.

So far as understanding what made Gilson *who he was* is concerned, we need to stand in his shoes. In that sense, the historian's task is like the phenomenologist's. But if we remained on the descriptive level in ascertaining Gilson's *achievements,* all we would know at the end of it was what he thought he achieved, and so what? Gilson always claimed that his achievement lay in giving *the* accurate historical interpretation of the thought of Thomas Aquinas. Even if that is objectively the case, history moves on. History is a positive science in that respect. Gilson said himself, in 1939, that his first book, about Descartes, published thirty years earlier, was "now out of date." He did not rewrite his own book on Saint Thomas seven times over sixty years because he thought history and interpretation stand still. Building on the revolution in understanding Aquinas, which Gilson helped to create, historians now know more about the historical Thomas Aquinas than he did. You will not be hearing much here about the "true" interpretation of Thomas's theology because this is a book, not about Gilson the mediaeval historian, which is where memory has currently buried him, but about Gilson the living philosopher, who taught timeless truths. What matters about Gilson's Thomism is not so much that it was true to Thomas as that it was true to reality.

Gilson's combination of "fideism" and realism issued not only in the historical description of Aquinas as a theologian but also in a very interesting Thomist philosophy. As a seasoned and reasoned opponent of rationalism, Gilson realized more than any other twentieth-century Thomist that doing philosophy is not a matter of constructing a system. It is, rather, a matter of experiencing reality and thinking about it. Thomas spoke of the beautiful as "that which pleases when seen." Instead of devising a "theory of every-thing" a priori from Thomist principles, Gilson made a series of ad hoc philosophical excursions into those avenues of reality which especially pleased him. And if reality is, in fact, more of a jungle of fiercely ad hoc animals than a stuffed system, this approach made him a better philosopher than the Thomist systematicians.

If Gilson was a Thomist, he was one who claimed he learned how to write about Thomas from Lucien Lévy-Bruhl's lectures on David Hume; one whose first great book was about Franciscan spirituality; one whose late pres-entation of the arguments for God's existence was influenced by Hume's *Essay on Human Understanding* and who drew on Pascal for his description of the vocation of the Christian intellectual. Gilson presented a way of doing Christian philosophy that was not prey to the pitfalls of the opposite error to fideism—rationalism. Very few Thomist philosophers have achieved this. To do so, one needs not only to nod piously at the "mystery of faith" but to experience reality as mysterious. And that takes some grit in the pearl.

A historical inquiry into Thomas and an inquiry into Étienne Gilson make for different narratives: I have planted my themes and chronology in the twentieth century. Therefore, the "Victorian voice-over," George Eliot's timeless moralizings about her characters' vicissitudes, had to be avoided. Having chosen the historical-narrative mode, it became impossible to make a detour into a timeless realm in which I could compare and contrast, for example, Gilson's analysis of Thomas's texts with those of later schools. This book is about Gilson, and not about Aquinas, Bonaventure, Descartes. A book following a synchronic order could have had a timeless chapter about the textual rights and wrongs of Gilson's interpretation of Aquinas or Siger of Brabant; one that grappled with the diachronies of Gilson's life could not. The only way to present the historian would have been to step out of history and test his historical theses against current historical hypotheses. That would have meant doubly stepping outside of the time in which Gilson lived, into the past that he studied, and into analyses of the past that post-date his work.

We begin by jumping into the cauldron of the modernist crisis, the epoch in which Gilson grew to intellectual maturity. Here we see all four of the great themes of his life, the Catholic republicanism that led him to believe in the intrinsic relation of nature to grace, and thus of reason to faith, his aesthetic realism, always directed to *mystery,* and his sense of the dramatic, mobile quality of existence. In the subsequent chapters, the themes branch off, reappearing on stage at their own volition, for a person's biography is a spiritual drama but it is not a continuous *story.* Novelists tell stories, but biographers cannot quite do so, because human lives are too ad hoc for such a treatment.

Gilson served his apprenticeship in philosophical realism by studying textual, historical facts. We will see how Gilson's first, historical studies of Descartes and Thomas Aquinas led him toward a realistic epistemology, which does not provide its own foundation, or "script," but requires the prompting of faith. Gilson worked as a historian for a quarter of a century before he began writing philosophy books. Rather than noting all of Gilson's historical writings, the book leads in with a few that best symbolize his historical research, like his studies of Descartes and Thomas. Chronology enables one to show how one thing leads to another, and I have selected for description those Gilsonian histories that had some causative influence on his philosophical thought.

In the midst of the modernist crisis, the Parisian Gilson learned to love the new art forms that were being invented by Picasso, the cubists, and the expressionists. Appreciation for the modernist painters helped Gilson to write his first truly beautiful historical book, his study of the Franciscan Bonaventure. However much he protested the historical accuracy of his Thomism, Gilson's own philosophy was profoundly colored by a Franciscan spirituality that inches towards the sur-real and trans-rational. In the 1920s, Thomism became fashionable in France, its promoters putting themselves forward as defenders of reason in their culture war against "irrationalism." Gilson was at edge with this self-understanding. It was in the mid-1920s that Gilson wrote his first defense of the intrinsic urge of the natural human mind for supernatural vision.

If this set him somewhat apart from contemporaries like Jacques Maritain, the debate about the possibility of Christian philosophy that took place in France in the early 1930s made the two men friends. It also initiated Gilson's transition from historian to philosopher. He began to argue that Christianity *can* combine with philosophy, because Christians make better realists than do their nonbelieving friends. Henri de Lubac was almost alone in appreciating the uniqueness of this presentation of Christian philosophy, that Gilson was staking the debate on the heightened metaphysical reality of nature as revealed in the Old Testament scripture, not on the epistemological foundations or spiritual edification supplied to the philosopher by his religious beliefs. In that debate, and in the brilliant books that flowed out of it, Gilson used arguments that look historical but are really neat philosophy, a philosophy of "graced factuality." It was in the mid-1930s that America recognized Gilson's achievement as one who had shown the unity of faith and reason. This book contends that American Catholics saw a valuable part of the man, but not the whole. Great actor that he was, he was well-enough attuned to his audience to know what they could hear and what they could not. The "Loisy problem" was outside their auditory range.

As the Second World War approached and the drums of the French rationalists beat louder in their support for Hitler's campaign against social modernism, Gilson argued ever more clearly that realism is grounded, not in the epistemic clarity of intuition, but in the simple mystery of facts. This elite intellectual gave some energy in the mid-1930s to writing popular social and political journalism, trying to turn the tide away from the French dream of a new dictator who would issue the command for the entire French population to attend the Mass. Some of Gilson's historical, mediaevalist opinions, such as his conceptions of Averroës and Dante, have been surpassed by contemporary scholarship. But if one sees these writings for what they are, as products of the late 1930s, their timeless value emerges. For now one can see what Gilson was trying to get at, politically and philosophically, by posing Averroës as a rationalist and Dante as an advocate of an emperor who need take no spiritual, or moral, advice from the church.

It was not by accident that Gilson discovered his existential Thomism in occupied Paris in 1942. It was the summit of forty years' thought about the errors of paleo-conservativism and about how to ground reason in a faith to which the call of the transrational sounds like music. Gilson's priest friends, like the Dominican Marie-Dominique Chenu, had followed him in working out historical, factual, and existential interpretations of Aquinas's thought. Others, like de Lubac, had taken his idea that grace speaks from within nature to their hearts. De Lubac's *Surnaturel* (1946) can be seen as a successor volume to Gilson's defenses of Christian philosophy. Thus there came about, in the late 1940s, the French "nouvelle théologie," followed almost immediately by its condemnation. De Lubac's "intrinsicism" was stigmatized in the encyclical *Humani Generis* (1950). It was at a Thomist Congress in 1950 that one of the triumphant opponents of new theologies indicated to Gilson that *L'être et l'essence* had the modernist tinge. At the very same time, the remnants of Charles Maurras' monarchist party began a campaign against Gilson that led to the loss of his retirement pension.

Throughout the 1950s, a rather embittered Gilson began to move still further away from this reactionary Thomism, with its rejection of a "graced nature," to form an epistolary friendship with de Lubac, the disgraced author of *Surnaturel,* and to write a sideways attack on what he saw as a contemporary, political version of "extrinsicism" in Maritain's propagandizing for world government. He did not just compose counterblasts, but a philosophy of particularity.

He also turned the rudder of his existential philosophy explicitly toward the mystery of the beautiful, writing seven books about philosophy of art and aesthetics between 1950 and 1967. The beautiful was the boundless sea on which he sailed in these years in which, his teaching now on one side, he could write and meditate about what really mattered. These were also what I call "grumpy years" for Gilson; for the only aspect of the spirituality of the Second Vatican Council with which this paradoxical Pascalian Thomist resonated was the encouragement it gave to philosophical pluralism. As Randolph Churchill tactlessly remarked to Pius XII, "None of us is infallible." We conclude by briefly considering the vivid current life of Gilson's thought within contemporary theology, especially that inclined to theological aesthetics.

The four themes are, in fact, continuous throughout Gilson's life; but chronologically, they cross and recross, appear, disappear and reappear. I tell this diachronic tale, which does not make a neatly rounded "story," because the spiritual drama of a man's life is the most direct way of making the philosophy accessible. Gilson might concur with Hans Urs von Balthasar's remark that the truths of Christianity are summarized, not in the catechisms, but in the lives of the saints.

# 1

# Draper's Son, Catholic and Republican

A crisis occurred in France in 1902 through 1914—a crisis about modernism. It affected Étienne Gilson at the time, and for always. To understand him, we have to look at what happened; but we need to do more, and, in a way, less, than that. The more objectively photorealistic a war movie is, the less true it is to the *experience* of war. Lacking the omniscience of the movie camera, combatants only see what is going on in their immediate vicinity. An aerial and yet telescopically naturalistic overview of the modernist crisis would likewise play false to how it was experienced by one nineteen-year-old French onlooker, Étienne Gilson. An exhaustively objective account of modernism would not necessarily help us to understand how Gilson felt about it. What we need is not just a detached comprehension of what modernism actually was but also what Gilson believed was going on. What influenced Gilson was what the modernist crisis looked like to him, and what it represented to him. He was nineteen when it began and thirty when it simmered out. He was to have a near lifelong sympathy for Alfred Loisy, one of the authors of French theological modernism. Gilson could write vitriolically about French paleo-conservatives seventy years after the events that we shall now describe. We will pinpoint several different viewing positions on modernism and observe where Gilson stood in relation to them. The first is the cultural and political environment of the French modernist crisis.

## The Cultural and Political Environment of Modernism

A purely theological definition of modernism is not the best place to begin, because what people experienced at the time was a thicket of entangled theological and *political* issues. So the first angle on the modernist crisis relates to its cultural and political concomitants in France. To understand what was going on politically, we have to retrace our steps to 1792.

In the textbooks of the history of ideas, modernity begins in the *cogito*

11

of Descartes. French Catholics of the early twentieth century dated the Fall from Grace at 1792, the year designated by their Patriot countrymen as Year 1 of the Revolutionary calendar. Catholics later associated the post-Revolutionary order with the political enfranchisement of Jews and Protestants. In 1801, the Emperor Napoleon and Pope Pius VII signed a concordat, which gave the French government the right to select the bishops of France. The papacy retained a veto over the nominees. It was seldom exercised. The concordat made the French state the paymaster of its Catholic clergy. Discomforted neither by their economic subjugation to the state nor by the loss of the autonomy of the episcopate, the Catholics of France were offended by the political freedoms granted to others. Of *Liberté, Égalité,* and *Fraternité,* it was *Liberté* that stuck in the gullets of the faithful. In the hearts of most French Catholics, and equally in the imaginations of most republicans, Catholicism and political liberalism were irreconcilable. The Catholics objected, not to the clergy's having become state employees, but to the fact that the state did not employ a king. A cleric who called himself a republican "was looked upon as a traitor to his priesthood."[1]

The anticlericals and the churched each made an act of faith in a political order. The great French positivist sociologist Auguste Comte argued that positivism would not hold society together unless it acquired a religious aura; society must now feel for its scientific directors the awe it had once invested in its confessors. Radical republicanism was inspired by this Comtean vision. On the other hand, while offering notional assent to the creeds promulgated by the ecumenical councils, French Catholics gave real and imaginative assent to a creed that included an affirmation of the divine right of kings. Just as the positivist and republican ideal of politics was theological, so the Catholic monarchists' ideal of religion was political.

The fact that the republicans and the Catholics of France were two warring sides of the same coin is symbolized by the Catholics' acquisition of Charles Maurras as an apologist. Maurras was an atheist whose intellectual master was Auguste Comte. He admired Catholicism for its political illiberalism. For a quarter of a century, from around 1900 until 1927, Maurrasianism and a very large section of French Catholic opinion found common political ground.

The strongholds of the French church were in the rural south; the urban and industrialized north belonged to the denizens of reason and progress. Caroline Juliette Rainaud was a Burgundian, born in 1851 in "Cravant, a

---

1. Chadwick, *History of the Popes,* 294.

small medieval village in the department of l'Yonne about halfway between Auxerre and Avallon." That is, she came from the south, which in the 1790s had been the military stronghold of "White" resistance to the French Revolution, and retained that allegiance. Caroline Rainaud attended a primary school run by Ursuline nuns, owing her religious education to Mother Saint-Dieudonné, who called her "one of my first daughters and one of the most faithful."[2] She was good with her hands, a facility that came to the fore when she married Paul Gilson, a Parisian merchant. Caroline presided over the draper's shop; she was the controlling center of the union. The marriage of Catholic south and mercantile, intellectual north bore fruit in a family of five sons. The third son was born in their flat above the shop, in 1884. Abbé Escaré baptized him Étienne. From the time that he was mature enough to form an opinion, the boy carried both the flag of the republic and that of the church. With a mother who created clothes and hats, Gilson's first impression of his religious faith came from an artist.

Leo XIII (Pope from 1878 to 1903) was not disposed to subscribe to the Gallican creed. He wanted French Catholics to cease to identify themselves as the victims of a revolution past and as the victors of a revolution to come. He wanted them to ally themselves with the state to which they belonged. Many of the 162,000 clergy and nuns in France were teachers, both in religious and in state schools.[3] In 1879, France elected a republican government, whose minister of education, Jules Ferry, was a "free-thinker to his finger-tips." He asserted the control of the state over its schools. Leo XIII's initiative for republican-Catholic ralliement came about in the face of a government determined to exercise its right to regulate its clerical employees and, upon their inability to comply with the altered laws, to expel them from France. Many Jesuits preferred expulsion to relinquishing their educational tasks. Instead of rebuking the government, Leo XIII urged French Catholics to reconcile themselves to the republic. "By the State," he said in *Rerum Novarum* (1891), "We here understand, not any particular form of government prevailing in this or that nation," as, for example, the *ancien régime,* "but the State as rightly apprehended; that is to say, any government conformable in its institutions to right reason and natural law, and to th[e] dictates of the Divine wisdom." In 1892, in *Aux milieu des sollicitudes,* Leo "tried to persuade the French church to be less uncompromising."

2. Shook, *Gilson,* 3–5.
3. McLeod, *Religion and the People of Western Europe,* 49.

This papal exhortation, known as the *Encyclique du Ralliement,* was diluted in its episcopal dissemination.[4]

Alfred Dreyfus (1859–1935) was a Jewish officer who was accused in 1893 of conspiring against the French government. The "Dreyfus Affair" dragged on until 1906, when, the evidence against him having been shown to be forged, he was pardoned. Conceiving Dreyfus's allies as liberals with no love for the armed forces, and being profoundly anti-Semitic, a majority of French Catholics were noisily convinced of Dreyfus's guilt. Even Catholic observers, such as Yves Simon, considered that "the persecution of the Catholics at the beginning of this century was determined in large measure by the attitude of the Catholics during the Dreyfus case."[5] That is, French Catholics brought the subsequent vengeance of the seculars down on their own collective collar.

Leo XIII had encouraged the faithful to engage in the print media. The contributors to the *Univers,* edited by Louis Veuillot, required little papal stimulation in their mission to extirpate liberalism within and without the church. Founded in 1840, the Augustinians of the Assumption took, in addition to the customary vows of poverty, chastity, and obedience, "a vow to struggle mightily for the kingdom of God." In 1883, they established *La Croix,* a daily newspaper with a circulation of half a million. *La Croix* purveyed the "most extreme journalism" ever composed by a "religious order in the history of Christendom" and on behalf of French Christendom.[6]

At the outset of the Dreyfus Affair, the editor of *La Croix,* Father Bailly, stated in an editorial: "Free thought, advocate of the Jews, the Protestants, and all the enemies of the Church, stands in the dock with Zola, and the Army is forced, in spite of itself, to open fire against it." In 1899, Leo "compared Dreyfus to Jesus on Calvary." He required some of the crucifiers to cease editing *La Croix.* The Augustinians' antics continued and played into the hands of the republican government, which took them to court in 1900 on a charge of "having subsidized Nationalist candidates in elections" and had them convicted, and dissolved.[7]

In 1901 a bill on the "Contract of Association," ostensibly concerned with the freedom of association of clubs and syndicates, was used to limit

---

4. Chadwick, *History of the Popes,* 293, 298.
5. Simon, *The Road to Vichy,* 70.
6. Chadwick, *History of the Popes,* 383, 384.
7. Weber, *Action Française,* 33; Chadwick, *History of the Popes,* 385–86; Bury, *France, 1814–1940,* 194.

that freedom: associations containing foreigners or governed by them must seek government approval. Those religious orders and congregations that failed to gain authorization would be dissolved. An additional clause forbade a member of an unauthorized congregation to teach: by December 1902, twelve thousand schools had been closed. Most congregations were refused permission for free association; fifty-four male congregations and eight-one female ones were dissolved. The dispersal of the religious orders began. In 1904 a new law forbade teaching by any religious congregation, illegal or legitimate. Jesuits, Dominicans, and others had to relocate their own houses of study outside of French soil, the anti-republican flame burning ever the brighter in their embittered breasts.

The education minister directing these reforms was Emile Combes. A former seminarian, he was Comte *redivivus* and in political power. He was "a fanatical anti-Catholic who...had a dream of a national Church where all the curés would be like Rousseau, where Rome would have no authority but the State would direct a religiously tinged moral code. This could not be achieved without exploding Catholicism; which he wished to do."[8] Leo XIII had meantime been succeeded by Pius X, renowned for his handling of the modernist crisis.

## The Church's Conception of Modernism: Faith, Reason, and Politics

Another angle on modernism is how it looked to the church: that is, quite simply, as heresy. At the First Vatican Council (1869–1879), the constitution *Dei Filius* had affirmed that the existence of God can be rationally demonstrated. *Dei Filius* condemned fideism, the notion that the existence of God is sheerly a matter of faith. In *Aeterni Patris* (1879), Leo XIII upheld Saint Thomas Aquinas as the exemplar of the Catholic mind, which elaborates the truths of reason in the light of faith. *Aeterni Patris* calls for a reform of "philosophy, in order that sacred theology may receive and assume the nature, form, and genius of a true science."[9] The Pope's ideal of faithful reasoning was effected in the manner of officialdom. The management of seminaries changed hands. The new Scholastics produced a diet of textbooks that were handy for training curial bureaucrats. These manuals appear to have been wanting in the way of the intellectual and spiritual formation of priests.

8. Chadwick, *History of the Popes,* 387.
9. Bourke, "'Aeterni Patris,'" 7.

Neo-Scholasticism was the means through which the church articulated its own theology and by which it discharged its objections to modernism. The Scholastics pictured the Bible as a series of propositions dictated by God to Moses, the prophets, and the apostles, each divine dictate containing in full the dogmas that were later to be built upon them by the Catholic Church. And so, those with a Scholastic mindset enculpated certain historians for distinguishing too clearly between the original meaning of biblical documents and the dogmas that the church had read out of the Bible. Because they seemed to tie the truth content of the biblical documents to the era of their production, these men were also charged with historicism. A related charge was propounding an immanentist conception of God, that is, conceiving the divine as the force driving the historical process of revelation forward.

Alfred Loisy (1857–1940) records the occasion upon which, "in his most majestic manner," Cardinal Richard "lift[ed] his hand impressively and said: '*You are a subjectivist!*'"[10] Subjectivizing religious faith was another charge. Fideism was also a cause for indictment as a modernist. Others were condemned for arguing that Catholic political culture must take a modern and not a mediaeval form. Loisy would be excommunicated because he was believed to be a subjectivist, a fideist, a historicist who had separated the content of the Bible from that of Christian dogma, and an immanentist. These numerous crimes amounted, in the eyes of the church, to undermining the objective and supernatural basis of Christianity.

The modernist crisis could be said to be about theological ideas, like those expressed in Loisy's *L'évangile et l'église,* published in 1903. But Loisy was not especially fortunate in his timing. The fact that *L'évangile et l'église* was published when the French church was under siege from a republican government meant that church authorities conflated theological and political error. The embattled church authorities perceived their different assailants as one single monster. Politics tinged the French church's "theological" conception of modernism. Secular movements seized the opportunity to settle their own political scores by denouncing other lay people, some non-Catholic, for modernism; they were heartily thanked by the church for so doing. French modernism had its own cultural "*haeccitas*": what the church in France saw itself as fighting was, simultaneously, theological heresy and political error.

Catholic anti-modernism was not the condemnation of a single book, but a basic option, the decision to set one's philosophical compass against

10. Loisy, *My Duel with the Vatican,* 254.

fideism, subjectivism, historicism, and political liberalism. Pius X's encyclical *Pascendi* (1907) decreed that what "We are pleased to name 'the Council of Vigilance'... be instituted without delay" in every diocese. In order to quell the storm, seasick ecclesial bureaucrats set up a new "Inquisition" that "methodically burned that Catholic spirit which was attempting... to make contact with the new age." The ferocious measures taken against individuals suspected of modernism aroused great sympathies in some French bystanders. Gilson himself later wrote that, if the "race of denouncers and heresy hunters is not dead... the Modernist crisis was their golden age."[11]

When one takes into account the facts that the innovators were trying to speak to serious problems, that this intention was disregarded by church authorities, and that those authorities erred in some of their denunciations, the modernist crisis can take on the aura of a tragic opera. The atmosphere of the time was emotionally charged, not to say melodramatic. Not only Loisy himself, but many bystanders, some of impeccable orthodoxy, saw him as a victim. This helps us to figure what the modernist crisis *meant* to French Catholics in the first decades of the twentieth century.

Some will find it ironic that the church went to the defense of eternal and objective theological truths while working hand in glove with political thinkers who were not merely secular, but avowedly positivist in their philosophy. But if the reasoning that church officials brought to bear in politics was anything to go by, the two machines of theological "reason," as then conceived, and positivist political "reason" were well fitted out for one another. The church meted out justice to errant Christian theologians in the same way that a state does to political criminals. "Faith" hovered above this *raison d'État* ecclesiastical theology like a ghost cut loose from its machine. Some will have grown up to feel that it was no wonder that men like Loisy reacted into fideism.

## Loisy's Problem: How to Reconcile
## Biblical History with "Eternal" Dogma

Gilson thought that the problems the modernists tackled were real ones, that there was something wrong with the orthodox portrayal of dogma and doctrine. So, of course, did they. A further aspect of modernism is what it meant to those who taught some variant of it. They wanted to

---

11. Pope Pius X, *Pascendi Dominici Gregis,* paras. 3, 18, 35, 55; Balthasar, *The Office of Peter,* 259; Gilson, *Le philosophe et la théologie,* 66.

change the theological outlook of their times, to do theology in a different way. Why? What did they see as being at fault in the late-nineteenth-century exposition of Christian doctrine? Loisy, Lucien Laberthonnière, and Baron von Hügel were each regarded in the Roman Curia as a subjectivist, but each of these men had touched upon subjectivity in answer to different questions. In order to understand what modernism was, one has to ask what questions were in the minds of each protagonist, what problem they were trying to solve, and how.

Alfred Loisy recalled the four years given to the study of Christian doctrine in his diocesan seminary at Châlons-sur-Marne as an era of "mental and moral torture." His first, amiably spiritual professor of philosophy was dismissed on a suspicion of liberalizing his seminarians. The "new professor, a devotee of scholasticism, introduced a textbook exempt from all compromise with modern philosophy." Loisy made a fist at studying the *Summa Theologiae,* but the outcome was unfortunate. Without having learned from the "devotee of scholasticism" that Aquinas's study of the Trinity is the contemplation of a mystery, Loisy found here only "exercises in logical subtlety" that "had upon me the effect of a huge logomachy."[12]

At the bidding of Abbé Escaré, the seven-year-old Étienne Gilson was enrolled by his pious mother in the Petit Séminaire Notre Dame Des Champs, a primary school run by the Christian Brothers. Abbé Victor Thorelle took Étienne under his wing, compelled him to join the choir, and impressed upon him a devotion to Wagner and Claude Debussy.[13]

The writings of Aquinas did not percolate so far as the Petit Séminaire. Gilson left there "after seven years of studies, without having heard even once . . . the name of Saint Thomas Aquinas." Most of the clergy who had any intellectual principles shared them with their secular counterparts. The young philosopher attended Notre Dame des Champs from 1895 until 1902. He said that "I do not know today in any detail what philosophy I would have been taught if I had stayed at Notre Dame des Champs. I know enough to say with certainty that it would not have been that of Thomas Aquinas. . . . The professor of philosophy at the Petit Séminaire was called l'abbé Ehlinger, that at the Lycée was called M. Dereux, but the main difference was that one taught in a soutane and the other in a frock-coat; otherwise they said more or less the same thing. A change of professors

12. Loisy, *My Duel with the Vatican,* 66–67, 78.
13. Shook, *Gilson,* 8.

does not change the history of French philosophy, because both taught with clarity a sort of spiritualism of which Victor Cousin would not disapprove." In 1902, having observed that teachers have long holidays, realizing that he had no vocation to the priesthood, and surmising that he must teach in a secular Lycée, Gilson took himself off for a year-long apprenticeship in the Lycée Henri IV.[14] He had freely selected secular education at just the moment when most of his young compatriots were to be compelled to undergo it. He had received an education that made the neo-Thomist orthodoxy of the time alien to him.

In his seminary at Châlons-sur-Marne, Loisy had taken refuge from Saint Thomas in the study of Hebrew. Once ordained, he went to teach Old Testament literature at the Institut Catholique in Paris. Loisy's doctoral thesis, *The History of the Old Testament Canon* (1889), earned him the odium of the crusading, anti-liberal *Univers*. In "The Biblical Question and the Inspiration of the Scriptures" Loisy denied the Mosaic authorship and the inerrant historicity of the Pentateuch. The investigation of biblical literature and archaeology had taught him two things. The first was that the Bible contains historical inaccuracies. Second, by studying each biblical book in relation to its historical context, Loisy saw that there is an internal *growth* of the religious ideas within the biblical literature.

Contemporary Scholasticism seemed to Loisy to turn a blind eye to the historical study of scripture. How could one reconcile this *historical* data with the *theological* doctrine that the scriptures contain the extra-temporal pronouncements of God? Loisy tried to do so by claiming that "the absolute notion of Biblical inspiration"[15] is a Protestant, not a Catholic, tenet. A church can evolve in a way that a revealed proposition cannot. Loisy imagined that the idea that revelation is given in slow stages to a historical community chosen by God was one to which Catholics might instinctually turn. Far from it: Loisy's writings aroused the concern of the cardinal archbishop of Paris. He departed in disgrace from the Institut Catholique just before Leo XIII issued *Providentissimus* (1893), which reaffirmed the divine wording of the scriptures.

14. Gilson, *God and Philosophy*, xii; Gilson, *Le philosophe et la théologie*, 22–23. In 1826, Victor Cousin wrote to the best known of German philosophers, "Hegel, tell me the truth. I shall pass to my country as much as it can understand." The idealist ungallantly replied. "M. Cousin has taken a few fish from me, but he has well and truly drowned them in his sauce." Cited in Zeldin, *France, 1848–1945*, 114.

15. Loisy, *My Duel with the Vatican*, 149–50.

While Adolf Harnack made use of his Chair of Theology in Berlin to define *religion* as a moral inspiration for individuals, a convent chaplain was composing a treatise to demonstrate that his own social and evolutionary conception of inspiration makes better sense. Loisy thought that the current state of biblical studies compelled believers to a choice between Harnack's liberal Protestantism and a Catholicism cognizant of its own *historical* roots. As he saw it, the choice was between reducing Christianity to a moralism that ejected Hebraic history from Christian theology, as Harnack did, or accepting a gradualist notion of inspiration and thereby retaining the Old Testament. A gradual inspiration struck him as the kosher Catholic option. This was not what most Catholic professors of theology thought. Loisy believed that they avoided the decision by extracting an ahistorical revelation from the scriptures, ignoring the historical conditioning of the human authors of scripture.

The Thomist seminary professors considered that their conception of revelation was rational. They conceived it as God-imparted propositions so as to defend the objectivity and thus the truth of divine revelation. But Loisy believed that their devotion to rationality merely paralleled the rationalism of their secular contemporaries. One of Loisy's unpublished chapters claims that

> the Scholastic theology derives directly from Greek rationalism; only it has introduced a modification, in supposing that it was in virtue of the Christian revelation that truth in its completeness entered the mind of man, and further that the philosophical version of revelation, that is to say, theology itself, was a precise rendering of the divine and ultimate truth. On the other hand, human reason, repulsed by theology and divorced from faith, has never left off believing in its power to solve all problems; it also . . . assumes the right to judge dogmatically concerning matters beyond its province. Nothing copies more slavishly the spirit of certain Scholastic theologians today than the spirit of the popular rationalism.[16]

As Loisy saw it, in 1902, both secular positivism and Scholasticism were "know-all" logical systems. The latter had the additional demerit of leaving no room for faith as such.

Loisy's reason had thriven on positive facts in which his faith put down no roots. His seminaries had trained him as an empirical historian but had not shown him how to connect Loisy the empiricist with Loisy the believer. He saw the problem and was looking for a solution to it. The higher ration-

16. Ibid., 184.

alism of the Scholastic professors had given the first generation of Catholic biblical critics scant means by which to relate contingent facts of history to the "logomachy" of revealed doctrine.

Following Saint Thomas to the letter, the seminary professors taught that scripture is propositionally revealed to its authors, by God. This enabled them to pinpoint the objectivity of faith: the objective data of faith reside in the revealed propositions of scripture. Once one starts conceiving the biblical texts as works of their own time and their contents as developing in history, where does one place the *objectivity* of faith? For the Scholastic rationalists, Christian dogma does not need a tradition in which to grow, because it is already packed inside the box of the Bible. All that remains to be done is to lift the eternal propositions out of the box and deduce their a priori implications.

Loisy picked up Newman's *Essay on Development* in 1895. He read it with "enthusiasm," because it enabled him to argue that faith remains absolute, while history evolves on the level of phenomenal facts that a positive scientist–historian can study. The objective datum of faith, outside and above the "empirical" texts of the Bible, remains the same, even as the biblical writers develop their ideas. Newman's metaphors of "vital," biological growth gave Loisy a way out of the conceptions of tradition of the Protestant and Scholastic rationalists. He would contrast the "living development" of doctrine with its "purely logical elaboration."[17]

Harnack's *The Essence of Christianity* (1900) finds the timeless Gospel in an ethical teaching of love of God as Father, and of neighbor, to be practiced by individuals. It disentangles Jesus's ethical message from its Jewish setting. Since Catholics would naturally regard this as an aberrant conception of Christianity, Loisy imagined he could use it to demonstrate that they needed an evolutionary notion of inspiration. He promptly published a section of his manuscript as *L'évangile et l'église* (1903). His book put itself forward as a defense of Catholicism against liberal Protestantism. Loisy could see that it would do no good to denigrate the Catholic-Thomist conception of a "timeless," propositional Gospel. He would proceed against that target indirectly, by criticizing a liberal Protestant idea of the timeless essence of Christianity.

*L'évangile et l'église* attacks Harnack's "arbitrary" attempts to separate "'what is traditional from what is personal, the kernel from the bark, in the

---

17. Gouhier, *Études sur l'histoire des idées,* 139–42, citing letters of Loisy dated December 4, 26, 1895; ibid., 134–36.

preaching of Jesus about the kingdom of God.'" Harnack avowed that "the spirit and his God are the whole content of the Gospel." But, says Loisy, the Gospel "does not have that individual...coloration." Rather, the Gospel of the Kingdom was informed by the dynamism that would evolve into the Catholic Church: "if there was one thing that was completely alien" to Jesus's "authentic teaching," he writes, "it is the idea of an invisible society, formed...by those who have faith in their heart in the goodness of God.... Jesus' Gospel already had the rudiments of social organization, and that kingdom had already assumed the form of a society. *Jesus announced the kingdom, and it was the Church which came.*'[18]

Harnack was looking behind the Gospels for Jesus who makes sense to intelligent moderns; but by the turn of the century, such Protestant rationalism was coming under fire. In *The Quest for the Historical Jesus* (1900), Albert Schweitzer argued that Jesus taught no moral message that would seem rational to a twentieth-century Protestant theology professor. Jesus was, he said, an apocalyptic visionary who died disappointed of his Father and of the Kingdom he preached. Schweitzer's historical idea of Jesus as an apocalyptic visionary was intended to make it impossible to envisage Jesus as Harnack's rational moralist. Where Harnack offered a rational message that is loosely connected to the historical Jesus, Schweitzer provided a historically grounded picture of Jesus, in which it is irrational for a modern person to believe.

Loisy saw that Harnack's theology could be set up as a stalking horse for any ahistorical system, like the Scholastic version of revelation. Loisy thought that one could use Schweitzer's conclusions against Harnack. He tried to use Schweitzer to prove that ahistorical rationalism does not fit Catholic faith. Loisy was deploying the fact that Schweitzer found the historical Jesus irrational to show that Harnack's rationalist moralism is insufficient to grasping the meaning of Jesus. Schweitzer himself believed, however, that Jesus's apocalypticism makes him "a stranger and an enigma to our times" and that Jesus died disappointed of his kingdom. Loisy's contention is that it takes faith, not reason, to believe in Christ's Church. For faith, Loisy said, "if the idea of the heavenly kingdom is real, the Gospel is divine and God reveals himself in Christ." Conversely, for "the logic of reason, if the idea of the kingdom is inconsistent, the Gospel fails as a divine revelation, Jesus is only a pious man who...died the victim of an error."[19]

18. Loisy, *L'évangile et l'église,* 43–44, 92, 153.
19. Ibid., 101–2.

The abbé-historian was playing a dangerous game. His Catholic critics suspected him of fideism, that is, of making reason and faith mutually exclusive. Loisy seemed to his critics to be denying that there is objective, external, historical evidence for Christian belief. They thought he was disjoining what empirical research knows about biblical history from what faith believes about it. They read Loisy as claiming that what faith believes about Jesus is not to be derived from the empirical facts of Jesus's life.

The Holy Office of the Inquisition and the Congregation of the Index of Prohibited Books swiftly went to work. Pius X called the odious object "religious neo-reformism," that is, neo-Protestantism; it was first termed *modernism* in an admonitory pastoral letter issued by the bishops of North Italy.[20] By December 1903, five of Loisy's books, including *L'évangile et l'église,* had been placed on the Index.

Loisy himself "did not suspect" any problem in treating history on the analogy of physical science.[21] For him, a historical fact was just the "quantitative" datum. Abbé Lucien Laberthonnière tried to ease the dilemma by examining the difference between a "quantitative," or positive, fact and one that is qualitatively significant for faith. The book in which Laberthonnière reapportions the balance between faith and facticity in the Bible, *Le réalisme chrétien et l'idéalisme grec* (1904), was set on the Index in 1906. Laberthonnière's endeavor to distinguish between the quantitative historical fact and the fact that has the quality of faith was seen to subjectivize faith, that is, to displace faith from external facts and relocate it in believers. In the battlefield of the modernist crisis, any attempt to discuss the relationship of faith and history brought one under fire. The relationship between faith and facticity was at issue, and it had become impossible to discuss it.

Those who condemned Laberthonnière believed that historical facts belong among the (nontheological) proofs of faith, like proofs of the existence of God. On no account, then, may one describe the facts to which the Bible refers as data of faith, because one thereby eliminates their externality. Here *externality* means having the quality of "rational—proof to anyone, believer or not." This is why Laberthonnière's *Le réalisme chrétien et l'idéalisme grec* fell foul of the Congregation of the Index of Prohibited Books. Laberthonnière was believed to be subjectivizing the historical proofs, by making them data of faith rather than of reason.

---

20. Chadwick, *History of the Popes,* 354.
21. Gouhier, *Études sur l'histoire des idées en France,* 139.

Gilson was well acquainted with Abbé Laberthonnière and with his book. So was Loisy, who regarded it as an exercise in "Protestant illuminism." If something was remiss in Loisy's theological education, it was not the immediate consequence of the anti-modernist campaign to set it right. "The priests whom we knew personally because they mixed in the world of philosophers and whose religious zeal we admired," said Gilson, "found themselves sooner or later disavowed by the Church, while those who triumphed over them in the name of orthodoxy, proclaimed a philosophy whose language was no longer of our time."[22]

The mentality of the first decade of the twentieth century was positivist. When Thomists defined *revelation,* they sounded rather positivistic: they made eternity sound static, the impartation of revelation look like the mechanical impartation of propositions, and the eliciting of dogma from scripture like the progression of a syllogism. In order to experience sympathy for Loisy, one would have had to possess a more empirical spirit than did the contemporary Scholastics. When biblical scholars studied the biblical history, they used empiricist criteria. When Loisy tried to show that Catholic faith grows, he used an empirical metaphor, the growth of a physical organism. Laberthonnière saw that Loisy's own idea of temporal growth was quantitative, not qualitative. So Loisy himself ended up extricating faith from history. In France, the modernist crisis was thus a violent dialogue of the deaf, among people who shared the same cultural mentality. Was there any other way to picture temporality and eternity, any way of altering the positivist paradigm?

That is how one young French Catholic philosopher experienced the problem of modernism. Gilson sensed that Loisy's question was genuine and had gone unanswered by authority. Ecclesial authority had said "no" rightly enough, but its "yes" was somewhat less well prepared. Moreover, was the real problem of the time a cognitive one, a need to find a new theory of knowledge, or was it a metaphysical one, a need to find another way of conceiving what is actually there?

Until the church had driven Loisy from her fold, he was too Catholic to stand outside it and ask himself if the story it told was for real. He worked under two disadvantages: he was no philosopher, and he suffered the limitations of a narrowly cultural Catholic perspective. Henri Bergson had neither of these drawbacks. He was a genuine philosopher and a secularized Jew. It was he, and not Loisy himself, who taught Gilson how to begin to think through the problems that Loisy had raised. When Gilson formally

---

22. Loisy, *My Duel with the Vatican,* 274–75; Gilson, *Le philosophe et la théologie,* 69.

matriculated at the Sorbonne in 1904, he had already been auditing the classes of brilliant lecturers such as Bergson and Lucien Lévy-Bruhl for several years past.

## Henri Bergson: Epistemologist Intuition or Musical Metaphysics?

In 1902 two young romantics who had vowed to commit suicide if materialism proved to be true were rescued from this fate by Charles Péguy's insistence that they go to hear Henri Bergson lecture at the Collège de France. A generation of Catholics, lay people and seminarians, who had been enjoined to avoid fideism, and a multitude of the churchless, who had been repelled by the church's rationalism, packed the lecture theater to the doors to hear Bergson discourse. Raïssa Oumancoff and Jacques Maritain heard Bergson say that intuition makes metaphysics possible.

In his *Essay on the Immediate Data of Consciousness*, Bergson argued that positivism looks good so long as we *visualize* reality. When we portray the real as a series of points in space we can construct a geometry of reality, in which every cosmic point is predetermined. Conversely, when we *sound out* our experience, we discover an area of pure duration, a condensed time within time, which is free. Bergson often described this creative freedom by analogy to the spontaneity of music. "Pure duration," he said, "is the form which the succession of our conscious states assumes when our ego lets itself *live* . . . [our ego now ] forms both the past and the present states into an organic whole, as happens when we recall the notes of a tune, melting . . . into one another. . . . [E]ven if these notes succeed one another, yet we perceive them in one another. . . . We can thus conceive of succession . . . as a mutual penetration, an interconnection and organization of elements, each one of which represents the whole, and cannot be distinguished or isolated from it except by abstract thought."[23]

Bergson considered that "the essence of the message which it was his mission to deliver"[24] was an epistemic contrast between a geometric intellect, unable "to comprehend life,"[25] and an intuition which hears the organic movement of life. This is how Jacques Maritain understood him.

For those who had crossed the threshold into the seminary, Bergson offered a novel style by which to convey the truths of faith, softening the

23. Bergson, *Time and Free Will*, 100–101.
24. Gilson, "Compagnons de route," 279.
25. Bergson, *Creative Evolution*, 165.

lines effected by the Scholastic educational bureaucracy. One such was the young Sulpician Lucien Paulet, a close friend of Gilson, who was teaching in the Grand Seminary at Issy. Étienne and Père Lucien went to Bergson's lectures together and spent hours in debate upon the professor's meaning.

Gilson was not primarily attentive to what Bergson was saying about epistemology. He went to the Collège de France readied for a philosophical tone poem: "To understand by what experience many people acceded to *metaphysics,* between 1900 and 1914," he writes, one must think of "Bach, Beethoven, Schumann, Wagner. Disciples of Bergson, . . . their lives were passed under a musical enchantment in which they were the . . . passionately complicit victims. Some of them still remember, as unforgettable events, two revelations . . . in 1900, *La damoiselle élue,* conducted by Taffanel, and the prelude of *Tristan [and Isolde]* directed by Gustave Mahler. Like the first reading of the *Essai sur les données immédiates de la conscience,* these dazzling discoveries inflected the curve of a life-time. We came to metaphysics already heavy with all the music of the world, and drunk with that of our time."[26] A new metaphysical paradigm could be drawn out of this experience of reality as music.

In the overture to *Creative Evolution,* Bergson asks, "What is the precise meaning of the word 'exist'?" Existence is found to be the structuring impetus of time. At the bottom of reality, and propelling it forward, is "pure duration," a continuous and unitary flow of motion. Bergson likens the evolution of the different species to "a musical theme" that had "been transposed . . . into a certain number of tones and on which, still the whole theme, different variations had been played." The underlying order of reality, he claims, is not geometric, spatial, and predetermined, but temporal, as "in a symphony of Beethoven, which is genius, originality, and therefore unforeseeability itself." Bergsonian time is not clocked but experienced. He argued that our consciousness knows it by "twisting on itself."[27]

But for Gilson, since the "universe" that Bergson "proposed for our reflection was fluid, moving and continuous, like that of music," those of "us, who knew from our daily experience how a theme contains its development, no twisting in on ourselves was necessary to attain a mobile continuity too pure for spatial partition. Through music, we were already in it, like fish in the sea."[28] Gilson understood Bergson to be talking, not about how we know what is there, but about the musically ordered structure of reality.

26. Gilson, "Compagnons de route," 282–83. My italics on *metaphysics.*
27. Bergson, *Creative Evolution,* 171–72, 224, 237.
28. Gilson, "Compagnons de route," 283.

What impressed Bergson's musical student was the philosopher's tranquil overcoming of Kant's prohibition upon metaphysics. "No philosopher was less taught at the University of Paris around 1906 than Aristotle, but we learned him from Bergson at the Collège de France, and we did not know it"; and neither did he. Many years afterward, Gilson traced Bergson's philosophical lineage back to Felix Ravaisson-Mollien, author of *L'essai sur la métaphysique d'Aristote* (1837): "The idea which Ravaisson set at the bottom of Aristotelianism" Bergson wrote, "'is that instead of diluting his thought in the general, the philosopher must concentrate on the individual.'"[29] That is, on the mysterious fact.

## Social Modernism—or Action Française?

Where Bergson took individually experienced time as the key to the creativity activating the cosmos, Auguste Comte thought of ideas as emerging from set stages of humanity's social evolution toward positivism. Fr. George Tyrrell asserted that the thought of Aquinas was produced by the civilization of the Middle Ages. Tyrrell complained that Leo's promotion of Thomism, in *Aeterni Patris,* makes "the medieval expression of Catholicism its primitive and its final expression." In effect, for Tyrrell, Thomism can be reduced to mediaeval culture. He felt it was absurd to expect anyone living in a modern liberal society to think as Thomas had done.[30] Assigning the former Jesuit to the cohorts of the modernists, Pius X responded to Tyrrell's contentions by denouncing what he called "social modernism," that is, liberal individualist society, as a corollary of doctrinal modernism.

Charles Maurras agreed with Pius as to the evils of social modernism. Like Comte, Maurras believed that monotheism begets the virus of individualism. Both men considered that mediaeval Catholicism had modified the disease endemic to Christian monotheism. Comte had attempted ralliement with the Jesuits, "the outcome of which was a comic fiasco." Maurras, who created the Action Française during the Dreyfus Affair, "with a view to combating the pernicious effects of individualism" and to welding "an alliance between positivists and Catholics,"[31] had some success in the latter aim.

In 1905 Combes instigated the disestablishment of the church. The 1801 Concordat was repealed. If the state would no longer pay the clergy, said Pius X, neither would it select the bishops. The act ordered that all church

---

29. Ibid., 279, 277.
30. Quoted in Daly, "Apologetics in the Modernist Period," 82.
31. Sutton, *Nationalism, Positivism, and Catholicism,* 1.

buildings be handed over to "associations" of lay people. In *Vehementer Nos*, of 1906, the anti-modernist Pope condemned the separation of church and state; in *Gravissimo officii*, he forbade the clergy to allow their property to be managed by devout lay people.[32] The state reclaimed its property, and the church was materially bankrupted.

Received with initial protest, and then valiant submission, by the French episcopacy, not widely welcomed by the laity who would henceforth discharge their clergy's upkeep, Pius's actions delighted Maurras. He stated his "profoundest admiration for *Vehementer Nos* and *Gravissimo officii*." The Action Française attacked the repeal of the Concordat and mobilized resistance to state inventories of church property. The object of the republican government's assault recognized an ally. What did it matter if the apologist was an atheist: "As a member-priest remarked, 'If one is not politically a Catholic, one does not join the Action Française: metaphysically, you can be whatever you like.'" The southwestern priest who wrote to Maurras, "You are completely right to say 'our philosophy of nature in no way excludes the supernatural'"[33] typifies one Catholic reaction to him.

Marc Sangnier exemplifies a different response. He created the *Sillon* in 1894 in order to give Catholics an arena in which to discuss democratic values. At the age of twenty, Gilson was enthusiastic about the *Sillon*'s effort to create a "sincerely Republican" and "social" Catholicism. These were the politics called for by Leo XIII. Gilson recalled that "there were many of us who felt a heart-felt union with Marc Sangnier and solidarity with him in his battles." These began in 1904, when Sangnier published an article urging Catholics to choose between the "Social Christianity of the *Sillon*" and the "Monarchical positivism of the Action Française." Maurras hit back at some length in the *Action française* newspaper. The collected pieces, *Le dilemme de Marc Sangnier* (1905), opens with a preface that repeats the phrase "I am Roman" like an incantation: "I am Roman, because without my Roman guardian, the second barbarian invasion, which took place in the sixteenth century, the Protestant invasion, would have made me a type of Swiss." The apologist claimed that Catholics and positivists may share the same societal vision: "Joan of Arc incarnated a . . . miracle, but the operations of that holy girl have been found to be conformed to all the most subtle laws of the tactics of those times. Where did she learn them? It matters little. She knew them. This social Christianity thus attains a certain de-

---

32. Chadwick, *History of the Popes,* 394.
33. Sutton, *Nationalism, Positivism, and Catholicism,* 96; Weber, *Action Française,* 35, citing Abbé Appert; Maurras, "Le dilemme de Marc Sangnier," 39.

gree of positivism. Monarchist positivism: it had to have been by the anointing at Rheims that Joan began the salvation of the country. Exactly, and trait for trait, this is the program of the Action Française. Like Joan of Arc, we say that there must first be a king, an authority. . . recognized by all."[34]

In 1907 Pius X's decree *Lamentabili* condemned sixty-five modernist propositions. In 1908 the encyclical *Pascendi* devoted a paragraph to the erroneous "apologetics" of *L'évangile et l'église*. *Pascendi* proscribes the "poison" disseminated by the modernists, men who feel "no horror at treading in the footsteps of Luther." Loisy was excommunicated in the same year.

In 1909 Pius beatified Joan of Arc, kissing the tricolor at the ceremony. In 1910 the Pope condemned the *Sillon*. The principal objection Pius urged upon his "Venerable French Brothers" was that the "priests and seminarians" who belonged to the movement were learning "democratic habits," which had issued in a lack of "docility" to themselves, who "represent hierarchy, social inequality, authority and obedience, antiquated ideals to which their souls, smitten with another ideal, cannot conform themselves." Moreover, "*the breath of the Revolution has passed through*" men who say that "*the great bishops and kings who have created and governed France so gloriously have given to their people neither true justice nor true happiness, because they did not have the Sillonist ideal.*" The *Sillon* had erred in attaching "'its religion to a political party,' said the Pope in words that could have been applied to the Action Française,"[35] but were not. The Sillonists were convicted, finally, of failing to come to the aid of the church under duress.

Gilson was dispirited: "Did there remain as the only possible political attitude for a French Catholic that of the royalists or the conservatives? If there was one, we could not see what it was." A year later Pius X named Maurras "a good defender of the Holy See and of the Church." Partly because antimodernism had such cultural concomitants, Gilson's youthful sympathies became so engaged in Loisy's case that it was not until sixty years later that he was able to "see him objectively (dead) for the first time."[36]

---

34. Pezet, *Chrétiens au service de la cité*, 27–33; Gilson, *Le philosophe et la théologie*, 64–65; Sutton, *Nationalism, Positivism, and Catholicism*, 2; Maurras, "Le dilemme de Marc Sangnier," 26, 35.

35. Chadwick, *History of the Popes*, 398; Letter of Pius X on the *Sillon*, August 15, 1910, in *La démocratie religieuse*, 167–68, with Maurras' italics; Weber, *Action Française*, 66.

36. Gilson, *Le philosophe et la théologie*, 65; Sutton, *Nationalism, Positivism, and Catholicism*, 100; Gilson to Henri Gouhier, July 19, 1963, in "Lettres d'Étienne Gilson à Henri Gouhier," 473–74. Gilson had just read the essay by Gouhier cited above.

## Gilson's Loyalty to Bergson

The childhood source of Gilson's existential philosophy was not pedagogical. It may have been an experience that he dated from his fourteenth or fifteenth year. He became aware that his need to explore every "road, footpath, summit or valley accessible to me from my father's house in the summer holidays . . . expressed . . . my love for it." Here, "in the June sun," he had an "unexpected meeting with a miraculous bank of little wild orchids, flowering vanilla." Gilson experienced this love in relation to things, such as the "humble flint," rather than for intelligent people, because, he said, if you take away thinking, talking, doing, one is left with the fact that "all entities do at least this, that they are." One cannot intellectualize the humble flint. Gilson would never be noted for hostility to fideism.

Gilson spent the later years of the modernist crisis as a Lycée *professeur*, teaching philosophy to schoolchildren. He remembered "often having said to my pupils that the supreme philosophical question in my eyes was to know 'why there was something rather than nothing.' I had not just read it in Leibniz, I had rather made it my own, as if it spontaneously flowed from my own thought, so intimately mine that I could never have borrowed it from someone else. It was much later, retrieving it in the writings of Martin Heidegger, that I became aware of my involuntary theft." Very long after those schoolmastering days, Gilson claimed that Leibniz must have "known this marveling in contact with this mysterious act which we call being, that in virtue of which one says of entities that they *are*."[37]

At the behest of the Ministry of Public Instruction, Gilson taught in the Lycée of Bourg in 1907, in the Lycée of Rochefort-Sur-Mer from 1908 until 1910, in the Lycée Descartes, in Tours, from 1910 to 1911, at the Lycée Saint-Quentin from 1911 to 1912, and finally in the Lycée in Angers. Despite the church of Pius X and the maneuvers of an omnipotent education ministry, Gilson remained "always first a Catholic, then, with equal fervor of a different order, a Frenchman of the Third Republic."[38]

The yearning of Jacques and Raïssa Maritain for truth had been stimulated but not satisfied by Bergson's philosophy. They believed that they must decide between relativism and unstinting faith in an authority that teaches

---

37. Gilson, *Constantes philosophiques de l'être*, 146–47. Gilson retracted the description of this youthful summer from the manuscript of *Constantes* that he left for posthumous publication; the editor replaced it.
38. Shook, *Gilson*, 6.

truth. *Pascendi* launched their journey toward the church of Saint Thomas Aquinas. They began their Catholic lives under the tutelage of the Dominican friar Humbert Clérissac, who had gone into exile under Combes's laws, and who was an impassioned enthusiast for monarchism, Maurras, and the Action Française.

In 1913 Maritain gave a series of lectures at the Paris Institut Catholique, "castigating the Bergsonian philosophy with the severity of the preacher of a crusade" and "shocking certain of his auditors when he treated as a 'poison' a set of ideas which for many of them, as for himself, had been their intellectual liberation." Maritain's talks were intended to inoculate the seminarians in his audience against the "application of Bergsonianism to religious and dogmatic matters." He "denounced" as "a peril to the faith" the "ruinous doctrine which corrupts the life of the Christian soul in the measure that it is radically incompatible with the Thomist doctrine that is the . . . 'only philosophy of the Church.'"[39]

Bergson nauseated the anti-modernist conscience because his demarcation between scientific understanding and intuition made certain Catholics remember Loisy's divide between empirical knowledge and faith. The clear line that Bergson drew between intellectual knowledge of facts or ideas, on the one hand, and intuitive vision, on the other, reminded the anti-modernists of Loisy's distinction between the empirical science of history and the constants of faith, outside and beyond history. Once the two are thus separated, it was thought, there are no external, factual proofs of faith, and faith is therefore relegated to "subjective" belief. The objection to Bergson was that his epistemology promoted fideism.

For Bergson, human language expresses scientific knowledge only; he did not believe that intuitive vision can be put into words. If one applied this philosophical attitude in theology, then it would be impossible to define the objects of faith in verbal propositions, or dogmas. The Catholic antifideists considered that if the human mind does not have the ability to express the constants of faith in propositional language then dogmatic formulas cannot contain ultimate, unalterable truths. The solution to modernism would then appear to be the Thomist epistemology, the principle that human reason knows objective truth and can state it in objectively true propositions. For Maritain, the uprights of objectivist Thomist philosophy upheld the rooftop of faith.

Maritain's strictures on Bergson's epistemology were published as *La*

---

39. Barré, *Jacques et Raïssa Maritain,* 174–75.

*philosophie bergsonienne* (1913), earning the congratulations of Pius X and Charles Maurras's benefaction.[40] Bergson's works were placed on the Index in 1914. In the "same year, Bergson was elected to the Académie Française, following a widely publicized debate over his candidacy launched by the royalist Action Française."[41] Forty years later, when they fell out over aesthetics, Gilson said that he could never forgive Maritain his book about Bergson.

Gilson's friend Abbé Paulet overlaid the statutory Scholasticism with a Bergsonian tinge. He was for that reason removed from seminary teaching; this "heart devoured by the love of Christ threw himself into the parochial ministry, without feeling himself diminished."[42] Lucien Paulet was killed in action in 1915. Gilson kept his photograph throughout his life. The biographical fact which best explains Gilson's intellectual development is what Paulet's photograph represented to him.

Gilson considered that the faults of omission in official Thomism had helped to provoke the modernist crisis, with its ruin of lives. "Here," he wrote, "is the wound of that troubled epoch: a truth which the guardians had lost. They were astonished that others refused to see, but they showed something else instead of it, and they did not know themselves where the truth lay. When I try today to understand the Modernist disorder in philosophy, it is first of all there," in the neo-Scholastics' misinterpretation of Thomas, so that a priest with "philosophy in his blood" looked elsewhere for inspiration. Lucien Paulet had conveyed to him a "strong bias against manuals of philosophy" that would stay with Étienne until his own death. Gilson's verdict was that "modernism was a tissue of errors made by responsible people but we should not forget the responsibility of another order of those who began by frequently permitting the truth to be misunderstood or ignored. They had travestied it to the point that it had become impossible to accept it."[43]

---

40. Ibid., 176.
41. Antliff, *Inventing Bergson*, 4.
42. Gilson, *Le philosophe et la théologie*, 50.
43. Ibid., 50, 59–60; Shook, *Gilson*, 21; Gilson, *Le philosophe et la théologie*, 60.

# 2

# Beginning with Descartes

## Lévy-Bruhl Teaches Gilson "*Chosisme*"—Thingism

During his final year at the Lycée Henri IV, Gilson slipped into the Sorbonne to hear its eminent professor of sociology lecture on David Hume. He realized that, "to me, to understand any philosophy would always mean to approach it as I had seen Lucien Lévy-Bruhl approach that of Hume." Gilson's year between school and university (1903–1904) was devoted to military service and to the consumption of Lévy-Bruhl's newly published *La morale et la science des moeurs,* which the young man termed an "almost incredible book." Gilson entered the department of sociology in the Sorbonne, a bastion of Durkheimian positivism, regarded by the Catholic poet Charles Péguy as the "citadel of the errors of the modern world." But Gilson admired the way in which Durkheim "conceived social facts . . . like things." For Durkheim himself, that meant the sociologist should look, not from theory to reality, but from social practice to theory, a thoroughly realist dicta.[1]

Gilson "did not have the technical formation of an historian." Instead, through his apprenticeship to Lévy-Bruhl, he acquired the skills of a historian of ideas, learning to place philosophical writings in their historical context and never to impose a theory upon a text to which it was alien; "his intellectual curiosity and taste for realities disposed him to appreciate the importance of documents." Lévy-Bruhl appealed because Gilson was already afflicted with the "incurable metaphysical malady" of "*chosisme,*" "thingism."[2]

Gilson intended to be an undergraduate for three years, rather than four. Once his heart had decided upon a plan, he had the stamina to carry it

1. Gilson, *God and Philosophy,* xiii; Shook, *Gilson,* 11; Barré, *Jacques et Raïssa Maritain,* 79, citing Raïssa Maritain; Gilson, *Le philosophe et la théologie,* 31; Lévy-Bruhl, *Ethics and Moral Science,* 79.
2. D'Alverny, "Nécrologie Étienne Gilson," 426; Gilson, *Le philosophe et la théologie,* 24.

inexorably to its conclusion. Gilson intended to marry Thérèse Ravise, which required that he graduate and attain the meager salary of a Lycée *professeur.* No Pelagian, Gilson attributed his "success" to "Providence": "in three years," he told his *Maman,* "the good Lord has given me the two greatest temporal happinesses possible: the love of Thérèse and success in the agrè-gation." A few years after first encountering him in the lecture halls of the Sorbonne, Gilson asked Lévy-Bruhl "for a subject of a thesis," and "he ad-vised me to study the vocabulary and, eventually, the matter borrowed from Scholasticism by Descartes." Where his priest contemporaries pored over the Scholastic manuals, and Maritain became a Thomist under the spiritual direction of Père Clérissac, Gilson recorded, in 1940, that he was guided toward the *Summa Theologiae* by "a Jew" who "had never opened a single one of the works of Thomas.... But he was, besides many other good things, a man of an almost uncanny intelligence, with a surprising gift of seeing facts in an impartial, cold, and objective light, just as they were." "Nine long years of preparation"[3] went into the production of the "mas-terpiece" that would give him entry into the guild of historians of ideas. Meanwhile, he would earn his family's keep by teaching philosophy to schoolboys.

Lévy-Bruhl edited the *Revue philosophique de la France et de l'étranger* and was thus called upon to supervise the publication of students' coming-out pieces. In 1909, Gilson provided the doyen of positivist sociologists with "Sur le positivisme absolu," which argues that if philosophy accepts the legitimacy of positivism, it will relinquish its own proper tasks: all it will have left to do is document the history of science. Like pacifists, "fideists" are a combatative bunch of people. Étienne's first published article con-cludes: "In the Middle Ages, one said: '*Philosophia ancilla theologiae.*' Phi-losophy is liberated from this servitude. Today, one says: '*Philosophia ancilla scientiae*'; this second servitude is no better than the first. Philosophy is the servant of no one. Left to itself, neither isolated from science nor absorbed into it, it can follow the work already begun over many centuries; just as science does, but from its own proper perspective, it achieves increasingly rigorous approximations to the truth."[4] Gilson's doctoral thesis is about how physical science came to take precedence over metaphysics. It num-bers Descartes as the first philosopher to mutter "Philosophia ancilla scien-tiae," albeit under his breath.

3. Gilson to Caroline Gilson, September 14, 1907, in Gilson Correspondence, Uni-versity of St. Michael's College Archives, Toronto; Gilson, *God and Philosophy,* xiii.
4. Gilson, "Sur le positivisme absolu," 65.

## Descartes' Opponent

French doctoral candidates submit a major and a minor thesis. Gilson's major thesis treats the theme of liberty in Descartes in relation to the doctrine of God and to anthropology. His minor dissertation, the *Index scholastico-cartésien,* is an "index" of Descartes' Scholastic terminology. In his last year of schoolmastering, in Angiers, and amid the pleasurable disruption of the birth of his first child, Jacqueline, Étienne taught himself "how to read medieval manuscripts properly,"[5] had the final texts of the theses printed, and prepared for his *Viva.* The defense took place in January 1913: the victim survived his trial, although his supervisor arraigned him on the charge of having, in one instance, supplemented Descartes' text with his own opinion. *La liberté chez Descartes et la théologie* was published some months later. The year 1913 also saw the birth of Cécile, a second daughter for Étienne and Thérèse.

Gilson is not employing a doctoral candidate's diplomacy when he states, in his preface, that many of the "guiding ideas" of the work were supplied by Lévy-Bruhl.[6] Along with Abbé Lucien Laberthonnière and Maurice Blondel, Lévy-Bruhl had derived his conception of Descartes as being a new kind of physicist rather than a new kind of metaphysician from L. Liard. Liard gave these men the idea that Descartes' metaphysics was invented to serve his physics.[7] Lévy-Bruhl's Catholic student sets out to explain how Descartes performed this feat within a theological milieu. Descartes studied from 1609 to 1612 at La Flèche, a Jesuit college whose curriculum was designed to inculcate Scholasticism, which meant Aristotle as read by Thomas Aquinas, as interpreted by the Spanish Jesuit Francisco de Suarez (1548–1617).

As a contemporary of Galileo and a proponent of the new physics, Descartes wanted to extirpate the Aristotelian philosophy of nature in which mediaeval cosmology was rooted. He launched his attack with all the resources gained in three years behind enemy lines among the combatant Aristotelians of La Flèche. It is Gilson's aim to show how Descartes deployed the language and the methods of mediaeval Scholasticism against the Scholastic attribution of purpose to nature. A teleological conception of nature had been integral to mediaeval physics and was still alive at the trial of Galileo in 1632. In 1630, Descartes wrote to Mersenne about God's freedom, telling his friend that God is not bound by the "eternal verities."

5. Shook, *Gilson,* 55.
6. Gilson, *La liberté chez Descartes et la théologie,* 4.
7. Marion, "L'instauration de la rupture," 15.

Such truths as that the two sides of an equilateral triangle are equal to the sum of the third, or that man is a rational animal, are not intrinsically true of themselves, true in a manner that renders their truth independent of God's free will. To the contrary, the reality, truth, and eternity of the "verities" are dependent upon a free and undivided act of the divine being. How then do we know, queried a scandalized Mersenne, that God will not reverse the eternal verities? Because, Descartes replied, His will is immutable; the reason for this infinite immutability transcends our understanding.[8] Descartes claims that this free God might have chosen to create a different set of "eternal verities."

Two thought-pictures are important here. The first derives from the Greek philosophers, through the Scholastics: the will naturally moves toward the good. The second localizes this paradigm in reference to the Baroque controversies about freedom. The seventeenth-century Jesuit apologists located freedom in indifference with respect to ulterior motivation. A truly free will is one that can choose between alternative goods: it does not gravitate naturally toward one or the other, because neither presents itself as the perfect good. A truly free will is indifferent in respect of the goods laid before it. Descartes is telling Mersenne that God is indifferent with respect to the "goods" of the "eternal verities." He says that God's will, understanding, and power operate in a single and indivisible act. What purpose does God's liberty of indifference serve in Descartes' philosophy?

Gilson's search for Descartes' agenda leads him to Thomas Aquinas's conception of divine creativity. In order to set out the workings of divine causality, Aquinas marks a distinction between God's will and His understanding. Through his understanding, God knows the good; this good is not external to himself but consists in his own essence. The divine knowledge of the good, God's self-knowledge, is the basis upon which divine volition proceeds: the divine will is thus guided by reason. If the divine will is guided by a reasoned knowledge of the good, then God creates with intelligible purposes.[9] God creates a nature that serves final ends and that can be known not only by the divine understanding but also, since it is informed by reasoned aims, by human minds. To will something is to make it happen, whereas to know a thing is to know its purpose: the willing is the power of bat upon ball, the understanding is the direction in which it is aimed. One attributes efficient causality to the will and final causality to the understanding.

8. Gilson, *La liberté chez Descartes et la théologie*, 21–24.
9. Ibid., 82–85.

Gilson's second chapter is titled "L'Adversaire de Descartes." Descartes' adversary is Aquinas. He criticizes each of Aquinas's examples of "eternal verities." Descartes wishes to eliminate an explanation of nature which includes final causality. The Cartesian God has his freedom of indifference so that He may be seen to operate through efficient causality alone. If God does not create with reference to reasoned goods, or ends, then the human physicist is sovereignly free to effect a complete explanation of nature in terms of "how" it works.

As to the "why" questions, Descartes will, in the second edition of his *Meditations,* published after the Galileo trial, strike a more mediatory attitude than in his 1630 correspondence with Mersenne. Rather than emphasizing the divine freedom to create alternative "eternal verities," Descartes now leans piously upon God's unknowable infinity. Even if God does work in nature to a purpose, the finite human mind cannot grasp the final aims of an infinite God. Although, Gilson says, Descartes cannot be designated a voluntarist, because Descartes identifies God's mind and will, nonetheless, in terms of human knowledge of God, the philosopher has subsumed the divine reason into the divine will by the tactical device of the divine infinitude. This entails that human beings can only know the efficient, and not the final, causality of the Creator: and if, as Gilson says, "the world has been produced in the order of efficient causes, and not the order of finality, it is the order of efficient causes . . . which a genuine physics should retrieve."[10]

## Cardinal de Bérulle

Gilson places the source of Descartes' "*metaphysica ancilla scientiae*" in the hyperpiety of the French Oratory. Cardinal de Bérulle was the founder of this institution. Setting his face against the debate-mongering of the Jesuit scholastics, de Bérulle planted the roots of French Oratorian piety, not in the thought of Aquinas, but in that of Augustine. De Bérulle published his conception of the divine liberty in the *Discours de l'état et des grandeurs de Jésus.* De Bérulle's theological style is constrained neither by the rules of Scholastic dialectic, nor by any specially rational methods of argument: devotional feeling, based on the authority of Augustine and the church Fathers, carries him through.

The cardinal was a figure of spiritual influence, taking at least two former pupils of the Jesuits under his wing and redirecting their pious energies in a

10. Ibid., 91–94, 138, 95.

non-Scholastic direction. He first encountered Descartes in 1626, a meeting out of which Descartes gained a spiritual director and ecclesial encouragement to design a new metaphysics. Descartes, who had not hitherto put his metaphysical ideas to paper, had by 1629 drafted the first edition of his *Meditations*. Guillaume Gibieuf was a "doctor of the Sorbonne, priest, and superior of the congregation of the Oratory"[11] after de Bérulle's death. The Jesuits had taught Gibieuf to argue, and de Bérulle realized that this facility would be useful to the Oratory. He set his young pupil into the field to make a reasoned case against theological rationality.

Gibieuf's *De libertate Dei et Creaturae* (1630) draws on a hyperbolic arsenal of "superlatives and capital letters" in an onslaught upon any who would set limits to the liberty of God by suggesting that it acts with reference to an end, good, or reason: "Where St. Thomas tranquilly declares that *in Deo est liberum arbitrium*, Gibieuf intones a hymn to divine liberty: *Liber est Deus, immo liberrimus, et si quid liberrimo liberius esse potest!* There are not enough words to celebrate the grandeur of God, and far from thinking with saint Thomas that certain words are properly used of the Creator, because of the positive reality which they signify, Gibieuf judges that his perfections are exalted beyond words. To say that God is One, the Universal, the All, takes us nowhere: such words leave us as far as possible from his true nature." Gibieuf's Deity is Independent of reasons and ends: He cannot, therefore, be constrained by understanding or will, taken in the merely human sense of the terms.[12]

Descartes did not read his conception of divine liberty out of the text of Gibieuf's treatise—he had described it to Mersenne before that book was published—but the friendship between the two men from 1626 to 1629 was sufficiently intimate to be termed a "collaboration." The "divine libertarians" both use God's Infinity as a cutting knife, which curtails comparison between creaturely and divine perfections. Both refuse to find such limiting perfections as understanding and will in God, on the ground that God's Unity overwrites the Scholastic or rational distinction between divine will and understanding. Gibieuf brushes off the insult to divine Majesty implicit in asking why God willed the order of creation. For the mediaeval Scholastics, the tree of final causality had spread out from God's creativity into the purposive order of creation. Descartes learned how to cut that tree off at its root under the supervision of the exceedingly spiritual theologians of the Oratory. Lévy-Bruhl's contention that Descartes sought in

11. Ibid., 173–74, 178.
12. Ibid., 196–97, 199.

his metaphysics merely plastic material for his physics, and the conception of Descartes as the "lay missionary" of the Oratory are not opposed but "complementary," the doctoral candidate affirms. The philosopher was able to "adapt the theology of the Oratory to the physics of efficient causality" because the Oratorian's Neoplatonic determination to raise the One above human reason produced a Deity perfectly formed to serve a mechanist physics uncoupled from final causality.[13]

The Oratorian's hyperspiritualism could have been built for collaboration with mechanist science. There is a kind of ghostly similarity between Gilson's seventeenth-century characters, Descartes, Cardinal de Bérulle, Mersenne, and the ecclesiastical-political controversialists of 1907–1913, the hypersupernaturalist clerics playing into the hands of their positivist political supporters. Gilson the PhD writer is of course too intent on his historical task to remark on it. The only trace it leaves is the unified conception of the political, metaphysical, and supernatural in his own later Thomism.

Gilson concludes his thesis by dismissing a hypothesis, held at that time by Espinas, which proposed that Descartes was a doughty defender of Catholic orthodoxy. We have, Gilson states, no reason to doubt the "reality and sincerity of Descartes' religious convictions." But is the desire to combat atheism or libertinism the guiding motivation of his work? Descartes "respected the Church and above all feared it"; he was "less worried about defending it than about defending himself against it."[14] Philosophy and theology were not peripheral concerns for Descartes; rather, they were helpful adjuncts to the requirements of the new physical science that it was his central aim to set forth. As Gilson's minor thesis showed, Descartes plundered the vocabulary of mediaeval theology; but in his methodology, the doctrine of God is determined by the force of naturalistic reason.

## "Metaphysics Stems from Theology"

Gilson said that his first book "is now out of date, but its nine long years of preparation taught me two things: first, to read Saint Thomas Aquinas; secondly, that Descartes had vainly tried to solve, by means of his own famous method, philosophical problems whose only correct position and solution were inseparable from the method of Saint Thomas Aquinas." The lesson Gilson had learned was to compare Descartes' conception of the

13. Ibid., 205, 208, 210.
14. Ibid., 436, 439.

relation of philosophy and theology with that set out by Aquinas. He may have preferred to keep that insight to himself, before his Sorbonne jury, but Gilson's head was too close to his heart for him to keep close counsel. He recounted to a friend that "during the defense of my thesis, V[ictor] Delbos asked me, 'Why have you written in your title *et la théologie* instead of saying: *and scholastic philosophy?*' I replied on the hoof, without reflecting, 'because, for me, metaphysics stems from theology.' Delbos had the goodness not to push it further. . . . I saw the abyss open under me!"[15]

Jean-Luc Marion feels that *La liberté chez Descartes et la théologie* both overestimated the likeness between Aquinas and Suarez and also overstretched the continuity between Aquinas and Descartes. There is some truth in this: Gilson was not just Descartes-baiting in his first book. He confidently told an interviewer in 1925 that Descartes' thought relied upon that of the Scholastics: "if my hypothesis can be verified, then the traditionally accepted *rupture* between the Middle Ages and modern times is *canceled out;* the continuity of the philosophical tradition from ancient Greece to modernity is established; and the Christian thinkers who have been exiled for too long from the history of philosophy are given their real position in it." Fighting talk from a young professor of the history of mediaeval philosophy! One reason why the fight seemed important was that the "traditionally accepted rupture" between the Renaissance and the Mediaevals meant, in many secular minds, that real philosophy, like real art, began again at the Renaissance, after the interruption of the "Age of Faith," Scholastic bigotry, and two-dimensional painting. A much older Gilson would remark to a friend who accepted that Descartes was at least partly motivated by religious considerations that his own "Descartes has remained exactly that of Lucien Lévy-Bruhl. When I was young, the impossibility of bringing philosophers into agreement contributed to my turning to the history of philosophy, where I hoped it would be possible. I have lost that illusion since."[16]

As to the apparent overestimation of the continuity between Aquinas and Suarez, Marion states that by the time Gilson composed his 1930 *Études sur la rôle de la pensée médiévale dans la formation du système cartésien,* Gilson had recognized the exigency of creating a hermeneutic of continuity in discontinuity, as between Descartes and the Scholastics: A decade and a half after the publication of *La liberté chez Descartes,* Gilson was able, Marion says, to recognize that Descartes' borrowings from Augustinian tradi-

15. Gilson, *God and Philosophy,* xiii–xiv; Gilson to Henri Gouhier, September 23, 1959, in "Lettres d'Étienne Gilson à Henri Gouhier," 468.
16. Lefèvre, *Une heure avec . . . Étienne Gilson,* 69; Gilson to Henri Gouhier, January 22, 1956, in "Lettres d'Étienne Gilson à Henri Gouhier," 463.

tion, such as the notion of innate ideas, are modified by their function within Descartes' own epistemology.[17] Gilson's *Études sur le rôle de la pensée médiévale dans la formation du système cartésien* is a compilation of articles. The first is the one Marion draws on for this analysis, "L'innéisme cartésien et la théologie." It was published in 1914, one year after *La liberté chez Descartes*. An interesting episode did intervene between the book and the article.

## A Suarezian Defense of the Action Française: Pedro Descoqs

In 1905 the Oratorian abbé Lucien Laberthonnière had become the editor and legal owner of the *Annales de philosophie chrétienne;* the philosopher Maurice Blondel gave his financial backing to the journal. Gilson was often to be found in the *Annales* offices. Marc Sangnier's *Sillon* had neither the same "philosophy" as Laberthonnière nor an identical "social thought," but nonetheless shared the same "adversaries," who had two common characteristics: "they were self-proclaimed 'Thomists'" and, as Gilson records, "they ranged themselves in politics on the side of Charles Maurras."[18]

Maurras' immediate "goods" served ever-more-distant final ends, like the man who sees himself reflected in a receding hall of mirrors: he admired Thomas Aquinas because he found in him a reflection of Hellenism. Maurras too believed in a "natural law," the "mathematical" one laid down by Auguste Comte in the formula "'human society is composed of families and not of individuals.'" Why, he had demanded of Sangnier, should a Catholic refuse to share such natural truths with a "positivist Monarchist"? "The one says: Here is the law of nature . . . the other: Here is the law of the One who made nature. Divided on the origins of things, they agree on the content of the law they have received." Maurras let slip one flaw in the affiliation when, insisting that it is not monarchy, but "hereditary government" that is "immutable in politics," he added, *"This is what divine right is for those for whom nature is divine.* It is the essential resting place of the nature of human societies, which is to be composed of families and not of individuals, to unfold over the course of centuries, and not to be concentrated in one human life."[19]

The Spanish Jesuit Pedro Descoqs, who had suffered persecution under Combes's reforms in the form of exile to the Channel Islands, was moved

17. Marion, "L'instauration de la rupture," 16, 19, 21–22, 28.
18. Gilson, *Le philosophe et la théologie,* 66.
19. Maurras, "Le dilemme de Marc Sangnier," 34–35, 95–96.

by Maurras' attack on the *Sillon* to write three articles discussing the compatibility of Maurrasianism and Thomism. As a Suarezian, Descoqs "allowed the political sphere a considerable degree of theoretical autonomy" and was ready to detach what he called "political society" from "religious society." Descoqs was motivated, not merely by speculative considerations, but by the practical need of the church for allies. He concludes that the Action Française is suited to this role: "'M. Maurras has nothing closer to his heart than to bring about the triumph of the Church, at least in society if not in individual souls. And, insufficient as that may be, is it not, all things considered, already a great deal?'"[20]

The author of *Le réalisme chrétien et l'idéalisme grec* dedicated the 1910 edition of the *Annales de philosophie chrétienne* to discussions of Descoqs' thesis. Laberthonnière shows that Maurras and his cohorts admired the church because they believed it could shore up society against the "anarchy they saw as inherent in Christianity itself." The Oratorian describes Maurras' Jesuit defender, Descoqs, as being one step worse than the casuists pilloried by Pascal, in suggesting that "'without believing in God, one can be orthodox.'" Descoqs answered with *À travers l'oeuvre de M. Maurras*. Laberthonnière retaliated by claiming that the Jesuit "was influenced by a false theological notion of some state of pure nature and therefore imagined that the State could be self-sufficient in the sense that it could be properly independent of any specifically Christian sense of justice." He had advanced upon a dangerous course. Gilson records that

> the *Annales de philosophie chrétienne* was not lacking in aggression, but there is scarcely a doubt what precipitated its downfall. When Fr. Laberthonnière took Fr. Descoqs S.J. to task over the question of the *Action Française,* I did not doubt an instant that his fate was sealed. It could be that there was no correlation at all between the two facts.... But on this precise point, no doubt is possible for me, and...I was not alone in the prognostication. Laberthonnière published in 1911 a little forty-two page pamphlet, *Autour de L'Action Française:* his friends were always sure that his enemies would never forgive him.

In 1913, Laberthonnière accepted Gilson's "Notes sur Campanella" for publication. Before it saw print, the Roman Curia placed the entire *Annales* series (1905–1913), including Gilson's piece, on the Index. Laberthonnière was forbidden to teach or to publish for the rest of his life. Gilson was "distressed when the hand of ecclesiastical authority fell heavily on the Cath-

---

20. Sutton, *Nationalism, Positivism, and Catholicism,* 118–19, citing Descoqs.

olic scholars whom he knew and admired." In mid-January 1914 "the Congregation of the Index found that seven of Maurras' books and the *Revue de l'Action Française* were 'truly very bad and deserving of censure. . . .' On January 29, Pius X accepted their decision, but he reserved the right to decide when the decree should be made public."[21] The decree had yet to be retrieved from the Vatican filing cabinets when Benedict XV became Pope, and he decided to leave it there.

In his memoirs, Gilson held up his hands in faux-naïve perplexity at how "a highly qualified interpreter of Thomist theology [was] . . . able in conscience to sustain the notion that the 'best political regime' defended by Charles Maurras was the same as that which had been taught by saint Thomas in his treatise on *Princely Government?* . . . by what secret route [did] Thomist philosophy . . . furnish a theological justification for Maurras' political doctrine?" The "secret route" from Thomas to Maurras was the replacement of Aquinas's teaching that kings must take into account "the supernatural good of 'blessedness in heaven'" with that of Suarez. Suarez considered that "civil power and civil law" must aim, not at "the eternal beatitude of individuals" but at "the realization of a 'common good' that was temporal . . . and limited to the sphere of civil society."[22]

The debate between the Oratorian and the Jesuit indicates the distance between Aquinas and Suarez; but as Bergson liked to say, "It takes time for a lump of sugar to melt." Gilson's first book, *Le Thomisme: introduction au système de saint Thomas d'Aquin,* first delivered as lectures in 1913, still slants Thomas's idea of divine creation in a Suarezian direction; Marion seems to overestimate Gilson's intellectual development between 1912 and 1914. Catholic political "Suarezianism" would continue to disgust Gilson. But in 1913, three years after the condemnation of the *Sillon,* Gilson probably did not see the precise route which his own historical journey would take; such episodes may have hardened his orientation. One did not require expertise in Baroque political theory to grasp that Maurras, "like Comte . . . was vividly interested in Rome, but not in Jerusalem" and thus that he was twisting ecclesial authority to political ends: "Saint Thomas is the common doctor of the Church; to demonstrate that his political doctrine is the same as that of Charles Maurras will be to prove that Charles Maurras' political

    21. Laberthonnière, "Une Alliance avec l'Action Française," cited ibid., 189; Laberthonnière, *Positivisme et catholicisme à propos de l'Action Française* (1911), ibid., 199; Gilson, *Le philosophe et la théologie,* 68–69; McCool, *From Unity to Pluralism,* 164; Weber, *Action Française,* 222–23.
    22. Gilson, *Le philosophe et la théologie,* 67; Sutton, *Nationalism, Positivism, and Catholicism,* 83.

thought is that of the Church, and thus that *all* French Catholics . . . are held in conscience to approve the monarchist politics of the Action Française."[23]

## Comparing Cartesian and Thomistic Anthropology

"L'innéisme cartésien et la théologie" (1914) is striking in its exposition of the enduring Gilsonian style, in which every sentence is gripped within a steel clasp. It exhibits what would become a characteristic Gilsonian antithesis: Saint Thomas's positing of the substantial unity of soul and body, with its epistemological concomitants, versus the "Platonic" or "Augustinian" identification of the human person with its soul, and the doctrine of knowledge through innate ideas which, Gilson says, necessarily follows from it.

The first section, which describes the Thomist anthropology and epistemology, reiterates the chapter heading from his doctoral thesis, "L'Adversaire de Descartes." According to Thomas, each of the organs of the human body falls into position when it is animated by a rational soul. Without the soul, it would be, not a specifically human body, but merely the material for one. Likewise, when it is stripped of a body to inform, the rational soul is divested of its natural condition. Neither the human rational soul nor its body is of itself a complete whole, or substance: each is "inclined," or directed toward the other, and the "object" or goal of this mutual embrace is "the constitution of that *unum per se* which is called man." Gilson identifies substantial being with integrity: neither rational soul, nor body, taken alone, are beings. The anthropological fraction is the soul or body, taken by itself: the anthropological integer is the human *being*. If the rational soul is conceived as extrinsic to the body, propelling it from outside, as a motor does a boat, then "Socrates" "is not *one,* and by consequence is not a being, because all things possess being in the degree that they possess unity." If the soul becomes itself when it exercises its rationality through the body, then we must say neither that the soul knows, nor that the body knows, but rather that, perceiving through his senses and thinking through his intellect, the *man himself,* the singular *being* constituted by the union of body and soul, knows.[24]

The rational soul, exercised by the whole human being, has a specific field of inquiry. The "man" who is a union of soul and body knows the "quiddity," that is, the "nature existing in corporeal matter." Because its

23. Gilson, *Le philosophe et la théologie,* 68.
24. Gilson, "L'innéisme cartésien et la théologie," 457–59.

object is the universal in the particular, sensible fact, human mental process relies upon phantasms that it draws from those objects. The Platonists may be right about how we will know in heaven, but "here below," according to Saint Thomas, "there is no intelligible truth without a turning of the spirit towards the phantasmata, that is, without the body participating in the acquisition of knowledge." We do not see God immediately, but rather know him through the mediation of his effects in the sensible world. Gilson states that three Thomist theses follow from this definition of the embodied, human act of knowledge: first, that there is no a priori knowledge of God; second, there can be no innate ideas; this is because, third, such ideas would be, to invert the metaphor, "foreign bodies" within the substantial union of the knowing soul and the perceiving body.[25]

It is otherwise for Descartes, for whom matter is defined by mathematical principles and cannot be informed by such a spiritual principle as the "rational soul." The summation of the 1629 *Meditations* is the Sixth, in which Descartes posits, as required by his physics, a "real distinction between the human soul and body." Once "one concedes that the body is only extension, all the phenomena of physics can be explained by extension and movement; substantial forms, real qualities, occult forces and all other such things are abolished."[26]

The feature of Thomist epistemology that requires spirituality-in-materiality is the phantasm. Phantasms are defined by Saint Thomas as "*similitudines individuorum*," likenesses of individuals. They carry the material image of the object to be known to the one who knows: they represent the "material individuating conditions of the object" to be known. But they do so immaterially: the mind does not receive phantasms like a bee picking up pollen. The sensible object does not offer a literal image of itself to the senses in the shape of a phantasm. As Thomas explains them, phantasms are not material duplicates of the object from which they are drawn; the similarity is intentional, that is, in the directedness from the object: "the phantasm is . . . placed between matter and spirit, at the mysterious frontier where the spirit enters into contact with things without ceasing to be itself." Phantasms have this "mixed nature," between the physical and the spiritual, because they are the "point of connection" between the "two heterogeneous realities" of intellect and sense. If the act of knowledge really were a physical reception of particle copies of things, the phantasm would be its cause. As it is, according to Thomas, the act of knowledge

25. Ibid., 461, 464.
26. Ibid., 466.

consists in the exercise of the human agent intellect upon the phantasms. The phantasm is "not the cause of knowledge" but the matter upon which the real cause of knowledge, the agent intellect, works.[27]

According to Gilson's 1914 lithograph, epistemology between Aquinas and Descartes is a series of accommodations to Platonism, which progressively dismantles the conjunction that Thomas considered requisite for knowledge. Aquinas's successors were not as subtle as he in explaining the boundary status of the phantasm. For Duns Scotus, the senses play the role of a mere stimulant to knowledge, accessories to the cause, rather than vital protagonists. His influence leads Francisco de Suarez further to depreciate the instrumentality of the phantasm. Because he thinks the phantasm is entirely material, it cannot really contribute to the act of knowledge: instead of finding, with Thomas, that the phantasm is the basis upon which the agent intellect forms a sensible species, Suarez makes the agent intellect work upon itself. If the phantasm is too material to form a bridge between the intellect's conceptions and its external object, one will have to attribute to the intellect some more spiritual access to truths. Although Suarez does not explicitly teach the existence of innate ideas, his abandonment of the functions of the phantasm creates the breach through which innate ideas enter epistemology.[28]

The Jesuits who taught Descartes at La Flèche were, Gilson says, Suarezians to a man. Moreover, those who retained for the phantasm some epistemic function, in the tradition of William of Ockham, defined it as a copy that carries by virtue of its physical likeness to the thing its "spiritual quality." It was easy for Descartes to make a mockery of " 'these little images flying through the air called *intentional species,* which have exercised the imagination of philosophers.' "[29] If knowing does not require phantasms, then the material senses can be excluded from a role in the human act of understanding.

When, in the seventeenth century, Catholic orthodoxy took up the cudgels against skepticism, deism, and atheism, its argument for the existence of God was a priori. "If," as Gilson says, "innatism made progress from St. Thomas to Descartes, that is because atheism had done so also." God innate within the human mind and atheism are two sides of the coin of Baroque philosophical theology. Cardinal de Bérulle was an "instinctive" Platonist, who taught that God paints the image of his Son in our hearts, using our soul as the workman, our heart as the palette, our spirit as the

27. Ibid., 470, 471, 468.
28. Ibid., 480.
29. Ibid., 474.

brush, and our affections as the colors. Père Gibieuf taught explicitly the doctrine of an innate idea of God in the soul. Descartes' intimate friend Mersenne had in 1623 composed the *Quaestiones in Genesim,* which contends that all men universally consent to the idea of God, and they could not do so unless it were innate in them as the idea of a perfect being. Mersenne feels it sufficient "textually to reproduce" Anselm's ontological argument for the existence of God. The idea of a perfect being includes the idea of an existent being; or, "exists" is contained in the idea of "God." Although this idea is innate in the human mind, Mersenne concedes that not everybody sees it. This is because original sin has sullied its purity; the mercy of God has nonetheless made us capable of recovering it, even in our fallen state.[30] By contracting the knowing faculties to the intellect, feeding upon its innate ideas, Descartes was able to cover the tracks of his path to an omnicompetent physics in the mantle of impeccable Catholic orthodoxy. The Cartesian doctrine of innate ideas was able to take the field left empty when Thomas's conception of the phantasm was relinquished. In his 1914 "L'innéisme cartésien et la théologie," Gilson homes in on battlegrounds that would occupy his attention throughout his life, and he determines their layout in the way in which he always would.

30. Ibid., 484–85, 490, 493.

# 3

## Ad Fontes

### Gilson's Erasmian Method

The original inspiration of the neo-Thomist movement was not the historical study of Saint Thomas's intellectual and spiritual personality. What it wanted was not so much a return to Thomas Aquinas as a revival of Thomistic theories. It cheerfully repackaged Thomas's thought to bring it into line with educational good practice, as then conceived, and updated it to make the best use of it against modern philosophy. For instance, in the first half of the twentieth century, the most influential manual for students of Saint Thomas was Joseph Gredt's *Elementa philosophiae aristotelico-thomisticae* (1909). The two volumes begin in logic, go on to philosophy of nature and to psychology, and conclude in general metaphysics or "ontology."[1] This is why the broad school is known as *neo*-Thom*ism*.

Gilson's sense of who Thomas was, and his own Thomist philosophy, were fed by his response to neo-Thomism. To understand what kind of case he was making, we need to know about the rival versions of Thomism from which he learned and with which he argued. From decades of thinking through why it is historically inaccurate to detheologize, theorize, and epistemologize Saint Thomas's writings, Gilson worked out why one should not do these things to reality.

### The Origins of Roman Thomism:
### Eclecticism and Anti-Kantianism

The neo-Thomists hoped to construct a timelessly true, or perennial, philosophy. The Thomism of the Spanish philosopher Jaime Balmes (1810–1848) drew on Leibniz, Thomas Reid, and Descartes. More characteristically,

1. Prouvost, "Les relations entre philosophie et théologie chez É. Gilson," 418.

48

his contemporary, the Italian Jesuit Vincenzo Buzzetti, juxtaposes the philosophies of Thomas and Aristotle.[2] His confrère Mattheo Liberatore (1810–1892) used the notion of common sense against idealist epistemology.

Eclectic in their choice of Thomas's allies, the neo-Thomists were one-sided in their selection of Thomas's adversary—namely, modern epistemology. The *bête noire* of the neo-Thomists was Kant. Thus Liberatore's *Della conoscenza intellettuale* (1857) "defended the Thomistic theory of knowledge against Italian idealism."[3]

Both Liberatore and Gaetano Sanseverino (1811–1865) became Thomists during the Italian revolution of 1848–1850. They were converted to Thomism by casting about for a philosophy that could counter the ill effects of social liberalism, made evident to them by the national-democratic uprising. Sanseverino's methodology is manifest in his *Elementa philosophiae christiana*. The book has two parts. "Subjective philosophy" deals with the human soul "as the subject of knowledge" and comprises logic, dynamology, ideology, and criteriology. "Objective philosophy" contains natural theology, cosmology, anthropology, and ethics.[4] The genus "Roman Thomism" was thus conceived.

Joseph Kleutgen taught at Rome from 1838. He sounded the clarion call for a return to a premodern philosophy in *Die Theologie der Vorzeit* (1853–1874) and *Die Philosophie der Vorzeit* (1860–1863). *Vorzeit* means "pre-Enlightenment," as opposed to the "new times" of the Enlightenment—*Neuzeit*. Kleutgen showed himself to be a "thorough-going Neo-Thomist" in that "faithful to tradition, he strives to transcend it." In the 1940s and 1950s, when Gilson was criticizing more recent Roman Thomists, he took the argument back to the sources, to Kleutgen and Sanseverino.[5]

From the mid-nineteenth century, the rector of the Roman College, Luigi Taparelli, was a "pioneer of neo-scholasticism." Taparelli won two seminarians, Giacchino and Giuseppe Pecci, to his doctrines.[6] As bishop of Perugia, Giacchino Pecci made his diocesan seminary into a seedbed of Thomism: as bishop of Rome, his third encyclical was *Aeterni Patris*.

---

2. Buzzetti's lectures were called "Institutiones sanae Philosophiae juxta Divi Thomae atque Aristotelis inconsussa Dogmatica." See Riet, *Thomistic Epistemology,* 1:30.

3. Ibid., 35.

4. Ibid., 33, 56.

5. Ibid., 63–64. On Kleutgen, see ch. 10 herein, "Gilson's Theological Thomism"; on Sanseverino, who serves here as a stalking horse for Garrigou-Lagrange, see ch. 13, "Facts Are for Cretins."

6. McCool, *From Unity to Pluralism,* 5.

McCool argues that Leo XIII viewed the Scholastics somewhat unhistorically, as a collective mind: "*Aeterni Patris* gave the impression that all the Scholastic Doctors had the same philosophy and theology. St. Thomas was the best of them, but there is no difference in essence between the philosophy that structures his theology and the philosophy of St. Bonaventure. Nor does the encyclical show any awareness of historical development within scholasticism itself."[7] The claim is important, because, if true, it would mean the approach of *Aeterni Patris* has nothing in common with that of Étienne Gilson. The evidence for it is that both Liberatore and Kleutgen assisted in writing this encyclical. But some features of *Aeterni Patris* indicate that Leo inclined to think that the most striking historical facts are outstanding characters. *Aeterni Patris* begins by noting individuals who used reason in the service of faith, like Justin Martyr and Augustine. Leo states that "among the Scholastic Doctors, the chief and master of all towers Thomas Aquinas, who, as Cajetan observes, because 'he most venerated the ancient doctors of the Church, in a certain way seems to have inherited the intellect of all.' The doctrines of those illustrious men, like the scattered members of a body, Thomas collected together and cemented, distributed in wonderful order, and so increased with important additions that he is rightly and deservedly esteemed the special bulwark and glory of the Catholic faith" (*Aeterni Patris,* para. 17). Leo's encyclical returns over and again to Thomas Aquinas, the man who best integrated the diverse ideas of his predecessors. *Aeterni Patris* has only one reference to Scholasticism. Leo does not employ the term *scholasticism* as a shorthand for Aquinas; and he makes a cautionary observation about "Scholastic doctors."

## The Traditions of Commentary on Aquinas

Nonetheless, as Gilson later considered, *Aeterni Patris* does not pay much attention to the difference between Thomas and his commentators, like Cajetan (1469–1564). Leo regarded "Cajetan and Pope Sextus V...as defenders of St. Thomas' own philosophy"; his encyclical does not indicate "that the diversity among contemporary Thomists...was of great philosophical significance."[8] The eclectic neo-Thomists found one source of equivalences to Thomas's thought in what it called "the traditional philosophy," that is, Aristotle, and some selected outbreaks of common sense

7. Ibid., 11.
8. Ibid.

among the moderns. Their second source of inspiration was the tradition of early modern Thomistic writing.

The Dominicans and Jesuits, such as Cajetan, Banez, John of Saint Thomas (1589–1644), and Suarez, had created an exegetical canon within which their disciples read the mediaeval writers. The commentaries created the intellectual paradigm in which Aquinas's thought was understood. It was this commentarial tradition that tended to the invention of an abstract collective essence of "Scholasticism," and it did so increasingly after 1907, when, with a repeated citation of *Aeterni Patris*, Pius X's *Pascendi* prescribed "the scholastic philosophy...which the Angelic Doctor has bequeathed to us" as a remedy against modernism. Encyclicals have consequences beyond their literal language, and if *Aeterni Patris* did not substitute a monochrome Scholasticism for Thomas Aquinas, the seminary culture which the modernist crisis called into being did. The canonical interpretations became part of the cultural paradigm of a "reinvigorated Thomism," which "functioned principally under the two modes of commenting on authorities and opposing deviants." "Thomism" was promoted as the exclusive norm by which modernism, the "synthesis of all heresies,"[9] could be kept at bay. But what was taught as "Thomism" was an amalgamation of mediaeval and baroque ideas.

For the neo-Thomists, the great philosophical error of modernism was its elimination of that right relation between the human mind and reality which Saint Thomas called truth. It was because they conceived of modernism as an attack upon rationality that seminary professors gave philosophy a central, if "paradoxical," position in their curricula: for the most influential Thomists, those who taught in Rome, there is "no theology without philosophy"; but "the very fact of the importance of this stage of clerical formation itself conferred an almost complete autonomy upon it, since reasoning already permitted one to approach truth."[10] If, as the Roman Thomists read in Aristotle, knowledge begins in the senses, rising thence to concepts, and if, as the Vatican I constitution *Dei Filius* states, reasoned metaphysics is the statutory prolegomenon to faith, then, as the manual writers considered, Thomas Aquinas *ought* to follow the same order.

### The Roman Thomists: Second and Third Generations

What sort of metaphysics was in play? In the Suarezian tradition, metaphysics is not a "science of existence" but one of "possible essences," that

---

9. Pope Pius X, *Pascendi Dominici Gregis*, para. 45; Fouilloux, *Une église en quête de liberté*, 40–41, 52; Pope Pius X, *Pascendi Dominici Gregis*, para. 39.
10. Fouilloux, *Une église en quête de liberté*, 54–55.

is, conceivables, ideal potentialities. Suarez's emphasis on logic and ontology influenced some neo-Thomists.[11] For the first "Roman Thomists," like Kleutgen, metaphysical science is of possible rather than actual essences. Possible worlds are a more perfect tool for analysis than the real and contingent one. This is especially so if one's ideal of scientific knowledge derives from Aristotle's logic, in which *necessary* truths are the only ones that can be deemed valid.

The Roman Thomists had two strongholds, the Angelicum, for Dominicans, and the Gregorian, for Jesuits. Pius X's adviser, Louis Billot, directed the latter until his vigorous anti-modernism was rewarded with the cardinal's hat in 1911. His student Guido Mattiussi succeeded him. Mattiussi's efforts "culminated in the reduction of Thomism to twenty-four theses." This pedagogical directive was ratified by the Congregation of Studies in 1916. In 1922, Mattiussi was joined at the Gregorian by Charles Boyer (1884–1980), whose "philosophy course for seminarians (in Latin)" became a best seller. The Dominican Père Édouard Hugon (1867–1929) composed a six-volume manual of Thomistic philosophy, the *Cursus philosophiae thomisticae* (1903), which states that "the natural order demands that we depart from the concrete and sensible, in order to elevate ourselves to the abstract and the invisible. Natural philosophy must thus precede metaphysics."[12]

Père Réginald Garrigou-Lagrange (1877–1964) arrived at the Angelicum in the same year as Hugon, 1909. He etched the stamp of his character upon the place for fifty years. "As a young Dominican," Garrigou-Lagrange had "read the *Disputations* of John of St. Thomas aloud to his director, Father Dehau, who was almost blind: 'As he read it aloud, it became for him the beginning of a long intimacy with the great commentator.'"[13] Garrigou-Lagrange would, in time, produce his own multivolume commentary on Aquinas's *Summa Theologiae*.

His first book, *Le sens commun, le philosophie de l'être et les formules dogmatiques* (1909), was originally composed in the service of anti-modernism. In its later editions, it brings not only Henri Bergson but also his disciple at the Collège de France, Édouard Le Roy, within its sights. These philosophers are rebuked for their agnosticism, nominalism, empiricism, idealism, evolutionism, pantheism, and Heraclitanism, that is, for supplying the intellectual underpinnings of doctrinal modernism. Their philosophical errors

11. McCool, *From Unity to Pluralism,* 29, 31–32.

12. Fouilloux, *Une église en quête de liberté,* 41, 50; Hugon's *Cursus* is cited in Prouvost, "Les relations entre philosophie et théologie chez É Gilson," 418.

13. De Lubac's note in de Lubac, ed., *Letters of Gilson to de Lubac,* 106.

result both from the denial of "the objective validity of the principle of identity or non-contradiction" and from their ignoring the fact that the "'philosophy of becoming' was clearly condemned in the first proposition of the Syllabus of Pius IX." "Very different from all of these," Père Garrigou-Lagrange writes, the "traditional philosophy... admits the absolute immutability of the first principle of reason and of reality or being,... recognizes the existence of God," and "must see... in common sense a rudimentary philosophy of being." The "traditional philosophy," shared by Aristotle and Saint Thomas, is "realist conceptualism or moderate realism." The two-volume *Dieu, son existence et sa nature: solution thomiste des antinomies agnostiques* (1914) elongates the thesis that moderate realism drives all of its opponents into *reductiones ad absurdum* from the axis of the principle of noncontradiction and has iron-clad, logically necessary proofs of the existence of God at its disposal. Père Reginald claimed that "the 'philosophical sciences' ought to be taught in the order followed by Aristotle: logic, natural philosophy, psychology, metaphysics, and theodicy." The "chevaliers of the concept" often harbored a "penchant for mysticism": in 1917, the Roman Thomist became the first occupant of an Angelicum chair in ascetic and mystical theology.[14]

The professors of the Angelicum and the Gregorian readily attained the ear of the Holy Office. This resulted in their conceiving themselves as "invested with a portion of the Magisterium of the popes whom they served, and consequently to confuse their personal positions, conveyed in numerous official texts, with the doctrine of the Church."[15] In the mythology of post-Scholastic Catholicism, Garrigou-Lagrange has assumed the lineaments of an Inquisitor, and with what justification we shall eventually discover.

Humbert Clérissac led Jacques Maritain into the cathedral-church of the *Summa Theologiae* through a porch over which the Dominican commentators stood guard; Maritain would always remain a spiritual devotee of the commentators. Maritain was given the chair of the history of modern philosophy at the Institut Catholique of Paris in 1914. The Institut was staffed by such Thomists as the Jesuit Pierre Rousselot (1878–1915) and the Dominican Antonin Sertillanges (1863–1931). Maritain was not a career academic; his wide influence came about through the Thomist study circle which he led, through his books, and through contact with this great spiritual personality. Whereas the "first wave" of Thomism inspired by *Aeterni*

14. Garrigou-Lagrange, *Le sens commun*, 7, 13, 39 ff.; Garrigou-Lagrange, *God: His Existence and His Nature*, 169–70, 165–66; Garrigou-Lagrange, *Le sens commun*, 14, 25; Riet, *Thomistic Epistemology*, 1:314; Fouilloux, *Une église en quête de liberté*, 55.
15. Fouilloux, *Une église en quête de liberté*, 49–50.

*Patris* was restricted to a clerical milieu, Maritain helped to create a Thomism that entered lay consciousness. His "Cercle Thomiste" attracted "an elite of intellectuals, artists, and writers"; its annual retreat was "one of the intellectual highlights of Parisian intellectual life between the two Wars."[16]

With Père Humbert's death, in 1914, Maritain had taken Garrigou-Lagrange as his mentor in Thomism. The Dominican preached the annual summer "retreat" of Maritain's Cercle Thomiste every year from its inception, in 1921, until 1937. The young Yves Congar frequented the Cercle in the early 1920s. He later recollected its "spiritual attitude" as one of "an intrepid and absolute faith in the most minute details of the texts of Saint Thomas and above all those of John of Saint Thomas." All of the "fatal" "deviations of Kant or Descartes" were thus "self-explanatory," brought about by "ignorance of a particular distinction made by John of Saint Thomas." Maritain seems to have wanted to recruit Gilson; but a Sorbonne student told him that Gilson was "irritated" by the "fanatical figures, especially women," within the Cercle.[17] Gilson did not become a member of the Cercle.

Maritain refers with such an aura of certainty to John of Saint Thomas in *The Degrees of Knowledge* (1932) that one 1980s doctoral student imagined that John must be some sort of relative of the Angelic Doctor. The *Degrees of Knowledge* is a seriously argued development of Roman Thomism. Its key idea, that the empirical sciences, mathematics, and metaphysics constitute three ascending degrees of abstraction from matter, is found in *Le sens commun* and in *Dieu, son existence et sa nature,* which trace the notion back to Aristotle's *Metaphysics.* Maritain makes his debt to Garrigou clear in his footnotes. He expanded his dialogue with Aquinas into a conversation with his contemporaries: no historian, he intended to exhibit Saint Thomas as the "apostle for modern times."[18]

Garrigou-Lagrange's former student, the Dominican Marie-Dominique Chenu, recalled his Roman teacher's having remarked, in a flight of logical fantasy, "After all, the Incarnation is just a fact."[19] Gilson's objection to Roman Thomism would come down to this: its making free play with the

16. Barré, *Jacques et Raïssa Maritain,* 178, 194; Chenaux, "La seconde vague thomiste," 140–41, 153.

17. Congar, *Journal d'un théologien,* 34–35; Roland Dalbiez to Jacques Maritain, June 5, 1923, cited in Chenaux, "La seconde vague thomiste," 154.

18. Garrigou-Lagrange, *Le sens commun,* e.g., 47–48, 103; *Dieu, son existence et sa nature,* 135. "Saint Thomas d'Aquin apôtre des temps modernes" was the title of a lecture given by Maritain in 1923; it was published as a book, with the same title, in the following year.

19. Chenu, *Jacques Duquesne interroge le Père Chenu,* 38.

facts of Aquinas's texts and, following from that, its logical imperviousness to facticity, its fatal lack of "choisisme." Rightly or wrongly, Gilson attributed this flaw not only to Kleutgen and Garrigou but even to Maritain, who became his friend.

## The Tradition of Louvain

At Pope Leo's suggestion, the University of Louvain created a chair of Thomistic philosophy in 1882. An intellectual disciple of Joseph Kleutgen, Desiré Mercier (1851–1926) was the first to hold it. In 1893, Professor Mercier was given his own graduate department, the Institut Supérieur de Philosophie, otherwise known as the École Saint Thomas d'Aquin. Here he "set up a psychological laboratory," for "along with psychology, epistemology was . . . Msgr. Mercier's favorite branch of philosophy." Mercier was determined to demonstrate that neo-Thomist philosophy can breach the domain of the positive sciences. For all of his faith in the empirical foundations of Thomism, Mercier's "epistemology. . . remained a theory of Aristotelian science,"[20] that is, science as conceived in Aristotle's logic.

Like Père Hugon and Joseph Gredt, the Louvain school marched through the land of philosophy on its way into the *Summa Theologiae*. Mercier's manual of Thomism, the *Cours de philosophie* (1905), travels through cosmology, psychology, criteriology, ontology, theodicy, logic, to ethics, and ends with a bit of history of philosophy. It links cosmology, psychology, and ethics with the experimental sciences.[21] The Louvain enterprise reflects the cultural optimism of the century ending with the First World War.

Monsignor Mercier's academic career came to an end in 1906 when he was appointed archbishop of Malines. The Thomists of Louvain were faithful to the tradition he founded. It was through the writings of the Louvain historian of mediaeval thought, Maurice de Wulf, that the notion of a "Scholastic synthesis" gained some currency at the outset of the twentieth century.

## The Saulchoir Dominicans

Upon their expulsion from France in 1904, some French Dominicans made for Belgium, where they reestablished their studium at Saulchoir.

---

20. Riet, *Thomistic Epistemology,* 1:129, 126, 129.
21. Prouvost, "Les relations entre philosophie et théologie chez É. Gilson," 418.

Under the regency of Père Ambroise Gardeil (1859–1931), and for many decades afterward, the atmosphere of the Saulchoir studium was pervaded by his book *Le donné révélé et la théologie* (1909). *Le donné révélé* centers upon the "*coherence* between the concrete experience of the faith of the Church and its scientific conceptualization."[22]

When Antoine Lemonnyer took the regency in 1911, with the assistance of Pierre Mandonnet, Saulchoir turned to the historical study of Aquinas. Mediaeval intellectual *history* became the forte of Saulchoir, with the attempt to "restore Thomas to his epoch" and with the presentation of the *Summa Theologiae* in the context of Gothic architecture and the merchant communes, rather than in the "timeless perfection" of its commentarial aspic. Père Garrigou-Lagrange supervised Marie-Dominique Chenu's doctorate, on contemplation in Aquinas. After its completion, Père Chenu came to float in Saulchoir's studium "like a fish in water." As an admirer of Bergson, *experience* was not a word at which Chenu took fright.[23]

Gilson was attracted by Saulchoir's historical mentality. He wrote to them in 1923, praising the work of the *Revue des sciences philosophiques et théologiques,* and offering them "two" copies of his forthcoming book on Bonaventure.[24] Even after the young professor wrote again, commending Saulchoir's "strong taste of intellectuality and hard work," Père Mandonnet rejected his offers of collaboration in Saulchoir's new edition of the *Summa Theologiae*. Père Chenu said that Gilson was refused admission to the Saulchoirist project because "some do not consider M. G's 'Thomism' to be . . . absolutely 'pure.'" In 1923, Saulchoir created the Société Thomiste, which published the *Bulletin Thomiste*. It ran a hostile review of Gilson's *Le Thomisme* (1919, 1922), which delayed the author's adhesion to the Société. But Saulchoir was a magnet for Catholic intellectuals, and Gilson eventually became a "habitué, and a close friend of Chenu." The Dominican and the "*universitaire*" layman would both "contest the intention of the Louvain school to reconstruct a Thomist philosophy independent of Christian theology." Chenu initiated the friendship by finding an English translator for Gilson's *Le Thomisme*.[25]

---

22. Conticello, "Métaphysique de l'être et théologie de la grâce," 450. My italics.

23. Fouilloux, *Une église en quête de liberté,* 127–28; Conticello, "Métaphysique de l'être et théologie de la grâce," 437, 447.

24. Gilson to Père M.D. Roland-Gosselin, April 27, 1923, in Gilson Correspondence, "Letters to and from Marie Dominique Chenu" file. Although it is filed with Gilson's letters to Chenu, the content has led scholars to believe that the "Révérend Père" to whom it was addressed was Roland-Gosselin, not Chenu.

25. P. Chenu to Père Raymond Louis (the French Dominican Provincial), January 18, 1925, cited in Chenaux, "La seconde vague thomiste," 156; Fouilloux, *Une église*

## Gilson's First Book about Thomas Aquinas

Along with his doctorate, Gilson had gained a posting as assistant professor of philosophy at the University of Lille. In his first semester, in 1913, Gilson gave what he called a "modest course of lectures" on Aquinas. Fernand Strowski, editor of the *Revue des cours et conférences,* "was impressed by the novelty of an entire course on St. Thomas being offered in a provincial university,"[26] audited a few, and bought the rights to the series; half had been published when the Great War put an end to such lighthearted publishing enterprises.

Gilson's "modest course of lectures" was reproduced as *Le Thomisme: introduction au système de saint Thomas d'Aquin.* The book was printed in 1919, by which time he was teaching at the University of Strasbourg. Gilson published six editions of this book between 1919 and 1965: he called it "l'oeuvre d'une vie entière." Although he described the first version as "a monument elevated by the author to his own ignorance," the profile of the 1919 edition of *Le Thomisme* is preserved in that of 1922, and the additions that version makes are carried into the great version of 1927, and so forth.[27] Throughout the expansions, rearrangements, elaborations, deepenings, and new departures which it achieved in its six editions, the home key of *Le Thomisme* does not mutate. That is like saying that the home key of a children's song is preserved within a Wagnerian opera. But it was the *simplicity* of the book that allowed for its continuous expansion.

The neo-Thomists had treated the *Summa Theologiae* like a jigsaw puzzle that could be taken apart and reassembled in a "common-sensical" or a logical order. This reordering had left a mysterious hole at the center: the missing piece was the revealed faith for which all of the other pieces were cut. It was because of that missing shape—omitted because of the idea that to "confuse philosophy and theology" is to "misunderstand the thought of Saint Thomas"[28]—that, whatever the efforts by Vatican officials to stuff that irksome gap with authority, the puzzle had come to pieces during the modernist crisis. The 1913–1919 *Le Thomisme* is Gilson's own contribution to the resolution of the modernist controversy.

---

*en quête de liberté,* 129; Conticello "Métaphysique de l'être et théologie de la grâce," 434; Marie-Dominique Chenu to Étienne Gilson, November 5, 9, 1923 (the second letter in response to a lost but evidently affirmative reply from Gilson), both in Chenu Papers, the Saulchoir Archive.

26. Shook, "Maritain and Gilson: Early Relations," 9.

27. Prouvost, "Les relations entre philosophie et théologie chez É. Gilson," 413; Gilson, *Le philosophe et la théologie,* 102.

28. Gilson, *Le philosophe et la théologie,* 102.

As Bergson had often done, Gilson claims to have two types of opponent. On the one hand, there are those unnamed secularists who consider that, since Thomas was a theologian, "whatever is philosophical in his work is necessarily contaminated." These anonymous secularists play little part in the book. It was not written for them. On the other, there are those neo-Scholastics who believe that Saint Thomas's philosophy "exists in and for itself, independently of the theological speculation with which it is eventually associated."[29]

Gilson's disapproval of the Thomism of the manuals, and his opposition to the Louvain and the Roman schools, is articulated in the layout of the first edition. Following the narrative order of the *Summa Theologiae, Le Thomisme* begins with the striking *entrée* of God, rather than sliding up the scale through nature or logic to the divine. Like the *Summa Theologiae, Le Thomisme* sets off with the arguments for the existence of God, proceeds to the divine attributes, and from there descends to the creation, the angels, and man.

In 1913 to 1919, Gilson's defense of his exposition is historical, or textual: this was Thomas's own procedure. Gilson did not believe that a philosophy that extrapolates ideas from the *Summa* and lays them out in an order judged appropriate on Aristotelian grounds is authentic Thomism. When *Le Thomisme* was composed, at Lille, the modernist crisis was passing through its "crucial years," during which Gilson "moved...in what one could call peri-modernist circles"; the intellectual priests whom this "faithful and fervent Catholic" knew in those days "generally had an aversion for the theological tradition." By situating Thomas's rational demonstrations within the order of faith, Gilson gave them a framework that might have made sense to one who was drawn to fideism or to Bergsonism, from 1903 to 1914. Gilson himself would be "called a 'fideist,' and the label was meant as a criticism."[30]

Gilson says that "first philosophy," the search for the first causes and final ends of the universe, and revealed theology are each sciences of God. But they are different sciences, because "where reason can take hold, faith has no role at all to play...one cannot know and believe at the same time, the same thing: '*impossible est quod de eodem sit fides et scientia.*'" Gilson distinguishes two ways in which philosophy and theology differ from one another. They vary first by the "principles of *demonstration*" they employ:

29. Gilson, *Introduction au système de S. Thomas d'Aquin,* 16.
30. Bars, "Gilson et Maritain," 259–60; del Noce, "Thomism and the Critique of Rationalism," 733.

"the philosopher borrows his arguments from the causes peculiar to things." Thus, for example, in each of the "Five Ways," Saint Thomas raises a question about the causal principles observed in the world around us. When Saint Thomas gives demonstrative reasons "it matters little whether religion has or has not directed his observation to that which he has to demonstrate": the only justification for such reasons is philosophical. The "theologian's argument," on the other hand, "is always taken from the first cause of things, which is God": theologians state that something is true *because* it is God's revealed word. In the second place, philosophy and theology differ in terms of "*order* followed": philosophy is spurred by the meaning which it finds in creatures to rise to God, whereas in theology "the consideration which comes first is that of God, and that of creatures follows upon it." Saint Thomas is made to see by theology and argues like a philosopher: "We are," says Gilson, "looking at a system which, historically speaking, consists in an ensemble of philosophical demonstrations ordered according to a theological plan and in view of theological ends."[31]

Saint Thomas's two *Summas* conduct, Gilson claimed, a "rigorous philosophical investigation" of God, angels, and man: they do so on theological territory, on the ground illuminated by the light of faith, given by God to the author. Far from being sterilized against it, Saint Thomas's theology fertilizes his philosophy. It is because "Saint Thomas was essentially a theologian" that "he constituted a new and original system of philosophy."[32] Eighteen years after *Le Thomisme* was originally composed, Gilson would begin to press that point against the secularists.

The two *Summas* are not the only stories Aquinas told. What about his commentaries on Aristotle, and his "opuscules," his short treatises on philosophical problems? These commentaries had been used to create the picture of Thomas as a straight philosopher. Although it is sufficient to glance at the footnotes to any of Gilson's books about Saint Thomas to realize that he does not disqualify Thomas's commentaries on Aristotle's *Metaphysics, Ethics, De Anima,* and so forth, "as an historical source of Thomas's own philosophy" Gilson does "refuse to establish, on their basis, the philosophical thought of the angelic doctor." "Is it absolutely certain," Gilson asks ironically, "that the Commentaries are . . . the philosophical work par excellence of Saint Thomas?" The "most perfect form in which" Saint

31. Gilson, *Introduction au système de S. Thomas d'Aquin,* 18, citing Aquinas, *Quaetiones Disputate de Veritate* XIV, art. 9, ad Resp; ibid., 22–25.
32. Prouvost, "Les relations entre philosophie et théologie chez É. Gilson," 414–15; Gilson, *Introduction au système de S. Thomas d'Aquin,* 23.

Thomas's philosophy is "clothed," that is, the two *Summas*,[33] ought to be the measure by which we interpret his procedure as a whole.

In the 1913–1919 *Le Thomisme*, Gilson does not tell us much about what is new in Thomas's philosophy. His conception of the function of the divine "ideas," or eternal verities has not advanced beyond the Suarezian notion described in *La liberté chez Descartes*. He still conceives the Thomist doctrine of creation as the reproduction of ideal essences contained in God. Having taken his auditors through the steps of the "negative way," stripping time, potentiality, matter, and composition from God, Gilson observes that "God is thus not only his essence: he is also his being . . . the *quod est* is identified in him with the *quo aliquid est*." If each creature's essence is its "final purpose," God's essence is existing. He is outside of nature, which receives its existence from beyond itself. Here Gilson finds the chord out of which many of his masterpieces will be orchestrated: "Between the being *[esse]* of God and the participated being that we are, there is no common measure, and we can say, to take up an Augustinian formula, that the creature *has* his being, whereas God *is* his being. There is thus a properly infinite distance, which separates the two modes of existing and . . . we can call God by the name which he gives himself [Exod. 3:13]: He who is." By comparison with what Gilson will later make of the metaphysical implications of this statement, this is indeed "perfunctory"; but the principle is there to be developed. In the 1913–1919 edition Gilson's Thomas weds a Christian God to an Aristotelian nature:

> The God of Saint Thomas is . . . that of Saint Augustine, and it is not enough for Augustine to have been influenced by neo-Platonism for his God to be identified with that of Plotinus. Between Platonic speculation and the theology of the Fathers of the Church, Jehovah, the personal God was interposed, who acted through intelligence and through will, who freely posited outside of himself a real universe chosen by his wisdom from amongst an infinity of possible universes. Between the freely created universe and the creator God there is an impassable abyss and no continuity other than that of order. . . . [W]e are at the antipodes from neo-platonic philosophy. . . . The distance between the two philosophies is less perceptible if we turn from God to man. We have said that the God of Saint Thomas . . . is not the God of Plato but the Christian God of Augustine; we can add that the man of Saint Thomas is not the man of Plato but the man of Aristotle.[34]

33. McCool, *From Unity to Pluralism*, 169; Prouvost, "Les relations entre philosophie et théologie chez É. Gilson," 414; Gilson, *Introduction au système de S. Thomas d'Aquin*, 23–24.
34. On the divine ideas, see Gilson, *Introduction au système de S. Thomas d'Aquin*,

From the start, Gilson cut through the rationalist interpretation imposed upon Thomas's texts by the Religious Orders in order to reclaim him as a religious thinker. The God of Thomas's metaphysics cannot be extracted and viewed separately from the God of his theology, because, historically, the metaphysics has been set a new object to describe, by revelation.

In the *Bulletin thomiste*, Père Pierre Mandonnet noted the reversal of the order of the manuals with disapprobation. He criticized the 1919 and 1922 editions of *Le Thomisme* on the grounds that Aquinas "classifies the sciences according to their degree of abstraction," as can be seen from his Aristotle commentaries, which list, in serial order, "posterior analytics (logic), physics, sense and sensation, ethics and metaphysics." Such is the "order implied by the conditions proper to human nature and its faculties," and such is the order that an exhibition of the doctrine of the *Summa* should follow. Ignoring Gilson's distinction between theological order and philosophical demonstration, Mandonnet argues that "transporting" the theological order into philosophy turns the arguments for the existence of God into a priori deductions.[35]

Thus began Gilson's life-long skirmishing with the three rival versions of twentieth-century Thomism: Conceptualist-Suarezian, Roman, and Louvainiste. He did not treat all of his contemporaries to disparagement. Gilson liked Sertillanges and Rousselot; his antipathy to Cajetan is "known to everyone. John of Saint Thomas comes out of it little better. He often cites Garrigou-Lagrange, nearly always in order to fire a rocket at him. He doffs his hat to A. Gardeil in passing."[36]

Gilson stands out as an Erasmus among the neo-Thomists, a scholar who returned to the sources. This was not simply due to originality. Gilson was lucky to have received a secular training in the history of ideas at the Sorbonne and to embark upon a properly historical study of Thomas at the moment when this step could best be taken. He nonetheless created his moment, not by the project of returning to the original mediaeval texts, for the example of Saulchoir shows that this was in the air, but by seeing the mediaeval Christian thinkers as *individuals*. When we speak of Gilson's Erasmian approach to Thomas, and to the other mediaeval authors, we do not mean that he abstained from the scholar's normal recourse to secondary literature. By 1913, others had trod the historical path into the Middle

---

76–77; on Exod. 3:13, ibid., 59. Noonan, "The Existentialism of Etienne Gilson," 418; Gilson, *Introduction au système de S. Thomas d'Aquin*, 171.

35. Mandonnet, Review of Gilson, *Le Thomisme* (1923), 135–36.
36. Bars, "Gilson et Maritain," 259.

Ages, and he cites them. Gilson's contribution to the progress of historical knowledge has survived because he treated his subjects' uniqueness as a metaphysical principle.

What was the principle? It is not too far from the nominalism for which Père Garrigou-Lagrange had taken Bergson to task. Gilson had, after all, modeled his presentation of Thomas on Lévy-Bruhl's way of interpreting David Hume. Nor did he not automatically regard *nominalism* as a term of abuse. As Gilson put it, much later: "When the inopportune works of historians disarrange received ideas, the exacerbated philosophers accuse them of nominalism. This is a little bit too easy. A nominalist is someone who replaces essences with names, and it is wrong to do this when essences genuinely exist, but one is not a nominalist, in the pejorative sense of the term, if one refuses to see an essence which is not truly there. 'Scholasticism,' . . . or 'the Middle Ages' or the 'Renaissance' are not essences susceptible of definition but names signifying historical realities which are the objects of analysis and description."[37]

But perhaps the principle had better be named *realism* than nominalism. Gilson's plucking of his writers' individuality out of the syntheses in which the neo-Thomist philosophy had submerged them was due, Kenneth Schmitz says, to his "metaphysical realism" in the "very domain of the history of ideas": he knew that "the fabric of history does not consist simply of facts, nor of ideas; it is made of persons: of saints, theologians, philosophers, and historians, of artists, musicians and poets, of political, military and ecclesiastical personages."[38] Gilson had the training in the location of ideas within a historical context that the neo-Thomists lacked; he knew and valued the arguments that would stick with a professional readership; and he had wider intellectual tastes than many of the clergy. Something must have given him the courage to portray Saint Thomas as a theologian.

37. Gilson, "Compagnons de route," 289–90.
38. Schmitz, *What Has Clio to Do with Athena?* 14–15.

# 4

# "Under the Ensign of
# Saint Francis and Saint Dominic"

In the years when Abbé Thorelle was nourishing Gilson's love for pictures and for music, and as Gilson made his patient way through the Sorbonne to schoolmastering, Paris was a matrix of modernist art. Gilson felt that Bergson's philosophy had a "deep tendency to be realized in beauty." Bergson's God was, Gilson claimed in 1917, "comparable to an artist."[1]

## Modernist Painting

According to the Russian expressionist painter Wassily Kandinsky (1866–1944), the two movements that changed the face of art, the cubism of Picasso, and "Futurism, Dadaism, and Expressionism," "were born practically on the same day" in "1911–1912." Cubism and expressionism share a rejection of the typifying feature of art since the Renaissance, the attempt to make a picture lifelike through the illusion of three-dimensionality. They eliminate the means by which the appearance of naturalism had been achieved, scientific or mathematical perspective. When the expressionist Ernst Ludwig Kirchner started to paint in two dimensions, in 1905, it was a way of insisting that a painting *is* a *painting*, not a natural object at second remove. As Jean Metzinger and Albert Gleizes put it in their manifesto, "Du Cubisme" (1912), once a landscape is "reproduced" in a painting, it belongs to "a different kind of space" than that of natural, physical reality.[2]

The expressionists wanted their pictures to be transparencies in which emotional, aesthetic, or spiritual values could be seen. Whereas Kandinsky

1. Gilson, "Art et métaphysique," 243; Gilson, early lecture notes on Bergson lectures, "Introduction à la philosophie Bergsonnienne," 1917, in Gilson Papers, University of St. Michael's College Archives.
2. Dube, *The Expressionists,* 104, 39; Gleizes and Metzinger, "Cubism," 7.

expressed his spiritual perceptions through unconstrained, lavish colors, cubists like Picasso and Braque impose a geometrical *form* on their designs. It required a mathematical imagination for Delaunay to paint the "Eiffel Tower" series, by which cubism entered the popular imagination. Cubism is the art of analytic painters, expressionism the art of the synthesizing vision characteristic of religious minds. Debate between these outlooks was well known in French intellectual society. In 1915, in his first essay on the philosophy of art, Étienne Gilson made it clear that he did "not at all intend to range" himself "amongst the partisans of *expression* against those of *form*."[3]

The two movements overlap. Cubism burst on the world in Picasso's *Demoiselles d'Avignon;* but that painting is more expressionist than cubist. The first exhibition to be described by critics with the new word *expressionist*, held in Berlin in 1911, included works by Picasso, Braque, Vlaminck, Matisse, and Dufy, artists who are usually designated as cubists or fauves.[4]

Bergson once told Gilson that it is no good having just one intuition: we must have two of them at once. Where such a fusion comes about, whether in Bergsonian metaphysics or in visual art, it travels beyond lyrical self-expression toward *symbolism*. The German expressionists were influenced by African sculpture. So was Picasso. What attracted him to it was that it captures the idea of a figure rather than imitating its literal shape. The "more symbolic" forms of African art showed him how to replace "visual appearances" with an "art that is simultaneously representational and anti-naturalistic." By 1909, Picasso had given cubism its "most lucid expression" by fusing "the principles" of "African art with the more painterly lessons learnt from Cézanne."[5]

Kandinsky claimed that each of his colors conveys a specific symbolism. His color symbolism is comparable to Eastern orthodox iconography. It is a visual spirituality of light. A "fairy-tale power and splendor" was present for Kandinsky when he first saw Monet's *Haystack*. Realizing that Monet's "painting" is simply that, "the object was discredited, as an indispensable element of a painting." He first painted his experience of "fairy-tale" when he realized that "nature and art are ... organically ... different from each other." "Picasso's *collages*" exemplify "the Cubists' obsession with the 'tableau-objet,'" that is, the idea of the painting as an "entity with a sepa-

3. Gilson, "Art et métaphysique," 254.

4. Golding, "Cubism," 53–54; Dube, *The Expressionists,* 18; Lynton, "Expressionism," 38.

5. Gilson, "Compagnons de route," 281; Lynton, "Expressionism," 39; Dube, *The Expressionists,* 72; Golding, "Cubism," 56, 62.

rate life of its own, not echoing . . . the external world, but recreating it in an independent way."[6] Between the Italian Renaissance and Picasso's *Demoiselles d'Avignon,* European artists more often understood a painting as a laboriously produced *sign* than as a *symbol.* Whereas the sign points away from itself, the symbol mysteriously compacts within its own individual substance a microcosm of the universe as a whole. The modernist artists recaptured the mediaeval sense of a picture as a symbol; a painting is for these men an aesthetic "sacrament." An apprentice mediaeval historian had something to learn from the artistic atmosphere they created.

As the proponents of an art that is both anti-naturalistic and realistic, the expressionists and the cubists were aesthetic symbolists. The cubist manifesto indicates that these painters hoped to achieve, not a nonrepresentative art, but one that is more intensively and universally representative: when "the light of organization" burns in a painting, they said, it "does not harmonize with this or that state of affairs, it harmonizes with the totality of things, with the universe: it is an organism."[7]

Its critics believed that modernist art was just the effusion of the artist's subjective feelings, that expressionism equals "the use of art to transmit personal experience." French conservatives saw avant-garde painting as an excrescence of the romantic exaltation of the subjective ego. For Pierre Lasserre, art critic to the Action Française, romanticism was born in Jean-Jacques Rousseau's egotistical "social nihilism," his individualistic subjectivism.[8]

The French royalists also held Bergson responsible for the depredations of modern painting. In lectures delivered at the Institut d'Action Française in the winter of 1910–1911, and published in the *Action française* newspaper, Lasserre attacked the "Bergsonian" aesthetic as a Romantic "egoism of the individual": "Rather than derive their themes from nature as the classicists did, the romantics take the self alone as their subject, a self . . . mired in its own lurid imagination. . . . Since a conception of beauty 'excludes the absurd,' and beauty is derived from the study of natural laws operative in the universal order, an art of beauty, rather than egotism, is eminently reasonable. Thus for the classicists, 'observation of the truth, study of nature, have always been the fundamental rule.'"[9]

The royalists felt that avant-garde art was untrue to the French genius. Lasserre "supported Maurras' association of French art with a rationalist

6. Kandinsky, *Concerning the Spiritual in Art,* 36–45; Kandinsky, "Reminiscences," 26, 23; Golding, "Cubism," 66.

7. Gleizes and Metzinger, "Cubism," 5.

8. Lynton, "Expressionism," 42; Lasserre, *Le romanticisme française,* 14, 16, 57.

9. Antliff, *Inventing Bergson,* 21.

tradition rooted in the Cartesianism of the seventeenth century and... Greco-Roman culture." The modernists countered with an anti-Cartesian aesthetic. In *Du Cubisme,* Gleizes and Metzinger, both admirers of Bergson, "claimed to express the organic 'light of organization' in their paintings even as they condemned *la lumière de la raison.*"[10]

For Kandinsky, the endeavor to find in art an autonomous, spiritual world led by 1912 to abstract painting. Kandinsky interpreted the new impulse of the arts toward abstraction as a rejection of contemporary cultural materialism. He praised Debussy for eschewing the "material tone so characteristic of program music" and trusting "in the creation of a more abstract impression." An admirer of Rudolf Steiner, Mme Blavatsky, and Bergson, Kandinsky hoped that the revolution in the arts was the herald of a more spiritual age. Ever since the wayward abbot Joachim of Fiore (1145–1202) intuited that the meaning of the unity of the Old and New Testaments is the three successive ages of Father, Son, and Holy Spirit, numerous charismatic movements have imagined that the age of the Spirit was coming to birth in themselves. The "Spiritual Franciscans" of the thirteenth century were the first of these. In 1913, Kandinsky wrote of his discovery of abstract expressionism, "Here begins the great epoch of the spiritual, the revelation of the spirit. Father-Son-Holy Spirit."[11] Instead of an eschatological new age, 1914 witnessed the outbreak of the First World War.

## Cubist-Expressionist Aesthetics—from the Trenches

Caroline Gilson feared that military service would lead her sons astray; she may have been looking in the wrong direction for occasions of sin. Just before his call-up, in 1914, Gilson wrote to her that "it would be a lot easier had I never got mixed up with our holy mother the church, as you think it to be. I have never failed to observe my religious duties. What is true is that I have not, since the present pope [Pius X] came on the scene, considered myself to be very orthodox. But I am doing my best. I am giving all my good will, and I don't believe I can do much more." In the same month Abbé Lemire, the editor of the *Cri de Flandres,* was suspended for putting an interpretation on *Rerum Novarum* which diverged from that of the Holy Office. Gilson was not favorably impressed by the Curia's readiness to use

10. Ibid., 10, 12.
11. Kandinsky, *Concerning the Spiritual in Art,* 16, 13; Lynton, "Expressionism," 46; Cohn, *The Pursuit of the Millennium,* 100–103; Kandinsky, "Reminiscences," 39.

the rapid-strike mechanisms of suspension and excommunication: "I assure you again that all you have asked me to do, I have done. Besides, the pope is dead! I may be more comfortable with his successor." Once at the front, Étienne was able to use his knowledge of Albert the Great's *Commentary* on the *Sentences* of Peter Lombard to offer a dying man the opinion that confession to a layperson is permissible, in extremity, and that the shame of so doing is sufficient to relieve the penitent of much of his guilt. The lay confession was, he told Maman, "a source of enormous consolation to both of us."[12]

In 1915 Gilson published "Art et métaphysique" "from the war-front." His article suggests that artists use nature as a stimulus but not as a model. He commends "cubism and futurism" for their efforts to shake off the traces of photography from art, for showing to what extent pictures "can become independent of the given physical world."[13]

Lasserre's neo-classicist aesthetic assimilated art to philosophy, since he considered that artistic "beauty is derived from the study of natural laws operative in the universal order." For such a rationalist philosophy of art, beauty and truth are achieved in the same way and are measured by the same standard. Gilson argues that art and metaphysics gain the same end, the intuition of the trans-cognitive, by entirely different means. If we are not to identify art and metaphysics, the first error we must clear out of our paths, Gilson says, is the idea that the purpose of art is the "exact representation of nature."[14]

For Bergson, understanding functions below the level of intuition. As Gilson notes here, parroting a Bergsonian truism, "Within the fleeting continuity of reality, understanding cuts out of things that which it designates by its own terms, and in so doing, it gives itself the necessary conditions of language and of action." Understanding makes its "cuts" for a practical purpose. Gilson observes that the artist's intuition differs from our quotidian attitude to natural objects in that the only aspect of things that he sees is their potential to arouse "emotion" in us. The artist thus creates an intensive symbol of affectivity. To do so is to "substitute for the given object a constituted object, more apt than the first to fulfill that function" of releasing emotion in an audience. Whereas "nothing in the universe of objects . . . is constructed in order to move us," art is affectivity made concrete. "The artist," Gilson claims, "uses sensible things to introduce us into a world

12. Shook, *Gilson*, 66–67, 76.
13. Gilson, "Art et métaphysique," 267, 255.
14. Antliff, *Inventing Bergson*, 21; Gilson, "Art et métaphysique," 245–46.

where each form . . . can . . . express a determinate spiritual significance."[15] The artist's model is his own "schema" for expressing emotion as form. Affective forms do not supply knowledge; they give us aesthetic perception.

If aesthetic experience does not provide information, does it follow that we cannot make objective judgments about works of art? Gleizes and Metzinger believed it to be so. Their manifesto asserted that "henceforth objective knowledge at last regarded as chimerical, . . . the painter will know no other laws than those of Taste."[16] Gilson's attitude falls close to the cubist manifesto. "Art et métaphysique" finds that "works of art do not offer themselves to us as representations of the interior or exterior world which are comparable in the degree that they are exact or profound, but as beings which form a scale in the degree of their perfection." The degree of beauty of an artistic work depends on its "structure of perfection," its internal ordering. There is, Gilson argues, a hierarchy among works of art, better and worse symphonies, and sculptures. He offers small comfort to the rationalist proponents of aesthetic value: his artistic hierarchy cannot be "known," as one can know a true proposition; it can only be "perceived," that is, experienced in the senses. Each person's sensing is unique to himself.[17] Whose senses are sufficiently refined to estimate the degree of perfection of an artwork? Individuals of Taste, as the cubists had declared.

The mediaevalist was taken prisoner at Bois de Ville-devant-Chaumant in February 1916. He was detained in two camps, at Ströhlen and at Burg. Having acquired a stockpile of the works of Bonaventure, Gilson's "enforced leisure" also went toward his first great biography of a historical individual.[18] He also entertained the officers in both camps with lectures on Bergson, in which he contrasted Aquinas, Descartes, and Comte, who make a rational "effort to exhaust the real," with Bonaventure, Pascal, and Bergson, as philosophers who attempt "to attain the real" suprarationally.

Gilson's lecture notes state that the "soul seems like the blossoming of that interior power which is liberty." The evidence that the "fundamental power" of free creativity "is the soul itself" is the "appearance of novelty in the world." "There is," Gilson advised his audience, "a case where we see a free act taking place before our eyes. It is that of art. A work of art is a free

15. Gilson, "Art et métaphysique," 244, 248–49, 250–51.
16. Gleizes and Meitzinger, "Cubism," 18.
17. Gilson, "Art et métaphysique," 263–64, 266; Diodato, "Note Sull' Ontologia dell' Arte di Étienne Gilson," 613.
18. Lefèvre, Une heure avec . . . Étienne Gilson, 70.

act made concrete. It is unforeseeable, it has no causes." The freedom which each of us discovers in his own "I" is "the furthermost wave in the sea of the *élan vital*...the avant garde of the *élan vital*." Bergson's *élan vital* is the creative "personality" of nature. If we "enlarge our horizon...[t]he whole world comes to appear to us like a consciousness, a deep 'I', and like this 'I', life is creative of new realities."[19]

Gilson pressed on with the development of his aesthetic. From the officers' prison camp, he mailed Lévy-Bruhl "Du fondement des jugements esthétiques." Here he returns to the question of the objectivity of aesthetic judgments, rejecting all of the classicist solutions to the problem and aligning himself with the Romantic adulation for creative personalities.

*Du Cubisme* suggested that "Cubist space puts the beholder in immediate contact with the artist's personality," reflecting "the personality back upon the understanding of the spectator." Gilson interprets aesthetic appreciation as a matter of "arousing" in oneself "an analogous intuition, corresponding to that which originated the work in the artist."[20]

"Art et métaphysique" had studied artworks from the point of view of their effect upon an audience's psychic state. Before we can really hear "Claude Debussy's *Préludes* for the piano," it claims, we must achieve an interior silence, which readies us for "the new state which a work of art must introduce into us," creating a space for "the condition to which the work is intended to lead us." Wagner's operas commence with "minutes of obscurity and silence" so that the audience can prepare itself for an "aesthetic intuition" in which "we model our psychic 'I' on the will of the artist expressed in the work of art."[21]

"Art et métaphysique" assumed that there *is* such a thing as "Beauty," with a capital B. Taking more seriously the implication of the principle that aesthetic experience is an event between an audience and an artistic object with its maker, "Du fondement des jugements esthétiques" argues that "Beauty is not an abstract entity subsisting in a-temporality, it only exists actually in those who perceive it and relatively to them."[22]

Gilson cuts down the classicists' armory of objective bases for aesthetic judgments. Aesthetic judgments find no objective foundation by being measured against generic types, for, he asserts, "in the order of art as in the

19. Gilson, notes on 1917 Bergson lectures, Gilson Papers.
20. Antliff, *Inventing Bergson,* 48; Gleizes and Metzinger, "Cubism," 8; Gilson, "Du fondement des jugements esthétiques," 533.
21. Gilson, "Art et métaphysique," 256–57.
22. Gilson, "Du fondement des jugements esthétiques," 545.

zoological order, the genres are posterior to the individuals." "General laws of art" are so "vague" as to be useless.[23] One may judge a talented copyist by his assimilation of traditional techniques, but this standard falls short of works of genius, by which the techniques are invented.

What does that leave us with, as the measure of artistic value, but the personalities of great artists? Gilson concludes that "if the understanding of a work is the more perfect in the degree that one can retrieve from beneath its exterior the emotion from which it originates, it is difficult to deny that in a similar way the communion of a great artist with great works of art must be more intimate than it is for an ordinary person. He must benefit from his faculties of artistic creation and from the particular revelation which he receives concerning the rapport of the man to his work." Artists of genius are fallible—Wagner did not like Debussy[24]—but they are nonetheless the best-equipped judges of beauty that we have.

Henri Bergson had a metaphysics and an epistemology of mobility. He compared spatial and intellectual cognition to a "series of snapshots" that remains external to the reality it aspires to know. Because reality is, at bottom, a temporal "propulsion," one knows it by "adopt[ing] its ceaselessly changing direction." Ernst Ludwig Kirchner said that his first step toward expressionism was "invent[ing] a technique of grasping everything while it was in motion."[25]

When he sat for his portrait before Jacques Émile Blanche in 1912, Bergson led their conversation away from cubism, which he disliked, toward the "Giaconda's smile." Jacques Blanche asked his sitter about cubism because these artists were attempting to capture the Bergsonian duration on canvas. They endeavored to do so by superimposing, juxtaposing, and multiplying the "same" figure in many postures. Gilson realized that such efforts go back to the beginning of art. He argued that the "most ancient designs that we have, cave paintings, are already interpretations, not copies of nature; they witness to an art of selection, of linear arrangement, and of synthesizing postures in order to produce the impression of movement."[26]

The cubists' effort to harness their painting to Bergson's metaphysic had the drawback that the philosopher claimed that time is the bearer of quality, whereas space is merely quantitative. Kandinsky realized that to attempt to achieve pictorial "mobility" is to assimilate painting to music, the art of

23. Ibid., 527–29.
24. Ibid., 541–43.
25. Bergson, *Creative Evolution*, 305; Bergson, *An Introduction to Metaphysics*, 59; Dube, *The Expressionists*, 38.
26. Antliff, *Inventing Bergson*, 39; Gilson, "Art et métaphysique," 246.

time. He saw in the "modern desire for rhythm in painting, . . . for setting color in motion" an application of "the methods of music" to painting.[27]

Kandinsky's desire to fuse the arts of painting and of music was rooted in a quasi-spiritual experience of the "fairy-tale" hour of sunset, when "the sun melts all Moscow into one spot which, like a mad tuba, sets one's . . . whole soul vibrating. It is only the final note of the symphony which brings every color to its greatest intensity, which . . . forces . . . all Moscow to resound like the *fff* of a giant orchestra." In Kandinsky's "fairy-tale" moment, color was transformed into sound. What the expressionist's eye *saw* in Moscow was realized, for Kandinsky, in Wagner's *Lohengrin*.[28]

For Gilson, the most nonrepresentative form of art is music. The painter, he says, still must compare his "white-gold" with the "ray of light." Although the writer "does not at all use language in the same way as other men," that is, for "practical purposes," he is nevertheless compelled to draw his words from "ordinary language." Music rises above this, since it "creates from whole cloth the works which it produces and the very fabric with which it constructs it. . . . Musical sounds are not utilisations of physical elements, elaborated and ordered in relation to aesthetic ends, but realities whose origin and essence is exclusively aesthetic." Since the origin of "musical sounds" is "exclusively aesthetic," having "no meaning outside of the domain of art," Gilson says, "they permit the musician to elaborate works" which are "totally expressive of beauty."[29] Like Kandinsky, he discovered in music the presence of a "fairy-tale," self-sufficient, supra-reality.

Bergson had said that "*Wherever anything lives, there is, open somewhere, a register in which time is being inscribed. . . . Time is invention or it is nothing at all.*" Because both bring about novelty, time is a symbol of creative energy. For Bergson, time as pure duration *is* creativity. So he does not, according to Gilson, identify nature as such with God: "God, in Bergson, is . . . not the world. This is not a pantheism in the strict sense. [God] is the creative energy of the world. The artist is neither a painting nor his collected works, but whatever he passes through has his creative power, and above all the *movement* which leaves pictures on its way. God is the *élan vital* which passes through and leaves the trail of the universe behind it." Speaking as an aesthetician, Gilson argued that the symphonies of César Franck exhibit, not an "original knowledge of what already existed," but rather a "new" creation. He writes, "The artist is not just a skillful artisan who captures the energies of the physical universe for our use, nor a savant or a philosopher, mirrors in

27. Kandinsky, *Concerning the Spiritual in Art*, 19.
28. Kandinsky, "Reminiscences," 23, 26.
29. Gilson, "Art et métaphysique," 255.

whom the universe is reflected; he is one of the creative forces of nature. He brings beings into existence which other men can know but which they do not have the power to create; if he himself had not existed, they would not have existed." Gilson could halfway concur with the Romantics' "religious" devotion to artist-personalities because the artist makes things that are new; or, at least, as he put it in 1915, "nature grows through man," because it "is elevated, through the personality of the artist, to total spirituality."[30]

At the close of the war, Gilson was deposited by the ministry in Lille for a year. Here he reviewed a few books by a man who differed from Bergson in the misfortune of having been a Catholic priest who had lost his faith. The reviewer notes with empathy the author's criticisms of the weapons of dogma—the "*Imprimatur,* the Index of Works and the Inquisition of Opinions"—and finds that he "could not read" Loisy's "little book without being moved by the profound sincerity and absolute intellectual honesty of the author." The reviewer lets the merits of the Comtean church, which Loisy now recommends, serviced by a "clergy of professors and intellectuals," speak for themselves.[31]

Étienne Gilson became professor in the history of philosophy in Strasbourg in 1919. He wrote the program notes for a series of symphony concerts, one of which was *La Mer.* He defends Debussy's use of new tone scales: "All chords and tones are legitimate if they... satisfy the ear and stir the imagination." Gilson had taken a stand against neo-classical aesthetics on the ground that the common-sense human impulse to allow "reason the satisfaction of strictly limiting the domain of the irrational" does not wholly work in the area of artistic judgment.[32]

## Gilson Appointed to the École Pratique des Hautes Études

In November 1921 Gilson was appointed *chargé de cours* in the undergraduate Faculty of Letters at the Sorbonne. In December, he was also posted to the postgraduate École Pratique des Hautes Études, where he worked in the Fifth Section, Religious Sciences of the History of Doctrines and Dogmas. From 1923, the section was run by the Sanskritist Sylvain Lévi. The scion of a family of tailors formed a close friendship with the cloth-merchant's son. With a nod at one aspect of Indian thinking, Gilson said

30. Bergson, *Creative Evolution,* 16, 341; Gilson, notes on 1917 Bergson lectures, Gilson Papers. Gilson underlined *le mouvement*. Gilson, "Art et métaphysique," 253–54.
31. Gilson, Review of *La discipline intellectuelle,* by Alfred Loisy, 130–31.
32. Shook, *Gilson,* 101; Gilson, "Du fondement des jugements esthétiques," 526.

that "if I had a chance to come back as someone else, I would want to come back as Sylvain Lévi." Hinduism was not Gilson's native genius; at Louis Massignon's doctoral Viva, at the Collège de France in 1922, he wanted to know, "Do the fakirs *really* perform the rope trick?"[33]

While still in Strasbourg, Gilson had received a manuscript about Descartes from a Sorbonne student. Once in Paris, he took over the supervision of Henri Gouhier's doctoral thesis. Gilson became the editor of the series *Études de philosophie médiévale*, published by Joseph Vrin, and in which most of his own books and those of his friends, such as Gouhier's *La pensée religieuse de Descartes* (1924), were published.

## Individual Characters

Henri de Lubac suggests that "it would be wrong to assume that" Étienne "had become a Thomist" by 1925. One reason was that Gilson felt himself a lone defender of "mediaeval studies" at the Sorbonne. In the academic world in which he lived, the history of philosophy jumped from Hellenism to the rebirth of rationality in the modern era. Lest Thomas be treated as a solitary incursion of reason within the superstitious bog of mediaeval culture, Gilson had to argue both that one cannot understand Thomas without reference to his contemporaries and that mediaeval philosophy as a whole had as much intellectual splendor as that of the age of Descartes, Kant, and Comte.[34]

One of the projects Gilson carried over from his Descartes thesis was to show that the "moderns" had a foot in mediaeval Christian civilization. To legitimate his position, Gilson needed to show that one cannot understand the early modern writers without knowing their mediaeval forebears. Thus, in "De la Bible à Françoise Villon," of 1923, he argued that "the first poet of modern times" drew on Isaiah, Saint Paul, and Bonaventure for his theme of the fall of the powerful. A four-finger exercise, from the following year, picks out the "Franciscan" elements in Rabelais.[35]

A second task was to depict the individuality of the mediaeval philosophers. "When the first, miserable edition of *Le Thomisme* appeared," Gilson

33. Interview, 1975, quoted in Shook, *Gilson*, 108; D'Alverny, "Nécrologie Étienne Gilson," 27. Seated in the jury, Gilson, who had read the thesis on al-Hallaj, whispered this question to a famous sociologist, who couldn't think what to ask. Massignon replied, "Yes, of course."

34. De Lubac, ed., *Letters of Gilson to de Lubac*, 218; Chenaux, "Le seconde vague thomiste," 154–55.

35. Gilson, "De la Bible à François Villon," 30; Gilson, "Rabelais Françisain" (1924).

said, "it was greeted with a striking criticism" by a theologian who "observed that the book had no object, because the philosophy of Saint Thomas was simply that of his times." The author had it in mind that religion is at the back not only of civilizations but of human characters. In his 1920 "Essai sur la vie intérieure," he wrote, "That which confers value on religion and assures its continuity, is that it is essentially productive of personalities; it is literally a maker of men."[36] Gilson is claiming that Christianity fulfills the aspirations of aesthetic Romanticism, producing great individuals. The Christianity in which the mediaeval writers were planted trained each of them to grow along their own, idiosyncratic lines. Just as, for Gilson the aesthetician, understanding a work of art entails communing with the great mind which created it, so, for the mediaeval historian, historiography is about the grasp of personalities, in their uniqueness.

Gilson devoted four Sorbonne seminars, in 1921, to Augustine, asking "what Augustine had meant in a number of his texts, what the role of faith had been in the thought of medieval Christians, and whether more than one manner of Christian thinking could be described as philosophical. These issues established the pattern of Gilson's philosophical (and theological) thinking during the next half-century."[37] He spent the 1920s meditating on the individuality of the mediaevals and on what constituted their common ground.

## Different Ideas Balanced within the Minds of Individual Characters

At the outset of the 1919 *Le Thomisme,* Gilson stated a principle he learned from Victor Delbos and employed in many of his biographical studies:

> When the historian of philosophy pushes his researches far enough, he makes the great systems appear as works of reconciliation, and as . . . efforts to harmonize divergent minds. Each of them, cultivated exclusively for itself, appears incompatible with the others; it engenders a strongly co-ordinated but poor system. One generally encounters a great complexity at the origins of philosophies, and that of St. Thomas does not make an exception to this rule. Like many others it is born in the consciousness of an epoch and in that of a man,

36. Gilson, "Compagnons de route," 289; Gilson, "Essai sur la vie intérieure," 55.
37. Shook, *Gilson,* 106.

in the conflict of spiritual tendencies which seek to create a harmonious equilibrium amongst themselves. This conflict is the Thomist problem itself.[38]

Thomas's system is balanced over against Averroistic rationalism and Bonaventurian fideism.

Gilson means, further, that the personality of every philosopher contains such contraries, and that the historian who reduces a system to a single essential idea makes his gains as a philosopher at the expense of the historical facts. He told an interviewer in 1925 that "the real philosophy of Descartes, Saint Thomas, or Bonaventure, is always a system of theses of which any one, taken by itself, would ruin the equilibrium of the doctrine, if left to develop on its own account."[39]

When his interviewer, Frédéric Lefèvre, asked him to distinguish his orientation from Maritain's, Gilson noted that Maritain's work "is not only that of a philosopher, but also of an artist." Maritain's "method," Gilson said, "consists in bringing the men back to their pure ideas." As Gilson observed, however, either one approaches ideas "in a-temporality, and one is outside history; or one moves in history, that is to say in time, and there one never encounters ideas in a pure state, but only men and systems of extreme complexity." Was he a historicist? Gilson replied, "I do not introduce historicism into metaphysics, and I attempt to avoid metaphysicism in history."[40] Gilson seems to have been at this juncture an Erasmian individualist with respect to the history of ideas.

## Saint Bonaventure: The Franciscan Way

Gilson's first enduringly beautiful book is *La philosophie de saint Bonaventure* (1924). One Louvain Thomist found it "even more disconcerting" than *Le Thomisme*. Gilson had meditated on the strangeness of Bonaventure's writings since the Great War. After discarding three attempts to describe these texts, he had decided that the only way to interpret Bonaventure was as "a spiritual son of Saint Francis, whose work is . . . an abstract expression of his interior life and personality."[41] Gilson pictures the Franciscan

38. Gilson, *Introduction au système de S. Thomas d'Aquin* (1919), 7; nearly the same words are used in the 1927 edition, *Le Thomisme: introduction au système de saint Thomas d'Aquin*, 13.

39. Lefèvre, *Une heure avec . . . Étienne Gilson*, 71.

40. Ibid., 71, 73–74.

41. Van Steenberghen, "Étienne Gilson, historien de la pensée médiévale," 500; Lefèvre, *Une heure avec . . . Étienne Gilson*, 70.

General as a philosophical expressionist. Expressionist art is the opposite of the classical realism admired by Pierre Lasserre. The art of abstract expressionism *expresses* the artist's mind and heart, rather than reproducing a copy of an external object.

Bonaventure the "philosopher," says Gilson, "cannot be separated from the man."[42] Born in Bagnorea in 1221, and assuming the Franciscan habit in his adolescence, Bonaventure's career as a philosopher at the University of Paris came to an end in 1257, when he was made Master General of the Franciscan order. The new Franciscan General was immediately confronted with the delicate problem of how to deal with his predecessor. Jean de Parme had become enamored of the prophesies of Joachim of Fiore. He had become the hero of the Spiritual Franciscans, with their literal, rigorist adhesion to the letter of Saint Francis's instructions for his friars' conduct. Others regarded Jean as a heretic; hence his sudden disposition as Master General. Bonaventure seems to have given orders for Jean de Parme's imprisonment.

The problem of how to adhere to Francis's "primitive ideal" did not languish there. Laying to one side Francis's first rule, the *Regula Prima,* and with it the dreams of the too-spiritual Franciscans, the new master general proposed to follow Francis's second rule. Even the attenuated *Regulata Bullata* required the sinuous skills of the commentator. Saint Francis would have conceded that his friars "could not preach without being able to *read* the sacred Scriptures and without knowing how the Church interprets them. But he appears to have failed to conceive of the necessity of writing four large volumes of Commentaries on the Sentences in order to be a good Franciscan Preacher." Bonaventure, that is, overrode Francis's literal intention that his friars be "instructed" but not "intellectuals." Intellectuals require books, and convents in which to house them: thus, *absolute* poverty disappeared along with the ideal of Franciscan friars who would simply sing the joys of the Creator. Bonaventure had to work out how to be a Franciscan in different circumstances from any which Francis had envisaged. His solution was to be true to the spirit, not the letter, of Francis's teaching.[43] This was an innovative kind of "spiritual Franciscanism."

According to Gilson, Saint Francis's personal experience consisted in near-constant experience of the presence of God, the highest "ecstasy" bestowed upon a human being in this life. The light of grace remained with Francis even in those brief moments when he was deflected from attention to God, "transfiguring" every creature in "the universe" into "precious

42. Gilson, *La philosophie de saint Bonaventure,* 43 (hereinafter cited as *Bonaventure*).
43. Ibid., 45, 57, 68.

effigies of God." The man who "walked on stones with fear and trembling, for the love of Him who is the corner-stone," and who "could not cut down a tree . . . without remembering Him who died on a tree . . . lived permanently in a forest of symbols."[44] The artistic revolution that erupted in Paris during the immediate prewar years turned back from naturalistic to symbolic art forms: one who had witnessed this was likely to find the key to Francis in his symbolic vision.

Gilson the aesthetician had claimed that art "is a *poesis,* that is, an activity that produces new realities." Now he underlines the inventive character of Francis's symbolic imagination, based as it was on the saint's direct communion with the Creator. The whole mediaeval world credited itself with symbolic vision, but the "thirteenth century biographers could easily gauge the distance which separates the allegories perceived, experienced and loved by Saint Francis from the hotchpotch of stale formulas known to tradition and deposited in the contemporary bestiaries." Francis "came down from Alverna penetrating the essence of creatures and fully deciphering their secret."[45] He saw Christ within all creatures.

This is Gilson's key to Bonaventure's philosophy. The saint would transform the "letter" of Francis's life into the "spirit" of an intellectual system. Bonaventure would transpose into philosophy the living experience of the saint whose basic intuition was the transparency of creation to the Creator. Bonaventure, the Franciscan who visited Alverna in order to write the *Journey of the Mind to God* (1259), the author of two lives of Saint Francis (1261–1263), the sermon "Christus omnium magister," and of the mystical theology of the *Hexaemeron* (1273), devoted his own mind to the translation of Saint Francis's experiences into a theological system. "If Francis had only felt and lived, Bonaventure would think," Gilson writes. The "personal intuitions of that spirit so detached from all science" would be expressed in the "philosophical ideas" of the Parisian Master.[46]

There is evidence for this in every philosophical step that Bonaventure took. Even his epistemology, in which reason is required to abstract itself from sense perception and from material images and in which the mind ultimately devotes itself to the "divine light" alone, can be seen as a transposition of Franciscan asceticism into philosophy. This was not a matter of a Parisian intellectual neutrally surveying the contents of someone else's spiritual experience. Even the most rigorist among the Franciscans had to concede his "humility and sanctity." Bonaventure's own piety and prayer,

44. Ibid., 72–74.
45. Gilson, "Art et métaphysique," 254; Gilson, *Bonaventure,* 73.
46. Gilson, *Bonaventure,* 69.

modeled on that of the founder of his order, was expressed in his "entire philosophy," which is nothing other than the rational articulation of "his experience of Franciscan spirituality."[47]

One reason some mediaeval historians found Gilson's book about Bonaventure so "disconcerting" was that he did not merely insist that the philosopher was, before all else, a theologian, but located the basis of his thinking in a spiritual experience. If Gilson's "Bonaventure" had been transported into the mid-twentieth century, he might have been suspected of theological modernism.

Bonaventure had learned his Augustinian theology in Paris from Alexander of Hales and Jean de la Rochelle. Albert the Great was lecturing in Paris when he was a student, between 1245 and 1248, and Gilson surmises that the man who passed onto his bovine Dominican student a reverence for Aristotle made his thoughts known to the Franciscan. Against Mandonnet and de Wulf, who proposed that Bonaventure was a forerunner to Saint Thomas, hampered from reaching the same conclusions by the lack of available translations of Aristotle, Gilson argues that Bonaventure's antipathy to the Philosopher was early and rooted. Bonaventure utilized the rite of passage into theological mastery, his *Commentary on the Sentences of Peter Lombard* (1250–1251), adversely to comment on Aristotle.[48]

There are for Bonaventure "three and only three metaphysical problems, creation, exemplarism, and the return to God through the mode of illumination." The Augustinian's conception of metaphysics was, Gilson thinks, deliberately systematized in opposition not only to the rationalism of Averroës but also to the mediating position of Aquinas. When Jean of Peckham attacked Saint Thomas "under his eyes," the Franciscan General was "complicit" in the action. Although this line of attack is far from the forefront of the book, *La philosophie de saint Bonaventure* has a nice line in sideswipes against those such as Père Mandonnet who appeared to have exaggerated the resemblance between the Angelic and the Seraphic Doctors. One can, the author says, synthesize the Thomistic and the Bonaventurian demonstrations for the existence of God "only by adopting . . . a bastard point of view which is neither that of Saint Bonaventure nor that of Saint Thomas Aquinas."[49] There speaks the historian.

47. Ibid., 80, 70, 75.

48. Van Steenberghen argues, to the contrary, that Bonaventure was a "Neoplatonizing" Aristotelian. See "Étienne Gilson et l'université de Louvain," 13. The article lists all of Van Steenberghen's anti-Gilsonian reviews and articles.

49. Gilson, *Bonaventure,* 140–41.

In Bonaventure's conception, the first steps to God are brute or unexamined faith; the midway landing is philosophy, and the summit is theology. If the house of human knowledge-and-belief exists for the purpose of the vision of God given on its topmost floor, then any philosophical stairway which closes the door at its last step could only be climbed for the sake of climbing and returning, climbing and returning. The philosophy that locks its upper exit makes itself self-sufficient at the expense of showing its visitors nothing at all. The purpose of philosophy is, Bonaventure says, the knowledge of God: a philosophy that sets itself apart from faith and theology cannot achieve that. Bonaventure saw that it is necessary formally to distinguish knowing and believing: knowledge presupposes sight, belief its absence. Nonetheless, he finds that a philosophy within philosophical limits is no philosophy at all and is, therefore, a false and idolatrous enterprise.

How then can we know without believing? If the philosophical act cannot achieve its truth without theology, knowing and believing appear to remit their formal distinction. Bonaventure answers that God, the object of philosophy, is neither "integrally known" nor "integrally knowable."[50] Demonstration is a philosophical exercise, and Bonaventure does not deny that it can be exercised successfully in relation to the existence of God.

For Saint Thomas, a philosopher's demonstration of God's existence works from the sensible world. The senses enable us to reconstruct a concept of God. According to Thomas, this concept, however incomplete, is entirely an object of knowledge. But for Saint Bonaventure, the demonstration of the existence of God is drawn out of an infused and innate idea of God.

Bonaventure can thus conceive the philosopher as having a "global representation" of God, within which some areas are clearly intuited and others are obscure. Part of this synthetic whole can be known by the philosopher and part of it must be believed. For Bonaventure, our rational idea of God is immersed in an act of belief. Knowing thus contains an apperception of believing, as the perception of an orange as globular cannot exist without the apperception of the half which we cannot see: nothing is known or grasped unless all is given. Thus, as Bonaventure conceives it, philosophy "cannot be what it should be except under the condition of coexistence with faith."[51]

Bonaventure accepted that there was a rightly directed philosophy among those of the Greeks, such as Plato and Plotinus, who maintained the doctrine

50. Ibid., 106.
51. Ibid., 106–7, 110.

of the Ideas and thus found in this world a "universe of images," in which "things are simultaneously copies and signs, without right to an autonomous nature."[52] Bonaventure's exemplarist metaphysics is constructed to override Aristotle's denial that Ideas can exist in separation from Things.

It is as if Aristotle were the classicist, insisting that a picture must be a figurative copy of an object, and Bonaventure the expressionist, for whom art is the immediate making visual of emotion. But here, God is the Artist. For Bonaventure, the images and signs in the world about him radiate from the Word of God. A symbolic universe is a structure of resemblances to God, emanating centrifugally from the "resemblance" par excellence who, "taking resemblance" to God to "its extreme limit," is identical to God. Christ, the Word and Image of God, is the prism in whom all of the "archetypes" are contained and through whom they are refracted into creation. By "knowing himself," God

> expresses in himself, by an entirely interior act, the Son or eternal Word, who is the resemblance of the Father, precisely because he issues from an act of knowledge. But having proffered this interior word, God can express externally a new resemblance through the signs which manifest it, and these signs will be creatures, words in which he exteriorises from himself the eternal archetypes conceived through the thought of God. . . . The proper term which designates in this doctrine the resemblance engendered by an act of knowledge is the term *expression*. And, under this term, which he uses constantly, Bonaventure always represents the generative act which we designate precisely by the term *conception*, even though usage has attenuated its primitive force.

Each of the multiple levels of being and of knowledge reflects the divine act in which God generates the Word by knowing Himself: "the divine truth . . . is capable of expressing everything through an exemplary mode of resemblance."[53] What human minds posit as the "exemplars" of creation are, within God, a single "Expression," Christ the Word; taken in relation to *our* understanding, and in its multiple material incarnations, the "Exemplar" becomes the "ideas." In itself, in Christ, reality is *one*.

Gilson describes Bonaventure's metaphysic as an "expressionism." It has Christ at its "perspectival centre," teaching that, since the "principles of being are . . . the principles of knowledge" and nothing can *be* without the Christ-Archetype, nothing "can be known without him."[54] The beauty of the metaphor of expression is that it enables us to picture one and the same

52. Ibid., 98.
53. Ibid., 144–45, 147, 151.
54. Ibid., 159, 145.

thought, pulsing through and unifying the varied motifs of creation. As a thought-picture, "expression" makes us imagine the expansion of a single thought, from God the Father, through the eternal Word to the least of God's mineral creation.

## God's Self-Expression

Gilson had argued in 1917 that it "is from the perfection which" the artist "expresses that the work derives its own." He relates aesthetic judgment not to artistic works but to their creators. Aesthetic apprehension is, he has said, communion with the author of works of art: "The work of art and the one who contemplates it both testify to their own dignity in so far as both participate in that of the artist; the work is thus the sign of unity between us and the fertile spirit who has preceded us in the way of interior perfection, the sign which he sends us, inviting us to raise ourselves up to him."[55]

In Gilson's early theory of art, aesthetic perception is directed at the very act of artistic expression; the work of art simply mediates between the audience and a human creative act. It is the act of artistic expression which, incarnating the energy of time, carries that "fairy-tale," or magical quality, the creation of a new spiritual landscape. Likewise, as he sees it, Bonaventure teaches that human understanding of the world, as God's "work of art," is communion with the divine act of self-expression.

Gilson insists that it was Bonaventure, and not Thomas, who pictured God as an Artist. Thomas was, he says, "above all" concerned about the "static" aspect of God's infinite perfection. For Thomas, God's "fecundity is eternally fulfilled": the act of creation yields no additional "evidence" of God's perfection. When Thomas's God knows himself, knowing therefore the eternal Ideas, He knows himself as "imitable by creatures." For Thomas, God's divine ideas are relatively colorless "possibles," hypotheses about how creatures can and will resemble Himself. Gilson contrasts this essentialist reading of Thomas on the divine Ideas with Bonaventure's notion of God. For the Franciscan, the "knowledge which God has of the ideas participates in the fecundity through which the Father engenders the Word; he insists on employing for the ideas themselves the same word 'expression' which traditionally characterizes the generation of the divine Word. This is why Saint Bonaventure does not hesitate to take to its conclusion the comparison

55. Gilson, "Du fondement des jugements esthétiques," 546.

between the divine wisdom and the natural fecundity of creative beings when a Scriptural image provides him with an occasion for it." Bonaventure's God is an "Artist" because His very act of self-knowledge is an act of engendering, expression. The engendered "Word is the art of the Father."[56] He expresses himself in all things, making the world a picture. Gilson's Suarezian-Thomist God is, by contrast, "*amusiké*" in his mode of creation.

For Gilson the aesthetician, artists aim to produce individuals, not examples of generic types. He liked paintings that glow with their own unique power of being; after visiting the Metropolitan Museum of Art in New York, he told his wife that "I was most impressed by the Manets; they are prodigious; they carry the art of existing by themselves to a point rarely achieved in painting." It is because Bonaventure's God produces each particular thing "for itself and distinctly" that "it is the mode of knowledge of the artist which determines his mode of production; if thus God produces distinct things, it is because he knows them individually."[57] It does not follow, for Bonaventure, that we advance through the multiplicity of individuals to the unity of God.

Having determined that, since he "contains their resemblances in himself," God must "know things through himself," the next step is to say that God is "the light or the supreme expressive truth of things." In God, the Ideas are one, not multiple as they are in creation. A created individual, that is, an "expression" of God's light, functions for us as a medium or "intermediary" between the "knowing subject and the thing known."[58] What is *really* known through creatures is thus, not finally the creature, but its Creator.

Once, on entering a Russian peasant home, Kandinsky found it so beautifully adorned that he felt himself to be *inside a picture*. When he painted its "tables and different ornaments . . . the *object dissolved itself*": the expressionist's "ability to *overlook* the object" flowed from this experience, in which the distinction between the painting and the objects it might represent disappeared. Similarly, for Gilson's Bonaventure, every created thing can be "dissolved" into the Divine Picture, or Picture-Making act. His philosophy tends toward abstraction from natural objects. For Bonaventure, the Ideas are not *really* multiple; their multiplicity resides in our way of thinking about them, not in themselves. It is only because of matter that what is *one* in God is many in created reality. The Franciscan "vainly tried to find a sen-

56. Gilson, *Bonaventure*, 158–59, 145.
57. Gilson, "Du fondement des jugements esthétiques," 527; Gilson to Thérèse Gilson, November 26, 1926, in Shook, *Gilson*, 153; Gilson, *Bonaventure*, 148.
58. Gilson, *Bonaventure*, 151–52.

sible comparison which would permit one to imagine" the relation of his Artist God to creation: "The most he can approximate to is that of a light which would be both its own illumination and its own radiation . . . [T]hus the divine truth is a light, and his expressions of things are like luminous radiations oriented towards that which they express; but it is a limping comparison because no light is its own irradiation and we can only imagine what would be an *intrinsic iridescence*."[59] The Bonaventurian artist-expressive God exercised a "fairy-tale" captivation on a man of aesthetic sensibility.

But Gilson was no less analytic minded than he was aesthetically gifted. One of his Sorbonne students of the early 1920s heard "the rising tide of Thomism" in Gilson's lectures. Gilson could see the perils in the degree of ontological uniformity that Bonaventure attributes to reality. Gilson names Raymund Lull, Descartes, and Comte as Bonaventure's heirs in the quest for the unification of the sciences. He does not expand on the topic. He just makes the telescoped observation that Bonaventure "founds the act through which God knows the ideas upon the act in which his self-thinking expresses them. This is to distance oneself from Saint Thomas' theorism, in order to enter the way which engaged Duns Scotus, that of a God whose creation determines the essences, and to await for a Descartes to arrive at their free creation." Gilson's book is a rounded description of a philosophy which, in its determination to be "radically incompatible" with Aristotle and because it is planted in Franciscan experience, proposes that we cannot understand the created forest of symbols without believing it to be reducible to its Uncreated Symbol.[60]

The Franciscan General gave three arguments for the existence of God. The first is that moving beings presuppose stimulation by an immobile being. The second is that it is requisite for finite and imperfect beings to be caused by the infinite and perfect. The third is that God is innately present to our minds. The arguments are intended to be circular, in the sense of beginning from our knowledge of and love for God, for we should not desire perfect wisdom unless we already knew and loved it. The first and the second arguments thus reduce to the third. Our belief could be said to

originate from a purely sensible given when we observe at the beginning of our reasoning that there exist movable beings, composed, relative, imperfect, contingent; but all these insufficiencies only appear in things because we already possess the idea of the perfections which measure them. . . . All knowl-

59. Kandinsky, *Concerning the Spiritual in Art*, 31–32; Gilson, *Bonaventure*, 152–53.
60. Dalbiez to Jacques Maritain, June 5, 1923, cited in Chenaux, "La seconde vague thomiste," 154; Gilson, *Bonaventure*, 159.

edge comes from an anterior knowledge, and the apparently immediate and primitive observation of contingency presupposes the preliminary knowledge of necessity. And, necessity is nothing other than God; the human intelligence knows experimentally that it already possesses the knowledge of the first being in the moment that it attempts to demonstrate it.

Bonaventure does not take Platonism to lunatic extremes. He appreciates that if we want to make a sensible assessment of the world around us, to decide how many trees to cut down in order to build a priory, the material content upon which our assessment is based cannot be innate. But when we wish to make a necessary and universal judgment, none of the mutable material supplied to our minds by the senses and imagination suffices to give certitude. In such cases, we do not test our ideas against sensible experience but interpret sensible experience in the light of our ideas. God's immobile perfection sits on the throne of Bonaventure's epistemology, for it is the secure ground of knowledge. It is necessary that we "see the truth in the eternal reasons" within the mind of God "for our thought to be capable of really attaining the truth." Although this analysis might have sounded plausible to Plato, Bonaventure's inspiration was, Gilson says, not primarily philosophical, but derives from the spiritual experience of a man who repeatedly commented on the Johannine epistles: "the doctrine of eternal reasons is . . . religious, in the affective meaning of the term . . . [M]an can know no truth without God, but he cannot see God. It is precisely this self-presenting action at the heart of thought by a transcendent energy, whose source remains hidden to us, that the Bonaventurian doctrine of eternal ideas is designed to explain."[61]

The experience out of which Bonaventure's metaphysical epistemology is drawn is *not* the vision of the eternal reasons in the mind of God, but that of knowing the truth of all else in their light and by their standard. Bonaventure's favorite activity was *reductio* or *resolutio:* tracing a line back to its origins. The "reduction" of our experience of truth takes us back, neither to an immediate intuition of the Ideas, or eternal reasons, nor to the direct vision of the divine light which, as Bonaventure believes, illuminates them. Rather, the "reduction" leads us to the "apperception" of both the intuition of the Ideas and the vision of the divine, as being the object from which each of these flows. Gilson writes that

> this indirect apprehension by the thought of an object which escapes us, but whose presence is implied in the effects which unfold from it, receives in the

61. Gilson, *Bonaventure,* 124, 127, 374, 372.

doctrine of Saint Bonaventure the name of *contuitus*. An intuition would be precisely the direct vision of God which is denied to us; a contuition in the proper meaning of the word is only the apprehension in a perceived effect the presence of a cause which we cannot intuit... [W]e attain only the contuitions of God, in things, in our souls and in the transcendent first principles which we apprehend. *Haec lux est inaccessibilis, et tamen proxima animae etiam plus quam ipsa sibi. Est etiam inalligabilis et tamen summe intima;* always present, always active, the motor and the regulator of the least operations of our thought, it nonetheless remains transcendent and inaccessible within us, because it can never be transformed here below into a known object.

If we "reduce" our experience of truth to the primitive condition of necessity and universality, that experience is an innate proof of the existence of God. Bonaventure is sufficiently confident in the Anselmian argument for the existence of God to affirm that even idolaters, who attribute false properties to their gods, affirm the existence of God.[62]

Is "God" then not a description but a name? Bonaventure is not giving what Kant would call an ontological argument for God, demonstrating God's existence on the ground of our knowledge of His essence. What even the mind of the idolater "contuits" as innately present to it is neither the definition nor the essence of God, which we cannot know, but His *existence:* "the idea" of God is in Bonaventure's "eyes only the mode of the presence of the *being* in thought," and it is "because the necessity of the divine being communicates itself to thought that a simple definition can become a proof." If we recollect our experience of the knowledge of necessary truths, this demonstrates that such mental operations require the illuminative presence of the divine and perfect Being. "The human intellect turns towards itself and reflects on what it is," and learns that it possesses "resemblances" to things, in *true* judgments; it is thus that the "human spirit knows God simply in reflecting on itself."[63]

Gilson told Frédéric Lefèvre in 1925 that it was impossible for him to choose between Bonaventure and Thomas: "My preference, which is not secret but openly avowed, is given to neither of them exclusively, but to the Christian thought of which they are both profound representatives." On one occasion, in the Bonaventure book, Gilson steps out of the role of biographer. He remarks on a principle that might yield common ground between Bonaventure and Thomas: "Desire for God," he says, "is not an artificial sentiment which philosophy extrinsically introduces into our spirit, it is a

---

62. Ibid., 385–86, citing *In Hexaem* 12.11; ibid., 123.
63. Ibid., 130, 360–61.

natural sentiment, a given fact which we have to take account of; the whole of true philosophy consists in explaining it." The desire for God, observed by "introspective experimentalism,"[64] or tested out in experience, could be recognized equally by an Aristotelian or an Augustinian.

When *La Vie catholique* praised Gilson's achievements as a mediaeval historian, one cleric wrote in to warn readers against a professor who had garnered his knowledge of Christian culture from the *outside*, being "étranger" to the Temple of Catholic worship. Gilson, by then a daily communicant, retorted in the November 1924 issue of *La Vie catholique* that he placed his entrance to the "'chapel'" "'under the ensign of *Saint-Francis Saint-Dominic.'*"[65]

There were always two sides to Gilson's mind. Aesthetically, he was a "Franciscan," vastly preferring nonfigurative art to classical realism. His experiences of beauty had no small connection with his religious life. But Gilson was also a "chosiste," dedicated to the fact and the *thing*. The aesthetic dimension of his religious and cognitive life inclined him to realize that what ultimately matters intellectually cannot quite be figured.

## Gilson Founds a Journal of Mediaeval Studies

Gilson was used to frequenting the Bibliotèque Nationale, relieving the pleasure of examining its manuscripts by conversing with another habitué of that salon, the Dominican Gabriel Thèry. One evening in 1925, the two mediaevalists inspired one another with the plan for a journal. The *Archives d'histoire doctrinale et littéraire du moyen age* published its first issue in 1926. Gilson and Père Gabriel Thèry were the directors. Vrin was the publisher. He would frequently call the lay director "mon purgatoire."[66]

In the same year, Gilson was promoted to *professeur sans chaire;* the Sorbonne provided no chairs for historians of *mediaeval* philosophy. He conceived his task as filling in the lacunae in the Sorbonne's instruction in the history of philosophy. If Gilson had been unperturbed by those critics who believed that all of the architects of the "scholastic synthesis" had the same philosophy, he was shaken by Thèry's comment, about the first editions of *Le Thomisme* and *La philosophie de saint Bonaventure,* that he was transmuting theologies into philosophies. But at least, Gilson felt, he had "respected

---

64. Lefèvre, *Une heure avec...Étienne Gilson,* 70; Gilson, *Bonaventure,* 89.
65. Gouhier, "Post-Face: Etienne Gilson,"153. Italics in *La vie catholique.*
66. D'Alverny, "Nécrologie Étienne Gilson," 426; Shook, *Gilson,* 139.

the principle of my Sorbonne teachers that the history of philosophy does not consist in fabricating a doctrine in order to attribute it to the philosopher of whom one speaks."[67]

## Saint Thomas: The Dominican Way

The 1927 *Le Thomisme* contains a preface that spurns De Wulf and Mandonnet's advice to improve the work by "inverting the plan which we have adopted." As in his book about Bonaventure, Gilson defines the subject's intellectual project by portraying his life. In 1244, Thomas accepted the "Dominican vocation . . . to serve God through teaching and absolute poverty. To be a friar Doctor, remained Saint Thomas' ideal until the last months of his life." Saint Thomas's basic gesture, which expresses his unique experience of the good and the true, the "figure" in which he "most clearly represents himself" is that of the Doctor. A Doctor *teaches*. This practical orientation requires one to have something to say; it is founded on contemplation of truth: "the function of the Doctor is naturally oriented towards a double object, interior and exterior, according as it is turned to the truth which the Doctor meditates on and contemplates or to the auditors whom he teaches." For the Dominican, theory and practice are not at odds with one another: knowing something readily issues in the desire and the ability to convey what one has learned; a good man wants to share his learning, and this act of communication is charity. There are doctors and Doctors, in the degree that their quest for truth progresses further among the goods of wisdom: "The Master *par excellence* can only teach Wisdom par excellence; that is to say, that science of divine things which is theology."[68]

The phenomenology of Thomas's Dominican experience supplies one reason for the rejection of the advice to "construct the Thomist encyclopedia of the sciences," different to that built by Saint Thomas in the *Summae*. The object Thomas sought to contemplate and to convey is "the plenary science of divine things," conferred upon him by faith. "So if we want to look for the Doctor of philosophical truth within the complex personality of Saint Thomas," Gilson asserts, "it is only in the interior of the theologian that we can hope to find him."[69]

Thomas wanted to "go beyond the confused mass of the commentaries"

67. Gilson, *Le philosophe et la théologie*, 105–7.
68. Gilson, *Le Thomisme* (3rd ed.), 9, 16–17, 34–35, 38.
69. Ibid., 9, 39.

to find a "direct translation of the Greek text of Aristotle." He "rigorously attached" himself "to the letter" of the Philosopher's writings, so as to plant its secular spirit within Christian theology. His Augustinian contemporaries were preoccupied with the danger of Averroës and of Latin Averroism: assailed by rationalism, they locked the doors of the castle of revelation. Thomas recognized that Augustine is, in this respect, not a safe keeper of the keys to the drawbridge, for he is allied with the Averroists, on the ground of Platonism. In Thomas's view, what was actually endangered both by Christian Augustinians and Averroists is the reality and intelligibility of the sensible world. He turns to a different ally in order to "prolong" into the thirteenth century the "battle which . . . Aristotle originally engaged against Plato."[70] The leaven of Aristotelianism that expands in Thomas's philosophy is realism.

Thomas the theological Aristotelian neither "isolates" faith and reason "in water-tight compartments" nor conflates them. If Christian theology is to get the benefit of the substructure of Aristotle's realism, then it must leave a rational demonstration to be itself. Thus, when Thomas takes over Aristotle's argument for the existence of an unmoved mover from the requirement that movement of potentiality to actuality cannot proceed within an infinite series, he gives the most difficult version of the proof, which eschews the question of movement in *time*. It is, therefore, not only the most "philosophically exhaustive" proof but also independent of the revealed word of Genesis. For Bonaventure, one of the cardinal sins of Aristotle, and of Averroism, is the false doctrine of the eternity of the world. Thomas tells the Augustinians that, since creation in time is conditional upon God's unknowable will, it is not a matter for philosophical demonstration; he reminds the Averroists that we cannot *know* that the world is eternal, since there is no "essence" of time upon which we could form the judgment.[71]

The 1927 edition is over-layered upon the first two versions. The center of his picture of the Thomistic God, at this time, is the Creation. Thomas's five ways have three defining traits. Unlike the Augustinian or Anselmian proofs, they are "extroverted," each referring to "the empirical observation of a fact." Second, each concerns "causality" and is therefore marked by "necessity." Third, this empirical observation does not count the causes, as they span out in mounting sequence, but refers directly to any one given cause. The fact that it is *given* is important: "it suffices to assign the single

---

70. Ibid., 32.
71. Ibid., 49, 75, 130–38.

complete sufficient reason of the particular *existence* of any empirical given in order to prove God."[72]

Thus, when we turn from the proofs to the nature of God, the way of analogy will lead us to a God who "appears to us as a living source of efficacy whose acts flow eternally from his being, more precisely, whose operation is identical with his being." Such a God, whose essence is limpidly the act of his existence, knows the forms of things, not by knowing the reduplicability of the contents of his mind, but by knowing the communicability of his own existence: "inasmuch as God knows his essence as imitable by a determinate creature, he possesses the idea of the creature."[73] What is imitated by the creature is the divine design as goodness, voluntarily communicated to dependent beings.

Thomas's God "concreates form and matter." But more than that, He effects being: "God is not only the cause of the form that clothes things, but of their being itself, in virtue of which they exist, in such a way that ceasing for a single instance to depend upon their cause, they would cease to exist." The divine creative act must be "perpetually" operative, in order for the contingently existing world to be. This divine causality permeates each natural movement: every action of God's creatures is that of an "instrument in his hands."[74]

But Thomas sets his face against the Platonic attribution of all causal efficacy to God. As the workman uses his hacksaw to cut a piece of wood, and the hacksaw is the second cause of the sawing but the worker the first, so God drives all of the formal causes in nature, using each to its appropriate end and through its own potentialities. This is only an analogy, Gilson says, "for the divine influence penetrates the second cause much more completely than that of the worker his tool. God confers on all things their being, their form, their movement and their efficacy; and nonetheless this efficacy belongs to them from the moment that they receive it, and it is through their operations that it is accomplished." The really active and causational "universe of Aristotle," Gilson now claims, "requires a God such as that of Dionysius the Areopagite." For this universe is not moved by "force," propelled from potential to actuality whether it wants to go or not. It is, rather, moved from within, by its own real agency, which "desires to imitate" the divine "goodness" of which it is the communication.[75] The center of the 1927 *Thomisme* is creation.

72. Ibid., 91–92.
73. Ibid., 118, 128.
74. Ibid., 170–71, 173.
75. Ibid., 176–78.

## A Modernist "Aesthetic" Historiography

Many of the modernist artists and writers of the 1920s experienced a rupture between themselves and the Western tradition of which they were the heirs. The American poet Allen Tate spoke of seizing the tradition "by violence." Writers of a conservative temperament wanted to situate themselves within history, because they saw in it a means of transcending themselves, as "subjective," idiosyncratic personalities. And yet, they associated themselves, not with a linear, chronological history, but with a more fragmentary "tradition," one that was not constructed on the lines of pure temporal progression. Frank Kermode describes T. S. Eliot's theory of tradition as "Cubist historiography, unlearning the trick of perspective and ordering history as a system of spatial alignments." A "canon" such as Eliot was looking for is "a site where the diachronic is organised into a synchrony, or . . . where the aspect of time is reconciled with the aspect of the timeless."[76]

In 1926, at the International Congress of Philosophy in Harvard, Gilson put himself across very differently than he had done when Frédéric Lefèvre interviewed him a year earlier. He gave a lecture defining three different approaches to the history of philosophy. For some, Gilson said, the history of ideas is research into the nexus between philosophical texts and particular stages of civilization. Others bypass the "concepts and images" in which a philosophy is articulated in order to retrieve "the original intuition which engendered it": these treat the philosopher as "a hero." A third position, with which Gilson clearly identifies himself, considers philosophy as a "wisdom": "truth depends neither on society nor on the creative genius of the philosophers: it is just truth." Great philosophers survive the civilization whose ideas they "synthesize," and it is their effort to find the "timeless element" that makes them the "perpetual contemporaries of all human reason."[77]

Gilson had not changed his mind about what he was doing. For he had also told his interlocutor of 1925 not to "neglect to signal how considerable has been the influence of the great Bergson on me: he showed us in the flesh and bones what it is to be a philosopher. I followed his courses for three years and I saw the work of philosophical thought taking place in front of me."[78] In 1925, depreciating "pure ideas," he was describing his

76. Tate, "Religion and the Old South," 322; Kermode, "A Babylonish Dialect," 237; Martindale, "Introduction: The Classic of all Europe," 9.

77. Gilson, "Le rôle de la philosophie dans l'histoire de la civilization," 170, 172, 174.

78. Lefèvre, Une heure avec . . . Étienne Gilson, 65.

endeavors as a historian, already in progress. At Harvard, in 1926, he was foreseeing his work to come, as a philosopher. Although it is tempting to make one or the other the patron saint of, respectively, his historiography and his philosophy, Dominic and Francis conspired in both.

# 5

# Reason and the Supernatural

## The Parti de l'Intelligence

In 1918 the French people had elected a coalition government, the *Chambre bleu*. In continental Europe of the 1920s the call of ideologies was too strong for such cooperation to endure. Intellectual upheaval sometimes leads intellectuals to write manifestos. The left-intelligentsia was first into the fray. A group led by Romain Rolland, which named itself Clarté, issued a manifesto in May/June 1919 calling for an internationalist and democratic future, in which reason would reign. A month later, in July 1919, Henri Massis published in *Le Figaro* the manifesto of the Parti de l'intelligence. The manifesto was signed by the Action Française leaders, by Maritain, and by Thomist clergymen such as Joseph de Tonquédoc. This signaled that Catholics and secular conservatives were joining arms in fighting "intellectual Bolshevism."[1]

Like the Clarté manifesto, that of the "Party of Reason" called for internationalism and for faith in reason, if not in democracy. It stated that the Parti de l'intelligence aimed at "rebuilding public spirit in France through the royal ways of reason and classical methodology, the intellectual federation of Europe and of the world under the aegis of a victorious France."[2] The manifesto combined French nationalism with internationalism.

The Catholic Thomists and the atheists who united in the Parti de l'intelligence shared a belief in the human mind. According to Étienne Fouilloux, both were critical of "anti-intellectualism and...irrationalism. Amongst the themes which bring reason into play, both of them put nature in the foreground: nature of man in society for the Maurrassians; nature of the

---

1. Prévotat, "Autour du parti de l'intelligence," 169–71; Weber, *Action Française,* 501–2.
2. Prévotat, "Autour du parti de l'intelligence," 174.

world and of man created by God for the Thomists, but accessible in its purity just by using one's mind. In both cases, the laws which govern nature are foundational, although their origins differ." In 1926, Père Réginald Garrigou-Lagrange composed a preface to Aquinas's *On Princely Government,* aiming to show its contemporary relevance. He states that the sociality of the nature of man "is deduced from his definition: 'rational animal.'"[3]

In the 1920s Thomism was a fashionable philosophy in France, a country in which both fashion and philosophy are of singular significance. It won over men such as Gonzague Truc, who professed loathing of the "dark veil of Golgotha." Truc's *Le retour à la scholastique* (1919) was well received by Léon Nöel, in the *Revue néo-scholastique de Louvain;* Maritain called it "an astonishing witness to the attractive power and properly human and rational value of the scholastic discipline."[4]

The conservatives' war on social modernism proved intellectually and socially compelling: "Parisian students," "professors and authors of renown," and every "lover of belles-lettres" read *L'Action française.* The movement "exercised . . . an almost complete dictatorship over Catholic intellectual circles. Whoever came out as a democrat in these circles was doomed to be the object of an ironical and scornful pity; . . . In order to appear up to date . . . you had to denounce liberal errors with an air of self-satisfied superiority" and "scoff at liberty, equality and fraternity." Within "Maritain's circle," as Yves Congar records, "everyone who was anyone belonged to the Action Française."[5]

Massis records that the same "sentiments and ideas" that had led him to create the Parti de l'intelligence "presided over the birth of the *Revue universelle.*" The *Revue* was founded in 1920 by Maurras and Maritain. It was edited by Massis and Jacques Bainville and carried the contributions of Pierre Lasserre, Garrigou-Lagrange, and Cardinal Mercier. It was to be, Maritain said, "from one side a platform for the ideas of the Action Française in the political order, and from the other side a platform for Christian, and especially Thomist, thought in the philosophical order." Maritain was in charge of the philosophy section of the *Revue universelle.* Some of his key works of the 1920s, such as *Réflexions sur l'intelligence*—which Gilson had just read

3. Fouilloux, *Une église en quête de liberté,* 72; Garrigou-Lagrange, Preface to *Du gouvernement royal,* by Thomas Aquinas, viii–ix.
4. Chenaux, "La seconde vague thomiste," 139, 158–59.
5. Simon, *The Road to Vichy,* 42–43; Congar, *Journal d'un théologien,* 34.

when he was interviewed by Frédéric Lefèvre—and *Trois réformateurs* (1925), first came out as articles in the *Revue*.[6]

Maurras summed up his own credo in two words, "Politique d'abord," politics first. His religious supporters envisaged their concordat as a pragmatic tactic. Whereas, as Père Réginald said, Thomas taught that political deliberation considers ends, political "execution," or action, considers the "lowliest means." And thus, "in the order of execution, but not in that of intention, one can say: *'politique d'abord'*: for in order that social life be possible, the city or country must be habitable and agitators must be expelled or called to their senses."[7]

These lines formed part of Garrigou's defense of monarchism. Democracy, he says, requires moral and intellectual perfection in its subjects, whereas monarchism operates on the assumption of human imperfection. Since "the virtuous and the competent are extremely rare," a monarchical government is the most down to earth choice for "a great people, whose interests are very complex, a people who not only have an economic life, but also a superior intellectual and artistic life"[8] such as, one imagines, the French.

When the Parti de l'intelligence manifesto was on the drawing board, Massis and Maritain had agreed that the program for the Action Française of the 1920s would entail fighting anarchy, rather than defending royalism. Attempting to persuade Maritain to sign it, Massis had assured him that Action Française support against anarchism was so important that "we should not be ungrateful" to them, "out of concern for orthodoxy." The manifesto sheds any reference to the traditional French Catholic faith in monarchy. Massis told Maritain, apologetically, "To Catholics, I fear that the Catholic perspective will appear to have been conjured out of sight, a little, or submitted to 'politics first'; but to unbelievers, who can be brought together by the program of a defense of reason, our Catholicism appears prohibitive in that it nonetheless dominates the whole set of propositions."[9] Pascal might have said that Massis was being somewhat Jesuitical, since the manifesto contains no reference to Catholic principles. Maurras was given Massis's document to edit, and removed any stain of religiosity from it. The willingness of Catholic intellectuals to bargain with him indicates that,

6. Massis, *Maurras et notre temps,* 104; Fouilloux, *Une église en quête de liberté,* 70, quoting Maritain's *Carnet de notes* (1920); Chenaux, "Le seconde vague thomiste," 152.
7. Garrigou-Lagrange, Preface to *Du gouvernement royal,* xxii–xxiii.
8. Ibid., xxvi.
9. Prévotat, "Autour du parti de l'intelligence," 172, 176.

though Maurras' political royalism was a rationalist dream, his extrinsicist ecclesiology was a bit of hard real *politique*.

## The Socialists Come to Power

In 1920 the French radicals dusted off their slogan "No enemies to the Left." This enabled them to form a pact with the socialists. When the Cartel des Gauches triumphed in the 1924 elections, the socialist Edouard Herriot became prime minister. The cartel's 1925 efforts to withdraw the French embassy to the Vatican bore fruit only in a statement by the French cardinals and archbishops "attacking the very principle of a secular—hence atheistic—State." When the Action Française interpreted this as a victory for its own principles among the episcopate, *La Croix* "commented, 'The truth is both simpler and more complicated: the declaration is a victory of common sense; but it was the Action Française which, for twenty-five years . . . maintained against one and all these common sense positions.'" While Prime Minister Herriot was thus preoccupied, in 1926, the French franc collapsed. The radical-socialists summoned the financial wizard Poincaré and gave the new president emergency powers by which to overrule Parliament.[10]

## The Vision of God Fulfills Human Desire

Maurras soothed the religious with the Thomist slogan "Grace presupposes nature," that is, grace respects the natural and thus the political order. The conception of supernatural grace and of reason as external or "extrinsic" to one another, common among Thomists at this time, made sense of their alliance with the nonbelieving secularists. Because their idea of natural reason was not deeply rooted in their religious belief, they could unite with the secular defenders of intelligence. Nature came "first" in the same sense that politics did, that is, before, and outside of, revealed religion.

In *La morale et la science des mouers*, Lucien Lévy-Bruhl had made fun of the eighteenth-century philosophers' idea of a universal "human nature": The Greeks' "man," he said, was a Greek; the Christians' idea of "humanity" is rather different from this. While no Thomist could follow Lévy-Bruhl in concluding that the idea of universal humanity is an "empty axiom," those

10. Weber, *Action Française*, 157; Bury, *France, 1814–1940*, 259.

who forgot that "human *nature*" is not an a priori idea but exists within a drama of creation, fall and graced redemption, did not do full justice to their Christianity.[11]

Not all secularists, or conservatives, were willing to collude in the Maurrassian front. In 1925 the philosopher Louis Rougier published *La scholastique et le thomisme,* arguing that Thomas unified his faith with Aristotelian reason by "the surreptitious transformation of a logical distinction posited by the Stagirite between essence and existence into a real and ontological distinction." Gilson's co-editor, Père Thèry, believed that Rougier had "borrowed . . . lavishly from Gilson's writings" and said so publicly. In the same year, Lasserre attacked Maritain's mediaevalist "archaism." Maritain did not fail to respond; such were the unprepossessing first steps in the French debate about whether a specifically Christian philosophy can exist.[12]

Père Simon Deploige had succeeded Monsignor Mercier as president of the Institut Supérieur de Philosophie. In 1911, he issued an attack upon Lévy-Bruhl's *La morale et la science des mouers,* that "almost incredible book" which inspired Gilson's academic career. The Louvain Thomist described the opposing sides in the title of his book as *Le conflit de la morale et la sociologie.* Maritain republished the sally in 1923 in his *Bibliotèque française de philosophie,* with a preface by himself. Gilson did not like the book because it exhibited the brand of reductionism espoused by the devout, the demolition of an adversary through the critique of their moral motives. Deploige "accused Durkheim of dishonestly laying claim to ideas which had first come out of Germany. . . . [T]his . . . offended Gilson." He considered, moreover, that Deploige was instrumentalizing Thomas for purposes that were not his own: Gilson "wondered whether Deploige had found in Thomas what Thomas had put there."[13]

11. Lévy-Bruhl, *Ethics and Moral Science,* 54–58.
12. Chenaux, "La seconde vague thomiste," 163; Shook, *Gilson,* 348; Chenaux, "La seconde vague thomiste," 165–66.
13. Shook, *Gilson,* 114–15. Canon Van Steenberghen considers that, since the original debate between Durkheim and Deploige took place in the pages of the *Revue néo-scholastique* in 1907, it is very unlikely that Gilson recalled the incident in 1923. See Van Steenberghen's "Étienne Gilson et l'université de Louvain," 6. Nonetheless, Shook repeated his claim in a later article, "Maritain and Gilson: Early Relations." The evidence that Gilson's feelings toward Deploige remained hostile is the sustained importance of Lévy-Bruhl's book within his own intellectual development. He was still quoting Lévy-Bruhl's *Ethics and Moral Science* in *God and Philosophy* (p. 107, eighteenth-century "natural religion" as rationalized deism) and would cite Lévy-Bruhl's dicta on the ability of theoretical ethics to dictate practice to Maritain in the 1950s.

He seems to have forgotten to respond to Maritain's friendly inquiry as to whether he would like to have a copy of Deploige's book. In his epistolary encounters with Maritain, which date from 1923, Gilson skirted some of their disagreements with a prudent modesty. When Maritain mailed him his 1924 piece on "Le Thomisme et la crise de l'esprit moderne," Gilson thanked the author politely and told him that it "introduces all sorts of nuances . . . which are too deep for a mere historian to get into."[14]

The historian welcomed some of Maritain's corrections to the second, revised and enlarged edition of *Le Thomisme* (1922). In the third edition, of 1927, he replaced his earlier statement that, for Thomas, the "proper" object of the human intellect is the essence in the sensible thing with Maritain's suggestion that the knowledge of sensible things is the "connatural," but not the *proper,* end of human intellectual inquiry.[15]

In the letter in which he mentioned Deploige, Maritain warmly concurs with Gilson's insistence that "the two *Summas* are not a work of philosophy but of theology." But he takes issue with Gilson's assertion that Saint Thomas teaches both that the vision of God is beyond the natural grasp of the human creature and that this vision is the fulfillment of human nature. "How," Maritain asks, "could a logician as rigorous as Thomas Aquinas contradict himself"[16] by saying that supernatural beatitude, or grace, fulfills our natural capacities but is beyond them?

This was a topic upon which the commentators had meditated creatively. Maritain's mentor, Père Garrigou-Lagrange, based his extrinsicism on John of Saint Thomas's contention that, if the human intellect were actively related to "God as He is in Himself," that is, related to God *through its own nature,* rather than passively submitting to divine illumination, it would simultaneously be "*essentially natural*" and "*essentially supernatural*": "this would," the modern commentator thought, blur the distinction between God and creation, entailing that "the natural and the supernatural order are not *essentially* and necessarily distinct."[17] Thomists had, not only political, but also theological, reasons for keeping nature and the supernatural "distinct."

Maritain advised the author of *Le Thomisme* that "this is one of the questions in which the Thomistic tradition can be of the utmost service in

14. Gilson to Jacques Maritain, November 25, 1924, in Gilson and Maritain, *Deux approches de l'être,* 27–28; Gilson to Jacques Maritain, November 6, 1924, ibid., 23.

15. Letters between Gilson and Maritain, March 11, 19, 1923, ibid., 16–21.

16. Maritain to Étienne Gilson, November 25, 1924, ibid., 26–27.

17. Garrigou-Lagrange, *God: His Existence and Nature,* 150.

grasping Thomas' own thought." Ignorance of that tradition leads to the "unforgivable" error of identifying the *natural* beatitude possible for a state of pure nature with "*supernatural* beatitude."[18] For Roman Thomism, the idea of a natural desire for God is sheer Pelagianism. That is, it fancies that human beings are by themselves capable of crossing the border between created nature and divine, free, grace. Five days later, Gilson replied with this paradox: "The necessity for the supernatural is inscribed in human nature in the form of a desire which man does not create in himself." He agrees to study Saint Thomas's texts further. Gilson has a not yet fully articulate intuition that grace can be freely present to nature, without denaturing it.

De Lubac's assertion that Gilson "took no part whatever in the publications and celebrations that accompanied Pius XI's encyclical *Studiorum Ducem*" is inaccurate. Composed for the six-hundredth anniversary of Thomas's canonization, *Studiorum Ducem* was celebrated by a Thomist congress in Naples, at which Gilson gave a "magisterial" paper.[19]

He never gave up, and his inexorability bubbled with joie de vivre. "L'humanisme de saint Thomas d'Aquin" mischievously redirects Maritain's touché, that the *proper* end of the human intellect is not the sensible, to the natural desire for the supernatural vision. It sets out the Pascalian paradox of the "disproportion between human thought and the nature of its objects." On the one hand, we cannot think without thinking *about* sensible objects; our intellectual gaze is locked into the vision of concrete, material objects. On the other hand, what we are looking for in sensible objects is their intelligibility, which our minds unlock by a nonmaterial process. Because it requires a brief elevation into pure intelligibility, the process of unlocking meanings within sensible things makes us experience our entrainment to the sensible as an untoward imprisonment. Our act of understanding sensible things constantly gives us an awareness of a horizon beyond that act. The very working of the agent intellect on sensible images tickles us with the consciousness of an excess, over and above sensible knowledge. "Riveted to the sensible," we constantly feel a meaning, "perhaps a morality and a mysticism, latent at the heart of things,"[20] which is forbidden fruit to the embodied mind.

Aristotle, the Greek humanist, therefore knew both that the ultimate end

18. Maritain to Étienne Gilson, November 25, 1924, in *Deux approches*, 26.
19. De Lubac's note in de Lubac, ed., *Letters of Gilson to de Lubac*, 218; Chenaux, "La seconde vague thomiste," 162.
20. Gilson, "L'humanisme de saint Thomas d'Aquin," 980–82.

of human contemplation is the "sovereign Good" and that such beatific contemplation is inaccessible to us. This discouraging fact is the "experience upon which" Thomas "goes on to build the order of Christian Wisdom, a new Humanism founded on the indissoluble synthesis of reason and revelation." His humanism holds together the paradox of an "order of reason," "superior" in its own domain, finding its fulfillment in an "order of revelation," superior in its realm. The paradox is that nature itself longs for the supernatural and sovereign good. Gilson repeats a phrase that had especially offended Maritain: "This is why, not only are all the legitimate aspirations whose satisfaction is required for human happiness inherited and fulfilled by beatitude: but inversely, all that is already true, good and just for natural reason finds itself sanctioned in advance and legitimated by the certitude that *nature itself requires* the supernatural in view of its complete perfection."[21] The ethics of Christian humanism sanctions the natural ethics of Greek humanism by rooting itself in the desire to which it tends and fulfilling it.

In 1927 Maritain published Massis's *Défence de l'occident* in his Roseau d'Or series, with, by that date, some reluctance. He did not write the manifesto of the Parti de l'intelligence, but he had shared its notion of reason. Gilson never did: when Massis asked him "to engage in a new crusade for the defense of the West," he excused himself on the ground that he was a Thomist.[22] In French Catholic intellectual circles of this time, the idea that natural reason presupposes grace tended to be accepted among the "Augustinian" heirs of Bonaventure, such as Blondel and Père Laberthonnière, rather than by Thomists, although some Thomists, such as Rousselot, espoused it. Gilson's aesthetic sense put him on their wavelength, leading him to suspect an opaque sign of God's grace in the disequilibrium between what human reason *can* achieve and what it *desires* to grasp. Gilson observed that Thomas's "philosophical humanism . . . consists in the considered effort to do justice to the beauty of man and to ensure the integral development of his nature": the hidden "pull" of grace within human nature is what gives humanity its aesthetic "form." "L'humanisme de saint Thomas d'Aquin" concludes with a reference to Comte's endeavor to "make a religion out of positive philosophy," impossible, because, Gilson says, "philosophy has never given rise to any religion whatsoever."[23] Only revelation can give the human mind, and thus the human sciences, the internal coherence which we desire.

21. Ibid., 980, 979, 982–83.
22. Prévotat, "Autour du parti de l'intelligence," 174; Gilson, *Les tribulations de Sophie*, 47–48.
23. Gilson, "L'humanisme de saint Thomas d'Aquin," 977, 987.

## The Action Française Condemned at Rome

The Belgian Catholic Universities of Louvain and Liège were especially susceptible to royalist influence: "By the mid-1920's, the *Action française* was selling some five hundred copies daily at Louvain, and more than that at Liege." Cardinal Archbishop Mercier, now retired from his chair of Thomistic philosophy at Louvain, "received" Maurras and wrote to tell him "how much he enjoyed dipping from time to time in *Trois idées politiques, L'avenir de l'intelligence,* and *La politique religieuse.*"[24] In July 1925 the journal of the Catholic Association of Belgian Youth published a poll that placed Maurras first among the Catholic student heroes of the past quarter-century; the cardinal archbishop of Malines trailed miserably behind. Belgian student enthusiasm for the Action Française led to its first serious setback, for the result caused consternation in the hierarchy.

In August 1926 Cardinal Andrieu, archbishop of Bordeaux, submitted to the Pope a list of objections to the Action Française. The royalist right were on the verge of losing their religious legitimization. Its many Catholic co-workers, such as Cardinal Billot, Père Garrigou-Lagrange, and Jacques Maritain, "found themselves placed in a situation which can only be called irregular."[25]

As rumors of an imminent condemnation spread, the *Action française,* on December 15, 1926, imprudently proclaimed "OUR FAITH FROM ROME. OUR POLICY FROM HOME."[26] On December 20, Pius XI condemned the Action Française, forbidding Catholics to adhere to "the school of those who place the interests of parties above that of religion and who want to submit the second to the service of the first," from "establishing, favoring, or reading the journals directed by the men who write them and who separate themselves from our dogmas and our moral doctrine, and who cannot escape our reprobation."

Summoned to the Vatican in March 1927, Maritain spent two unpleasant hours in the headmaster's study. Within two months, he had published *Primauté du spirituel,* in which he asserts the "rights of the City of God over the terrestrial city," that is, the rights of the church over the Action Française. At a second meeting, in September 1927, Pius XI laid upon the Catholic philosopher the tasks of writing directly against the Action Française, defending the apostolate of the laity, and denouncing anti-Semitism. The condemnation freed him from his persona as a crusader against the modern

---

24. Weber, *Action Française,* 489, 224.
25. Barré, *Jacques et Raïssa Maritain,* 343.
26. Weber, *Action Française,* 234.

world. The "first Maritain," the author of *Antimoderne* and *Trois réforma-teurs,* was released to become an "artist, a free man, a revolutionary," the author of *Humanisme intégral.*[27]

In an article of 1931 Chenu would defend Gilson's assertion that the "historical significance of Thomism" lies in Saint Thomas's "tranquil confidence in human reason." Chenu criticized the "'baroque' scholasticism" which during the modernist crisis had "feared the infiltration of Protestantism whereas more far-sighted people emphasized the central importance of faith and the religious life" on dogma, and upon Thomas's "authentic theology." "They are certainly no disciples of Thomas Aquinas!" Chenu wrote: "And still less are those who, because of a strange collusion whose keynote is anti-modernism . . . , tie the great tradition of the mediaeval doctor to a certain kind of positivist intellectualism, using Thomism as the battering ram of their pseudo-religious integrism." Gilson wrote to tell Chenu how much he enjoyed this article. Chenu was attacking the clerical first fruits of *Aeterni Patris,* a Thomism that allied itself with social anti-modernism. From 1927, the younger generation of French Catholic Thomists ceased to call themselves believers in "reason" and announced their faith in "Christian Humanism." With the papal condemnation of the Action Française, a new kind of Thomism began to blossom; for a second time, a "pontifical intervention" would "create a Thomist Renaissance" in the writings of Gilson, Maritain, and Chenu.[28]

27. Maritain, *Primauté du spirituel,* 25; Congar, *Journal d'un théologien,* 34.
28. Chenu, "Les sens et les leçons d'une crise religieuse," 370, 376–77, 380; Gilson to Marie-Dominique Chenu, February 14, 1932, in Chenu Papers, the Saulchoir Archive; Chenaux, "La seconde vague thomiste," 167.

# 6

# Christian Philosophy

## Gilson Founds the Pontifical Institute of Mediaeval Studies in Toronto

When Yves Congar was a student at Saulchoir, Père Chenu told him that "Gilson is like God: he communicates himself through participation."[1] Gilson had the born teacher's ability to enable others to experience his thought processes as their own, because he himself thought his listener's thoughts, his interlocutor's questions becoming his own. From the 1913–1919 *Le Thomisme,* many of Gilson's books had their birth as lectures, either at the Sorbonne, in Toronto, or in one of the numerous European and American universities that invited him as a guest speaker. He had a terrific ability to rise to an audience; he would show his humanist side at Harvard, while the theologian would be uppermost at Aberdeen. The fact that he wrote for an audience enforced his clarity and narrative verve and his inclination to size down his adversaries in a witty epigram. A good teacher must be an actor, and Gilson the performance artist sublimated his artistic sensibility into this work.

Saint Michael's College, Toronto, desired to put *Aeterni Patris* into practice and had recruited Thomist scholars like Fr. Gerald Phelan to work for them.[2] They were after a bigger fish. Gilson had been performing as a visiting professor in American universities since 1926. At the end of January 1927, he spent three days at Saint Michael's College. The Toronto Institute of Mediaeval Studies would open in the autumn of 1929. Gilson had many projects on hand when his third child, Bernard, was born. He was the director of the institute for the rest of his life: he spent the first semester of each academic year teaching there until 1959.

1. Congar, *Journal d'un théologien,* 58.
2. Shook, *Gilson,* 193.

Having assumed the directorship of the Institute of Mediaeval Studies, Gilson spent the next decade as an apologist for Christian philosophy. Just before the institute opened, the director published an article advertising the enterprise. Gilson writes that "Saint Michael's College is now trying to organize...a regular laboratory for mediaeval research." A "Catholic thinker" ought to be "so wholly permeated with mediaeval thought that anything he says or does...should be but a natural...and spontaneous expression of that everlasting tradition itself." It is *religion* that can best "explain the wonderful beauty of mediaeval art and mediaeval life."[3] As Gilson conceives them, the mission of the Institute of Mediaeval Studies and the project of Christian philosophy are directly analogous. The metaphor of the "laboratory" will eventually enable him to experiment on his claim, made at Harvard in 1926, that "the philosopher finds himself, in the presence of ideas, as before necessary essences, whose content escapes the free choice of his will."[4]

## Neo-Thomist Attitudes to Christianity and Philosophy

Canon Fernand Van Steenberghen was convinced that "there are Christian *philosophers*, but there are not Christian *philosophies*." This stern partisan of Louvain was sure that the mediaevals saw the matter in the same light: "neither St. Augustine, nor St. Bonaventure, nor St. Thomas," he said, "dreamed of elaborating philosophies...which were specifically Christian. Faithful to the thought of its founder, Msgr. Mercier, the School of Louvain always defended that position, with a twofold aim: to show that the Christian thinker could practice science and philosophy in the rigorous sense, as scientific methods; and consequently, to maintain common ground between Christian and unbelieving thinkers."[5] The Louvain school considered that reason is not true to philosophical science if it operates within the field of theology. Unless philosophers who are Christians argue on intrinsically rational grounds, how can they converse with opposing positions? In their project of ensuring that believers and agnostics share a level philosophical field, the Louvain Thomists pictured human rationality on a linear model, drawing an equation in which the line of reason ends as that of faith begins:

3. Gilson, "Mediaevalism in Toronto," 738–40.
4. Gilson, "Le rôle de la philosophie dans l'histoire de la civilization," 174.
5. Van Steenberghen, "Étienne Gilson et l'université de Louvain," 12.

| Nature | Supernature / Grace |
|---|---|
| Reason | Faith |
| Philosophy | Theology |

For the Louvain school, faith cannot enter the first arena without lifting it off its rational foundation. As they see it, unless it is demarcated from faith like this, reason cannot prove God's existence.

Few Neo-Thomists appear to have doubted that modern skepticism and agnosticism are expressions of immorality. Neo-Thomism did not fear to allow faith to cross the demarcation line in the form of moral influence upon reason. Père Garrigou-Lagrange said that, upon leaving a lecture at the Sorbonne, we are tempted to think, with Saint Paul, "They have made themselves inexcusable" (Rom. 1.20); when the Roman Thomist affirmed that "philosophy, as a science distinct from the positive sciences, cannot live long without religion; on this we are in agreement with the positivists,"[6] he meant that metaphysics cannot survive the absence of the morally stiffening effects of religion.

This attitude was not intended to imply any concession to fideism. Cardinal Mercier put it like this: "Revelation is *morally* necessary to humanity to conserve its patrimony of speculative and moral truths. But it is not *physically* necessary, and in all cases, the existence of God cannot be the object of an act of faith."[7] Fallen humanity is liable to err as to the existence of God. But we cannot *believe* that God exists because we can *know* it. Thomas affirmed that one cannot believe and know the same thing at the same time and in the same way. This entailed, for Mercier, that reason and faith have different objects, a God who presides over nature, known to philosophy, and a Trinitarian God, presiding over the distribution of grace, and known by theology.

## Laberthonnière: Christianity Makes for Realism

"The manner in which the supernatural is represented" by Scholasticism, wrote Père Lucien Laberthonnière in 1901, is what "gives rise to all the...misunderstandings." The Oratorian considered that a conceptualist philosophy is not easily paired with biblical realism. In *Le réalisme chrétien*

6. Garrigou-Lagrange, *Le sens commun*, 93–94.
7. Cardinal Mercier, *Traité élémentaire de philosophie à l'usage des classes,* Louvain, 1925, quoted in Gilson, *Christianisme et philosophie,* 87.

*et l'idéalisme grec* (1904), which Gilson described as "the best of his books," Laberthonnière designates the Greek "genius" as "abstraction." "All men by nature desire to *know*," said Aristotle in the first line of his *Metaphysics:* the italics are Laberthonnière's. The "philosophy of concepts" was born in the Greek pursuit of scientific knowledge. It is "idealistic" because it is "embarrassed" by the real and conceptually inassimilable "individual": "There is only a science of the idea which is universal and which, because it escapes time and space, can be defined. There is no science of the particular, of the individual." Beginning in "thought and sight," Greek philosophy must end in a "world of ideas." But in the Christian universe, "existences do not flow out of an essence; they are not deductions; they are facts, they are created. They cannot be explained logically and statically; they are explained historically or dynamically. It does not suffice for God to think, so to speak, for the world to come into being, it is necessary for God to act. The world is not a consequence of which God is the principle, it is an effect of which God is the cause." The Greeks deified the process of logical thought: Aristotle's God is a "supreme idea," a mind-God. For the biblical realist, "God is the eternal action of an eternal life," who "is not only present to the world as an ideal . . . , a final cause," but is "really and actively present as an efficient cause." Because it responds to the God who *acts* in Genesis, the "light" of Christian philosophy "shines on each individual life in its singularity."[8]

*Réalisme chrétien* made its way to the Index of Forbidden Books. It could have helped Gilson to picture the "beyond of contemplation" that Bergson indicated. Gilson concurred with Laberthonnière in considering that Christian realism is a gift to philosophy by grace. His intellectual life came to be governed by two principles, Christian philosophy and realism.

## The First Debate (1928): Idealist Philosophers vs. a Christian Realist

It all started in 1926, when the competent Sorbonne historian Émile Bréhier published *L'antiquité au moyen age.* This was the first volume of his *Histoire de la philosophie,* in which Bréhier "denied any influence of Christianity on the history of philosophy. In 1928 he defended his thesis in some lectures" at the Institut des Hautes Études "in Brussels under the

8. Laberthonnière to Marcel Hébert, cited in de Lubac, *At the Service of the Church,* 182; Gilson, *Le philosophe et la théologie,* 63; Laberthonnière, *Le réalisme chrétien et l'idéalisme grec,* 15, 18–19, 17, 53–54, 65, 69–70, 98.

title, 'Is there a Christian Philosophy?'" Bréhier laid down the gauntlet with the contention that Christianity and philosophy are incompatible, because the one is purely "mysterious," the other purely rational.[9]

When his Sorbonne colleague Léon Brunschvicg outlined to him the contents of his most recent book, *Progrès de la conscience* (1927), Xavier Léon remarked, "C'est la querelle de l'athéisme." Brunschvicg's thesis was that "*It is in history that the spirit conquers, naturally and necessarily, the consciousness of its eternal actuality.*"[10] By March 1928, Xavier Léon, secretary of the Société Française de Philosophie, had recruited eight philosophers to pursue the gambit.

Brunschvicg was, not an atheist, but that more complicated creature, an idealist. His idealist version of theism was intended to surpass what he described as the Christian metaphysical practice of projecting worldly objects like craftsmanship and paternity into a "supernatural" sphere, which it names "God." But, he claimed, once the philosophers of the seventeenth century had replaced this "physical metaphysics" with a "mathematical physics," the "axis of religious" life was shifted from its hinges. Thenceforth, the idealist philosopher argued, "the drama of the religious conscience" has been its effort to reconcile the God of Abraham with the God of the philosophers. The Abrahamic, premodern God was conceived in the imagination. This was so even in the hands of the metaphysicians who "prolonged" common sense nature into an "objective" supernature. Brunschvicg is arguing for something akin to the "demythologized" Christianity that was being put forward by Rudolf Bultmann at the same date. Unlike the German neo-Kantian, the French idealist recognized this as an attempt to abolish Christian doctrine. Brunschvicg's new theism will revere the *Verbum ratio,* the rational Word, and abhor the *Verbum oratio,* the spoken word, which engenders "myths of local revelations and of miraculous finality, symbols of anthropomorphic finality." The new hinge is the "radical incompatibility" between the "*interiority of the Reason-Word* and the exteriority of the Language-Word." Brunschvicg wanted a more rational religion than Christianity as traditionally conceived.

Both Brunschvicg and Gilson, facing one another on the podium in March 1928, had cut their wits on Descartes; both could be sharp. Gilson told his one-time professor that "the great Pythagorean discovery, that everything is number, has never lost for me the effect of admiring surprise

9. Van Steenberghen, "Étienne Gilson, historien de la pensée médiévale," 495; Bréhier, cited in de Lubac, "Sur la philosophie chrétienne," 226.
10. Blondel et al., "La querelle de l'athéisme," 61, 64.

that it produced for its inventors." The Sorbonne had also taught Gilson "*chosisme*": empirical facts matter to reason. Gilson argues that science advances through "the lucky find," "unexpected" and unpredictable windfalls of facts, discovered in territory outside human thought. The source of this line in apologetics was not only chosiste empiricism. Gilson had told his fellow officers, in 1917, that "the artistic type and the saint" exemplify the force of free creativity: for Bergson, the personal liberty which is the élan vital in us "is a power of creation," a force for innovation.[11]

He went forthrightly to the cutting operation required to dispense with Brunschvicg's thesis. The great Christian metaphysicians and mystics, Gilson says, explicitly posited that God transcends imagination, and even human reason itself: "The hypothesis of a spiritual transcendence is only contradictory for reason when it is the imagination which realizes it; but the constant philosophical and theological doctrine of Christianity is precisely the refusal to accept such a realization as satisfying. *Deus qui melius scitur nesciendo:* in refusing to enclose God in a sphere of imagination or even in that of reason, this classical formula of Thomism thus excludes *a fortiori* spatial exteriority from the concept of God."[12] Gilson advances a negative theology against Brunschvicg's rationalist theism. God's transcendence to human thinking is more obvious to the empiricist Gilson than to his rationalist colleague.

But Gilson's main weapon against Brunschvicg's idea of God as an "Interior Reason-Word" is the principle of sufficient reason. Gilson's style of argument does not stray far from the mainstream Thomism of the late 1920s. When he crossed swords with his idealist friend, at this first debate of 1928, Gilson asserted that "the idealism of M. Brunschvicg is a conquest over a certain dogmatism which disguises imagination in reason; the dogmatism whose rights I vindicate is essentially a realism."[13] The "querelle de l'athéisme" indicated to Gilson that Christian philosophy could be vindicated by its realism.

Maurice Blondel also contributed to the 1928 debate. In response to Brunschvicg's sallies against the "clockmaker" and "Father" analogies for God, Blondel noted that the "sense of the Divine" which develops concrete imagery of that sort can easily exercise Dionysius the Areopagite's method of "negation" upon them. The God of "the simple," the God of Abraham, is only incompatible with a "philosophy which has cut itself off from its

11. Ibid., 60, 58; Gilson, notes on 1917 Bergson lectures, in Gilson Papers.
12. Gilson, in Blondel et al., "La querelle de l'athéisme," 59.
13. Ibid., 69.

natural roots." Reflection on our own, natural thought processes shows that they are prompted by the quest for the supernatural.[14]

## Augustinian Approaches to Christian Philosophy: The Natural Desire

Laberthonnière's dramatic, biblically realistic theology was his own creation. He drew his Augustinian philosophy from Maurice Blondel. Gilson told Henri Gouhier that, after being forbidden to publish his opinions, Père Laberthonnière persistently "invited" his young friends "to accept the passing aberrations of an ill-advised ecclesiastical politics." Rather than fixing his resentments on the church, the Oratorian developed a "strange obsession, the assiduous companion of his silence"; his "bad angel" attributed his misfortunes to Saint Thomas Aquinas. But he forgave Pierre Rousselot his Thomism, "grateful to him for having seen him to be, not at all a modernist but an Augustinian."[15]

Under Père Descoqs' supervision, and despite his keeping modern works "like that of Étienne Gilson on Saint Thomas Aquinas . . . shelved in a locked wall cupboard, which was opened only on holidays," a troupe of Blondelians graduated from the Jesuit philosophy scholasticate on Jersey. They went on, in the mid-1920s, to the Jesuit theologate at Fourvière, in Lyons, where Rousselot's disciple, Joseph Huby, welcomed them. When, in 1930, a Blondelian Jesuit sent him his first published article, "Apologétique et théologie," Laberthonnière liked the piece, but reproved Henri de Lubac "for having quoted Saint Thomas." As Blondel had hinted in the debate about "demythologization," so de Lubac claimed here that theology had been driven into a cul de sac by "believing that in order to remain supernatural, it must be superficial, and that thought becomes more divine in the degree that it is cut off from all human roots. As if the same God could not be the author both of nature and of grace, and of nature in view of grace!"[16]

Père Huby asked de Lubac to give a talk about the natural desire for the supernatural. Père Guy de Broglie had lately discussed Saint Thomas's use

14. Ibid., 55.
15. Gilson to Henri Gouhier, October 31, 1932, in "Lettres d'Étienne Gilson à Henri Gouhier," 472; Gilson, *Le philosophe et la théologie*, 64; "le pauvre Laberthonnière a été son mauvais ange," Gilson to Henri Gouhier, January 30, 1962, in "Lettres d'Étienne Gilson à Henri Gouhier," 473; de Lubac, *At the Service of the Church*, 20.
16. De Lubac, *At the Service of the Church*, 65, 16; de Lubac, "Apologétique et théologie," 366.

of this trope, in a manner the young Jesuit took to be "a form of passage from the theses in our manuals to the rediscovery of traditional thought." As de Lubac began to piece together his argument that Christian tradition prior to the commentators had taught a natural desire for the supernatural vision, he was motivated by a desire to reclaim the synthetic quality of theology which this Augustinian thinker took to have been lost in modern times. He was excited by a comment of Maurice Blondel's, which he read around 1932: "People are afraid of confusing things, when they should be afraid of not uniting them sufficiently."[17]

Rousselot's claim that Thomas had taught the "natural desire" had been rejected by the Roman school: "only the divine intellect refers directly to divine being . . . the created intellect refers to created being," as Garrigou-Lagrange put it.[18] The Roman Thomists found in the "natural desire" a displeasing recollection of the "illuminationism" of the nineteenth-century Italian philosopher Rosmini.

## Gilson on Augustine's Realism

Gilson's article "The Future of Augustinian Metaphysics" (1930) is a one-off defense of Augustinianism. Augustine, he says, conceives the "natural desire," not as a generalized wish to catapult from nature into supernature, but as an orientation, a finality, built into human nature by its Creator. God-given faith directs humanity on its journey through nature to God. Augustine's "*Nisi credideritis, non intelligetis* is and will always remain," Gilson claims, "the charter of every Christian philosophy." It is not uncommon for writers to identify Descartes' act of doubting introversion with Augustine's *si fallor sum* ("If I doubt, I am"). Both Augustine and Descartes sought certitude by turning within the mind, and so both are said to deal in an argument from the private, and unreal, to the public and the real. Gilson argues that Descartes' cogitations uncovered mathematical ideas, which have no real being, and used them as a test of reality. Descartes was no realist. But Augustine's inner journey never departs from realism, because he was a Christian philosopher. Being a Christian philosopher made him a thinker who "holds faith to engender reason." Augustine's introspection analyzes the "content of thought": what he found "within" was "empirical," given. His explorations are not merely private or subjective, but

17. De Lubac, *At the Service of the Church*, 35; Komonchak, "Theology and Culture at Mid-Century," 582.

18. Garrigou-Lagrange, *God: His Existence and Nature*, 149–50.

map out a "*metaphysic* of inner experience." How can an inner-directed survey discover the objectively metaphysical? When Augustine asks how he can know truth, he was inquiring about something *factual* and open to "empirical observation."[19] His inner and his outer worlds are both equally real, because both are given within faith, that is, given as *brought about* by grace.

How can Augustine's reflection on his own inner world tell us about something that is not just contained in that "private" world? Is Augustine's "God" merely an extension of his own capacity for true judgment? No, says Gilson, because he does not identify God with the first thing he knows. He argues *from* the "facts of inner experience" *to* God, as their cause: "the doctrine of divine illumination is not the vision of the First Cause, but an induction of the First Cause, starting from an effect, namely truth."[20] The experience of truth is given as a dependent fact. Augustine's argument from his knowledge of truth is just as much an argument from a created and objective effect as a demonstration of God that sets off from sensible objects, like Thomas's proofs. The objectivity of nature is founded in its created contingency: graced creation can be discerned as much inside as outside the human self. Gilson is trying to show that the Augustinian way, of knowing God through innate truths, is reconcilable with Christian empiricism. "Innatism" is not identical with Cartesianism, so long as one remembers that the 'innate ideas' are just as much given by God's creative grace as any outward fact.

There is no "Thomist realism," Gilson says, without Augustine's insight that "nature is given to the Christian in grace." To be "Christian *qua* philosophy a philosophy must be Augustinian or nothing," because Augustine attempts

> to show the presence in the heart of man of a contingency much more tragic and disturbing than that of the universe, because it is the contingency of our own beatitude. Even when we know... why we are capable of truths, we still need to know why we are capable of the desire of truth; we need to understand the presence in us of an appeal by God who, working in our soul, creates in us a fruitful restlessness, ... stirs our soul, and leaves in it no rest until it has finally put itself into His hands. That this opens a field of inexhaustible fertility to... metaphysical reflection is... proved by the recent controversies about the possibility of a natural desire of God in man.[21]

19. Gilson, "The Future of Augustinian Metaphysics," 290, 302–3, 306.
20. Ibid., 307.
21. Ibid., 308, 312.

Gilson's brief venture into "Augustinianism" overturns the Louvain and Roman paradigm of how nature and supernature are related. The picture becomes circular:

$$\uparrow \text{grace / supernature} \;\rightarrow\; \text{nature} \;\rightarrow\; \text{theology / supernature} \downarrow$$
$$\leftarrow \; \leftarrow \; \leftarrow \; \leftarrow \; \leftarrow \; \leftarrow \; \leftarrow \; \leftarrow \; \leftarrow \; \leftarrow \; \leftarrow \; \leftarrow \; \leftarrow \; \leftarrow \; \leftarrow \; \leftarrow \; \leftarrow \; \leftarrow$$

So far as the priority of grace is concerned, Gilson is in agreement with the "Augustinian" approach to Christian philosophy. The issue between Gilson and contemporary Augustinianism will be whether one can distinguish the thinker and the believer within a "thinking graced nature."

## Gilson's First Round of Giffords: February 16–20, 1931

Marie-Dominique Chenu said that Gilson endeavored both to "extract a *philosophy* from the expressly theological work of St. Thomas" and to "conserve the theological genesis of that supposed philosophy." Increasingly, between 1913 and 1927, Gilson had claimed that Thomas's work had a "theological genesis." Entering the lists against Bréhier, he will argue that, because Thomas sets off from theological mystery, his rational demonstrations attain a realism denied to secular philosophies. Genesis is the operative word, in the sense of a beginning. In 1930, Gilson was asked to give the Gifford Lectures on natural theology at the University of Aberdeen. The Gifford lectures are given over two years: Gilson gave his from February 16 to 20 and May 29 to June 2, 1931, and February 8 to 12 and May 30 to June 3, 1932. Delivered in French to an Aberdonian audience, the lectures were published as *L'esprit de philosophie médiévale* (1931–1932), "Gilson's most beautiful book."[22]

The Giffords are Gilson's most wide-ranging defense of Christian philosophy. They are also an exercise in theologically ordered apologetics. Like *Le Thomisme,* the lectures follow a theological order, beginning with a general defense of the notion of Christian philosophy and proceeding through God, to a creation perceived in the light of revelation as existentially contingent, to the efficient causes and final ends of human nature, on from there to ethics and concluding with the philosophy of history.

In the opening lecture, "The Problem of Christian Philosophy," Gilson sums up its opponents as secular rationalists who believe that philosophy

22. Chenu, "L'interprète de Saint Thomas d'Aquin," 44–45. My italics.

cannot be combined with anything so irrational as revelation *and* those neo-Scholastics who consider that Saint Thomas's philosophy was "constructed on a purely rational basis." The problem of "Christian philosophy" is how to hold the two terms together. If the nonbelievers abhorred irrationality, the neo-Thomists also feared and disliked it. To sink reason into faith is to fall prey to the fideism that had been outlawed by the First Vatican Council, against which the Thomist apologetics of the Manuals had been unleashed, toward which the excommunicate Loisy had leaned when he made the Bible a secular history which it took the church to sacralize and which every ordinand had since 1907 been under oath to forswear,[23] under the guise of modernism. Some Thomists had forsworn modernistic fideism so thoroughly that when Gilson spoke of Christian philosophy, they heard him say that faith must supplant the human mind.

Gilson understood contemporary Augustinianism to contend that to know in the light of faith is simply to *believe,* so that, for a "graced thinker," everything known is a matter of belief. He wanted to say, to the contrary, that grace does not effect a spiritual lobotomy, replacing ratiocination with belief, teaching us to *see* differently, but rather throws us into an unexplored territory, into which reason makes its way. Faith presents reason with unknown territory, giving reason the impetus to make a portion of it visible. Reason is the same in believer and unbeliever, but Christian reason is exercised on different premises, or territory. Gilson told his audience that "there is no such thing as a Christian reason, but there may well be a Christian exercise of reason." The paradox of the Christian exercise of reason is that finding oneself in an inexplicable situation encourages one to produce an explanation of it. It requires that faith and reason each operate in its own way: "Thus I call Christian, *every philosophy which, although keeping the two orders formally distinct, nevertheless considers the Christian revelation as an indispensable auxiliary to reason....* [T]he concept does not correspond to any simple essence capable of abstract definition; but it corresponds much rather to a concrete historical reality as something calling for description."[24]

There is no essence of a Christian philosopher that could make a ghostly appearance at the banquet to silence the rationalists; the question turns, for Gilson, on whether, in historical fact, any persons have used their minds in the way that he describes. In his second lecture, "The Concept of Christian

23. Gilson, *The Spirit of Mediaeval Philosophy,* 4; Gouhier, *Études sur l'histoire des idées en France,* 139.
24. Gilson, *The Spirit of Mediaeval Philosophy,* 37.

Philosophy," Gilson presents history as a laboratory within which the Christian exercise of reason can be made evident. To show that revelation has influenced metaphysics "would be to demonstrate ... experimentally, the reality of Christian philosophy." Christian philosophy is not an idea but the body of "rational truths discovered, explored, or simply safeguarded thanks to the help that reason receives from revelation"; that this exploration has been conducted is a fact of history.[25]

Two related facts are brought into play. The first "fact," which separates Aquinas from Aristotle, is the "event" of Christianity, the advent of revelation. The second fact is that the Christian mind works within a world shown to it by revelation, attempting to interpret a faith-given object. Manual Thomism, as with Hugon's *Cursus* or Mercier's *Cours*, began in a philosophy of nature identical to that of Aristotle. Gilson wants to depart from the neo-Scholastic conception that "Thomism ... is nothing but Aristotelianism rationally corrected and judiciously completed,"[26] because if he is going to prove that the fact of revelation has contributed to philosophy, he will have to show that Christian thinkers have been drawn to describe a world that Aristotle failed to see. They did not just prolong Aristotle's narrative; the drama which they describe has a fresh inception. Gilson uses his theological apologetics to argue that the Christian philosophers reinvented the genre of philosophy on a supernatural ground.

With that, Gilson went home to Paris and made a striking textual discovery. He unshelved a pamphlet that he had glanced at before but without sufficient attention for it to stick in his mind. In

> encountering the encyclical *Aeterni Patris*, ... I perceived that I was in the process of proving in two volumes, twenty lectures and I don't know how many notes, exactly what the encyclical was sufficient to teach me. ... This notion of Christian philosophy, which I had taken great pains to retrieve from the facts, and whose name my colleague M. E. Bréhier had put in my memory, by denying that it exists, had been imposed on me as the end of a long research, from which a little attention to the teaching of the Church could have dispensed me. ... After all, that is the title of the Encyclical; it was not me that invented it, and to imagine that I should abstain from speaking of *philosophia christiana*, well, the least that I can say to the Catholic philosophers who criticize me for doing so is that I find their attitude surprising.[27]

25. Ibid., 41, 35.
26. Schmitz, *What Has Clio to Do with Athena?* 9; Gilson, *The Spirit of Mediaeval Philosophy*, 8.
27. Gilson, *Christianisme et philosophie*, 129–30.

## The Christian Philosophy Debate (March 21, 1931)

A letter dated February 24, 1931, carrying the news that the Société Française de Philosophie intends to hold a public debate about Christian philosophy is the first in which Gilson addresses Jacques Maritain as "Cher Monsieur et *Ami*." The debate was held on March 21, 1931, with Xavier Léon once again in the chair. He told the audience that Gilson, who felt that no one's mind was ever changed by a debate, had agreed to participate out of friendship for himself. Gilson had fallen for a second sparring match with Brunschvicg, whom he described to Léon as his "cher enemi." Alongside him was Émile Bréhier, who considered that when, as in the Middle Ages, "there is a collision between them, faith tells one what is true" and thus "philosophy has only an illusory autonomy: it is controlled by dogma and must at once give way to its complaints." The Bergsonian philosopher Édouard Le Roy was also on the podium. The audience included Père Mandonnet, who agreed with the agnostics in demarcating Thomas's use of philosophical reason from his theological faith, and Gabriel Marcel, "his cane in his hand, looking pugnacious and making comments under his breath."[28] Blondel absented himself from the meeting. Père Laberthonnière was there to represent the Augustinian view that thinking and believing is a phenomenologically unitary act.

Henri de Lubac claims that the Oratorian

> "looked tense." . . . Everyone was biting his tongue to keep from mentioning Father Laberthonnière's name as the debate ranged on. Yet, wasn't it his "Augustinian concept" that "Gilson the Burgundian cheerfully, carelessly, and cruelly made fun of . . . ?" That . . . was the impression Laberthonnière took away with him, and confided to his young visitor a few days later, reiterating his position "forcefully": "Christianity is my whole philosophy, just as it was for Justin Martyr . . . The idea of an independent Christian philosophy came from the Middle Ages."[29]

In the transcript, Gilson's adverse comments on Blondelian "Augustinianism" are in fact brief, although they do include one joke. Gilson's opponents objected to the welding of Christianity and philosophy on the grounds that the only context reason can have is the laws of thought. It would not have been to Gilson's advantage to rebut this anticontextual notion of philoso-

28. Gilson to Jacques Maritain, February 24, 1931, in *Deux approches*, 43–44; Blondel et al., "La notion de philosophie chrétienne," 39; Nédoncelle, *Is There a Christian Philosophy?* 91; de Lubac's footnote in *Letters of Gilson to de Lubac*, 122.
29. De Lubac's footnote in *Letters of Gilson to de Lubac*, 122.

phy by ridiculing the psychological holism of Augustinianism. He distinguishes between Augustine's search for the "comprehensive" notion and Thomas's desire for the "precise" conception: "the one expressed the concrete, the other analyzed it," says Gilson. The "Augustinian spirit" looks to the complete human being, who is not a machine containing separate believing and reasoning mechanisms, each "purchased in a detached parts shop." The "truth" of Augustinianism is "the real unity of the concrete elements in the subject" in whom faith and reason operate. The Christian's "reason is that of a subject in which something non-rational is given, his religious faith." But, Gilson argued, "I wait to find a pure philosopher, the concrete realization of a unique concept, whose reason never visits any irrational neighbors . . . I ask myself if the philosophic life is not precisely a constant effort to bring the irrational within us into a state of rationality. . . . It belongs to the Christian to be convinced of the rational fecundity of faith." The "true meaning" of Augustine's *credo ut intellegam* and Anselm's *fides quaerens intellectam,* so Gilson argued, is "a Christian's effort to derive a rational understanding from his faith in revelation."[30]

Gilson wants to recapture the "true" Augustine from the Augustinians in order to make it plain that faith does not seek understanding so that they can look at one another: faith induces the mind to look at realities. Faith is the presentation of a spectacle to reason's sight. Believers hold on nonrational grounds that certain realities exist. The attempt rationally to elucidate them is Christian philosophy. If, in historical fact, the nonrational has generated philosophy, if there are "systems of rational truths, whose existence is historically inexplicable without taking account of the existence of Christianity, these philosophies must be called Christian."[31]

Bréhier took the stage to affirm that "Christianity and philosophy pose exactly the same problems" with entirely different methods. Christianity is both unoriginal in its concepts and irrational in its way of employing them. It borrowed the Greek notion of the Logos, the eternal rational structure of reality, and changed it into the agent of a "mysterious history, which can only be known through revelation, and which is thus extrinsically attached to that eternal notion, adding nothing to it." Gilson interrupted to object that Judaeo-Christian revelation had changed the course of philosophy by opening a window onto a world in which a single God, who is pure act, created the world out of nothing. Christianity "introduces the idea of a radical contingency of being, of existence, rather than of its intelligibility or

30. Gilson, in Blondel et al., "La notion de philosophie chrétienne," 45, 47–48.
31. Ibid., 48.

order as in Greek philosophy." His research has taught him that Descartes lived not in a Greek universe but in a Christian one: "for Descartes, for whom God is *causa sui,* creation extends to the external verities." To which his colleague retorted, "Descartes is too Christian!"[32]

Maritain now entered the game, and began by marking his "complete agreement with M. Gilson on the essentials of the debate." But a few theoretical precisions must be permitted to one who has listened to Gilson's strictures on "'rationalist' neo-Thomists." Thomas's philosophical arguments *are* constructed on purely rational lines. Maritain distinguished between the "order of specification" or "nature," of philosophy, and its "order of exercise," or its "*state.*" Philosophy is specified by its formal object, which is "intrinsically accessible to the human mind." What formally constitutes Thomist philosophy as philosophy is not theology but rationality: "philosophy as such, whether in the head of a pagan or a Christian, is directed by the same strictly intrinsic criterion, which is natural or rational."[33]

But, factually, this "nature" is always found in various states, as for example the psychic condition of a Christian. The nature of philosophy is exercised by people in different moral states, Maritain says. In the Christian philosophy debate, it was not Gilson but Maritain who weighed the ethical advantages of philosophizing in a Christian *state.* "In order to achieve its full, normal development in us," Maritain said, "philosophy demands many rectifications and purifications of the individual, an ascesis, not only of the reason but of the heart, and one philosophizes with one's whole soul, just as one runs with one's heart and one's lungs."[34]

Maritain is content to give Bréhier the pawn of a shared philosophical heritage: if the "supernatural facts given by revelation" had been "a sudden apparition of new concepts . . . no one would have understood them. . . . In order that the . . . supra-philosophical Logos could be usefully communicated to men, . . . a conceptual preparation was required . . . [T]he idea of the Logos had long been mulled over by philosophers." Within Gilson's strategy, his *cher ami* had offered up the queen. Gilson's idea that the light of faith prompts the Christian to notice that he is on different or new territory has been exchanged for the idea that the Christian philosophizes in a different moral state to the unbeliever.

The *cher enemi* made a two-pronged assault. Brunschvicg argued that what a philosopher discovers is outside of his believing state, and that Aristotle would never have become a Christian. Gilson was willing to bracket

32. Ibid., 51–52, 57–58.
33. Ibid., 59, 61–62.
34. Ibid., 63.

the revelation if he could make his professor see the novelty of Christian philosophy: "Whether this is a God, who said to Moses, 'My name is Being,' or indeed Moses or someone else whom we call Moses, had the religious intuition, 'the name of God is Being,' the result is the same, for the origin of philosophical speculation is not philosophical." In his relations with Maritain, Gilson "sometimes cedes, then regretted it, and did not always say so." His "impatience" was "restrained by courtesy and affection, and exacerbated by them." He conceded the pre-Christian preparations for Christian philosophy to Bréhier and to Maritain: one can imagine the gritted teeth through which Gilson added, "But does it not matter at all whether Christianity, or the Judaeo-Christian revelation, conveyed something new?" In conclusion, Édouard Le Roy suggested that the "true question" of the evening's discussion had been whether "Christianity introduced something new into" philosophy's "history": the Bergsonian philosopher concurred with Gilson that it had.[35]

After the debate, Étienne wrote to Henri Gouhier, "Brunschvicg and Mandonnet," the idealist and the Thomist, "unite in anathematizing me." The phrase "revelation engenders reason" expressed what he saw as the central issue in the debate. Gilson praised Maritain's contribution to the debate. But it is not entirely accurate to say that "Maritain's distinction between philosophy considered according to its nature and philosophy considered in its concrete state ... correspond[s] to Gilson's distinction between philosophy considered formally, or in the abstract, and philosophy taken as a concrete historical reality." For Maritain, the philosopher's "nature" operates in a new ethical or psychological context, if he is a Christian, whereas for Gilson the Christian philosopher's "nature" is set on new, supernatural ground, if he accepts revelation. De Lubac was one of the few to see that, despite both men's insistence that their "positions converge," in "practice, M. Gilson ... admits a much greater influence of Christianity than M. Maritain concedes. For the latter estimates that one must find, amongst the thinkers who precede Christ, at least some germs of *all* the philosophical truths which faith must illuminate": it follows that what Christianity gives philosophy is not "'revelation'" but "'confirmation.' Gilson's formula, that revelation generates reason, surely goes much further."[36]

---

35. Bars, "Gilson et Maritain," 260; Gilson and Édouard Le Roy, in Blondel et al., "La notion de philosophie chrétienne," 80 (Gilson), 83 (Le Roy).

36. Prouvost, "Les relations entre philosophie et théologie chez É. Gilson," 420; Wippel, *Metaphysical Themes in Thomas Aquinas,* 12; de Lubac, "Sur la philosophie chrétienne," 229–30. The words *revelation* and *confirmation* are quoted from Maritain's comments at the debate.

Gilson remembered Père Laberthonnière by such "memorable circumstances" as when the Oratorian had "told me that Saint Thomas was a 'malefactor.' A short silence, then, 'I hate him.'" But as we read that debate, and the *Spirit,* it may seem that Laberthonnière's distinction between Greek idealism, or epistemologism, and Christian dramatic and historical realism had made some impression upon Gilson's mind. As in *Réalisme chrétien,* Gilson takes revelation to point its finger at the concrete individual. Christian philosophy is the rational elucidation of a new and untoward fact, a miracle. Laberthonnière had accentuated the difference between an Aristotelian deity as an "It" and the *existent* Christian God: "God does not want us, know us, love us as *things;* he wants us, knows us, loves us—which for him is to make us exist—as *beings,* so that we, in our turn, might want him, know him, love him as Being. This implies a relation between him and us of known being to knowing being and, in consequence, a knowledge by us about him just as by him about us. But this knowledge does not at all resemble the knowledge of things."[37]

And yet, Gilson was no friend to Laberthonnière's philosophical mentor, Maurice Blondel. He was infuriated that Blondel published a critique of his position as an appendix to the minutes of the debate. Blondel accused Gilson of historicism, the same charge that stuck to Loisy. De Lubac's description of Laberthonnière's reaction to the debate may have been enhanced by Blondel's posthumous critique, in which the philosopher claimed that "there are no Christian philosoph*ies,* in the plural; there is only, as Justin the Apologist put it, '*the* philosophy of Christ, in the singular.'" The Thomist and the Augustinians were not in thorough-going disagreement. Blondel considered that Guy de Broglie's recent excavations of "the place of the supernatural in the philosophy of Saint Thomas" provided a "speculative possibility" of the orientation of consciousness to God, which is incomplete without Gilson's demonstration that it is "actualized in the facts."[38]

## The Giffords Completed: May 29–June 2, 1931, February 8–12, May 30–June 3, 1932

A month later, resting in France before returning for his second round of Gifford lectures, Gilson described to Maritain what he saw as the abyss

---

37. Gilson to Henri Gouhier, January 30, 1962, in "Lettres d'Étienne Gilson à Henri Gouhier," 473; Laberthonnière, *Annales de philosophie chrétienne,* 159.292, cited in de Lubac, *At the Service of the Church,* 180.
38. Shook, *Gilson,* 199–200; Blondel, Appendix to "La notion de philosophie chrétienne," 91.

between a Platonic or Aristotelian nature, in which given substances are ordered in relation to the Self-Thinking Thought, and the notion of nature in Christian philosophy, in which it is dependent for its existence upon a free act of divine creation. For Aristotle, nature is the constant round of the unfurling and furling of substance, from potentiality to actuality. Thomas includes this level of causality and adds to it the notion of a cause of being itself. Five days later, Maritain responded: "If you want to make your position completely impregnable," you should say that Moses was made to grasp the Being of God "*explicitly*" but that Aristotle himself saw that God is subsistent Being, albeit "*implicitly.*" Because his notion of Christian philosophy is grounded in historical innovation, Gilson has to make himself more vulnerable than Maritain would have preferred. He responded on April 21: "I think Aristotle did turn to the correct solution; he employed formulas which materially express the idea of pure Being, but we know from his collected writings that it was not the idea of the existence of *esse* that he had in mind. His system is healthy but it is thanks to the Bible that it has been completed." Two weeks later, before Gilson returned to Scotland, Maritain told his friend that

> for your thesis to be beyond attack, an expression like "Aristotle didn't arrive at Being" is too general; it is necessary to get a formula that is really technical and explicit about what this historical development achieved: Aristotle did not get to the doctrine of the real identity of essence and existence in God and its real distinction from everything else. This is Thomas' fundamental truth and without this doctrine his whole theory of the *Ipsum Esse Subsistens* loses its metaphysical value. The sad fact is that here Suarez is slipshod in relation to Thomas. . . . Some people will say to you: there are Christian philosophers who don't understand the cornerstone of Christian philosophy. To which you can reply: so much the worse for them—a Christian philosopher is not necessarily a good philosopher. The important point is that, in fact, the cornerstone was set in position thanks to Moses.[39]

His Scottish audience refreshed and ready for another stint of French philosophy in French, Gilson resumed his Giffords on May 29. He began with "Being and Its Contingence" and was "more severe to Greek theodicy than Père Laberthonnière had been," for the Oratorian "did not deny that there was monotheism among the Greeks."[40] The Gifford lecturer affirmed

---

39. Gilson to Jacques Maritain, April 15, 1931, in *Deux approches*, 46–48; Maritain to Étienne Gilson, April 20, 1931, ibid., 53; Gilson to Jacques Maritain, April 21, 1931, ibid., 58–59; Maritain to Étienne Gilson, May 5, 1931, ibid., 64–65.
40. Nédoncelle, *Is There a Christian Philosophy?* 88.

that the Greek philosophers were polytheists, because the being that their gods possess is not unique. "Even were it granted," Gilson says, "in the face of all the texts, that Aristotle's being as being is a unique being, it would still be true that this being is none other than the pure act of thought thinking itself. . . . [T]he attributes of Aristotle's god are strictly limited to those of thought. In good Aristotelian doctrine the first name of God is being, and pure being is reduced to pure thought; in good Christian doctrine the first name of God is being." Christian philosophy makes a discovery in the realm of reason, because of the revelation to Moses that God is "I am Who I am." Gilson told his audience: "No hint of metaphysics, but God speaks, *causa finita est,* and Exodus lays down the principle from which henceforth the whole of Christian philosophy will be suspended. From this moment it is understood . . . that the proper name of God is Being and that, . . . this name denotes His very essence. . . . There is but one God and this God is Being, that is the corner-stone of all Christian philosophy, and it was . . . Moses who put it in position." By exercising their reason on the Mosaic revelation, Christian philosophers since Augustine have recognized that there is an entirely transcendent act of Being as Being, "I am that I am," and that the "nature" that Aristotle described in terms of substances requires a "sufficient reason" for its existence.[41] By virtue of revelation, the Christian philosophers were able to distinguish a single Uncreated, or subsistent, Being, from created being.

Gilson and Maritain did not achieve agreement in their April 1931 correspondence about whether Aristotle had the notion of "creation." Gilson told his friend that nowhere does Aquinas attribute that idea to the Philosopher: although Aristotle does not deny creation *ex nihilo,* neither does he affirm it, and so Aquinas "avoided" applying "the word '*creatio*' to Aristotle's doctrine." Maritain returned his own reflection that "the ancients arrived at the recognition that there is a universal cause from which all things proceed and depend, and this conforms to the Catholic faith, but they did not *explicitly* say that all things proceed from this cause as by creation."[42] Maritain means that Christian philosophy fulfills what is potentially present in Greek thought. But Gilson finds that the realism of the Christian thinkers instantiates a substantially new philosophy. As he sees it, they don't just draw out the potentialities of the ancients, but reason on the other side of the chasm opened by revelation. Gilson makes use of the difference between Aristotle and Aquinas to show how a theology of *cre-*

41. Gilson, *The Spirit of Mediaeval Philosophy,* 50, 51, 53.
42. Gilson to Jacques Maritain, April 21, 1931, in *Deux approches,* 58; Gilson to Maritain, April 22, 1931, ibid., 62; Maritain to Gilson, May 5, 1931, ibid., 64.

*ation* can penetrate a natural philosophy of substance without overwriting its inherent principles: "The more one reads the mediaeval commentaries on Aristotle the more one is convinced that their authors knew exactly what they were about. St. Thomas can write his pages on the *Metaphysics* without once saying that Aristotle taught the doctrine of creation, nor yet that he denied it. He knew very well that Aristotle does not teach it, but what interests him is to...make clear that,...his principles, while remaining precisely what they are, are perfectly capable of bearing its weight."[43]

The fifth lecture, "Analogy, Causality, and Finality," begins with a curious question: If God is Being, is the real existence of all else subsumed into God's? "We must," Gilson says, "notice the abstract, non-realist and therefore non-Christian character of the difficulty." If God's Being is the cause of the existence of a system of secondary causes, then the first act it communicates is being itself: divine creation is the transmission of an activity originally exercised by God alone, that is, *existing*. All Christian philosophers attribute this self-communication of being to the divine goodness: as the divine act of Being causes existence in contingent beings, so, in one and the same act, it causes them to be good. Being creates by its own Goodness, and therefore creates things whose act of created being is good. When they discovered that it follows from this that goodness is an analogy between Creative Being and dependent beings, the mediaeval Christian philosophers were elaborating "the metaphysics of the Exodus."[44] The existential dependence of beings upon Being entails the analogy of goodness. It is because the two orders of being are existentially "incommensurable" that they are metaphysically "compossible." The answer to the "abstract and non-realist" question about the simultaneous existence of subsistent Being and contingent beings is analogy; it is only if two things are different in their being that they can be analogous. The revealed glimpse of God's self-sufficient existence makes one notice the oddity of the fact of existence.

Gilson restates on existential grounds what had been denied by Descartes on the ground of physical science: the good that God wills to bring about in creation is being itself, and thus "the universe was conceived by the Christian Middle Ages not only as sacramental, but also as oriented." The final causality that had been central for the "Aristotelian" Gilson of 1908–1919 has become the expression of existential causality. Nonetheless, Gilson makes light of the differences between Augustine, Thomas, and Suarez, because the "chief significance of the real distinction" still resides, for him,

43. Gilson, *The Spirit of Mediaeval Philosophy*, 424.
44. Ibid., 85, 94.

"in its relation to creation, where its use" is "to enable Christian philoso-phers to escape pantheism."[45] For Gilson, in 1932, existential dependence *says* "createdness."

"Christian optimism" is the fruit of meditation on Genesis. Augustine overcame Manichaeism by philosophical reflection on the biblical creation story. What is implicit in his recognition of the difference between Creator and his good creation is made explicit in Thomas's distinction between the creature's "essence" and its "existence." Gilson subscribes to the Aristotelian principle that unity is a mark of substantial existence. His thought experi-ment must elicit, not various Christian philosoph*ies*, but a single, substan-tial Christian philosoph*y*. The Gifford lectures make the Apologists and the Schoolmen unite around the "metaphysics of the Exodus." Gilson remarks that "it is very true that the obstinate concordism of the Middle Ages does not facilitate the task of the historian. . . . But if the mediaeval thinkers often let fall the differences it was because they knew that the differences tend to fall out of themselves; that the resemblances alone are really fruitful."[46]

The case can be seen in the notion of "divine providence" common to the mediaeval Christian philosophers. The notion of providence flows out of that of created finality, God's ordering of being toward His own goodness. This conception is absent from Aristotle's natural philosophy. Aristotle's

> First Mover . . . moves only by the love it excites—which it excites, observe, but does not breathe in. . . . *l'amor che muove il Sole e l'altre stelle* has nothing but the name in common with the first unmoved Mover. The God of St. Thomas and Dante is a God Who loves, the god of Aristotle is a god who does not refuse to be loved; the love that moves the heavens and the stars in Aristotle is the love of the heavens and the stars for god; but the love that moves them in St. Thomas and Dante is the love of God for the world; be-tween these two motive causes there is all the difference between an efficient cause . . . and a final cause.

The mediaeval conception of final causality is related to that of the Ideas within the divine understanding. Thomas, Bonaventure and Duns Scotus define the Ideas differently. For Thomas, the idea is "God's knowledge of his own essence as capable of being participated"; Bonaventure makes the idea into a divine "expression" of "the totality of possibles"; with Duns Scotus, the ideas, extended into plurality, are "the creatures themselves as creatable by God and existing in Him in virtue of their concepts of possi-

45. Ibid., 106; Noonan, "The Existentialism of Etienne Gilson," 419–20.
46. Gilson, *The Spirit of Mediaeval Philosophy,* 115, 146.

bles": when God knows the idea, He does not know Himself, but an "imitation" of his essence.[47]

Fifteen years later, in *L'être et l'essence,* these differences become the subject of a treatise on the logical steps by which philosophy became oblivious to being. In the Gifford Lectures, Thomas, Bonaventure, and Scotus are unified by their theological conviction of divine providence. This, the apologist states, is enough to show the "fundamental unity of Christian thought."[48]

When Gilson says that "all the great mediaeval epistemologies were, as we should say today, realisms," he means epistemically realistic: in a God-created universe, objects are expected to be *knowable.* But a Christian universe is not an entirely effective antidote against idealism. Augustine inherited from Plato a distrust of the senses and conveyed it to the Franciscan tradition. Bonaventure, Matthew of Aquasparta, and Roger Marston all agree with Augustine that "from our corporeal senses . . . no genuine truth is to be looked for," and thus that truth is to be sought in the illumination of the human intellect by an appropriate divine idea. Since we do not know the essence of the thing in its sensible encasement, but rather in the reference of our idea to its divine exemplar, we can, according to Matthew of Aquasparta, bypass the physically existent reality and go directly to God for information about its essence: "the intellect might very well know by means of the Ideas, even if things did not exist." Matthew makes his faith do the work of his rational knowledge of the existence of the world. Such realism as he retains is fideistic: "since Matthew of Aquasparta regards the doctrine of illumination as essentially theological . . . his epistemology is a philosophical scepticism saved by divine illumination."[49]

Gilson's disapprobation of August*inianism* seems to be getting the better of his claim for the unity, and the realism, of Christian philosophy. But the case he is making is that this type of philosophy has an inbuilt recuperative mechanism. Christian philosophers instinctively redress the exaggerations of their predecessors, restoring the equilibrium. Gilson continues the tale:

> Many years ago a friend of mine, who happened to be a sociologist, congratulated me for treating the philosophies of the Middle Ages as those of groups, of collectivities. But the fact is that the groups were all formed around individuals, and nowhere does this more clearly appear than in this particular case. By all Franciscan tradition Duns Scotus should have taken up the cudgels

47. Ibid., 75, 159–60.
48. Ibid., 160.
49. Ibid., 229–30, 234–35.

against St. Thomas and voiced the suspicion thrown on the sensible by the Augustinians of his Order; but judging the position to be philosophically untenable, he . . . simply rejected it, reserving the right to find some other means of saving whatever truth there is in St. Augustine's doctrine.[50]

"Christian philosophy" does not automatically redress the balance; individual Christians do. For Thomas, a creature's "state" is its nature, and the nature of the human being is to know through body and soul together: although it is discombobulated by original sin, human nature has not changed. Duns Scotus mobilized a more dramatic notion of "status": the "status" of a nature, such as that of man, is its "stable mode of being" at any particular time, the stability being guaranteed by God's wisdom. By virtue of its position in the Second Act of history, after original sin, humanity has now the "status" of a creature that is compelled to employ its senses to know objects: "Without an initial movement of the intellect by sensation there is no intellectual knowledge. But why? Perhaps—and this is an hypothesis to which Duns Scotus returns with . . . complacency—as a divine punishment for original sin; perhaps . . . because God desires this strict collaboration between our various cognitive faculties."[51] Some people in the Aberdonian audience may have been impressed by Duns Scotus's logic. For Gilson, the point is that the Franciscan used the resources at his disposal to drag epistemology back into a sense-based realism, even if that took nailing it to the mast of the divine will.

The Christian conception of human nature as a conjunction of sense and spirit goes back to Athenagoras. The second-century apologist attempts to justify the revealed doctrine of the resurrection of the body by the argument that man is made to contemplate God and cannot do it in this life. If he must, then, do it in the next world, it will not be as soul alone, for "*that which has received mind and reason is the man, and not the soul by itself.* Therefore the man, a composite of body and soul, must always subsist, and this could not be if he does not rise again." The significant novelty that Gilson espies is that Athenagoras defends the composite reality, not of the human species, not of human nature taken as a collective unit, which is what mattered to Aristotle, but rather of the individual person, who will rise again at the last day to contemplate God. "Athenagoras' expressions," Gilson claims, "show how deeply the Good News influenced philosophy. Created by God as a distinct individuality, conserved in being by an act of continuous creation, the man is henceforth the protagonist of a drama,

50. Ibid., 240.
51. Ibid., 252.

which is none other than that of his own destiny." For Aristotle, a nature is *individuated* by matter. The same nature is cut into many different pieces of dough; human beings are different because they inhabit different bodies, not because they have unique souls. Distinguish, then, Gilson says, individuation and individuality, and we may, with Duns Scotus, attribute individuality not only to God and to angels, but also to human beings, because, "in its root reality, the soul is individual and the cause of individuality.... [I]t is not simply *a* soul but *this* soul, and it is this essential individuality which individualizes the matter of the body and, along with the body, the whole man."[52]

The person gives individuality to its material body; the individuation of the soul around this particular nervous system is secondary, in the order of ethics. Christian personalism gives rise to an ethics in which moral norms are no less objective than they are for Plato or Aristotle, but in which the "source" of morality is "altogether interior" because it "expresses itself in us" through our "reason." The Fathers of the church and the mediaevals "would have been very much surprised to hear that their moral philosophy was not based on reason; perhaps...they might have been got to admit that it was 'laic.' But we shall find it very difficult to believe...that if this laicized ethic was so very different from the ancient, the fact that its authors were Christian priests had nothing at all to do with it."[53]

The lecture on "Christian Socratism" finds that the mediaevals found out how to direct themselves to their final end, to God, by practicing Socrates's injunction "Know thyself." All of nature is objectively analogous to God: human beings are capable of knowing that analogy in self-reflection. This is why human persons are made in the divine image. Gilson cites Thomas: "The image of God is found in the soul according as the soul turns to God, or possesses a nature that enables it to turn to God." Gilson turns to a point against which the commentators had insuperable objections: "That the desire to see God is natural the whole history of philosophy proves, and...the personal experience of every man who, from the consideration of the world, rises to the consideration of its cause.... [A]s many men as there are to know that God exists so many men will there be to desire to know His nature; so many men will there be to know neither rest nor beatitude while deprived of this knowledge."[54]

Maritain had told Gilson that the statement in the 1922 *Le Thomisme* that "human nature imperiously desires transcendence and the divine" "in-

52. Athenagoras, *On the Resurrection of the Dead,* cited ibid., 192–93; ibid., 196.
53. Ibid., 359, 363.
54. Ibid., 213, 260–61.

troduces confusions which I deplore."[55] He believed that Aristotle's conception of God contains implicitly what the Christian Aquinas knows explicitly. It is then difficult to say that we have a natural desire for the supernatural vision without destroying God's free will. If the beatific vision is the free gift of God, then human beings cannot achieve the supernatural by extending their human natures ever so far. How, then, could they desire a good that transcends their human potential?

The human intellect, says the more theological Gilson, has a created potentiality, which only God can actualize. Aristotle's God operates within a closed set of rules; Thomas's God can perform miracles within the order of second causes, because He created it: "Just as, for a Christian, all is miracle, so, in a certain sense, all is grace." Maritain had rapped Gilson on the knuckles for illogicality, because he said that although grace is a miracle, the desire for it is natural. The Christian "created essence" is more open to divine intervention than is the Aristotelian substance, *while retaining its nature*. The natural desire for God is present, Gilson thinks, in the "Anima capax Dei," of Saint Bernard, Anselm, and Thomas Aquinas. Gilson asserts that "the capacity that lies in human nature for the beatific vision . . . is part of human nature itself made to the image of God, from Whom it derives its power of knowing. The capacity for grace is also something more than a word; if human souls were not susceptible of grace God Himself could not bestow it. . . . [T]here is nothing in it at all that already belongs to the supernatural, . . . the obediential power . . . remains absolutely passive; . . . it expresses the distinctive character of a Christian nature, open . . . towards its Creator."[56]

Édouard Le Roy closed the debate of March 1931 with the statement that what is "genuinely novel in the Christian perspective is" that "the being of the world is essentially conceived as a history, and as a history open to the infinite." Gilson advised his colleague that he would deal with this in his Giffords. Against the idea that the mediaevals lacked a conception of what we today call *history*, Gilson argues that mediaeval poetry and architecture differ from our own, but we do not say that they had none. We say, rather, that there is a unique mediaeval understanding of art. Likewise with history: "We might well have guessed *a priori* that this was the case when we deal with a time when all minds lived on the memory of an historical fact, of an event to which all previous history led up, from which was dated

---

55. Maritain to Étienne Gilson, November 25, 1924, in *Deux approches*, 26.
56. Gilson, *The Spirit of Mediaeval Philosophy*, 378, 381.

the beginning of a new era; a unique event, which might almost be said to mark a date for God Himself, the Incarnation of the Word and the birth of Jesus Christ."[57]

The literalist of concrete facts asks, "How could a civilization believe in the fixity and permanence of things when its own sacred books—. . . the Bible and the Gospel—were history books"? Bergson had set in Gilson's mind the image of music as existence in motion; Augustine's *Confessions* indicate the rapid movement of time. Gilson says that "far from ignoring the fact that all things change, Christian thought felt almost to anguish the tragic character of the *instant*." Augustine's *City of God* bequeathed to the Middle Ages a picture of God as Conductor and Composer of history: "at many points the hidden sense will escape us; we may suppose that the 'ineffable musician' would often keep his secret back; . . . we shall decipher enough to be sure that all has a meaning, and to be able to conjecture how each event stands to the unique law that rules the whole." Saint Thomas makes a positive assessment of history: "there is," Gilson says, "as St. Thomas often notes," "a progress in the political and social order, just as there is in the intellectual order of science and philosophy, each new generation becoming the beneficiary of all the truths accumulated by its predecessors."[58] The business of the rational animal is to know truths; the accumulated legacy of knowledge is passed on, generation by generation. By what measuring rod could we judge that progress takes place? Gilson notes that Christians have a measure in our supernatural end: there is progress in our knowledge of our natural and of our supernatural end, that is, of God.

Gilson sums up his apologia for Christian philosophy by returning to the individual and his personal conversion. The "religion" of the mediaeval Christians, he claims, "brought with it no new philosophy, but it made them new men; and the new birth effected in themselves was bound to bring about a renaissance of philosophy."[59] He does not argue that Christian philosophy is the *only* real philosophy, the single genuinely philosophical exercise of human reason. Utopians may wish to legislate for the sole-sufficiency of one philosophy—*extra ecclesia nulla philosophia*. But for Gilson, Christian philosophy is a species within the genus philosophy, because, historically, it has worked and made its results known within the field of operation common to all human thinkers.

57. Le Roy, in Blondel et al., "La notion de philosophie chrétienne," 84; Gilson, *The Spirit of Mediaeval Philosophy*, 384.
58. Gilson, *The Spirit of Mediaeval Philosophy*, 385–86, 391, 388.
59. Ibid., 418.

## Aftermath of the Debate

Early in 1932 Maritain wrote to tell Gilson that the first volume of the Giffords "is itself a great work of Christian philosophy." The author had stated twice that, at the debate of March 1931, his friend "analyzed" and "established" the "existence" of Christian philosophy "much better than I could do."[60] Jacques approved of the *Spirit*'s critique of "Thomistic rationalism." He observed that "by virtue of the fact that he ... disengages pure essences, the danger for a Thomist is always that of taking such essences for what reality is like in its concrete condition, a gross error which Thomas never committed but which some of today's Dominicans ... do not always take enough care to avoid." Gilson developed that theme in *L'être et l'essence*. *The Spirit of Mediaeval Philosophy* is a more spontaneous expression of his personality. One of his Sorbonne students speaks of him as a "well earthed man, attached ... to the quality of wines and cheeses ... Gilson ... loved in St. Thomas, not only the sober elegance of a perfectly precise language, but also the fundamental fidelity to the definition which God gives of himself in Exodus ('I am that I am'). Not the first mover of the celestial sphere, not the idea of the good or the thought of thought, but the act of being itself."[61]

Gilson played in a return match against the clerical opponents of Christian philosophy at the second study day of the Société Thomiste, held at Juvisy in September 1933. Henri Gouhier sat beside him. The Saulchoir Dominicans came out in force: Père Mandonnet, sitting on Gilson's other flank, Marie-Dominique Chenu, who had in the previous year shifted from his elder confrère's position to that of Gilson,[62] and Père Yves Congar. Concerned to "emphasize the necessary autonomy of philosophical research," Mandonnet denied "any doctrinal influence by revelation on the elaboration of mediaeval philosophies," attributing the "superiority" of Thomism to Aristotelianism to "the philosophical genius of Saint Thomas." Questioned by the rector of the Institut Catholique in Toulouse, Bruno de Solages, as to whether "the influence of Christianity on the movement of philosophy is like the influence of a great philosopher or a school of philosophy introducing new ideas," Gilson replied that Justin and Saint Hilary discovered "a rationality which came to them from an extra-rational source." The neo-Thomist denial of the supernatural foundation of Christian philosophy is

60. Cited in Bars, "Gilson et Maritain," 243.
61. Maritain to Étienne Gilson, February 29, 1932, in *Deux approches*, 79–80; Gandillac, "Étienne Gilson: incomparable maître," 11.
62. Fouilloux, *Une église en quête de liberté*, 153.

summed up by Van Steenberghen: "The direct influence of Christianity is purely of the psychological order, and *limits itself to setting the Christian philosopher in the best conditions for elaborating*—not a Christian philosophy, which is a meaningless term—but a *true philosophy.*"[63]

There are no recorded instances of a Catholic philosopher scrupling to turn a papal encyclical to his advantage. Van Steenberghen claimed that "Leo XIII never spoke of 'Christian philosophy.'" But that Pope "spoke many times of '*philosophia scholastica*' and that it is why the editors of the Bonne Press in Paris gave this title to the pontifical document: *Epistola encyclica de philosophia scholastica.* They translated this as *Lettre encyclique sur la philosophie chrétienne,* doubtless in order to avoid the discordant term 'scholastic.'" Gilson was perfectly well aware that Leo only spoke of "philosophia scholastica," Van Steenberghen says, for when they debated the question at Juvisy, he asked "who introduced the subtitle of 'Christian philosophy' into the encyclical *Aeterni Patris?*"[64] Insofar as it is an exhortation to philosophical apologetics, *Aeterni Patris* can be found to underwrite the Louvain Thomists' program. It praises the Angelic Doctor in these terms: "clearly distinguishing, as is fitting, reason from faith, while happily associating the one with the other, he both preserved the rights and had regard for the dignity of each; so, indeed, that reason, borne on the wings of Thomas to its human height, can scarcely rise higher, while faith could scarcely expect more or stronger aids from reason than those which she has already obtained through Thomas" (para. 18). This has the ring of the neo-Scholastic "one after the other." On the other hand, Gilson believed that his attitude was in tune with Leo's comment that "so far is the super-added light of faith from extinguishing or lessening the power of the intelligence that it completes it rather, and by adding to its strength renders it capable of greater things" (para. 3). Gilson's perception of Thomas's philosophizing as a work empowered by faith was a response to anti-modernist rationalism, in which faith became somewhat extrinsic to reason.

63. Van Steenberghen, "La II journée d'études de la société Thomiste," 541; de Lubac, "Sur la philosophie chrétienne," 233; Van Steenberghen, "La II journée d'études de la société Thomiste," 546–47.

64. Van Steenberghen, "Étienne Gilson, historien de la pensée médiévale," 492.

# 7

# Newspapers and Utopias

Reformist politics are practiced by realists, who deal with the individuals out of which their nation is built and who strive to maintain an equilibrium among concrete forces within it. Utopian politics is for intellectualists, although they may have to impose their concepts on reality by force.

## The Aftermath of the Condemnation of the Action Française

With the condemnation of the Action Française, Maritain returned to his connatural spiritual springs, becoming, by 1934, "one of the rare persons to break the silence amongst Catholics" about anti-Semitism.[1] He was able to change direction because the Maurrassian politics were a superstructure upon his unworldly and devout nature. For others, the opposite situation pertained. Many abstained from the specifically proscribed sheets of the *Action française* but devoured "*Candide,* edited by Jacques Bainville and in which Léon Daudet wrote regularly; *Gringoire* in which pornography was harmoniously combined with polemics of an unheard of vileness; *Je suis partout* where names made famous by *L'Action française* were recognized, and which only later revealed its connections with the Nazis; and all those 'pious' local papers, the self-appointed defenders of religion against liberal and socialist sheets. . . . The spirit of L'Action Française made enormous progress during the thirteen years of its condemnation, . . . the work of Catholics who practiced submission to the letter of the condemnation."[2]

## French Public Schools Do Not Know
## What Morality to Teach

With the 1932 elections, Prime Minister Herriot formed a government of radicals and socialists. No stable government emerged: there were four dif-

1. Barré, *Jacques et Raïssa Maritain,* 448, 362–64.
2. Simon, *The Road to Vichy,* 64–65.

ferent cabinets between December 1932 and February 1934. The right ceaselessly fired upon them. A decade after the Great War, France was "well-nigh in a state of veiled civil war." Each of the factions suffered from a deficit of reasoned conviction concerning the moral basis of their policies. Yves Simon described the years of depression in France as a time when neither communism, socialism, nor liberalism inspired belief and when the government was "ready to follow any policy, because no one knew what was the good policy."[3]

For a hundred years, the French school-system had been geared to inculcating moral values. When they used education as a means of moral engineering, republican ministers simulated the methods of the church. They qualified this with the hope that children might be voluntarily induced to give rational consent to a socially agreed system of values:

the heart of the new primary education developed by the Third Republic was moral and civic training.... [T]he reformers wanted to create a society whose members would be more than oppressed subjects, held to the observance of the laws ... by fear of punishment.... Hippolyte Carnot, as minister of education in 1848, had distributed little books ... which combined republican propaganda with exhortations to virtue and philosophical explanations of why one should be both virtuous and republican.... Jules Ferry ... made this an integral part of the school syllabus. After 1881–2, the day's work had to be preceded by a little lesson in morals, in place of prayers. The ministerial instructions were drawn up by Henri Marion and the syllabus by Paul Janet, both professors at the Sorbonne. They declared that the lay teacher of morals should aim to complete what the priest ... began ... ; he had to ensure that every child "served an effectual moral apprenticeship." Whereas the Church ... stressed what separated Catholics from others, the lay school ... would show children ... "those essential notions of human morality common to all doctrines and necessary to all civilized mankind."

Ferry derived his faith in education as a means of producing good citizens from Auguste Comte. What values should the primary school teach? The successive governments of the Third Republic formed no stable hypothesis: "In 1882 Ferry laid it down that...'The teacher is not required to fill the child's memory, but to teach his heart, to make him feel, by an immediate experience, the majesty of the moral law.' But then in 1888 Octave Gréard ... said the method should not be emotional, but intellectual.... [T]hen again in 1923 the minister said that the approach should be to 'sen-

3. Bury, *France, 1814–1940*, 260; Simon, *The Road to Vichy*, 86–87.

sibility' and that the effectiveness of the teaching depended on its ... warmth of conviction. At this point ... the ministry seems to have lost courage, and ... declared that each teacher had better follow his own inclinations."[4]

It was into the moral vacuum created by the state's attempt to put ethics on the national curriculum that the *Action française* poured its steady drip of contempt for the ideals of the French Revolution. Whatever drawbacks a French monarchist could find in the philosophical antecedents and current practice of *Liberté, Egalité, Fraternité,* when they cut away at republican values, paleoconservative theorists left their followers in a state of moral cynicism. This evolution produced a tribe of "*realistic little cads,*" addicted to "the quarter of an hour of delightful hating" provided by the *Action française*'s satellite newspapers.[5]

## Maurras' Comteanism

In September 1932 the editor of the *Études de philosophie médiévale* was studying a manuscript, the first volume of *La jeunesse d'Auguste Comte et la formation du positivisme* (1933–1941). Gilson's editorial comment to the author was, "You have a style, happy man, and do not let other people put you off." The subject of Henri Gouhier's trilogy believed that the era of metaphysics has ended; the age of positivist sociology dawns in his own writings. The question left for Comte was how to unify the empirical sciences. His answer was to make Humanity the new center around which the separate sciences revolve. As against the "objective synthesis" of metaphysics, the new age of Humanity unifies its data by reference to a "subjective synthesis." The "subject" in question is collective humanity, the "Great Being." Maritain remarked in Spain in 1934 that Comte's "Great Being" "exhibits the logical end of the purely naturalistic idea of man."[6]

Maurras admired Comte's preference for collectivism over individualism. But he saw that Comte had yet to relinquish all traces of metaphysics. Sociology by itself cannot ground the objective existence of "Humanity." Maurras replaced Comte's religiose "subjective synthesis" with an exhaustively subjective "*patrie.*"[7] The French *patrie* is to supply the unification of the sciences.

4. Zeldin, *France, 1848–1945,* 177–80.
5. Simon, *The Road to Vichy,* 15, 152.
6. Gilson to Henri Gouhier, September 6, 1932, in "Lettres d'Étienne Gilson à Henri Gouhier," 467; Maritain, *True Humanism,* 15.
7. Sutton, *Nationalism, Positivism, and Catholicism,* 43–44.

In the spring of 1934, Gilson argued in a popular Catholic magazine that, because there "are in France millions of people who . . . are sincerely attached to Catholicism because they cannot conceive of *France* without it," "clericalism is one of the worst corruptions which menace" the church. The clericalists were the political obsessives who confused "the Two Orders" of state and church: "Of all the anticlerics I know," Gilson wrote, "that of my priest and religious friends is the most solid, and also the most intelligent."[8]

## *La vie intellectuelle* and *Sept*

The papal condemnation of Maurras' movement led to an improvement in genuine Catholic journals. In 1928, the *Nouvelles religieuses* became *La vie intellectuelle,* published by the Dominican Père Marie-Vincent Bernadot, and to which Gilson contributed. Gilson wanted to speak to a nonacademic Catholic audience. In March 1934, Père Bernadot launched the weekly magazine *Sept,* intending to give French Catholics, deeply divided since the condemnation of the *Action française,* a shared political and social vocation.[9] In his *Sept* articles Gilson "was not formulating theoretical social philosophy. Social philosophy was the emphasis of . . . Emmanuel Mounier's *Esprit.* Jacques Maritain . . . contributed a number of articles to *Esprit;* not so Gilson, who instinctively as a republican distrusted socialism in all its forms."[10]

Gilson confided to Père Marie-Dominic Chenu that when he wrote for *Sept,* "I know I'm outside my métier. I do not know if I'm obeying an interior counsel or being an idiot. I know I have a duty to fulfill."[11] Politics was a driving force for Gilson in that it ignited his emotions. But the *chosiste professeur* did not find it easy to speak directly on a concrete level. The Sorbonne professor shared one thing with his readers, that is, a lengthy experience of the French school system. It was from this common source that he composed his most effective pieces for *Sept.*

Gilson indicated that the educational experiment of the republicans, in which the element of Christianity was eliminated but that of Christian *morality* was retained, had to fizzle out; for as he claimed, Christianity and ethics make up an indivisible alloy. As a Lycée *professeur,* Gilson had had to teach ethics. On asking the headmaster how he was to do so "without

---

8. Gilson, "Le faux remède," 63. My italics. Gilson, "Les deux ordres," 160–61.
9. Prouvost's note, in *Deux approches,* 117.
10. Shook, *Gilson,* 218–19.
11. Gilson to Marie-Dominique Chenu, May 6, 1934, in *Deux approches,* 163.

religious authority or metaphysical principles," Étienne was told: "Your teaching must be essentially *practical*, and since everything which concerns the conduct of pupils relates to the Deputy Headmaster, if you have any doubts, address them to the Deputy Headmaster." The deputy headmaster, "or rather as the pupils said, the *Bison*,"

> counseled me to avoid subversive ideas, above all "liberty of conscience," for which my predecessor had been terribly abused and which rendered discipline impossible in his Lycée. 'In sum,' he concluded, 'preach good conduct.' I preached it. With what success, one can see. I had to return to my Deputy head, to ask if he could not intervene with one of my philosophy students, who was accompanied each day by a woman of easy virtue to the door of the Lycée where, with a view to the baccalaureate, he came to learn ethics. His strongly felt response was that "she doesn't come into the Lycée," and consequently, "this does not concern us." I asked him, in my naive candor, if he did not believe it opportune to inform the parents. And I obtained this second response, no less sagacious: "They would tell me: it is not against nature is it? So it's natural." I thus came to discover the foundations of ethics.[12]

*Christian* morals having been excised from France, the words *Liberté, Egalité, Fraternité* have lost their meaning, along with the "doctrine which contains the secret of their birth." The only ethical language left to the French is that spoken by the communists: the French must now choose between "the communist experience, with the frightful debasement of man which it entails" or Christianity.[13]

## France Advances to Revolution—and Retreats

In late 1933 Sacha Stavisky was on the brink of telling tales of parliamentary corruption. In January 1934 the *Action française* urged its readers to make a show of force against the republican government.[14] The exposure of the evidence of corruption was forestalled by the Russian financier's suicide. It was obvious to the royalist paper that Stavisky had been assassinated at the instigation of the chief of police and the prime minister, Chautemps. Chautemps' resignation and the enforced departure of the police chief merely whet their appetites.

12. Gilson, "L'état sans moral," 50–51.
13. Gilson, "L'état sans religion," 42–43.
14. Weber, *Action Française*, 321–22.

Maurras' deputies contacted the Duc de Guise and agreed that the moment for a royalist coup d'état had arrived. The Action Française's adolescent vanguard, the Camelots, began to riot outside the parliament buildings. In February 1934 all of the independent rightist factions held demonstrations in the Place de la Concorde, rioting simultaneously but not in unison. The largest demonstrations took place on the night of February 6. Present at the outset of the evening, Maurras ordered those of his troops in hearing to retreat to the "printing shop" to compose the next day's paper. His more physically energetic lieutenants such as Georges Cazelot were lost in the fray. Doumergue, rather than the Duc de Guise, was installed in power. He was voted "power to legislate by decree."[15]

Charles Maurras failed to seize his opportunity. His philosophy fit the nihilistic times, not only because he believed that "justice was a delusion" and "goodness, either of God or of men a dream"[16] but also in that his monarchism was "a species of defeatism," consisting in "a wish that things would happen in a way in which they are manifestly not going to happen."[17] Politics went on as usual; excluded from the Chamber, the socialists joined forces with the communists. When the radicals cast about for allies, a new left-wing bloc emerged, the Front Populaire, containing no enemies to the left of Stalin.

## The "Dream of the Baptism of Clovis"

The German Youth movement had helped to convey Hitler to the Reich chancellorship in 1933. Once "youth" is inured to immoralism, Gilson wrote in *Sept,* they are "ripe for the dictators," and having grown up on the cult of violence, they practice it in their control of the German universities. "The central role played by youth in the German revolution must serve as a warning." We are, therefore, "at a cross-roads: either re-establish a true order, or a fascist or communist dictatorship." Catholics are less likely to be seduced by communism than by a third position, the utopian fantasy of an instant draining of the quagmire into which France had been marched by the revolution. "There is," Gilson writes, "in the heart of many French Catholics, a dream which has never died: that of the baptism of Clovis." On his conversion to Christianity, the emperor Clovis (465–511) brought

15. Ibid., 337; Bury, *France, 1814–1940,* 268.
16. Weber, *Action Française,* 8.
17. Orwell, "Inside the Whale," 120–21. Orwell is speaking of the religion of D. H. Lawrence.

his entire army into the church with him. "With the techniques available to a modern civilization, one could do it better and more quickly. If one could find a Clovis, he would send all the French to Mass." But "those who, for political reasons, dream today of a dictator of the Right...must be told that Jesus Christ did not turn to Caesar to impose the faith on his apostles; he converted his apostles, and much later, Caesar himself was converted. It takes a Christian people to get a Constantine; the church does not win hearts through institutions but institutions through hearts."[18]

Gilson's first books had been biographies, which put the man before the idea. He is far from advising the Catholic readers of *Sept* to forgo politics. Rather, he wanted them to initiate the conversion of politics by conversion to a spiritual order. In a genuinely spiritual order, unlike Comte's "subjective synthesis" or Maurras' *patrie,* the individual takes precedence over the collective. The historical and political order, says the Erasmian realist, is the construct of individuals.

If we seek common ground between Catholics and nonbelievers, Gilson claims, some will advise us to begin by defining the French *patrie,* but "I do not think so. First because France is an individual and an individual cannot be defined; but above all because there is not, at the beginning of our history a France which creates Frenchmen, but a long series of Frenchmen who have created a France." Moreover, "the unity of France is not that of an absolutely simple essence; but rather the result of a compromise, or...an equilibrium. It results from many groups, 'spiritual families,' each of which contributes in part to the definition of France...Protestants, Jews, Freemasons, communists," each forms a unique "group" *and* "modifies itself" in relation to its ideal of France.[19]

There are also good souls who feel that prayer for the conversion of France is their only recourse. Gilson agreed that France, which is once again a *"pays de missions,"* must be rechristianised. But the one time admirer of the *Sillon* did not take "prayer, and doing your best as an individual" to be an exhaustive solution. If it is the only available way forward, that is because, socially, Catholics do not exist in France. They have not yet begun to create a Catholic social order. Gilson defines this as "an order of institutions created by Catholics to ensure the realization of Catholic ends for which the State does not take responsibility." If Catholicism has no party political footing, it can yet "do much for France; but it can only do so if it is given the means.... The end, is integrally to satisfy the demands of a full

18. Gilson, "La croisée des chemins," 54; Gilson, "Le faux remède," 62, 64–65.
19. Gilson, "Terrain d'entente," 83; Gilson, "Ordre catholique et unité national," 3.

Catholic life in a State which is not Catholic. The means are the ensemble of institutions, to be created or coordinated, so that the demands can be . . . satisfied. Once such an order exists, although it will be entirely a-political, one will not have to wait long to see that, without seeking it, the presence of such an order will weigh heavily on the life of the parties. In so far as it is not there, we have nothing to say and we can do nothing."[20]

## Grace Presupposes Nature—but Nature Presupposes God

For Maurras, "grace presupposes nature" means that nature is impermeable to grace. Supernatural additives sweeten the worldly aperitif but never alter the chemistry of the compound. Gilson retorted that an atheist's "nature" is different from a nature that exists within transcendence. The Christian cannot concur in the positivist's dictum that "what is religion for you is civilization for me," for he conceives of both of these entities differently. "Yes, grace does presuppose nature," Gilson wrote, "but politics, like the nature from which it arises, is first in need of being atoned for by grace. . . . It is God who first loved us." Between "the *nature* of integral nationalism, which," as Maurras cajolingly put it, "'does not exclude the supernatural' and that of Catholicism, which only fully finds itself in grace, no identity of methods is possible."[21]

Gilson did not deny that moral or political truth is accessible to an atheist. Rather, his contention was that such truths are not a halfway house to faith. Since the seventeenth century, the uneasy accommodation between church and state, in France, had been the political equivalent of Cartesian physicism, nature plus a supernatural add-on. As Gilson understood the matter, "nature" seen "naturally" is always going to be positivist nature; if one wants the type of nature which grace can perfect, one has to begin from the supernatural, from the God who created it. Just as Gilson proposed that philosophical apologetics for Christianity must grow out of the root principles of theology, so he claimed that neither "Christendom" nor the church can benefit from the employment of secular political principles taken as such. *Catholic* participation in the Parti de l'intelligence's defense of natural reason, or a pessimistic hope for the return of monarchical order to restore Christendom, is the same type of self-destructive ordinance as the rejection of the existence of Christian philosophy on the grounds of the

20. Gilson, Introduction, *Pour un ordre catholique*, 20; Gilson, "L'ordre catholique et la France," ibid., 100–107, 103–4.
21. Gilson, "Action politique et action catholique," 4.

autonomy of reason, or the attempt to swing a secular Cartesian around to Christianity by sharing his epistemology. One would not persuade Maurras to replace "Auguste Comte's fantasy of the Church" with the genuine article or make him any less "blind to what Christianity is" by sharing his political strategy.[22]

Gilson did not think that this entailed that Christians and nonbelievers live on different intellectual planets. In "Terrain d'entente" and "L'humanisme et les humanités," Gilson argues that the two can share a certain "humanism." He finds common ground between Christians and nonbelievers in a "humanism" that keeps faith with "realism" and with human freedom. Gilson may have found his common ground here because realism and freedom are the twin lights of Bergson's *Essai sur les données immédiates de la conscience*.

Recognizing that it is a value shared between Christian and humanist, Gilson asks what *freedom* means for the church. He considered ecclesial freedom more important than state recompense. He saw that the 1801 Concordat between Napoleon and Pius VII created a "Gallican Church, the pinnacle of the functionaries in the pay of the government." By taking the government's franc, "the Church in France paid with the price of the liberty to teach." Gilson asked, optimistically, "*What French priest today would not prefer to die of hunger?*" The state had used each ecclesial accommodation to "limit" the freedom of the church. Gilson said in 1934 that if a "new Concordat is in preparation," let the bishops who will accept or reject it remember that "*the complete liberty of our Catholic teaching is its reason for existence.*"[23]

## Action Catholique instead of Action Française

From 1926, the papal nuncio in France, Monsignor Maglione, steadily replaced bishops on their retirement with men who were more interested in social than political questions. In the next decade, forty bishops were appointed, many of them "tied to Action catholique," that is, to such Christian social movements as the *Jeunesse ouvrière chrétienne*. The appointments of Achille Liénart, a supporter of Catholic trade union movements, to the see of Lille in 1928 and of Monsignor Suhard, who believed that the

22. Ibid.; Gilson, "Par delà le Sillon et l'Action Française," 4.
23. Gilson, "Le prix de la liberté," 146–47, 150–51.

church's mission field lay among the urban proletariat, to the cardinalate in 1935 were signs of the times.[24] Gilson states in his "Action politique et action catholique" of 1935 that the Catholic's motto must be "*église d'abord*."

It has been argued that this turn toward Action catholique was just a new way of dressing up the same old "integralist" and "intransigent" Catholicism: "no longer directed to the nostalgic mirage of mediaeval Christianity, but towards the 'conquering utopia' of a new Christendom disembarrassed of monarchism. Catholicism first rather than politics first; Action Catholic rather than Action Française. A secular, rather than a sacred utopia, whose authentic charter was furnished by Maritain Thomism, in *True Humanism* (1936)."[25] This is a careless reading of Maritain's *True Humanism*. In that book, Maritain distinguishes between a utopia, or an *ens rationis*, the nonexistent, logical entity which he says "the mediaeval ideal of a consecrated Christian society" has now become, and the *analogical* notion of Christendom, which is a "concrete historical ideal" toward which groups of lay Christians should begin to direct themselves. He rates their chance of success as "highly improbable."[26]

Gilson's politics begin in what Thomas Masaryk called "small work," the performance of achievable local tasks. Grace "transforms the conditions of the existence" of nature and reason, but it does not permit us to put them into abeyance. Gilson claimed that "Catholics, who profess the eminent value of nature, because it is the work of God, show their respect for it by positing as their first rule of action, that *piety does not dispense with technique*. For the most vivid piety cannot use nature for God without technique."[27] Christians have to *create* their own social order through their institutions, Gilson argued, and he focused his attention on the institution he knew best, the schools. His later *Sept* pieces criticize those Catholic schools that substitute pious intentions for knowing something about what one is teaching. In order to put the church first in any fruitful way, one must be a true *humanist*. French Catholics made themselves susceptible to Maurrassianism by the notional quality of their realism, their inability to connect piety with techniques of practical living. Because these pious folk devoted

---

24. Cointet, *L'église sous Vichy*, 16–20.
25. Fouilloux, *Une église en quête de liberté*, 83, describing the opinion of Yvon Tranvouez, with which he does not concur.
26. Maritain, *True Humanism*, 121–22, 204, 237.
27. Gilson, "Action politique et action catholique," 4; Gilson, "L'intelligence au service du Christ-Roi," in *Christianisme et philosophie*, 142–68, 156. This article was first published in *La vie intellectuelle* in 1936. It is reprinted in English translation in *A Gilson Reader*, ed. Pegis, 31–44.

insufficient attention to "using nature for God" in their daily callings, they laid themselves open to the dark shadow fantasy of "practical" men who appeared to be capable of bulldozing their ideals into reality.

Gilson's early biographies had distinguished between the Thomist concept, drawn from sensible objects, and the Bonaventurian innate idea. For Gilson, utopianism is "*idea*logism." When he gave the William James lectures in 1936, he told his audience,

> Begotten in us by things themselves, concepts are born reformers that never lose touch with reality. Pure ideas, on the other hand, are born within the mind and from the mind, not as intellectual expressions of what is, but as models or patterns of what ought to be; hence they are born revolutionists. And this is why Aristotle and Aristotelians write books on politics, whereas Plato and Platonists always write Utopias. Ockham himself... was the perfect anti-Plato; yet, like all opposites, Plato and Ockham belonged to the same species. Neither one wanted to know up to what point the universals could be truly said to be real; Plato wanted them to be the very core of everything, whereas Ockham wanted them to be nothing. Ockhamism could not possibly be a reformation; it was bound to be a revolution.[28]

"Revolution," in 1936, meant fascist or communist revolution. Conceived in this light, the Franciscan way of "ideas" must go by the board. In the years preceding the Second World War, as Gilson traces the genealogy of "*idea*logism," he is exercised by the ethical and thus the political disorder created by the quest to unify the sciences around a single idea. He contrasts it negatively with Thomistic humanism and realism, the political way of the "reformers." As the 1930s drew on, an ethical impetus briefly directs him away from "Saint Francis" and toward "Saint Dominic." In order that one rightly use "nature for God," nature, with its secondary causes, must have more reality of its own than Bonaventure ascribed to it.

## Anti-Semitism and the Closure of *Sept*

Anti-Semitism increased with the tide of refugees from Germany and Austria. In the "I am Roman" speech with which Maurras had opened his offensive against Marc Sangnier and the *Sillon*, the journalist claimed that he approved of "Rome" because "without it, 'one reads the texts directly, one reads above all the letter. This letter, which is Jewish, acts for Judaism,

---

28. Gilson, *The Unity of Philosophical Experience*, 68.

if Rome does not explain it.'" Gilson responded to this in 1935: "for us, this letter is divine before being Jewish; we shall not freely accept the idea that the proper function of the Church is to make the divine word say something other than it does say. Luther and Harnack have already maintained that the Church has paganised Scripture; they were not being complimentary. In our times, Hitler and Rosenberg have concurred in suspecting the Jewishness of the Bible, and this is company in which neither Maurras nor ourselves wish to be seen," but he is flirting with them.[29]

The Front Populaire formed a government after the 1936 elections, with Léon Blum as the first socialist prime minister of France. The Catholic deputy Xavier Vallat greeted him in the Chamber with an observation about the historical significance of the occasion: "For the first time, this old Gallo-Roman country will be governed by a Jew." Gilson referred to the Italian "Mussolini problem, which is resolved in that Mussolini is not a Catholic," and to the problem of Hitler, which "is not resolved, for Hitler would be a Catholic," warning that "we will inevitably have in France a problem of the same type to resolve in the wake of a dictator."[30]

Maurras soon had a new dictator to champion. The Action Française's alliance with General Franco did it some good with the Holy Office. In the spring of 1937, Père Garrigou-Lagrange used his newly acquired role as qualifier at the Holy Office to threaten Maritain with the Index for an anti-Francoist tract to which Jacques contributed a preface, admonishing him to stick to metaphysics, although, the philosopher said, "'he does not hesitate to pronounce in favor of Franco and to approve the civil war in Spain.'" The editor of the Italian branch of the AF League, Robert Havard, hastened to argue that Catholic political equilibrium had been distorted by the condemnation of the Action Française and that this had brought about the leftist "deviations of publications like *Sept, Esprit, L'Aube* and *Le temps présent.*" On August 27, 1937, *Sept* was permanently closed down by order of the Dominican provincial general, Père Stanislas Martin Gillet, "for having offended dominant Catholic opinion, in particular by declaring that General Franco is condemnable for having started a civil war."[31]

29. Bury, *France, 1814–1940,* 277; Maurras, "Le dilemme de Marc Sangnier," 24; Gilson, "Action politique et action catholique," 4.
30. Cointet, *L'église sous Vichy,* 193; Gilson, "Le faux remède," 66.
31. Maritain, *Carnet de notes,* September 1937, quoted in Barré, *Jacques et Raïssa Maritain,* 455; Weber, *Action Française,* 248; Prouvost, in *Deux approches,* 117.

# 8

# Humanist Realism

## A Comparison of History as Finished and History as Living Tradition

When he was not speaking in Aberdeen on mediaeval Christian philosophy, Gilson was lecturing, at the Hautes Études, on Martin Luther. The curia was ever vigilant against the Bergsonian "poison." In June 1931 the entire oeuvre of the Bergsonian Édouard Le Roy, professor at the Collège de France, was set on the Index. Gilson feared that this public relations disaster would damage his own chances of promotion, or rather, as he put it to Maritain, the status of Catholics in that seat of learning. "Most successful professors in the French universities have aspired to the Collège de France, and Gilson perhaps more than most," because of his outpost in Toronto and the reluctance of the Sorbonne to provide full chairs for mediaevalists.[1]

He gave his inaugural lecture in the chair in mediaeval philosophy at the Collège de France on April 5, 1932. The late Scholastics and the Renaissance thinkers each accused the other of a failure in humanism, said Gilson, and they were both right, in different ways. Erasmus and Luther scourged the mediaevals for incorporating the Greek notion of nature into theology. Erasmus's "pure and simple Gospel" and Lutheran grace both require the expulsion of Aristotle's *Ethics*. For Luther, "nature" represents "works," the effort to win heaven by moral achievement; he opposes it to "grace." Gilson pays detailed attention to mediaeval poetry, waves his hand at "every mediaeval Cathedral," nods at Thomas and the Averroists, and digs into Augustine's writings, in order to argue for the close companionability of nature and grace in the middle age between Plato and Protestantism. Because Augustine "always recalls the presence of the natural subject to which"

1. Congar, *Journal d'un théologien*, 26–27; Fouilloux, *Une église en quête de liberté*, 27–28; Gilson to Jacques Maritain, July 16, 1931, in *Deux approches*, 70; Shook, *Gilson*, 205.

grace "is applied," his God, and that of Bernard, Anselm, and Thomas, "heals a nature; whereas that of Luther saves a corruption."[2]

Luther and Erasmus did not see eye to eye. Where the ardent German reformer condemned humanism as such, Erasmus stood for a different kind of humanism to that of his Scholastic contemporaries. He invented the type of historical research upon which Gilson and his colleagues at the Collège de France had built their intellectual careers. Erasmus appreciated that reading texts through the traditions of later commentators is a fine occasion for the sin of anachronism. In his "scrupulous attention" to documents, Erasmus treated "the past as past," that is, as "simultaneously fertile and closed."[3] This is what the moderns have understood by the "historical sense."

Gilson marks his debts to his teachers. Lévy-Bruhl had taught him to recover philosophers in their "individual difference." That is the Erasmian genius. But Bergson had led him "beyond the formulas in which the philosopher's thought is expressed" to "the simple movement which engenders them, traverses them, and confers an indivisible unity upon them." Gilson characterizes mediaeval humanism by its feeling for what, with a nod to Loisy, one may call the vital life of tradition, in which the "timeless" quality of ideas makes their original bearers live on into the present. Classical Latin was a dead language for Erasmus but a living tongue for the dog-Latin authors of the *Summae,* and "just as the Alexander of the *Chansons de geste* is a Charlemagne who conducts his barons into battle, so . . . Plato and Aristotle survive in Saint Bonaventure and Saint Thomas because they adopt their faith and their principles." The mediaeval mind "rediscovered" in Graeco-Roman antiquity "only the eternal present and that which maintains its permanence through time." Alcuin had told Charlemagne that there is no "difference between pagans and Christians . . . 'except faith and baptism.' In effect, for all the rest, they were men."[4] Gilson thus divides humanism into two kinds, the "Erasmian" and the "Bergsonian-Mediaeval."

The professor, who was sometimes labeled a historicist, concluded by expressing his hope that he would never traduce either Erasmus's idea of "history" or Bergson's notion of "the permanence of pure ideas," that is, "philosophy."[5] Gilson was never tempted by the Parti de l'intelligence's defense of pure nature. In the later 1930s, he builds a rampart for humanist

2. Gilson, "Le moyen âge et le naturalisme antique," appendix to *Héloise et Abélard,* 193; Gilson cites Luther's remark that "presque toute l'*Éthique* d'Aristote est le pire ennemi de la grâce," ibid., 203; ibid., 200.
3. Ibid., 220.
4. Ibid., 184, 222.
5. Ibid., 224.

realism, against a somewhat a-historical opponent that he called Cartesian-Thomism.

## The Beginnings of the Debate about Realism

Gilson had already begun his defense of realism at the Sorbonne. Père André Gilson attended his brother's courses there between 1929 and 1931. He wrote in his notebook, "If you establish yourself within thought, you will never connect with things, because everything will show up as thought."[6] Étienne Gilson would shortly be applying that opinion, not only to the writings of historical figures like Descartes, but to his Thomist contemporaries.

For the great modern philosophers, such as Descartes, the advantage of "establishing oneself in thought" was the solution of the epistemological problem concerning whether or not we have *certain* knowledge. The great endeavor of Kant's *Critique of Pure Reason* was to demonstrate the possibility of the synthetic a priori judgment. A synthetic a priori judgment binds together two different propositions with the knot of certainty. The Kantian judgment is rationally lawlike in itself, whether or not its empirical object is so.

When modern Thomists like Jaime Balmes, Joseph Kleutgen, and Cardinal Mercier took on nineteenth-century positivism, they chose "reason at the expense of experience" because reason alone gives certain knowledge. With Kant, Mercier held that the ground of certainty, the true judgment is "ideal" and not "real." With Aristotle, he took "ideality" to refer to the degree of materiality in which a real object is known. Only purely "ideational" judgments, those that transcend sense perception, are certain.[7]

Taking Mercier's lead, the Thomists of Belgium aimed to confront idealism by showing that, even if one begins in doubt, as Descartes had proposed, or, following Kant, starts from a critical study of mental categories, one will be led to affirm the reality of the external world. Because they hoped to turn the idealist critique against itself, the Louvain school called themselves critical realists. Msgr. Léon Nöel, Mercier's second successor in the chair of Thomistic philosophy at Louvain, was a leading proponent of critical realism; but the movement had many partisans.

Gilson thought it impossible for Thomism to flourish within a Kantian orbit. In his first essay against critical realism, "Le réalisme méthodique"

6. Shook, *Gilson*, 196.
7. Riet, *Thomistic Epistemology*, 1:161; on the certainty of ideational judgments, ibid., 138–39.

(1930), Gilson argues that Mercier and Nöel are under an "illusion" in imagining that "one can derive an ontology from an epistemology"; the "problem of discovering a critical realism is in itself as contradictory as a square circle." Since there is no right of way from thought to reality, "justification for St. Thomas' realism will never be obtained from any *Cogito*."[8] In 1932 Gilson published "Réalisme et méthode."

In the debate about realism, Gilson displays his typical "alternation of rudeness and courtesy, of irony and deep humility." The "passion" that he "dedicated to the truth which he wanted to serve ... is intense; ... he has confidence in his arms: but he knows that he puts his own heart at risk." In the sallies of the first half of the 1930s, Gilson assails theories but not persons: he calls Monsignor Noel a "true philosopher" whose *Notes d'épistemologie thomiste* are "penetrating." Gilson's biographer portrayed a professor at home at the Sorbonne with Sylvain Lévi and Henri Gouhier, and from behind whose lines he issued sharp retorts to the Louvain scholars.[9] Canon Van Steenberghen recalls otherwise: "Gilson's relations with Maurice de Wulf were always excellent." The canon was helping De Wulf with the sixth edition of his *Histoire de la philosophie médiévale* when he first met Gilson, in the summer of 1933. He records that "in the course of a promenade in the streets of Louvain, our guest asked me what I was working on at the moment." When Van Steenberghen cheerfully confessed to complicity in De Wulf's enterprise, Gilson replied, "'You are wasting your time'"; the vignette indicates that Étienne was not always shy in expressing disagreement. It was his Toronto colleague Gerald Phelan who initially "encouraged Gilson to respond flamboyantly to what both men regarded as a temporizing tendency toward idealism in current neoscholasticism."[10] In 1935 the Frenchman whose "dogmatic realism" was absorbed through wines and cheeses was made a *Chevalier de la Légion d'Honneur*. Later that year, the chevalier issued "La méthode réaliste" and "La vade-mecum du débutant réaliste."

## Gilson Begins to Write Philosophy alongside History

Gilson's "extensively documented accounts" of the "highly diverse philosophies" of Augustine, Thomas, Bonaventure, Duns Scotus, and William

8. Gilson, "Le réalisme methodique," in *Le réalisme méthodique*, 10.
9. Bars, "Gilson et Maritain," 239; Gilson, "Le réalisme methodique," in *Le réalisme méthodique*, 4–6; Shook, *Gilson*, 114.
10. "Les relations de Gilson avec Maurice de Wulf furent longtemps excellentes," Van Steenberghen, "Étienne Gilson et l'université de Louvain," 6; ibid., 10; Shook, *Gilson*, 188.

of Ockham had made it "impossible to claim, as de Wulf had done, that there was a common system of scholastic philosophy in the Middle Ages."[11] Demonstrating that Bonaventure and Thomas is each a unique thinker was originally a *historical* or "Erasmian" project. From the early 1930s, Gilson uses his demarcations philosophically, against the insertion of non-Thomist epistemologies into an updated "Thomist" metaphysic.

A curious feature of the debate with the neo-Thomists that he was inaugurating was its roots in an "Augustinian" perception on Gilson's part. He had claimed at Harvard in 1926 that "just as it suffices to go to the bottom of oneself in order to attain to another, so it suffices to reduce ideas to pure essences in order to render them necessary and universal. The philosopher operates this reduction." Against Mercier and Nöel, Gilson now argues that one cannot pass through the Cartesian "I think therefore I am" on the way to realism, because "there is an internal necessity of metaphysical essences and the progress of philosophy consists precisely in achieving an increasingly clear cognizance of the content of these essences. This is what came about with Descartes and the Cartesians. . . . Thus, in order to return to realism, it is not enough to go back to the person who took the first step on the road to idealism, for his step inevitably recreates the whole route of his successors."[12] The stages through which Descartes' ideas progressed in the hands of his successors are "necessary." As a metaphysical essence, the Cartesian method dispatches its practitioners into the territory of thought, from which there was no exit into things. The debate was not about the historical man Renée Descartes but about Cartesianism. Gilson is turning from history to philosophy.

In 1933 Gilson was invited to lecture at the Protestant faculty of theology in Paris. He was going to argue that Calvin dismantles nature. But he was not just being tactful when he told his audience that "perhaps it is of real importance that the one who poses the question is a philosopher, because one of the essential tasks of philosophy seems to me to be to define what I want to call *pure positions*."[13] As an apologist for "dogmatic realism," Gilson found it helpful to reduce his adversaries' positions to a pure state. His biographical studies continue to multiply, but he adds to this a new arsenal, containing the weapons of an *almost* ahistorical treatment of his foes' positions, taken as "essential" attitudes.

11. McCool, *From Unity to Pluralism*, 171.
12. Gilson, "Le rôle de la philosophie dans l'histoire de la civilization," 175–76; Gilson, "Le réalisme méthodique," in *Le réalisme méthodique*, 5–6.
13. Gilson, *Christianisme et philosophie*, 12.

Maurice Blondel had agreed with Brunschvicg that "one can no more speak of a Christian philosophy than of a Christian mathematics or a Christian physics." Gilson's talks to the Protestant faculty, published as *Christianisme et philosophie*, began by retrieving the catholic Augustine. Augustine "does not hesitate to say that if God had created it such as it now is after the Fall, it would still be sufficient to prove the infinite wisdom of its author."[14]

Gilson goes on to explain his objections to "Augustinianism." Instead of "damning philosophy," as Luther did, Augustinians "transfigure" it "into faith," speaking of "the philosophy and wisdom of Christians" "to designate what is really supernatural Christian wisdom." Gilson's audience was as well acquainted with that phrase as he was with *Aeterni Patris,* since it is, as he reminded them, repeated throughout *The Institutes of the Christian Religion.* Calvin's method is "an invitation to reason to establish itself on the interior of faith." The God-shaped hole from within which "our philosophy" operates is, according to the master of Geneva, an "innate knowledge" of the divine. But Calvin must say that the "innate idea" has been sunk into our minds by God's grace, for otherwise reason could "award itself merit for this knowledge." It follows that the "efforts of natural reason go for nothing" in effecting our understanding of God; reason has become indistinguishable from revelation. Because it can only speak the language of faith, Calvinist philosophy is lightly disguised theology. "Calvinism," Gilson says, "is a religious disqualification of the order of fallen nature, just as Kant's criticism will be a scientific disqualification of the metaphysical order." He touches the heart of his enterprise of the later 1930s when he says, with implicit reference to Blondel, that despite the objections that some "Catholics" make to the idea of Christian philosophy, "Philosophy is not just another science," like mathematics, "because it cannot be achieved without metaphysics, and metaphysics cannot be achieved without God."[15]

Gilson's four essays about the grounds of metaphysical realism were published in 1936 as *Le réalisme méthodique.* They defend methodological realism on the grounds that positing "esse . . . as distinct from percipi" is the "condition of" the "possibility of philosophy." Taken as a pure position, Cartesian idealism must abolish metaphysics, because if one founds oneself in thought, one's conception of *thinking* will have a nonphilosoph-

14. Blondel, cited in Nédoncelle, *Is There a Christian Philosophy?* 92; Gilson, *Christianisme et philosophie,* 19.

15. Gilson, *Christianisme et philosophie,* 25–26, 44, 60–61, 72–73, 38–39.

ical content. The paradigm method of Cartesian philosophy is not philosophy but mathematics. From "the fact that it identifies philosophical method *a priori* with that of a certain science, it necessarily terminates by emptying philosophy of all of its unique content and condemning it to scientism."[16] If we begin from thought, we conceive it after a paradigm taken from one of the sciences, and our metaphysics will be designed to fit that framework. Chapter three, "La spécificité de l'ordre philosophique," examines the historical progress of this "essential position." The mathematical paradigm flows out of the founding *Cogito* because, "for the mathematician, the problem of essence always takes precedence over that of existence; the true circle and the true triangle are the definition of the circle and the triangle, the empirical figures given in sensible experience are only approximations to their definitions. . . . [A] systematic application of the mathematical method to reality could have no other . . . result than the substitution of a certain number of clear and distinct ideas for the concrete complexity of things, the ideas themselves being conceived as the genuine reality." For Thomas, the concept is filled with the reality from which it is drawn, but never seizes it in its entirety; whereas for Descartes, "all substance is known because its content reduces to an idea." Rather than being a rough but good guide into existence, the clear and distinct idea repels anything which is extrinsic to it; mathematicism divides reality into two substances, the "understood" and the "real." The lack of fit between the two sets the deconstruction of metaphysics in motion. The "metaphysical epicycles" of Malebranchian occasionalism, Leibnizian pre-established harmony, and Spinozist parallelism each attempt to make an engine of unfitted parts run. Each is constrained to make God the "bridge" between the two substances; these seventeenth-century systems are "the best adjusted" ever invented, "because, working on pure ideas . . . they are not constrained by the complexities of reality."[17] Hume notes their failure to show how the "thought substance" can affect the external "sensed substance"; Kant's critique follows from that. Descartes' mathematicism had set the mind tasks it can perform, but Kant's paradigm science is physics, founded in "sensible intuition," and he leaves the mind no metaphysical matter on which to work. From "this moment on," Gilson says, "in despair of philosophy as a science, one begins to seek for its justification in an order which is alien to rational knowledge." The metaphysics of Kant is founded in moral postulates, that of Comte in Humanity.

16. Gilson, "Le réalisme methodique," in *Le réalisme méthodique*, 11–12.
17. Gilson, "La spécificité de l'ordre philosophique," ibid., 54, 56–57.

## Pilgrim's Regress: Substituting the Map for the Country

The French educational system was unique in "teaching philosophy to children," hiring a "special class of civil servants," such as Étienne Gilson, as "professional philosophers" to the Lycées. The Lycée *professeur* who touched the youthful lives of French philosophers from Simone Weil to Simone de Beauvoir was Alain (Émile Chartier, 1868–1951). Alain summed up his educational method in the phrase "Philosophy is not a system, it is a style." The philosopher aimed to teach, "not facts, but how to think."[18] The philosophy class was a training in verbal boxing. Composed in English to be delivered at Harvard in 1936, *The Unity of Philosophical Experience* is Gilson's most accessible work of philosophy. But it has some material foundation in a peculiarly French cultural context.

Gilson had claimed that "behind every criticist there is . . . a realist metaphysician," to whom the criticist turns a blind eye.[19] When he combined his analyses of the "pure positions" of Augustinianism and of Cartesianism, the road was clear to the William James lectures, which portray the criticist swerving round and round, as the metaphysician in him tries to get out. Gilson takes on the role of a scientist who demonstrates the reaction of one element upon another before an audience:

> One of the greatest uses of history of philosophy is . . . that it brings us their experimental demonstration. By observing the human mind at work, in its failures as well as in its successes, we can experience the intrinsic necessity of the same connections of ideas which pure philosophy can justify by abstract reasoning. . . . [T]he history of philosophy is to the philosopher as his laboratory is to the scientist; it . . . shows how philosophers do not think as they wish, but as they can, for the interrelation of philosophical ideas is just as independent of us as are the laws of the physical world. A man is always free to choose his principles, but when he does he must face their consequences to the bitter end.[20]

Gilson experiments first on "Theologism," that is, doctrines that are drunkenly dictated by a pious "feeling of the Glory of God." Such religious "intoxication" is "bound to wrong nature, for how could we find in piety a principle of self-restriction?"[21] "Theologism" is a "unified" philosophical

18. Zeldin, *France, 1848–1945*, 207, 209, 214–15.
19. Gilson, "La methode réaliste" (1935), in *Le réalisme méthodique*, 77.
20. Gilson, *The Unity of Philosophical Experience*, 121.
21. Ibid., 37, 53.

essence, and not the effect of historical conditions. Theologism renders natural agents impotent. Its first act is to expel efficient causality from nature.

Gilson gives three examples of the disease. The contagion of pious deprecation of second causes is first noted in the Muslim Al Ashari (873–935), for whom nature consists of "atoms without magnitude" that meet and go apart in a vacuum. Each atom owes its existence and its motion to direct divine causality. Bonaventure's favorite word was *reducere,* that is, "taking a thing back to God." He followed Augustine in conceiving all causality as implicit in divine causality, so that no effect falls outside the immediate range of God's first empowering action: "If, in the beginning, God created, together with all that was, all that was to be, the end of the world story was in its beginning, and nothing can really happen to it; in such a system God is the only efficient cause, and this world of ours is a completely barren world, just as in the doctrine of Malebranche, and of Al Ashari. This is exactly what St. Bonaventura wanted it to be. His piety needed a world which, like an infinitely thin and translucid film, would allow the all-pervading power and glory of God to shine forth to the human eye."[22] The world having been made so transparent to God as to be empty of natural order, theology replaces metaphysics.

William of Ockham had not Bonaventure's otherworldly faith; the fourteenth-century writer's theologism is combined with empiricism. He makes no exceptions for his philosophical conviction that only individuals exist, and so "decided to eradicate" realism with respect to universals

> even from the divine mind and to deny the existence of ideas . . . even in God. If the universals are nothing real, God Himself can no more conceive them than we can. A divine idea is always an idea of this and that particular individual which God wishes to create. If he freely decrees to create several individuals that resemble each other, the concrete result . . . is what we call a species.

The test of a sound theology is its ability to harbor a rational philosophical explanation of nature, including that "natural" fact which is the human mind in its characteristic act of seeking order, expressed in the discovery of universals. As Gilson puts it here, "The God of theology always vouches for nature; the jealous God of theologism usually prefers to abolish it."[23]

William of Ockham's theologism was engineered by his empiricism. He invented a "new intellectual disease: psychologism," the substitution of a

22. Ibid., 54.
23. Ibid., 74, 86.

description of the material process of thought for that of reality. For Ockham each human "intuition" is possessed of such cast-iron individuality as to be impermeable to conditioning by other intuitions. He conceives nature through the glass of a human psychology pictured as a process of discrete intuitions. His work left nothing behind it except "empirical sequences of facts outside the mind, and habitual associations within the mind, the mere external frame of a world order carefully emptied of its intelligibility." In taking the sensed matter of thought as the measure of metaphysics, psychologism substitutes "the map for the country." The road into skepticism has been followed to its end when, "having mistaken philosophy for reality itself, the best minds were surprised to find reason empty and began to despise it."[24]

It was Descartes' purpose to excavate a firmer grounding for philosophy than Aristotelianism and thereby to refute the skepticism of his contemporaries like Montaigne. By uncovering a steel flooring for philosophical knowledge in the certainties of mathematics, Descartes preferred knowledge to its real objects. Any aspect of reality that cannot be explained with the certitude proper to mathematical demonstration will be stretched, foreshortened, or eliminated. Mathematics is the most "evident" science, because it is the most "abstract." "Mathematicism" gives priority to method over reality; having cut its paper to fit the procedure that elicits certainty, the sole omission of this angular philosophy is to demonstrate that "everything can, and must be, mathematically proved."[25]

Abstraction, however, is an action before it becomes a concept, and its basic meaning is "not . . . to leave something out, but to take something in, and this is the reason why abstractions are knowledge." The stuff of certitude is not empirical; rather, clear and distinct ideas pave the floor of the mind and provide the measure by which empirical facts are judged. The thing is perfectly incarnated in its pure idea and may be reduced to it. For Descartes, "all that can be clearly and distinctly known as belonging to the idea of the thing can be said of the thing itself. As a matter of fact, it *is* the thing." God need fear nothing from mathematicism: "it is at least as certain," Descartes writes, "that God, who is a being so perfect, exists, as any demonstration of geometry can possibly be."[26] The soul, or rather the mind, is also safe, since the pure idea of myself is contained in the *Cogito*. The physical world *is* in danger, for pure thought does not contain the idea of body. Descartes was not in genuine doubt as to the existence of the material

24. Ibid., 90–91.
25. Ibid., 133.
26. Ibid., 145, 154, 182.

world, but since his agenda requires that the external world be molded into the forms of "geometrical extension," the Sixth Meditation begins with the fateful question: "Nothing further now remains but to inquire whether material things exist." During his peripatetic career as a visiting lecturer, Gilson had mastered the art of the pithy joke: "Descartes' demonstration was as good as it possibly could be; its only defect was that it was a demonstration. As soon as Descartes published it, it became apparent that, like Caesar's wife, the existence of the world should be above suspicion."[27]

Descartes' eager disciple Regius was surprised to be rebuked when he went one better than the master's faith that God is not a deceiver. Regius's claim that revelation alone instructs us that the world exists was given philosophical precision in Malebranche's *Conversations on Metaphysics and Religion*. Malebranche, who would have given no doctrinal or territorial quarter to Al Ashari, shared the Mohammedan's occasionalism. The existence of the world becomes an item of faith for the theologists, albeit that sensed objects have become a shadow-play caused by God's will to produce the appropriate reactions in our minds. Since no body can act upon another, Malebranche says, we must refer to the will of God for the existence, motion, and location of things.

A generation of British philosophers not remarkably found the convolutions of the Continentals incredible. In his *Essay Concerning Human Understanding* (1688), Locke laid waste to Descartes' ideas: "Now that the Cartesian mind was dead, the body was left without either a mind or a soul."[28] David Hume inherited Malebranche's "physical world" but not his theology. Once we divest the theologist's world of its divine puppet-master, there is no reason to attribute externality to it: external causality is found only in our psychological habituation to the association of one idea with another. The cycle of philosophical skepticism which began with Montaigne closes with Hume.

Kant starts again, with a new foundation for philosophical experience; his metaphysics and epistemology are neatly fitted into Newton's physics. Newton had ordained that space and time are absolute; Kant obediently ascribed the sensible intuitions of space and time to human thought. But Kant cannot be altogether true to his "physicism" if he wishes to account for God and immortal human souls. He must supplement it with a "moralism," in which "ought" decrees "is": "When, after cutting loose from metaphysics, ethics begins to dictate its own metaphysics, moralism appears on

27. Ibid., 201, 186.
28. Ibid., 175.

the scene. . . . The primacy of practical reason means that reason has to sub-scribe to a certain set of affirmations, through they be rationally undemon-strable, because their truth is postulated by the exigencies of the moral life."[29]

Like Descartes, Kant suffered the logical development of the essence of his philosophical experience in his disciples. Retaining the Kantian principle that metaphysical facts may be willed into being by moral exertion, and re-uniting in a single explanation the physics and the morals for which Kant had separate rationales, Fichte made the human will the agent of reality. Hegel found truth in "a progressive overcoming of all the partial contradic-tions from which its unity shall spring": the Law of metaphysics is War.[30]

Hegel, the historical idealist, believed that he had discovered the laws of social existence: every social group emerges out of a particular state of in-tellectual, political, and cultural development. Comte will claim that the history of social formations follows a necessary sequence, from a theological state, to a metaphysical state, to the contemporary "positive state." With his "Law of the Three States," Comte invented a new methodology against which to test reality: "There was nothing wrong in discovering sociology," Gilson finds; the fault lies in making the new science answer the questions of metaphysics. Comte's anthropocentring of science is legitimated by a device akin to Kant's metaphysically creative "ought." The difference is that, with Comte, the moral demand is suffused with emotion: we *ought* to *love* humanity. Comte's *Considerations on Spiritual Power* (1826) notes the requirement of a new clergy, to fuel the fires of religious devotion to human-ity: "The science of sociology thus gave rise to sociolatry, with love as the principle, order as the basis, and progress as the end."[31]

Gilson wanted to stir his American audience to the recognition that Hegelian nationalism animates the march of Italian fascism. If, as Hegel considered,

the state "is the march of God through the world," it is the only legitimate heir to the transcendent Idea; and nothing else, but the state, can 'sublate' social antinomies into its own unity. Thus understood, Hegelian fascism is much more than a political party; in Gentile's own words, it is, 'before any-thing else a total conception of life,' *una concezione totale della vita*. Schools ought not to teach it as politics, but as a religion, for "the state is the great will of the nation, and therefore its great intelligence." Such a "Statolatry,"

29. Ibid., 238.
30. Ibid., 249–51.
31. Ibid., 262, 271.

though it see itself as an antidote to the blindness of materialism, is but the advent of another blindness.

The reaction from skepticism into a particular ideology is now the engineer of communism and of fascism; and as Gilson states with reference to Marx, "It is not easy to start a new idea, but it is still more difficult to stop it."[32]

In 1925 Gilson had said that "that which is Descartes, and his system, not Cartesianism, is a reality; and finally since he is not his pure essence, but simply himself, one cannot reduce him to it without doing violence to the truth."[33] In 1936 the genial project of attending to the diverse individuals is replaced by a fighting position. That ideologism should have entered political history was not inevitable, but the progress of *idea* logism is *metaphysically* inevitable, and ineluctably increases in certitude as it has less and less to be certain about, because the thinking mind naturally seeks first principles. Frustrated by the denial of the transcendent intelligibility which it implicitly knows through its own operations, human thought identifies the intelligible with one of its regions.

Skepticism is a metaphysical impossibility, because if the mind cannot name the principle that is tantalizingly present to it as *being*, it will devolve the function of that principle to logic, mathematics, physics, the state, or some other tributary region of human thought. Lenin does not assault Hume in his *Materialism and Empirico-Criticism*, and Gentile lay waste to "the agnosticism of the Schools"[34] only because they were authoritarian personalities: they defined reality against a utopian idea out of a thwarted humanism, displaced from its metaphysical order. Comte goes the whole hog, dressing his positivist idea in the unifying costume of mediaeval religiosity.

The separate human disciplines, such as mathematics, physics, or the natural sciences, will only transcend conceptual reality if they plant themselves in the domain of being, the science of which is metaphysics. By exposing the conflagrations that occur when philosophy tries to work against them, Gilson claims to have proved six laws of "philosophical experience." The first is that "philosophy always buries its undertakers." The second law gives the reason for this potential for resurrection: "man is a metaphysical animal." The positive side of philosophy's refusal to lie down is the fact that human beings have spent twenty-five centuries looking for "an ultimate ground of all real and possible experience," finding it in such varied first causes as Democritus's matter, Kant's moral law, and Bergson's creative

32. Ibid., 294–95, 290.
33. Lefèvre, *Une heure avec... Étienne Gilson*, 74.
34. Gilson, *The Unity of Philosophical Experience*, 296–97.

duration. The first cause, or the ground of all experience, has been sought in something that transcends any particular experience: "our third law" is that "*metaphysics is the knowledge gathered by a naturally transcendent reason in its search for the first principles, or first causes, of what is given in sensible experience.*" To reduce philosophy to one category of knowledge is to amputate the body of metaphysics from a limb that, in itself, is lifeless. The organic life of metaphysics overgrows its parts. Gilson said, "Theology, logic, physics, biology, psychology, sociology, economics, are fully competent to solve their own problems by their own methods; on the other hand . . . and this must be our fourth conclusion: *as metaphysics aims at transcending all particular knowledge, no particular science is competent either to solve metaphysical problems, or to judge their metaphysical solutions.*" Immanuel Kant eschewed contact with reality in the manner favored by most professors before and since: "there was always some book between this professor and reality." And so it was for every philosopher who sought to universalize his findings by reference to a method rather than a result. Transcendent reason, looking beyond itself, seeks a "principle of unity" in individual objects. If it cannot find the principle of "unity-in-diversity" in reality, metaphysics looks instead to a principle "present in the human mind." Extroversion taken neat gives us unconnected individuals, whereas introversion gives us pure connectivity without factuality and multiplicity. The elusive object that metaphysics has sought, sufficiently individual to be present in all things differently, and sufficiently universal to unify all of its objects, is *being.* There is one root principle that "the mind is bound to conceive both as belonging to all things and as not belonging to any two things in the same way," and that is being. The fifth law is thus that "*since being is the first principle of all human knowledge, it is a fortiori the first principle of metaphysics.*"[35]

Gilson grounds the unity of philosophical experience in an "intuition" of being. "As soon as it comes into touch with sensible experience, the human intellect elicits the immediate intuition of being: X is, or exists; but from the intuition *that* something is, the knowledge of *what* it is . . . cannot . . . be deduced. . . . The intellect does not deduce, it intuits, it sees, and, in the light of intellectual intuition, the discursive power of reason slowly builds up from experience a determinate knowledge of concrete reality." Without this intuition, I cannot properly conduct the analytic, deductive, or inferential examination of my mental objects: "being is included in all of my representations," it is the single transcendent and yet encompassing reality, and so the science of being, metaphysics, is the source of all the

35. Ibid., 312–16, 318–19.

particular sciences. Maritain had long argued that the original sin of philosophy is nominalism, caused by the lack of the sense of being. The recurrent error of the metaphysicians, Gilson says, is to halt at one particular being, to take "*a* being for being itself," failing to see that being overflows its instantiations. His sixth and final law is that "*all the failures of metaphysics should be traced to the fact that the first principle of human knowledge has been either overlooked or misused by the metaphysicians.*"[36]

## Extrinsicism Cannot Put the Intellect in the Service of Christ

*The Unity* spoke of numerous intellectual pitfalls. C. S. Lewis's allegory *The Pilgrim's Regress* (1933) limits itself to two obstacles to conversion. In Lewis's imaginary country, the South, with its capital at "Claptrap," is peopled by materialists and psychologistic reductionists; the North is inhabited by idealists. Lewis's hero, John, wanders from South to North in search of the Island of desire and in flight from the Landlord. Wisdom asks John to consider who made the roads along which he travels:

> You have seen how we determine the position of every other place by its relation to the main road: and through you may say that we have maps, you are to consider that the maps would be useless without the roads, for we find where we are on the map by the skeleton of roads which is common to it and to the country....The people, indeed, say that the Landlord made these roads: and the Claptrapians say that we first made them on the map and have projected them, by some strange process, from it to the country. But I would have you hold fast to the truth, that we find them and do not make them: but also that no *man* could make them.

Gilson claimed in *The Unity* that Ockham's psychologism substitutes "the map for the country," mental conceptions of reality for reality itself. The metaphors are temptingly generic. Did Gilson read *The Pilgrim's Regress* in the 1930s? He did not refer to it directly until 1951, when in a work about aesthetics he spoke of

> a progress through art to something above art and therefore above humanity. In the setting of a bigger problem this is suggested by C.S. Lewis towards the end of *Pilgrim's Regress*—a work modeled on Bunyan's masterpiece and not unworthy of comparison with it....If God offers to men 'visions' whereby

---

36. Ibid., 320–21; Maritain, *The Degrees of Knowledge*, 1–2; Gilson, *The Unity of Philosophical Experience*, 323.

they aspire towards the highest truth, He does so either to supply for the law not yet revealed to them, or to recall to them that revelation which He has made and they have forgotten. Sometimes God offers 'visions' even to those who know His law, that He may draw them through the sweetness of desire awakened thus in their hearts. . . . But this beauty is offered only to awaken love, not to appease it. . . . For it is not Beauty they have seized, merely the sign set up to guide them. But God is never discouraged. He sends one vision after another, desire of which spurs these men afresh and brings back their former experiences, until at last, seeing what is left in their hands of all they thought to seize, they say, "Yet one more failure."[37]

The theme of the *Pilgrim's Regress* is a *moral* one: Lewis's hero has to learn the connection between his *desire* for the Island, and the Landlord's Rules. Allegory is more typically a device of ethics than of metaphysics. Reduced to their pure positions, Gilson's "historical" characters are as allegorical as the figures in Lewis's novel.

"Heaven forbid," he joked in 1939, that "I should once more re-open the never-ending controversy on 'Christian philosophy'!"[38] Gilson the Christian humanist seemed to have put theology to one side. One could read *The Unity*, or *Réalisme thomiste et critique de la connaissance* (1939), without realizing that the author was a proponent of Christian philosophy. Lewis's "romanticism" may give us a glimpse of the theology that is submerged within these books.

In 1936 Gilson had published *Christianisme et philosophie*, consisting of his lectures to the Parisian Calvinists, and "Intelligence in the Service of Christ the King." He told Chenu that engaging with Calvinism had led him "back to the problem of Christian philosophy, which literally horrifies me. It has unexpectedly. . . put me in the presence of the fact that there is behind the rejection of this notion, what seems to me to be a fatal theological error within Catholicism which, if it does not justify the Calvinists, excuses them. It is, if one wishes, Laberthonniére's famous 'extrinsicism,' against which he could, sadly, set only an equally illegitimate immanentism."[39]

"'You interest me exceedingly,'" says Lewis's Vertue: "'What are the principles of this community?' 'Catholicism, Humanism, Classicism,'" the Pale Men answer. When Vertue asks them if they "'believe in the Landlord,'" Classical tells her he has "'no interest in the question'"; Humanist

37. Lewis, *The Pilgrim's Regress*, 160–61; Gilson, *The Unity of Philosophical Experience*, 90; Gilson, *Choir of Muses*, 29–30.

38. Gilson, *Dante the Philosopher*, 306.

39. Gilson to Marie-Dominique Chenu, April 29, 1936, in Gilson Correspondence, "Étienne Gilson à M.-D. Chenu," University of St. Michael's College Archives.

knows "'perfectly well that the Landlord is a fable.' 'And I,' said Angular, 'know perfectly well that he is a fact.'" "'Angular is for me,'" Classical explains "'in one sense, *the* enemy, but in another, *the* friend. I cannot agree with his notions about the other side of the canyon: but just because he relegates his delusions to the *other* side, he is free to agree with me about this side and to be an implacable exposer (like myself) of all attempts to foist upon us any transcendental, romantical, optimistic trash.'" Neo-Angular, who defines himself as a "Scholastic,"[40] is a proponent of what Gilson called "Laberthonniére's famous 'extrinsicism.'"

Although his relations with Monsignor Nöel were "excellent," Van Steenberghen says, "in his two works on knowledge, above all in the second, he unleashed his Parisian verve and his caustic spirit," attacking the neo-Thomists with none of his habitual respect for persons. Bars recalls that "in *Réalisme thomiste* ... which appeared on the eve of the war, one had never seen Gilson so pugnacious before, in comparison with which Maritain's polemics seem almost anodyne."[41]

Augusto del Noce adversely compares the "positivistic" Thomism of Louvain with "Gilson's infusion of Augustinian spirit" into Thomism: "I said 'infusion of Augustine,' and I was just about to write 'Pascal.'" Gilson "strikes a blow against the habit of Catholic philosophers who, in the name of a certain Thomism, eliminate Pascal from the history of philosophy and relegate him to apologetics."[42] One cause of the acerbity of *Réalisme thomiste* was Gilson's belief that, by dint of their threadbare, mentalist metaphysics, the neo-Thomists had absorbed the positivism they sought to oppose. If it does not emerge *within* a metaphysics, an epistemology is a science of *how* one knows, that is, a purely empirical discipline.

Such epistemic positivism had to remain extrinsic to theology. Christian extrinsicism had proved defenseless against the emergent totalitarian ideologies. In Gilson's mind, Descartes typified such extrinsicism. In "The Intelligence in the Service of Christ the King," Gilson discusses the question of Christian philosophy in relation to the fall and redemption of humanity. How can fallen humanity use its intelligence rightly? By "taking itself as its own end, the intelligence has turned away from God, turning nature with it, and grace alone can aid both of them in returning to what is really their end, since it is their origin." Gilson's answer is like Pascal's. The human intelligence finds what it really is in Christ: "the great discovery or redis-

---

40. Lewis, *The Pilgrim's Regress*, 125–27.
41. Van Steenberghen, "Étienne Gilson et l'université de Louvain," 9; Bars, "Gilson et Maritain," 251.
42. Del Noce, "Thomism and the Critique of Rationalism," 744.

covery of Pascal is to have understood that the Incarnation, by profoundly changing the nature of man, has become the only means that there is for us to understand man. Such a truth gives a new meaning to our nature, to our origins, to our end. 'Not only,' wrote Pascal, 'do we understand God only through Jesus Christ, but we understand ourselves only through Jesus Christ. Outside Jesus Christ we do not know what life is, nor death, nor God, nor ourselves.'" The grace of Christ is interior to the metaphysical description of human nature given by Christian philosophy. Encouraged by the "favorable echo" this essay received at Saulchoir, and concerned by how far he was taking Thomist philosophy into faith-based theology, Gilson asked Père Chenu for his "imprimatur" on *Christianisme et philosophie*, before its publication.[43]

## Dogmatic Realism

*Réalisme thomiste* makes progress in the same philosophical experiment as *The Unity* but also professes to be a historical reclamation of Thomas's authentic position. Some Thomists had interpreted *Réalisme méthodique* as arguing that one must begin by *postulating* existence. The author was annoyed at being misunderstood: "I never realized just how profoundly classical metaphysics had been contaminated by Kant's *Critique* until a spiritual and intellectual son of St. Thomas Aquinas wrote in a Thomist journal that my position forced me to choose between either a critical realism or a realism reduced to the status of a mere postulate. The Thomism of Thomists who no longer understand the meaning of concepts like 'evident' and 'human consciousness' is in an advanced state of decay. The present book is therefore a critical analysis of Cartesian-Thomism."[44]

*Réalisme thomiste* takes on the modern Thomists from the Louvainistes, Mercier and Nöel, to Pedro Descoqs' Jesuit colleague at Jersey, Père Gabriel Picard, to the Dominicans of Saulchoir and Rome, Pères M-D Roland-Gosselin, Garrigou-Lagrange, and Charles Boyer, to the transcendental Thomism of Joseph Maréchal. The book is a part historical, part philosophical refutation of "Thomistic epistemologism," that is, the use of some way of knowing as a doorway into metaphysics. Gilson argues that this project is inextricably linked to Cartesianism. "Whoever sticks a finger into the machinery of the Cartesian method," he asserts, "must expect to be dragged

43. Gilson "L'intelligence au service du Christ-Roi," in *Christianisme et philosophie*, 147–49; Gilson to Marie-Dominique Chenu, April 29, 1936, in Gilson Correspondence.
44. Gilson, *Thomist Realism and the Critique Of Knowledge*, 24–25.

along its whole course."[45] By dint of his adverse reactions to the neo-Thomists' attempts to gain reality through intellectual dynamism, intuition, common sense, and logic, Gilson took a step toward existential Thomism.

The best-known adversary of extrinsicism was Maurice Blondel. He was a magnet to Catholic writers such as de Lubac and Joseph Maréchal, professor in the Jesuit house at Louvain. Drawing on Thomas and on Blondel, Maréchal argued that our minds have "a natural desire for the beatific vision." Human thought has an innate dynamism to an absolute and final end. The subject could not, without self-contradiction, tend to a goal it knew to be "unrealizable," and so, Maréchal argued, the existence of God must be possible. Our intellect participates in the idea of God toward which it is naturally oriented, and it could not do so unless that idea was "a manifestation of real being."[46]

Blondel had defined truth as the adequation of thought and *life*, or activity. Maréchal attempts to breach the Kantian proscription of metaphysics through the active or dynamic quality of thought. For Maréchal, the mind's dynamic progress to an *ideal* infinite gives coherence and structure to its empirical knowledge. In his system, God functions as the "noumenal absolute" that is the "a priori condition for the determination of every possible object in consciousness."[47] Maréchal rules by the ideal, not the empirical.

Gilson does not find that the existence of God is an actual, being-giving center to Maréchal's thought. He says that "the Thomist judgment implies an element of finality" because "Thomist 'intentionality' presupposes . . . an already completed union between subject and object."[48] It is possible, and conceivable, that God exists on the grounds Maréchal proposes; but the demonstration has been constructed by logic, not caused by existence.

Fr. Picard built his argument for the reality of world and God on an intuition that "I am": "it is only to the extent that we have an intuition of the self that we have an intuition of being," which in turn "puts us in possession of the absolute, justifies the evidence of the first principles, and assures us of the . . . trustworthiness of our minds." Gilson counters: "I am, therefore X exists, is not a valid inference." Even if the mind is so structured that it *could* know that "I am," that does not demonstrate that it *does* know objects, or that objects *do* exist. Gilson does not like the way in which Picard's "experimental proof" of the existence of the self becomes for him a generalizable principle. Such an "intellectual intuition" of self-existence must be

45. Ibid., 48.
46. Joseph Maréchal, *Cahier V,* 334, cited in Riet, *Thomistic Epistemology,* 1:266–67.
47. McCool, *From Unity to Pluralism,* 99–100, 105.
48. Gilson, *Thomist Realism,* 140.

legitimated by "downgrading the value of sensible knowledge in favor of some more or less Cartesian intellectual intuition."[49]

At the beginning of the nineteenth century, Jaime Balmes introduced Thomas Reid's notion of common sense into Thomism. Balmes considered that the return to "ordinary experience" was the best means of repelling skepticism with respect to the external world, for it is "unnatural" to doubt that the world exists; the skeptic, he said "is bound to go back to the common way of looking at things *as soon as he ceases to philosophize.*" The Thomist who thus averred that it was more important to be on the side of "humanity" than of "philosophy" was also a progenitor of the neo-Thomist demarcation between the "real" and the "ideal order," the latter standing for epistemic certitude on the ground of the principle of noncontradiction. "To the real truths," Balmes wrote, "corresponds the real world, the world of existences; to the ideal truths belong the logical world, the realm of possibilities." The ideal world is that about which true judgments are made. How then to advance from logical certitudes, which have only "hypothetical value with relation to the facts," to factual assertions? It is common sense, or a "natural instinct" that "*sees*" that the denial of the existence of Rome, for example, "is nonsense." The ideal principles themselves are "established" by the existence of God.[50] Common sense is the means by which Balmes proves the existence of "ordinary human nature"; "ordinary human nature" is the faculty by which common sense is exercised.

For the Roman Jesuit Mattheo Liberatore, common sense is the "natural" application of judgments. He scented fideism in the defense of Christianity on the basis of common sense, if that faculty is not legitimated by reason, and so he allied the ability closely to logic. Common sense is said to provide "a number of immediately evident truths, among which are the naturally known first principles, Aristotle's *koinai doxai* or 'common opinions.'"[51]

As Gilson notes, the "most sustained effort to integrate a doctrine of common sense into Thomism is that of Fr. Réginald Garrigou-Lagrange." *Le sens commun* attempts to root its "conceptualist-realist" understanding of common sense in what "Leibniz called '*quaedam perennis philosophia,*'" or the "traditional philosophy": this idea of common sense "can be easily disengaged from the writings of Aristotle and the great scholastics." Garrigou-Lagrange gave a wide scope to the objects of this faculty: "it perceives in being," he said, "the primary and speculative principles (the principles of identity, of non-contradiction, of substance, of *raison d'être,* of causality, of

49. Ibid., 92, 103, 98, 102.
50. Ibid., 28.
51. Ibid., 44; McCool, *From Unity to Pluralism,* 16.

finality, and also the first principle of morality...).'' The traditional philosophy is then the "justification" of this original, common-sense apprehension of being.[52]

Étienne's first line of objection to "common-sense Thomism" is a historical one. For Aristotle and Saint Thomas, the "sensus communis" was just the faculty that conjoins the objects of the diverse senses into a single psychological gestalt. It was Cicero who made a rhetorical use of common sense as a universal human faculty of knowledge. In order to compound the psychological and the rhetorical conceptions of common sense, Gilson says, the neo-Thomists made their way to Aristotle's *koinai doxai*, or common conceptions, which Thomas interpreted as referring to evident, and thus undemonstrable, principles. But *Le sens commun* gives no examples of Thomas employing common sense as a means of knowing the first principles. Gilson inquired of Père Garrigou, "Who are these scholastics?" and "Why, if realism had always been critical, did the scholastics fail to realize this until after they had read Kant, or why, if their philosophy had always been *the* philosophy of common sense, did the scholastics fail to realize this until after they had read Reid?"[53]

Gilson writes that "Descartes never denied that the existence of the external world was a *common-sense* truth.... [H]e expressly affirmed that it was." But if Garrigou was rather weak in the historical sense, does that make him Descartes' *de trop* disciple? Was Garrigou an idealist? Gilson appears to say so: "as soon as the problem of the existence of the external world was presented in terms of common sense, Cartesianism was accepted." Garrigou thought that unjust and, in reply to Gilson, restated his credentials as a realist.[54] He could not appreciate why, having consistently asserted, "with Aristotle and St. Thomas," that *"the formal object of the understanding is being,* just as the formal object of sight is color,"[55] anyone could accuse him of idealism.

By the word *being* Garrigou understood "intelligible being" or the "*raison d'être*" of objects. The first thing common sense garners from being is "the truth of the principle of identity: 'every being is itself.'" Common sense thus also apprehends the principle of noncontradiction, which is "a negative formulation" of the principle of identity. Common sense sees the

52. Gilson, *Thomist Realism*, 41; Garrigou-Lagrange, *Le sens commun*, 84–85, 104, 96.
53. Gilson, *Thomist Realism*, 36–37, 41.
54. Ibid., 48. My italics. Garrigou-Lagrange, "De intelligentia naturali et de primo objecto ab ipsa cognito," 137–54. I obtained this article in a translation done by Jason West, which contains no page numbers.
55. Garrigou-Lagrange, *Les sens commun*, 20.

reality of essences, an object's reason for being itself, the terra firma upon which we conceive that a pig *is* a pig, and not an apple (to supply an example). As Père Réginald puts it himself, "Every being has its *raison d'être*, that which it needs in order to be; to deny this would be to identify it with that which is not." Logical intelligibility, or the first principles, is thus the criterion by which we judge reality; for example, a "sensation which is the record of no sense perception would be contrary to the principle of contradiction; a sensation which is not the effect of a determining external cause would be contrary to the principle of causality." For the proper object of the human mind is not such real objects as pigs or apples, but first principles, which the mind achieves when it rises above conception and reasoning to judgment, attaining "the third degree of abstraction (abstraction from all matter)." Human reason is made for such abstraction, and thus, beyond the formal object of the intellect, as "the essence of sensible things," there lies

> the *formal and adequate object of the intelligence* which is fitting to it insofar as it is intelligence (dominating the body), is unrestricted *being*, that which permits it to know in a certain way all beings, and the *raison d'être* of all beings (Ia q XII, a 4). The being which is here in question is not precisely factually existent being, it is the being which is abstracted from the state of simple possibility and that state of actual existence, that is to say, whatever is or can be. It is thus that we conceive what man *is*, making an abstraction from actual existence; in the same way we judge that man is free and we can prove it: *because* it is reasonable. The object of intelligence is *real being which is divided into possible and actual.*

With such statements to his credit, Garrigou found, in response to *Réalisme thomiste*, that "I do not see a notable difference between this position of Professor Gilson and the traditional position of Thomists, which I have defended many times in nearly the same way."[56]

When he wrote *The Degrees of Knowledge*, Maritain had at hand Gilson's "Le réalisme méthodique" (1930). Maritain's second chapter is a defense of "Critical Realism." It cites with approval Gilson's statement that "every scholastic who considers himself a realist because he accepts" a "starting point" in the human mind is "in reality a Cartesian." Maritain uses the resources of Roman Thomism to defend critical realism. He contends that, when all else is denied, the principle of identity remains: "*I am conscious of*

56. Ibid., 20, 106–7, 108; Garrigou-Lagrange, *God: His Existence and His Nature*, 153–54; Garrigou-Lagrange, *Le sens commun*, 47, 52–53; Garrigou-Lagrange, "De intelligentia naturali et de primo objecto ab ipsa cognito."

*knowing at least one thing, that that which is, is.*" The principle of identity is a principle in logic, that something cannot be and not be at the same time and in the same way. Because it is a *logical* principle, "identity" holds both in relation to actual and possible existence. This is why the principle of identity is suitable for the "critical" argument that initially prescinds from reality; even before reality is given, this necessary law must pertain. This first principle which meets our minds supplies all the rest: "It is sufficient for each one of us to think for himself to experience . . . the absolute impossibility of the intellect's thinking of the principle of identity without positing (at least possible) extramental being, of which this first of all axioms expresses the bearing."[57]

Desmond FitzGerald says that it was Maritain's "characteristic gentleness" that led him to "minimize the disagreement with the Louvain School." Maritain's gentleness did not prevent him from admonishing Edmund Husserl for forgetting that "the first, absolutely unbreakable, apodictic certainty of the intellect is concerned with *possible* (metalogical) extramental being."[58] He was himself closer to realistic phenomenology than he realized.

Maritain's chapter concludes by asking whether Gilson is now convinced of the value of critical realism. The answer was no: if the act of criticism is taken to *add* anything to realism, the realism is annulled. With reference to the critical realism of Louvain, Gilson asks how could anyone call this "collection of basic positions" Thomist, given that Thomas "never used thought as a starting point, never founded his epistemology upon thought and never had to use it in order to reach existence?" If the preliminary act of criticism has any '*because* value,' then the act of self-reflection becomes a criterion by which one advances to the existence of the world; if it has none, then one is simply playing at doubt, a game of which Gilson accused Monsignor Nöel. For Gilson, the necessities of reason are not enough to give us reality, because they are not causes: "a necessity of thought does not," he writes, "guarantee the existence of a concrete, extra-mental reality."[59]

Garrigou-Lagrange's favorite prescription against Blondel's philosophy of action was the Angelic Doctor's realist definition of truth. It is upon this that Gilson takes his stand against a realism that casts off from the intelligibility of the first principles. He writes, "It is not enough to give mere verbal assent to the proposition that truth is an adequation of understanding and

---

57. Maritain, *The Degrees of Knowledge,* 86–87, 93, 114.
58. FitzGerald, "Étienne Gilson: From Historian to Philosopher," 36; Maritain, *The Degrees of Knowledge,* 124.
59. FitzGerald, "Étienne Gilson: From Historian to Philosopher," 36–38; Gilson, *Thomist Realism,* 80, 82–83, 171–72.

being. To give this formula its full realist meaning, we must go beyond the schema in which a being is reduced to an essence, which is itself reduced to the quiddity expressed in the definition. St. Thomas' whole noetic invites us to go beyond that . . . : a being's act of existence, not its essence, is the ultimate foundation of what we know to be true about it." Gilson is saying that, although the intellect takes definitions, or "quiddities," from essences, what causes its ability to do so is not, as Garrigou seems to say, that natures are definable. The justification of realist epistemology is rather that the metaphysical fact that the "essence . . . contains the form, the cause of the being of the existent, and the act by which form causes something to exist is the very heart of reality." It is the act of existence, involuted within, and inseparable from, an essence that causes our experience. Such experience is not purely rational or "ideal." The many "writers" who "never tire of citing the formula St. Thomas borrowed from Avicenna in which he says that being is the first thing encountered by the intellect" neglect that "the apprehension of being by the intellect consists of directly seeing the concept of being in some sensible datum." The Gifford lecturer had said of the mediaeval Christian philosophers, "the resemblances alone are really fruitful." He did not apply the same principle to his contemporary co-religionists; the notion of a philosopher's neutrality between "possible or real" existence was alien to him.[60]

Gilson reminds his readers that Kantianism is not a timeless philosophical problem. The critical philosophy emerged from the "historical experience" of Immanuel Kant as he surveyed the detritus of Leibnizian dogmatism left by Hume's treatise. Kant never came near the metaphysics of Aristotle, or of Aquinas. His notion of metaphysical *necessity* derives not from Aristotle's logic but from "Descartes, Leibniz and Wolff." Metaphysics as thus conceived is an "abstract rationalism devoid of any empirical content." For Kant, reason is pure to the extent that it is evacuated of sense information, and the purest reason is thus a priori knowledge. The description of the machinery of imagination, understanding, and reason in the first *Critique* has no bearing on the existence of empirical objects: "The critique is therefore a *transcendental* knowledge with regard to experience." It does not touch on the neo-Thomists' battle against skepticism about the existence of the world. Kant wants to defend a priori knowledge; existential questions are not germane to his inquiry, because he construes them as being merely empirical. He did not believe that designating the noumena as that of which

---

60. Gilson, *Thomist Realism* , 204, citing Aquinas, in I *Sent.*, dist 19, q. 5 a I, Sol.; ibid., 200, 196; Gilson, *The Spirit of Mediaeval Philosophy*, 146.

metaphysics cannot speak entails either calling the existence of the phenomenal world into question or attempting to demonstrate it. As Gilson says,

> Kant himself professes an immediate realism of the experience of external objects, given as such, in the *a priori* form of space; in other words, he affirms an immediate realism of the existence of a Kantian external world. As for the existence of another world, that of things-in-themselves which cause phenomena, he simply takes it for granted. . . . The transcendental point of view of the *a priori* conditions of the object of knowledge ignores, by definition, the empirical problem of the existence in themselves of known objects. The result is that . . . "critical realists" are today absolutely the only ones who pose the problem of the external world.[61]

If the neo-Thomists had engaged in battle with a fictitious enemy and had cut themselves off at the pass, marching around and around in a circular effort to demonstrate the undemonstrable, *why do we think the world exists?* One starts by planting oneself, not in Thomas's description of the mind's operations, but in his metaphysical account of human nature. It is no use, "while professing with St. Thomas and Aristotle that man is the substantial unity of soul and body," setting up "the problem of knowledge as if" one "did not know that man's body exists," an exercise which leaves us with the "impossible task of establishing a link between the material world and a disembodied soul." One need not then eschew epistemology. It may be more frightening to confront a real opponent, and the soldier may feel less than fully armed when he meets the legions of skeptics with the calm statement that "St. Thomas considers the existence of the external world to be self-evident." The way out of the circle of logical possibility engendered by the transcendental critique is the "turn to the testimony of experience," a maneuver we should perform "at the beginning of any undertaking": it will then be "difficult to designate by any other word than 'evident' the type of certitude we have concerning the existence of the external world."[62] Like Balmes, Gilson thinks that such certitude cannot be demonstrated to those who deny it, but he invokes, not common sense, but sensation as his witness.

All exist*ents* are singulars. How is the intellect to gain conceptual knowledge of exist*ence?* Drawing out Thomas's epistemology, Gilson explains that, since the "intellect knows universals . . . only in a phantasm . . . intellectual

---

61. Gilson, *Thomist Realism*, 155, 157–58, 161, 164–65.
62. Ibid., 190, 100, 180.

knowledge of universals requires the perception of singulars." We achieve the concept of existence through sensing singular facts: "In order for man to perceive being with his intellect, an existent must be given to him, an existent perceptible to his sensibility."[63]

Gilson was not the only modern Thomist to note that philosophy can only go past speaking of the *concept* of existence to the *fact* of existence if it abandons the heights of ideality for the lowlands of empirical sensation. Domet de Vorges (1829–1910) claimed that no Thomist should separate sensation and intelligence and that, since we know through this conjunction, "our experience continually convinces us that we know things which exist, whose existence we grasp directly." Urging that neither the Humean senses nor the Cartesian intellect know the existence of the world, but only "the *conjunctum*, man,... the only concretely existing knowing subject," Gilson takes over the baton from de Vorges's claim that "it is by means of a sort of metaphor that we say that the senses know this or the intellect knows that.... neither the senses nor the intellect knows; it is the individual man who knows by means of the senses and the intellect."[64]

## Maritain: *Sept leçons sur l'être*

The preface to Maritain's *Degrees of Knowledge* is dated June 11, 1932. June 11 was the date of Maritain's baptism, into Catholicism and into Thomism in the Roman style. The book brings that era of his life to a close. In September 1932 Maritain gave some lectures at the Institut Catholique in which he elaborates a new "intuition," that of being. Printed in 1934, *Sept leçons sur l'être et les premiers principes de la raison spéculative* was dedicated to Gerald Phelan, who had insisted that Maritain publish the lectures.[65]

*Sept leçons* begins with a question: Why isn't Thomist metaphysics as outdated today as, say, mediaeval physics? Since the answers to scientific questions perpetually create new paradigms, should metaphysics not do likewise? Borrowing a pair of words from the Catholic existentialist Gabriel Marcel, Maritain responds by distinguishing a "mystery" from a "problem." Mysteries differ from problems by their greater *ontological* depth. Whereas the "problematic" of the natural sciences progresses by replacing

63. Ibid., 190, 204.
64. Riet, *Thomist Epistemology*, 1:192; Gilson, *Thomist Realism*, 174, and 173, citing Domet de Vorges, *La perception et la psychologie thomiste*, 197.
65. Maritain to Étienne Gilson, August 12, 1934, in *Deux approches*, 120.

one paradigm with another, those who probe within mysteries can only deepen their knowledge of the same reality. That mysterious reality, the object of metaphysics, is existence itself. Maritain answers the question about the continuing relevance of Thomist metaphysics by designating it as an "existential philosophy."[66]

*Sept leçons* is an effort to deepen our understanding of the Aristotelian dictum that the object of metaphysics is being qua being. The book jettisons many of the accouterments of modern Thomism that were the objects of Gilson's campaign, such as the *sens commun,* with its weak bearing on existence, and the very terms *neo-Scholasticism* or *neo-Thomism,* on the grounds that they align Thomism with a problem-solving exercise, that is, with positivism. It gently differs from Garrigou-Lagrange's exposition of the principle of identity. By accentuating the fact that the principle of identity rests on an intuition of existence, Maritain labors to relate the first principles to existence.[67]

A short section in *Sept leçons* is titled "Digression sur l'existence et la philosophie." Here Maritain turns to the fact that the metaphysician approaches existence through his senses. The "res sensibilis visibilis," the visible sensed thing, Maritain affirms, "is the touchstone of judgment." The metaphysician, says the "Digression," must enter

> the depth of existence through a sensitive (and aesthetic) perception which is as pointed as it can be, and through an experience of suffering and of existential conflicts, in order to go to devour the highest, to the third sky of natural intelligence, the intelligible substance of things. Is it necessary to add that the condition of the professor who is nothing more than a professor, retired from existence and desensitized to this third degree of abstraction, is precisely opposed to the genuine condition of the metaphysician? Thomist metaphysics is called *scholastic,* the name of its cruellest ordeal. The scholarly pedagogue is his own worst enemy. He must perpetually triumph over his own intimate adversary, the Professor.[68]

Gilson will cite these very lines, but not until ten years after they were published.[69] *Réalisme thomiste* gives Domet de Vorges, and not Maritain,

66. Maritain, *Sept leçons sur l'être et les premiers principes de la raison spéculative,* 8–11, 30. I am grateful to Jim Arraj for pointing out to me the significance of *Sept leçons* within Maritain's intellectual development, and thus, by implication, in that of Gilson.

67. Ibid., 34–40, 65, 104–6.

68. Ibid., 29–30.

69. Gilson, *Le Thomisme: introduction a la philosophie de saint Thomas d'Aquin* (5th ed., 1942–1944), 505–7.

as his forerunner in noticing the irreplaceable role of the senses in Thomas's realism. The book treats Maritain purely as a representative of "critical realism," and its critique of that epistemic maneuver seems to be aimed right at him. Far from protesting his existentialist innocence, Maritain responded to Gilson's "well-deserved blow" to "Cartesian-Thomism and Kantian-Thomism" in the guise of a "*critical realist*," albeit one who insisted that his use of the term was "substantially in agreement" with Gilson's "dogmatic realism."[70] Gilson's reticence can be explained on aesthetic grounds. Treating Maritain's thought like a "pure position" that contained only one building block permitted him a greater clarity of exposition than dealing with a Maritain who subtly altered his emphasis a few months after publishing *The Degrees of Knowledge.*

Between 1932 and 1939, Gilson often asked Maritain to lecture at his Institute of Mediaeval Studies, and sometimes won him over to Toronto. The intellectual companionship between the two men became like a game of leapfrog, each resting on the other, and then jumping ahead into the Thomist philosophy of existence. Maritain asserted, in his Institut Catholique lectures, that it is an "intuition" of being "that makes the metaphysician." The sixth and highest law of metaphysics, in *The Unity,* is that "sensible experience" gives our intellect an "immediate intuition of being."[71] Gilson used the word *intuition* eight times in his concluding lecture at Harvard. Nor is the word absent from *Réalisme thomiste.* But does "intuition" have the same object for the two leap-froggers?

Maritain had claimed that he was using the word *intuition* in a "modern" sense and defined the activity it designates as "eidetic or ideational visualization." If, he says, Thomism is an "existential metaphysics," the existentiality renders it none the less *metaphysical.* For Maritain, metaphysics spelled the doctrines of analogy and first principles. The intuition of being leads to the formation of one "eidetic" concept, that of existence. So the intuition cannot be "centered on a concrete reality taken in its singular existence." If it were, the concept that "eidetic" vision forms would teach us that extramental existence is as singular as the particular existent out of which it is elicited. Rather than referring us to existence as univocal and identical throughout, our "eidetic visualization" of existence relates to existence as analogical, that is, as polymorphous and variegated. Once in our minds, the

70. Prouvost's note, in *Deux approches,* 134; Maritain to Étienne Gilson, August 16, 1939, ibid., 133. My italics.

71. Maritain, *Sept leçons,* 52; Gilson, *The Unity,* 320.

concept of existence "breaks up" into pluriformity "when one passes from its conceptual existence to its real existence."[72]

*Sept leçons* is more fascinated by the notion of an "intuition" of being than by the fact that it comes back to sense experience. Its excursus on sense knowledge is in a real sense a "Digression" because Maritain's main concern is that existence itself presents itself in analogous forms and that the notion of being is an "analogizing" one. For Maritain, the analogical concept of existence contains in itself the principle of the diversity of things. The fullest reason why the metaphysician knows that existence is multiple in reality is not because his senses inform him of the existence of a multiplicity of different sensible objects. It is because the "crystal liquid"[73] of the analogical notion of being shows being to him as implicitly containing an infinity of different intelligible forms. It is through the medium of the analogical concept of existence that the metaphysician exhibits the significance of the first principles, such as those of identity, finality, and causality.

The analogy of being is not the point of departure for Gilson's personal philosophy. He begins from the opposite end of matters, with sensible objects delivering the reality of individuals, and the understanding searching for universals: that the human person is a "conjunctum" of sensibility and thought is for this "Erasmian" and Pascalian philosopher truly a miracle. In Thomas's "doctrine," he writes, "only individuals exist." It is not the concept of being that indicates ontological diversity to us, but the individuals by which we are surrounded. Each individual existent essence, according to Gilson, is "revealed to the intellect by the sensible effects it causes." Thus, although Gilson, like Maritain, speaks of a "concept of being" and refers in *Réalisme thomiste* to its being grasped in "intuitive perception," intuition is for him more inescapably tied to sensation.[74] The divergence between the man whose first great intellectual experience was hearing Lévy-Bruhl lecture on Hume, and the poetic-visionary and signatory to the manifesto of the Parti de l'intelligence, created no breach between the friends until 1950.

Why was it that many neo-Thomists had come to see only one side of what Gilson called "the osmosis ... between sense and intellect in ... the knowing subject"? It may have been because, conceiving themselves as defenders of the citadel of Christendom, they thought *against,* and the enemy was irrationalism, first as philosophical skepticism, and later as theological fideism. "What makes man is not liberty, ethics, religion, sociability

72. Maritain, *Sept leçons,* 53, 66–67.
73. Ibid., 73.
74. Gilson, *Thomist Realism,* 191, 199, 205–6.

or speech, it is reason,"[75] said Père Garrigou-Lagrange, and this pledge to rational humanism sank to the core of his theological system. Against the denial of truth, men like Garrigou took their stand on the ability of human reason to extract quidditative definitions from essences, for the citadel was lost to the modernists without the true propositions that constitute doctrinal dogmas.

Domet de Vorges was, by comparison, something of an "agnostic," for he considered that the "notion of essence" refers to the "foundation (*fond*) of being, but since we know nothing of that foundation except that it is, we call the essence of the thing its 'being' (*être*)." For de Vorges, being is simply "the act and the mode of the essence."[76] Gilson was likewise tentative with respect to the total intelligibility of essences. Although we are alerted to them by their "sensible effects," essences are ultimately "unknown to us because the form," that is, the existence, "which confers their intelligibility upon them is purely intelligible" and "pure intelligibility escapes our intuition." *Réalisme thomiste* comes to ground in existence, which, according to Gilson, is never fully comprehensible to us.

For all the aggression of *Réalisme thomiste,* it is Gilson, rather than his interlocutors, who embraced the problem of modernity: "St. Thomas agrees with Kant in denying that man has an intellectual intuition of things in themselves, but he maintains, while Kant denies, that our knowledge by means of concepts does attain reality as it really is, although it does not exhaust the intelligibility of reality in the way an intuition would." Gilson's philosophy bypasses intellectual totalitarianism because his realism has a theological source: "For a realist philosophy, thought has no other content than that which its faculties permit it to abstract from things. . . . Nothing abnormal about that, and even less so in the Middle Ages, which because it was Christian, and the Christian world is a creation of God, not of man; Christian philosophy spontaneously envisages problems from the point of view of the object."[77]

In *Réalisme thomiste,* following in Maritain's footsteps, Gilson has almost achieved an existential Thomism. He was driven there, in part, by the Augustinian features of his thought; a reviewer of *Christianisme et philosophie* found in it a "'concealed Jansenism.'" Gilson had noted Bonaventure's

75. Ibid., 189; Garrigou-Lagrange, *Le sens commun,* 47. Religion is thus for Garrigou a "note" or moment lodged within essential human rationality.

76. Riet, *Thomistic Epistemology,* 1:194.

77. Gilson, *Thomist Realism,* 203–4; Gilson, "La spécificité de l'ordre philosophique," in *Le réalisme méthodique,* 64.

criticisms of a philosophy that would be independent of its theological end: the Franciscan condemns as idolatry any philosophy that takes itself as an ultimate. The "first intellectual duty" of the Christian is not "to pay homage to the intellect." The author was akin to one friend of Port Royal in considering that "to make the God of the philosophers pass before that of Abraham, Isaac and Jacob is to perform an object substitution whose consequences can be serious."[78]

---

78. Cited with contumacy in Gilson, *Le philosophe et la théologie*, 93; Gilson, "L'intelligence au service du Christ-Roi," in *Christianisme et philosophie*, 143; Gilson, *Le philosophe et la théologie*, 76.

# 9

# World War II History and Eternity

## Reason and Revelation

Père Marie-Dominique Chenu was one of the first contributors to Gilson and Thèry's *Archives d'histoire doctrinale et litteraire du moyen âge.* In an article of 1927, he showed how Saint Thomas invented the idea of theology as a science. In the early Middle Ages, scripture was taken as the *matter* of theology; theologians wrote *about* the Bible. From the mid-thirteen century, English and Parisian theologians began asking how theology argues, that is, how it is a *science.* Colonizing Aristotle's definition of science as reasoning developed from evident principles, Thomas defined the biblical articles of faith as the first principles of the science of theology. Theology is not just about scriptural revelation. It operates as a science by working through the revealed articles of faith. Flowing from revelation, the first principles galvanize human reason to create theology. Thomas's idea of theology-as-science exhibits the "fertile continuity" between revelation and reason.[1]

God's Revelation exhibits a field of *revelabilia* which theological reason cultivates. The *revelabilia* are that portion of revealed truth that, Chenu says, is contiguous to human reason. Thomas taught that human theological reason opens up "the virtualities of revelation," exploiting the terrain of the *revelabilia.* As knowledge, human theology depends upon God's self-knowledge. The revelation of God's "science" of himself yields the principles upon which theology works. Moreover, as an Aristotelian "science," theology conforms to human rationality: we have here a "perfect synthesis between the mysticism of the believer and the science of the theologian." Hinging on Thomas's "grace perfects nature," Chenu's article is a vindication of human reason: "with Saint Thomas," the author affirms with some

1. Chenu, "La théologie comme science au XIIIe siècle," 63.

173

pleasure, "the immense curiosity of human intelligence becomes a religious act, indeed the best exercise of faith."[2]

Gilson had asked Chenu for his "nihil obstat" on *Christianisme et philosophie,* in 1936, because he was both intrigued and concerned by the overlapping frontiers of philosophical demonstration of the existence of God and of religious faith in what God has "done." Could one say, he wondered, that Thomas "believed" in the existence of God, without denying the teaching of the "Vatican Council," that God's existence can be proven?[3]

In his Richard lectures, delivered in Virginia in 1937, Gilson deals with the same issue. Here he is speaking as an apologist for Thomism, not as an academic historian. The game in *Reason and Revelation in the Middle Ages* is to show that, of the Tertullian, Augustinian, Thomist, and Averroist "families," the Thomists have the most balanced conception of the relationship between philosophy and theology. For the Tertullian tribe, theology is a no-brainer: "since God has spoken to us, it is no longer necessary for us to think." The Augustinian family believe that "rational insight into the contents of Revelation"[4] enables us to *see* that the truths of faith are logically demonstrable. Chesterton noted that if a chap's aunts are his pals, then his pals are his aunts: if the function of philosophy is making faith transparent to reason, then philosophy *is* theology. Taking the contrary tack, the Averroists favor what is rationally knowable, that is, philosophy, to faith: theology is thereby subordinated to philosophy. Augustinianism and Averroism both make philosophy and theology inbreed, generating offspring that are neither genuine pals (philosophy) nor kosher aunts (theology).

Contemporary Augustinians, like Laberthonnière, customarily complained about Thomas's insistence that philosophy is something different from theology. Gilson has set up the different families' "problem" in such a way as to show *why* Thomas had to invent that distinction. The "trouble" of Thomas's time, Gilson says, "was that some theologians wanted to theologize in philosophy, whereas some philosophers wanted to philosophize in theology. . . . [T]he only way to bring that strife to a close was for Saint Thomas Aquinas to handle philosophical problems as a philosopher and theological problems as a theologian."[5]

The reason that Gilson gives for the distinction of theology and philosophy is that *knowing* and *believing* are psychologically different acts. Phenom-

2. Ibid., 58, 71.
3. Gilson to Marie-Dominique Chenu, April 29, 1936, in Gilson Correspondence, St. Michael's College archives.
4. Gilson, *Reason and Revelation in the Middle Ages,* 6, 19.
5. Ibid., 72.

enologically, knowing consists in understanding, grasping a datum, whereas believing consists in holding as true something which one *cannot understand* to be so: "I know by reason that something is true because *I see* that it is true; but I believe that something is true because *God has said it*."[6]

Gilson defines Thomist theology as a science "whose principles are articles of faith." The Thomist is said to divide theology into two categories: on the one hand, there are "revealed truths," which are also "attainable by reason alone," such as the existence of God, and on the other, there are truths that "surpass the whole range of reason." The latter can neither be collapsed into Averroistic philosophy nor be the subject of "necessary demonstrations of purely rational nature," as the Augustinian "theologism of the early Middle Ages" proposed. It is because theological science follows from principles that are articles of *faith* that it is not "a merely natural assent to some rational probability."[7]

Thomas distinguished philosophy and theology, but also united them at the level of the revealed truths that *are* accessible to human knowledge. The area where they come together is the *revelabile*. The "Thomist family" maintains that some of the truths God reveals are accessible to reason, that is, capable of becoming the object of human acts of knowledge. When a revealed truth is demonstrated by reason—as, for instance, when one proves the immortality of the soul—the psychological act of belief in the soul's immortality turns into a psychological act of knowledge. Because he sets out to prove the first category of revealed truths, transmuting belief into knowledge, the *revelabile* is, for Saint Thomas, "a presupposition to faith" rather than an "article of faith." The moment that a revealed truth ceases to be an object of faith and becomes an object of knowledge, then, psychologically, it ceases to be believed—it is *known*. The unspoken word, at the back of the book, is *creation:* "faith and knowledge grow into an organic unity because they both spring from the same source," for Thomas's family.[8] But has Gilson succeeded in showing that knowing and believing form an "organic unity"? He has given more energy to their psychological distinction than to their metaphysical unity. Gilson has drawn back, for the moment, from the overlap of belief and knowledge, at which *Christianisme et philosophie* had hinted.

To decipher the Latin phrases with which Gilson's 1936 "request for an imprimatur" is peppered, it is useful to have at hand the Latin of the Question on Faith, in the *Summa Theologiae*. In retracing Gilson's efforts to

6. Ibid.
7. Ibid., 76–78.
8. Ibid., 82–83.

figure how reason can be conditioned by faith, one needs to look, not only at the main body of the text of the *Summa,* but through the ins and outs of the objections and their replies. He is *noticing,* not just the details *as details,* but how they qualify the whole. The early phase of the art of Picasso and Braque is called analytic cubism: what Gilson is doing now, in his historical investigation of Thomas's writings, is to cut them apart, analyze them, and then resynthesize them as a whole. In the 1937 *Reason and Revelation in the Middle Ages,* Gilson's process is still, as it were, on the cutting table; it is not until 1942 that he achieved the fully tailored and synthesized object.

## The Saulchoir Model of Theology

Marie-Dominique Chenu became regent of the Dominican Studium at Saulchoir in 1932. For the annual homily given at the Feast of Saint Thomas in 1936, Père Chenu prepared a set of lectures defining the Dominican charism, from a Saulchoirist perspective. As a program for Dominican formation, *Une école de théologie: le Saulchoir* indicates that Thomist theology is a function of "Dominican religious life," a particular type of spirituality. Following Père Gardeil, Chenu terms the foundational principle of theology the *donné révélé.* This revealed principle is not to be found in a text, such as Denzinger, but in the "*presence* of Revelation in the Holy Spirit," or, again, in a "*presence* with the inexhaustible realism and the insistent silence which this word implies, for the eyes which consent to it." The *donné révélé* is the Incarnate Christ: "The Son of God is an historical person."[9] A modern Saulchoirist theology takes this historical fact as its "first principle."

Such a theology would construct itself as a *human* science, not on the basis of Aristotle's *Posterior Analytics,* but on that of history. Chenu is rather unkind to interpretations of Thomas that fix the master's ideas outside and beyond history. The "abstract intellectualism of the *Aufklärung*" has, the Dominican says, "contaminated modern scholasticism." It forgot that Thomas's work was an "*invention,*" that "'it is impossible to conserve without creating' (E. Gilson)" and that Saint Thomas's thought is "nuanced with a discrete relativism" in relation to its own time. A historical appropriation of Thomas need not submerge him in temporal relativity, for historical research works on three levels: the understanding of a thinker's milieu, the grasp of his personality, and, "the ultimate matter of the histo-

9. Chenu, *Une école de théologie,* 122, 124, 144, 137.

rian," the grasp of the "internal logic" of his "intuitions"[10] (difficult not to add "E. Gilson").

The advantage for "baroque scholasticism" in elevating itself outside of time is that it had all its answers pre-prepared inside a box; "refuting" its "adversaries by naming the counterpositions," a decadent Scholasticism "'philosophized on the philosophies instead of philosophizing on the problems (E. Gilson).'" A true Saulchoirist, Chenu says, does not "consider the *philosophia perennis* as a defined system of inviolable propositions, but as a body of master intuitions." Since "one does not philosophize by beginning from a set of propositions," the term *traditional philosophy* "sometimes... engages one in a facile philosophy, without struggles and without problems."[11] Chenu ascribes this facility to "*scholastique 'baroque*,'" that totalitarianism of reason with which Gilson engaged in *Réalisme thomiste*:

> Under the patronage of Leibniz, this qualification of *philosophia perennis* invites us to recognize... a certain ideal of intelligibility which marks modern scholasticism and which even today most often gives it its tonality. This scholasticism tends to define the intelligible under the strictly rational form: the intelligible is the concept which is analyzed and attributed; the bond of reality, its intimate structure is imagined as a network of concepts. The whole effort of its thought is thus brought to bear on the possible and its logical compatibility, since precisely the contingent existent is a failure to this ideal conceptualization and the truth which is its fruit. For the truth is that which is 'conceivable,' that of which we can have a clear and distinct idea, a 'notion.' Research into truth, the work of science, thus consists in bringing every proposition to the logical necessity of identity.... The principle of sufficient reason, the expression of this ideal of universal analysis, is itself reducible to the demands of a logical identity and can be brought back to the principle of contradiction.

Because it has sealed itself up in a "philosophy of essences," the "categories of Wolff" "still reign in the best Thomist manuals." This passage allows us to overhear the conversations which preceded *Réalisme thomiste* and which flowered in *L'être et l'essence*. Chenu did not, of course, say precisely to which baroque theologians he was referring, but he was incautious in alluding so caustically to those "for whom the whole of theology consists in being anti-modernist."[12] He was summoned to Rome in 1938, where ten theses had been prepared for his signature, by way of an anti-modernist commen-

10. Ibid., 141, 122–23, 125–26, 163.
11. Ibid., 123, 152.
12. Ibid., 155–56, 139, a "certain 'fixisme' dont toute la théologie consistait à être antimoderniste."

tary on Saint Thomas. The eighth thesis stated that "'although properly a theologian, St. Thomas was also properly a philosopher; for that reason his philosophy does not depend for its intelligibility and truth on his theology, and it states truths that are absolute and not merely relative.'"[13] Chenu signed this declaration. Assuring him, in March 1938, that he retained "the love of a great friend," Gilson told Chenu that the Dominican "Province in France does not seem to me to have only friends in Cisalpine Gaul," that is, in Rome: "it is really sad," he wrote, "that in a time in which the Church suffers so much from outside, some people take pleasure in trying to destroy it from within."[14]

## Humanism in Danger: 1937–1939

Gilson was thinking of Erasmus in May 1939. He told the readers of the Paris *Nouvelles litteraires* that if he had been alive today, this "citizen of the world" would probably have been a modernist "with reservations," because his "philologism had its limits: *philologia ancilla theologiae.*" This humanist breathed the air of reality. As one who "fled from Louvain, whose Catholic theologians made his stay untenable," and from Basel, from Paris, and from Zurich, "Erasmus is the patron of . . . the refugees from ideology who today add up to thousands." But he lived in a "happy time," which lacked "concentration camps for refractory intellectuals." States, Gilson says, "have become more accurate Inquisitors since, having decreed their own theologies, they are transfigured into Churches." Humanism is "in danger today," but, Gilson suggested to his Parisian readers, whenever France "has had to chose between Erasmus and Machiavelli, she has chosen Erasmus."[15]

In public lectures and in texts such as *L'impossible antisémitisme* (1937), Maritain contended with this evil on theological grounds. Père Garrigou-Lagrange let it be known to him through a mutual friend that, in his opinion, Monsignor Pacelli did not like Maritain's "excessively general propositions, where the *per se* and the *per accidens* are insufficiently distinguished; I recall this 'The hatred against the Jews and against the Christians comes from the same source'; this might be true in a specific country, at a specific moment, but it cannot be formulated in such a general way; for when it is

---

13. For a complete list of the theses signed by Chenu, see R. Guelluy, "Les antecedants de l'encyclique *Humani Generis* dans les sanctions Romaines de 1942: Chenu, Charlier, Draguet," in *Revue d'histoire Ecclesiastique* 81 (1986): 461–62.

14. Gilson to Marie-Dominique Chenu, March 29, 1938, in Gilson Correspondence.

15. Gilson, "Erasme, citoyen du monde," 1–2.

the Jews who hate the Christians, hatred of both cannot come from the same source."[16] Gilson avoided the generalizations the Roman Thomist so disliked, preferring to make declarations of loyalty to particular friends, as in his obituary tribute of March 1939 to "Mon Ami Lévy-Bruhl."

## Gilson Turns Back to Theology: 1939

The Averroës of *Reason and Revelation in the Middle Ages* would not have felt out of place in the *Action française*. Gilson's 1939 "Averroës" surmised that one needs "revelation" because "you will not civilize a tribe of Bedouins by teaching them metaphysics. If you want them not to kill, not to plunder, and not to drink" you must "appeal to their imagination." Like "most philosophers, he wanted social order, that he himself might philosophize in peace.... Averroës did not consider religion as merely a rough approximation to philosophic truth.... It had a definite social function that could not be fulfilled by anything else, not even philosophy. Such is the exact meaning of the texts where he praises the Koran as a truly 'miraculous' book."[17]

Averroës's Christian followers in the Latin West could not treat the production of social order as the ultimate test of faith; nor could they reconcile the Averroistic God with the Christian one. They took two different paths, depending upon the genuineness of their faith. Those whose faith was as actual as their rationality, such as Siger of Brabant, held that the "*necessary* results of philosophical speculation" and divine revelation are independent and, as it were, magnetically repellent. But when thirteenth-century Parisian philosophers were atheists, Gilson said, "the deism of Averroës was their natural philosophy": "the Averroistic tradition forms an uninterrupted chain from the Masters of Arts of Paris and Padua, to the 'Libertins' of the seventeenth and eighteenth centuries."[18] For the deist, revelation is so extrinsic to human reason as to contradict it.

Gilson asserts that Dante would not have put Siger of Brabant into "the fourth heaven of the sun," in the *Divine Comedy*, if Siger had not been a Christian.[19] Others had been found to explain Siger's position in the *Paradiso* by a late conversion to Thomism. Van Steenberghen argued in 1937 that, if one attributes the newly discovered treatise, the *Quaestiones de*

16. Barré, *Jacques et Raïssa Maritain*, 465.
17. Gilson, *Reason and Revelation in the Middle Ages*, 43, 50.
18. Ibid., 57, 60, 65.
19. Ibid., 60.

*anima,* to Siger, that will demonstrate that this Latin Averroist was ultimately a Thomist. The ascription of the *Quaestiones de anima* was a gift to those who believed that Dante's philosophy is the same as Thomas's. Gilson was "too perceptive to accept this revised version of events, and was delighted" when the Italian mediaevalist Bruno Nardi "mailed him an essay" arguing that "there were no good grounds" for ascribing the "anonymous" *Quaestiones de anima* to Siger of Brabant. Gilson told Nardi in 1942 that Van Steenberghen's "case seems to me to be desperate." But was it really because "Gilson sees with Nardi that it is *because* of the Averroist elements in Siger's teaching, not despite them, that Dante welcomes him as a thinker in the heaven of the Sun"?[20] Others, such as Père Mandonnet, had gone through elaborate contortions in order to reconcile the placement of Siger in Paradise with what they perceived to be Dante's Thomism.

Nardi's argument for Dante's Averroism set off from the poet's *political* philosophy, and Gilson believed that his demonstration from Dante's politics in the *De Monarchia* "is a perfect demonstration." If Dante was a political Averroist, then he considered the political order as outside and extrinsic to religious and ecclesial truths. It is within a fear of the political consequences of extrinsicism that I place a prickly book that Gilson published in the year before the war. Why else did he need to make an "astonishing scalp dance around P. Mandonnet" to show, in his *Dante and Philosophy* (1939), that Dante was no Thomist, for his *De Monarchia* proposes two separate, self-sufficient orders, the philosophical-political and the theological-pontifical? For Dante, Gilson says, "Philosophy and the Empire govern the entirety of human life in the realm of nature"; "there remains no element of the natural life of man over which the Pope can claim any authority." Gilson is no less acerbic about a strain in Dante's early thought which "suggest[s] that the miracles of Christ . . . become *possibili* when one sees how divinely miraculous are the splendor of philosophical knowledge and the efficacy of the philosophical ethic": "it will undoubtedly be recognized" that this "does not conform to the canon of Thomist apologetics."[21]

Along with Père Gardeil, Père Mandonnet had been one of the handful of French Thomist clerics who never supported the Action Française. He had, that is, no wish to make Thomism sound like Averroism. Others, such as the Italian philosopher Giovanni Gentile, had strategic reasons for want-

20. Peter Dronke's note in *Étienne Gilson's Letters to Bruno Nardi,* xvi–xvii; "Van Steenberghen prepara il suo II vol. di Siger, ma il suo caso mi sembra disperato . . . ," Gilson to Bruno Nardi, September 5, 1942, ibid., 6; Peter Dronke's note, ibid., xvii–xviii.
21. Gilson to Bruno Nardi, June 17, 1937, ibid., 4; Bars, "Gilson et Maritain," 261; Gilson, *Dante the Philosopher,* 150, 119.

ing to make an Averroist out of Dante. Gilson regrets that "Nardi does not seem to suspect that as an historian he is far superior to G. Gentile, whose immanentism is the scourge of . . . contemporary Italian scholarship with its abundance of learning and ingenuity." He finds that Nardi has taken an unjustified leap in inferring from Dante's political separation of the powers to an Averroism of the philosophical order: as Gilson sees it, Dante neither subordinates theology to philosophy nor maintains, like Siger, "that one thesis is necessary for reason and that a contradictory thesis is consonant with faith." In Gentile's version, Dante "revolted against 'the transcendency of the schoolmen.'" But, says Gilson, though Dante separated faith and reason, still, for him, reason and even political power, the emperor, are dependent on God, and that, the Christian God.[22]

He had told Nardi in 1937, "I don't believe that Dante was either a Thomist or an Averroist; he was Dante." He felt at that time that one could call Dante's thought a "Christian Averroism." But, Gilson wrote in 1939, although "I have long been inclined" to call Dante's thought Averroist, "when I have come to write on this question," the picture looked different. The most "personal" or idiosyncratic of Dante's ideas was, Gilson writes, "the natural incompleteness of the knowledge of the intelligible whose human character compels it to feed on sensible notions." Neither a Thomist nor a rationalist signatory to the Parti de l'intelligence, Dante "believes" in the "immortality of the soul" not because he "perceives it perfectly clearly" but "because he does not perceive it perfectly clearly." As a poet, Dante knew full well of the immortality of at least one soul: even the early, philosophical *Banquet* "is hallowed from its outset by the memory of a heavenly Beatrice who, although she is not yet what she will become in the *Divine Comedy,* is none the less already one of the blessed and, to Dante himself, a summons from the next world." Even in the *Divine Comedy* Beatrice awakens Dante's poetic sense for the supernatural through her "bodily beauty": that "excruciating beauty possessed by some bodies which promise more than a body can hold and other than a body can give." Dante feels for Beatrice the same enthusiastic, Bacchanalian love that Dido had for Aeneas, but the "carnal love" of the poet "is directed far less towards the beloved woman than towards the work which she inspires: . . . it is the poet's love for the woman whose presence liberates his genius and makes his song burst forth." Dante's poem is his register of the supernatural in this world. For there are "two classes of men" for whom physical beauty and

22. Fouilloux, *Une église en quête de liberté,* 72; Gilson, *Dante the Philosopher,* 163, 157, 299, 307.

the emotions it inspires are "redemptive": "the Saint, who perceives all beauty as a reflex of divine beauty, and the artist who, incarnating these emotions in his works, creates for them a body made to measure in order that they may express themselves in it and survive it."[23]

Gilson did not depart from Erasmus in 1939. His philosophical Erasmianism will consist, however, not in reflection upon individual characters, but upon the particular and factual presence of existence. From *God and Philosophy* through the 1942 edition of *Le Thomisme* to *L'être et l'essence*, Gilson turned back from the reality of nature to the priority of grace and fused the two preoccupations; the growth in Europe of a cancerous deformation of political anti-modernism perhaps concentrated his attention. The social anti-modernists had off-loaded some of their resentments onto Henri Bergson, to whom Gilson had listened with the enchantment of Debussy in his ears. He says that between "1905 and 1939," "through many uncertainties and at the cost of many false marches, a Catholic philosopher had to lose a lot of time in order to rediscover the notions which he always possessed." Gilson added that Bergson's "revenge" against his Thomist denigrators was to remind others of the notions of "being and of God": "The philosophy of Bergson facilitated our access to the authentic God of Saint Thomas Aquinas."[24]

In March 1940 Gilson delivered the lectures that were published as *God and Philosophy,* his first work of existential Christian philosophy. The book compares the conceptions of existence in Plato, Augustine, and Aquinas. Plato attributed existence to the necessary and intelligible. Mired in contingency and change, the material world has neither of these qualities. It is not the sensible world, but the Ideas, in their immaterial, immobile, intelligibility, that can really be said "to be."[25]

Plato's gods and his philosophy do not mix: the necessary Ideas and the personal gods of religious story are two separate orders of reality. Plotinus combined his "god" with the first principle of his philosophy at the expense of conceiving the divine One as transcending being itself, with its multiplicity. Such a Deity is not, Gilson says, the object of popular piety. By what criterion are Plato and Plotinus being assessed? We can go back to the "querrelle de l'athéisme," the "demythologization" debate with Brunschvicg of 1928, to see why Gilson is testing philosophy against its ability to make its

23. Gilson to Bruno Nardi, June 17, 1937, in *Étienne Gilson's Letters to Bruno Nardi,* 4; Gilson, *Dante the Philosopher,* 300, 139, 152, 159, 69, 59–60, 71.
24. Gilson, *Le philosophe et la théologie,* 121, 185, 187, 189.
25. Gilson, *God and Philosophy,* 23–24.

ideas and its religious stories work together. Gilson's next step was the investigation of the explosive area of the *revelabile*.

Not even Christian philosophers have always succeeded in harmonizing their philosophy with their religion. Knowing that God is "He Who Is," the supreme act of being itself, Augustine could conquer neo-Platonism, in his theology. Although Augustine saw that God is both act of being and cause of being, he did not realize that this religious insight required a philosophical reworking of the question of what it means "to be." When he had to say what existence is, he plundered the Platonic formulae: the existent is the intelligible, the necessary. Truth is known in its divine Idea. As a metaphysical repercussion of this immobilist epistemology, Augustine's idea of reality is "essential rather than existential . . . it exhibits a marked tendency to reduce the existence of a thing to its essence."[26]

Thus, beginning from the question of the 1928 debate, "Is the God of Abraham at odds with the God of the philosophers?" Gilson finds that one man, at least, overcame the antithesis. As Chenu so lucidly explains in "La théologie comme science au XIIIe siècle," revelation was a "fertile" first principle for the reason of at least one theologian. Aquinas, says Gilson, is the philosophical "pupil," not of Aristotle, but of Moses, to whom God exposed his self-knowledge, by *naming Himself*. Aquinas exercised his reason on the Divine Name. He asks, What is so perfect about how "He is," and *why* is "He is" a perfection? If the divine "*Qui est*" is a perfection, so is the *exist*ence of things. That made Aquinas ask "What is it to be?" This question led him to distinguish the static noun *being*, or *ens*, from the dynamic verb *to be, esse*. The noun *ens* describes the "substance," the stable character of a thing that we bring out in its conceptual definition, whereas the verb designates its "act," that is, its act of "to be," which is not the subject of conceptual knowledge.[27]

Once having divided the noun from the verb, the substance from the act of existence, how do we know this mysterious act of "to be"? It is not difficult for a philosopher to explain to his students what is meant by "substance." He can tell them that "the Oak oaks oakly." A "non-*ent*ity" is that sad personage so far lacking in idiosyncrasy as to be undefinable, and thus the teacher may expose *ens* as the object of definition.

Once having distinguished *ent*ity from *esse*, what type of intellectual act should one say knows the *esse*, the "to be"? In *The Unity of Philosophical Experience* (1936–1937), Gilson had spoken of a primitive "*intuition*" of

26. Ibid., 61.
27. Ibid., 63–64.

being. In *Réalisme thomiste*, (1939), he bluntly referred our knowledge of "existence" to the fact of our combined exercise of sensitivity and reasoning, placing "the grasp of attainment of *esse* in our act of *understanding*."[28] In *God and Philosophy*, he speaks of a sequence of acts, passing from conception through definition to *judgment*:

> we first conceive certain beings, then we define their essences, and last we affirm their existences by means of a judgment. But the metaphysical order of reality is just the reverse of the order of human knowledge: what first comes into it is a certain act of existing which, because it is *this* particular act of existing, circumscribes at once a certain essence and causes a certain substance to come into being. In this deeper sense, "to be," is the primitive and fundamental act by virtue of which a certain being actually is, or exists. In Saint Thomas' own words: *dictur esse ipse actus essentiae*—"to be" is the very act whereby an essence is.[29]

"To be" or *esse*, comes first in reality, because the act that makes a thing exist is also that which individualizes the common substance. A thing is no thing at all, no bearer of a substantiating act, unless it is a particular *exist*ent. *Ens* comes first in epistemology, because it can be conceived. The substantial quality of things, their oakeyness, is held in common with other oaks and is thus conceptualizable and definable, but also universal and nonparticular.

Substances require an explanation at a conceptual level; they lead to Aristotle's self-thinking thought, the eminent self-forming substance. But if, as Aquinas has it, each substance or *ens* stands in reality through its "habens esse," its "having being"; it requires a perfect act of Being to cause it to be:

> a world where "to be" is the act par excellence, . . . is also a world wherein . . . existence is the original energy whence flows all that which deserves the name of being. Such an existential world can be accounted for by no other than a supremely existential God. The strange thing is that, historically speaking, things seem to have worked the other way around. Philosophers have not inferred the supreme existentiality of God from any previous knowledge of the existential nature of things; on the contrary, the self-revelation of the existentiality of God has helped philosophers toward the realization of the existential nature of things.[30]

The Christian philosophers did not first adduce that all substances available for enumeration are contingent and infer from this a necessary first Cause

28. FitzGerald, "Étienne Gilson: From Historian to Philosopher," 51. My italics.
29. Gilson, *God and Philosophy*, 64.
30. Ibid., 64–65.

of existing. Rather, because revelation teaches us that God is the "existential act," the "being whose essence it is to exist," the philosophers were impelled to spell out the difference between substance, or *entity*, and act of *esse*, to exist. This philosophical elucidation is made on a theological basis: "it is only in the light of the revelation of the divine I Am that an alliance can be established between the God of religion and *l'être* of philosophy."[31]

## Differing Reactions to the Occupation of France

When German tanks bypassed the Maginot line, Maritain telegraphed President Roosevelt, on June 15, 1940, urging "the president to make a public declaration against Nazism to support French morale or that country would make a separate peace."[32] On June 17, as 7 million French citizens fled south before the Wehrmacht, Marshall Philippe Pétain seized power. A demarcation line was drawn between Occupied France, in the North, and the Free Zone, or Vichy France, of which Pétain became the chief administrator.

In July, Charles Maurras and his epigones apologized for having been "disrespectful, injurious, and even unjust to the person of the Pope and the Holy See" and accepted the justice of their condemnation. The prohibition on Catholic membership of the Action Française was lifted. Yves Simon wrote to his teacher from Notre Dame that "Fascism is a socialism which has been clever enough to fool the vigilance of the Church, as no other socialism has done." When Marshall Pétain went to Montoire on October 24, 1940, to propose a collaboration between Vichy France and Hitler's Germany, Maurras composed a "dialogue with himself":

Are you in favor of this collaboration?
I do not have to favor it.
Do you oppose it, then?
I do not.
Are you neutral?
No, not that, either.
Then, you admit it?
I have neither to admit, nor to discuss it . . . .[33]

31. Floucat, "Gilson et la métaphysique thomiste de l'acte d'être," 361.
32. Hellmann, "World War II and the Anti-Democratic Impulse in Catholicism," 95–116.
33. Simon to Jacques Maritain, 1940, in Simon, *The Road to Vichy*, xviii; Weber, *Action Française*, 468.

Based on his knowledge of *Mein Kampf,* another Frenchman notified the American people that his neighbors to the east do not undertake speculative circumambulations around political decisions: "as we see it, in her daily life as in her philosophy, Germany is the land of the primacy of the will." Urging the United States not to be delayed by "*reason*" in entering the war, Gilson wrote, "What France is now up against is a fixed will to conquer the world."[34]

During 1940 and 1941, Pétain's speeches against "the false notion of the natural equality of man" and in favor of an "hierarchic and authoritarian" state reflect Maurrasian principles. Maurras' bag-carrier "Georges Calzant would arrive as messenger to carry Maurras' opinions straight into the Marshall's inner sanctum." Admiral Darlan and Pierre Laval were influential members of the collaborationist wing of the regime, which advised the marshall to support Germany's efforts to extend the Reich to Great Britain. Both of them were impervious to the Action Française.[35]

Although it may have looked that way to some of Bergson's disciples, the Vichy régime was not simply Maurrassianism incarnate. Pétain himself was "not of the school" of Maurras; but, Henri de Lubac thinks, the fact that he was "at that time surrounded by men from l'Action française was not . . . a coincidence. For if he admired the Church, it was in the same way that Maurras did, as an agent of order and national cohesion." Vichy was not, precisely, a Catholic administration. The fervently Catholic Jacques Chevalier lasted about a year in its ministry of education. The tone at Vichy was set by Pétain's call for a national revolution that would purge the moral decadence of the Third Republic. The man behind the Parti de l'intelligence, Henri Massis, was the theorist of the national revolution.[36]

The idea of a national revolution charmed many French Catholics and their bishops. In February 1941 the Assembly of Cardinals and Archbishops exhorted the faithful to be loyal to the marshall. The congregations, exiled from France in 1903, were now given permission to return. Although it created good will among Catholics who saw it as a break with the past, the Vichy government's legitimization of the congregations grew out of steps taken under the Third Republic. Gilson had heard rumors in 1935 of a new concordat. Between 1942 and 1944 Pierre Laval devoted his

34. Gilson, "The French View of the War," 452, 454–55.
35. Weber, *Action Française,* 445–46; Cointet, *L'église sous Vichy,* 175, 178.
36. De Lubac, *Christian Resistance to Anti-Semitism,* 20; Cointet, *L'église sous Vichy,* 112.

energies to the project; he "said entirely spontaneously: 'My bishops, my prefects.'"[37]

A key issue for French Catholic intellectuals at this time was how Thomas's politics could speak to their situation. Maritain, who was in New York, was again first into the fray, publishing *À travers le désastre* in January 1941; the text was disseminated in Europe. By July 1941 Simon was convinced of the complicity of Thomism in the triumph of fascism, telling Maritain that "if St. Thomas were alive today, he would be for Franco, for Tizo, for Pétain; that's evident. St. Thomas, that's Garrigou. To do something practical in 1941, with St. Thomas, in politics, is a joke." His correspondent was advising de Gaulle that the moment at which Vichy France was invoking the "teachings of the popes and of the Catholic social school" was a providential "opportunity" for the Free French general "to reconcile . . . Christianity and liberty," Thomism and democracy.[38]

Maritain would later reproach Père Garrigou-Lagrange for taking "the side of Pétain to the point of stating that to support de Gaulle was a mortal sin." Garrigou was "very close" to such members of Pétain's court as Léon Bérard, Vichy's ambassador to the Holy See. Maritain received in May 1942 a letter of concern about his political sympathies from a French mother superior. He told her to tell "them who are concerned about me that it would be more appropriate to be disquieted to see Cardinal Baudrillart associated . . . with the worst politics of collaboration with the enemy, by Père Garrigou-Lagrange fighting politically for the Vichy government, a handful of traitors who try to corrupt French Catholic opinion through the radio and the press."[39]

Fourvière is a district in northwest Lyons. Gaston Fessard and Henri de Lubac were promoting Blondelian theology in the Jesuit house of studies there by the late 1920s. The war deposited Père Pierre Chaillet at Fourvière in December 1940. On the first of his "frequent visits to his cell," the Résistance leader Henri Frenay "asked him to write a religious column" for *Les petites ailes de France* (which later became *Combat*): "I always had the

37. "Pierre Laval . . . dit tout naturellement: '*Mes évêques, mes préfets,*'" Cointet, *L'église sous Vichy*, 313.

38. Simon to Jacques Maritain, July 16, 1941, quoted in Hellmann, "World War II and the Anti-Democratic Impulse in Catholicism," 100; Maritain to Charles de Gaulle, November 21, 1941, ibid., 103–4.

39. Maritain to Réginald Garrigou-Lagrange, December 19, 1946, cited in Komonchak, "Theology and Culture at Mid-Century," 601–2; Maritain to a Mother Superior, June 3, 1942, cited in Barré, *Jacques et Raïssa Maritain*, 503.

impression," Frenay recalled, "God forgive me if I slander the innocent—that plots were under way on every floor in and every cell of this Jesuit residence....I later discovered that Fathers Fessard and Lubac were working...along the same lines as we were. Even today I would not swear that other cabals of a very different tendency were not being hatched in the same honorable quarters. No doubt only the Almighty Himself knew about all of them."[40] As *Combat* began to instigate military operations, it had to forego its religious correspondent.

De Lubac and Chaillet were made to realize the necessity of spiritual resistance by the First Statute of Jews of October 1940. The Second Jewish Statute, of June 2, 1941, led to the first of the underground *Cahiers de témoignage chrétien,* Fessard's "France Take Care Not to Lose Your Soul!" The *Cahiers* were secretly published and distributed from November 1941; Jesuits such as Jean Daniélou would later dessiminate them in the occupied zone. After the Second Statute had become law, Léon Bérard was sent to the Vatican for reassurance that the statute was not objectionable to the papacy. Bérard returned with the news that "as someone from the Vatican has authorized me to say, there is no intention to quarrel about the Statute of the Jews." Bérard supplied a reference to the "*Secundae Secundae,* art. 9, 10, 11, and 12," in which Saint Thomas "recommends taking" in the Jews' regard "proper measures to limit their action in society and to restrict their influence. *It would be unreasonable,* in a Christian state, to let them administer the government and thereby reduce the authority of the Catholics. *From which it follows* that it is legitimate to forbid them access to public office; it is equally legitimate to admit them to the universities *(numerus clausus)* and professions only in a fixed proportion." Bérard's line in rationalization was a little esoteric; it was more commonplace to refer oneself to the Pauline injunction that "all power is from God." Maurice Lesaunier, the Sulpician director of a Carmelite seminary, rested his theological Pétainisme on this biblical basis, in *La conscience catholique en face du devoir civique actuel,* published with the imprimatur of the archbishop of Paris in 1941.[41]

In 1942 de Lubac gave a talk examining the "Causes of the Disappearance of the Sense of the Sacred." He gives four internal causes, each a type of extrinsicism. First, that children cannot reconcile what they learn from their "secular primary school teacher" and from their priest; second, the preference for opposing heresy to "nourish[ing] theology on 'mystery'";

---

40. Frenay, *The Night Will End,* 68–69.
41. Léon Bérard's comment is in Cointet, *L'église sous Vichy,* 205; Bérard's report is cited in de Lubac, *Christian Resistance to Anti-Semitism,* 92; on Lesaunier see Jacques Prévotat's note, in Gaston Fessard, *Au temps du prince-esclave,* 100.

third, the "'clear-cut' separation between nature and supernature," which cuts across the religious person's awareness that the "face of God mysteriously shines" in the whole world around her; and fourth, the rationalism that turns theologians into museum curators of the sacred, men who know that "everything is clear, everything explained. If there is still a mystery there, at least we know exactly where it must be placed." This profanizing theology has handed the world over to the powers that be. The consequence is that, "today…when the essential doctrine of the unity of the human race is attacked, mocked by racism, doesn't one feel torn at one's heart to see it so feebly defended, sometimes?"[42]

In 1939 Gilson had felt impelled to argue that "the autonomy of reason" is not, for Dante, "the right to adopt a line of thought that runs counter to the revelation of faith, and…the autonomy of the Empire by no means consists in the right to govern in a manner hostile to the Church." Taking part in a public celebration of Bergson in May 1941, Bruno de Solages, rector of the Institut Catholique at Toulouse, gave as an example of civil authority "Pilate, representing the occupying powers." In his opening discourse to the Institut in the autumn of 1942, the rector tackled the question of whether the civil authority is the highest to which a Catholic owes obedience: "in doctrinal and moral matters, it is the spiritual authority and not the temporal power which judges what is opportune and what is not." Will the national revolution bring about the restoration of the rule of mediaeval Christian society? Monsignor de Solages gave no answer to his rhetorical question.[43] His words lent some encouragement to Msgr. Jules Saliège, the first bishop to speak out publicly against the round-ups of Jews. Saliège's example was quickly followed by Monsignor Théas, bishop of Montauban.

In the summer of 1942 Père Fessard joined the offensive against Lesaunier's rationalization of spiritual and moral collaboration by writing *Au temps du prince-esclave*. The Jesuit distinguished two elements within the common good. The common good of a society has a material base, those things necessary to the "security" of its physical culture, and an "ideal" summit, those "universal values" that a particular society incarnates. It is morally right, Fessard says, to collaborate with an occupying power so far as the maintenance of the "elementary" or material common good is concerned. Nonetheless, a "slave prince," the ruling authority of an occupied nation, cannot compel "*unreserved* legitimate authority." It is only as prince

42. De Lubac, "Causes internes de l'atténuation et de la disparition du sens du sacré," 15, 17, 20–21, 23, 16.

43. Gilson, *Dante the Philosopher,* 305; Cointet, *L'église sous Vichy,* 236–37.

that he "merits respect and obedience." Insofar as a prince is compelled by a conquering nation to legislate against the superior "common good" of universal moral values, he is not prince but slave and can "legitimately be opposed."[44]

In September 1942 Gilson was wanting news of "young Franco Simone," who was probably in hiding with the Résistance, and needing to find a way of sending the bulky fourth edition of *Le Thomisme* to Bruno Nardi.[45] The 1942 *Le Thomisme* explains that the Thomist conception of the "common good" comes from Aquinas's idea of moral law. Moral laws exist in three forms: first, eternally, in God; second, as humanity's participation in that eternal law, that is, the "natural law," which is "literally written in the human heart"; and third, as the "human law," the general rules of conduct upon which human beings, acting in concert, as in a state, have agreed.

In Thomas's ethics, the human law decreed by princes or states "reduces strictly to the modes of application of the natural law." "Designed to prescribe the particular acts which the law of nature imposes on individuals in view of the common good, human laws are only obligatory in the degree that they are just." No matter what sacrifices he imposes, a prince is strictly to be obeyed so far as his laws are underwritten by natural law: "Conversely, if the State, or the prince, establishes laws which have no other purpose than to satisfy his greed, or his thirst for glory, he promulgates his laws without having authority to do so," and if his laws are unjust "no-one is held in conscience to obey them."[46]

At the reopening of the Institut Catholique in 1943, Monsignor de Solages observed: "'When in the name of morality, the Church intervenes in the affairs of human life, one often reproaches it for mingling in what does not concern it. But, in matters of morality, everything concerns it...I do not admit any other censor than that of the Magisterium of the Church.'"[47] This aristocratic Thomist was deported to a prison camp in Germany.

Noting that Thomas's political thinking is ideal, rather than descriptive, Gilson observes that Thomas's general thinking about politics "moves in an ideal world, where everything unfolds according to the demands of justice under a perfectly virtuous king." Thomas was a "monarchist," because, for the Dominican saint, "it was the essence of a king to be virtuous." In his preface to Aquinas's *De Regimine Principum* (1926), Garrigou had claimed

---

44. Fessard, *Au temps du prince-esclave*, 102–5, 108, 106.
45. Gilson to Bruno Nardi, September 5, 1942, in *Étienne Gilson's Letters to Bruno Nardi*, 6.
46. Gilson, *Le Thomisme* (5th ed.), 372, 373.
47. Cointet, *L'église sous Vichy*, 237.

that "the Common Doctor" of the church taught that democracy demands "a perfection in its subjects which it cannot give to them," whereas monarchy "can bend" to human "imperfection." In an aside, Gilson observes that Garrigou-Lagrange's "ingenious" anti-perfectionism was unduly optimistic, for "if there is, for Saint Thomas, a regime which requires that the holder of power be perfect, it is monarchy."[48]

Under pressure from Vichy, the French Assembly of Cardinals and Archbishops of "October 1943 criticized 'anonymous theologians,' warning against the proposals of the *Cahiers du témoignage chrétien* and indeed also against those of *Prince esclave....* Many bishops repeated to their clergy and diocesans, to beware theologians who do not have the mandate to guide the faithful." During the war, Gilson became "impatient" with the French hierarchy and "closer to God." His son Bernard deplored the "collaborationist tendencies" of the monks who taught him at La Pierre Qui Vire, and carried messages for the Résistance. Étienne responded by giving the monks lectures on the history of spirituality. Gilson said that he was "fundamentally against Vichy and Pétain from the first day of the disaster, that is, from the armistice...and I never looked for anything from that quarter."[49]

Many of his co-religionists hoped that Pétain would support them in their greatest theater of war with republicanism, the schools. Jacques Chevalier seemed the embodiment of this dream. Graduating from the Sorbonne in 1905 as one of Bergson's "favorite students," Chevalier wrote his doctoral thesis on *La notion du nécessaire chez Aristote,* progressing to the chair of philosophy at Grenoble in 1920. He saw the Spanish civil war as a "battle of Good against Evil"; his first educational program was elaborated for General Franco in 1937. In 1939 the philosopher published *Cadences,* which claims that modern philosophy declined because of its neglect of eternity. Bergson has provided a new philosophical grounding for religion: "*L'évolution créatrice* and *Les Deux sources de la morale et de la religion* have demonstrated that 'the force of obligation proceeds...from an aspiration and an élan whose end and principle are shown to us by the privileged spirits, the mystics, a Saint Thérèse, a Saint John of the Cross, as the Love who has made all, God.'"[50]

Chevalier had begun to influence Vichy education policy by September 1940 and became secretary of state for education in December 1941. His

48. Garrigou-Lagrange, Preface to *Du gouvernement royal,* xxvi–xxvii; Gilson, *Le Thomisme* (5th ed.), 459.

49. Cointet, *L'église sous Vichy,* 317; Shook, *Gilson,* 243–46.

50. Cointet, *L'église sous Vichy,* 107–9, 111 (citing Chevalier).

most striking proposal in this office was that the state primary schools' ethics class must refer ethical duties to God. Chevalier tried to preempt discontent among the teachers by explaining to journalists that "the idea of God does not only derive from faith: 'It derives first of all from reason. It can and must be evoked on the rational level, independent of all religious considerations.'" He sought agreement with the secularist *instituteurs:* the orientation of morality to God is a "recognition of one of the acquisitions of reason, because 'human thought has posited it as the sole possible base of morality.'"[51]

Chevalier was moved from the education ministry within a month of writing the decree. He was brought down by his broadcasts in homage to Bergson, who died in January 1941 (tributes which, the collaborationist press felt, neglected the opportunity to "show up a fine case of Jewish boosting and the jobbery of Jewish intellectuals"), by offense at his decree's infringement of teachers' liberties, and by Pétain's need to keep one who had so many useful contacts with Great Britain out of the public eye.[52] After the war, Chevalier would be condemned to hard labor for his collaborationist politics. His is a poignant example of the road Gilson did not take, that of making an immanentist, this-worldly theology out of Bergson's philosophy, instead of using Bergsonism within a revealed theology.

The education minister's successor, the Roman historian Jérome Carcopino, replaced the Chevalier law with one requiring history classes on Christian civilization. The French episcopate considered its confidence betrayed. In his *Sept* articles, Gilson had appealed for charitable donations to the Catholic "free" schools, impoverished since the withdrawal of the concordat. Carcopino introduced state aid for Catholic schools, which, as he indicated to Cardinal Suhard, does not come without "benevolent" supervision.[53]

## Chenu Condemned: 1942

In a letter of February 5, 1942, Gilson told Marie-Dominique Chenu that "the *revelabile* is effectively an *agent provocateur.*" Retreading this minefield, in which revealed theology and philosophical demonstration overlap, had ignited the insight that "saint Thomas alone has constructed an existential

51. Ibid., 120.
52. Ibid., 118, 121–22.
53. Ibid., 131, 138.

philosophy, because he alone has refused to posit *esse* without the *ens* which conceptualizes it, or to posit *ens* without reference to the supreme act of *esse*. His metaphysics is a doctrine of *habens* esse as suspended from *Ipsum Esse*." Gilson had simultaneously feared and been attracted by the sacred space of "*philosophy insofar as it is ordered within theology*" because it led him toward saying that Thomas *believed* in the existence of God, that is, toward the danger of fideism: "they are doubtless going to say that I have interpreted St. Thomas through the medium of Kierkegaard. P. Descoqs would make that assessment." Describing *God and Philosophy* as "the decisive stage in my interpretation of Saint Thomas," Gilson told his Dominican friend that, where the Scholastics, such as "Descoqs, Scotus and Suarez," "forget *esse*" and thus "condemn" themselves to a "metaphysics of the pure concept," the existentialists, like Kierkegaard and Jaspers, "forget the habens," the stuff of nature through which existence is expressed, bringing about "the condemnation of philosophy as such." Existentialism reduces metaphysics to silence, because existence, or *esse*, cannot be defined: "What one cannot conceive one cannot speak about.... [A]n existential metaphysics, which would only be that (= of pure *esse*) is impossible." If metaphysics mentions the unspeakable, it must listen to that which is almost out of hearing, beyond words and concepts. "Saint Thomas appears to me as a perfect equilibrium, but a concealed mystery is part of that equilibrium, and, as we conceptualize whatever we can, the danger will always be, for these interpreters, to break that equilibrium in conceptualizing his mystery, that is to say, in evacuating it." Something in Aquinas must escape the pedagogue who wishes to press him into the service of wordy religious apologetics. Gilson concludes, "This is why one cannot *teach* Saint Thomas."[54]

For many of those charged with ensuring doctrinal uniformity within the church, Thomism was precisely such a pedagogical tool. Marie-Dominique Chenu comments on the "detriment" to the Thomistic "equilibrium," brought about by "miserable abuse" wrought by exercising "the thought of Saint Thomas as an authoritarian arm against modernism."[55] Père Cordovani made it clear, in 1940, that the "modern tendencies" and "reformism" of Chenu and Yves Congar were still suspect. Early in 1942, *Une école de théologie* was placed on the Index. Monsignor Parente explained the action

54. Gilson to Marie-Dominique Chenu, February 5, 1942, in Gilson Correspondence. Gilson's italics.
55. Chenu, "L'interprète de Saint Thomas d'Aquin," 44. *Most* of Gilson's letter to Chenu is quoted on 46; with extraordinary tact, Chenu omitted the references to Descoqs.

in *l'Osservatore Romano,* February 9–10, by reference to Chenu's "relativism and subjectivism outside the norms of the School recommended by the Magisterium." Parente's article is the first to criticize a theologian for the practice of "Nouvelle Théologie." Chenu told Gilson that "the blow reaches not only the booklet but the house as well, and will certainly remove me from teaching." Gilson replied on February 27: "The news . . . would make me laugh if I did not know what a deep pain it is for you to be placed on the Index. I also think of the possible repercussions for your teaching activities and I imagine without pleasure the evil joy of those who have succeeded in engineering this little scandal. All very sad for you and for the Church. Without doubt, we have known for a long time that the Congregation of the Index is not identical with the Church, but it touches her closely, and the blunders of the one do not do good to the other." In a second letter, on February 28, Gilson wrote to Chenu that "we are once again suffering an attack of anti-Protestantism. Instead of correcting the evils and faults which the Reformers rightly noted, one can espouse their errors (Jansenism) or justify the faults. It is against this sclerotic notion of 'theology' that you protest with reason and force."[56] Gilson was disgusted. He "was never able to put Chenu's case out of his mind and he became sensitive to any displays of religious authority. He much disliked the tendency of . . . Charles Boyer to set forth the right and the wrong about papal documents almost as though he had written them himself."

On the instructions of Père Garrigou-Lagrange, Chenu was removed from his regency. He was forbidden to teach elsewhere. "Chenu's troubles . . . contributed to Gilson's hard attitude toward those French Catholics, including members of the hierarchy, who sympathized with Vichy and who were hostile to the *Résistance.*" Gilson once "told Msgr. Montini (later Pope Paul VI) that he had found only three doctrinal issues in Chenu's brochure. Enumerating the doctrines he asked: 'Which one of these, Monsignor, is out of line with Catholic doctrine?' Montini replied: '*Le propre de l'autorité, c'est de ne pas se justifier.*' 'His French,' reported Gilson years afterwards, 'was impeccable.'" Having promised to "try all possible angles" to have the teaching ban lifted, Maritain told Gilson that if Monsignor Montini could not help Chenu, no one could.[57] Gilson attempted to get permission for Chenu to teach in Toronto, while Maritain energetically pleaded his case

56. Fouilloux, *Une église en quête de liberté,* 90, 193; Chenu to Étienne Gilson, February 21, 1942, in Chenu Papers; Shook, *Gilson,* 248; Gilson to Marie-Dominique Chenu, February 27, 28, 1942, in *Deux approches,* 146.

57. Shook, *Gilson,* 248; Maritain to Étienne Gilson, November 15, 1945, in *Deux approches,* 140–41.

in Rome; these initiatives failed.[58] Although he was not alone in disapproving of *Une école de théologie,* the available evidence indicates that Garrigou-Lagrange was chief among those who instigated, perpetuated, and perhaps added to the sanctions taken against Marie-Dominique Chenu.[59]

## Thomistic Existentialism Distinguished from Experientialism

Gilson's end-of-term lecture for his 1943 course on the Latin sources of mediaeval Platonism includes a glowing reference to Jérôme Carcopino's study of the Roman mystery cults.[60] The lecture shows where Gilson thought the fault line between philosophy and religion lies. The historical thesis of "Le christianisme et la tradition philosophique" is that Plato and Aristotle equally influenced mediaeval thought: Plato's influence on the mediaevals was religious, whereas Aristotle's was philosophical. Aristotelianism did not supersede Platonism, because the two worked on different planes within the mediaeval mind.

Gilson makes a cheesewire cut between the Plato who analyzed the Ideas, in the *Sophist* and the *Parmenides,* and the author of the *Timaeus* and the *Phaedrus,* who depicted the individual destinies of believers. Plato knew that his writings contained two different elements: on the one hand, a philosophy that "contemplat[es] eternity," as in the analysis of the Ideas, and, on the other, myths that "tell stories which unfold in time." Plato's religious mythology, such as his imaginative tales about "the origin of souls and their future destiny,"[61] have to "come down" from eternity to time in order to connect with each individual's personal experience of the timeless Ideas. In order to express human experience, philosophy has to be translated into narrative.

As a philosopher, Plato relegated mythology to opinion. The mediaeval

---

58. Shook, *Gilson,* 258–59. Prouvost notes that Chenu's condemnation made it impossible for him to teach at the Toronto Institute of Mediaeval Studies; he says that when he showed Chenu Maritain's letter of 1945 about his case, in 1989, the Dominican was "astonished." "Unlike Gilson," Chenu commented, "Maritain hardly liked me at all." *Deux approches,* 142.

59. Congar, *Journal d'un théologien,* 112–13.

60. Gilson, "Le Christianisme et la tradition philosophique," 264. This article is described in the text as Gilson's "Leçon de clôture," Collège de France, "1943." I gather from this that the 1941 edition of the Saulchoir journal was published several years after its specified date, because of the war. The internal evidence also indicates that the piece was written after Carcopino's stretch at the ministry of education and after Gilson had made a close study of Chenu's piece.

61. Ibid., 255, 252.

theologians nonetheless delighted in Plato's myths of the afterlife, for here "the *pistis*" ("faith") of the philosopher and that of the Christian "believer can and must meet one another, for... they are applied to the same objects." Aquinas did not set aside a shred of this religious Platonism; but it was Aristotle that he drew on when he needed an impersonal and theoretical tool with which to "constitute theology as a science." In order "to objectivize theology completely," Thomas had "radically to detach it from the subjectivity of concrete spiritual lives," no longer "recounting histories, but formulating laws."[62] When mediaeval theology wanted to "objectivize" itself, it relied on Aristotle's definition of science; but when it reflected on the personal salvation of individuals, it turned back to Plato.

When he was describing the formation of priests, Chenu had to explain how philosophy works in the Saulchoir curriculum. He observed that Plato defined the genuine *philosophia perennis* in the *Theaetetus* when he found that "we are in a critical situation" with respect to the search for truth; "Augustine transmitted" such a genuine conception of philosophy to "Christianity as dramatic ardor and personal engagement." This is the conception of philosophy of one who, having read Gilson's *La philosophie de saint Bonaventure,* believes that the truth of Bonaventurian or Scotist Augustinianism lies in "the spiritual experience of St. Francis": wherever its philosophy may happen to be, a "theology worthy of the name is a spirituality which finds the rational instruments adequate to its religious experience."[63] Chenu's conception of metaphysics is that of a theologian.

Gilson was usually exigently attendant to his historical brief, at the Collège de France, but one can play games in the last lecture of term. He had begun by saying that the problem of the relation of Christianity to Greek philosophy can be tackled in various ways, one of which is that of a "philosopher discussing the problem as a philosopher, with a specifically philosophical method." He is not just giving a history lecture, but cutting out and defining some aspect of the essential positions of Plato and Aristotle, making the one to stand for "life," and the other for "knowledge." Plato recapitulated the meaning of his own personal experience when, "in the margin of his philosophy and under the form of myth," he retraced "the story of the soul since its divine birth, to follow it in its pilgrimage towards matter, and traces the way which can lead it toward God." Augustine pursues the same religious quest, because the God he "wants to know is the one to whom a soul who says 'I' can say 'Thou'"; the mythic or religious

62. Ibid., 252, 262.
63. Chenu, *Une école de théologie,* 155, 148–49.

impulse found its "perfect expression" in Bonaventure's *Journey of the Mind to God*.[64]

Unlike Augustine, Thomas "did not confess God, he taught him." To a philosopher, it appears that Saint Thomas intended to "detach" theology "from the subjectivity of concrete spiritual lives, for it shall no longer tell a story, but formulate laws." Thus conceived, the "science of God" is "so transcendent to the destiny of the individual as such that it is more speculative than practical. For this is what is really at stake" in the dispute between Thomas and Bonaventure. That dispute bears on "the initial option between two possible conceptions of theology," whether to be a "science of salvation in general" or "the instrument of salvation for each man in particular." If Greek philosophy and Christian thought form a "diptych," Gilson was drawn in 1943 to the Aristotelian side of the "two tableaux,"[65] whereas his Dominican friend found the Platonic picture more attractive.

Gilson's allegiance to Thomas was clear in the 1940s. His opening sentences are a disclaimer to a unitary approach to theology; the philosopher's "perspective" on that discipline is one among others. Without conceding an inch to the "anti-Protestant" obsession of his Dominican friend's superiors, Gilson did not plan to counterattack essentialism by recourse to existential experience. As he launched himself further into his philosophy of being, Gilson detached his conception of God from all personalism, whether, on the human side, the personalities of Saint Thérèse or Saint John of the Cross, or, on the supernatural side, from any trace of the "personality" that biblical anthropomorphism imparts to its protagonist. All of the creative energy which he had once ascribed to the artistic personality is now situated within being.

## The 1942–1944 *Le Thomisme*

Gilson published a tremendously enlarged edition of *Le Thomisme* in 1942. Two years later, the book was republished, with tiny corrections. The supplemented 1944 version, the fifth edition of *Le Thomisme*, is commonly regarded as the landmark book.[66] This new edition of *Le Thomisme*, "written and published...during the darkest period of the war, 1942–

---

64. Ibid.; Gilson, "Le Christianisme et la tradition philosophique," 250, 264, 260, 264.

65. Ibid., 262–63, 249.

66. It was this 1944 (5th) edition that was translated into English by Laurence Shook as *The Christian Philosophy of St. Thomas Aquinas*.

1944," was that in which "the thinking of Gilson on the metaphysics of St. Thomas' doctrine of *esse* as act of existing takes a virtual quantum leap."[67] Everything in the text of the great fifth edition, from God and his attributes, to the human person, his way of knowing and his ethics, comes back to *existence*.

Anton Pegis argues that it would be "superficial" to imagine that Gilson had in this book "developed from being an historian of philosophy to being a philosopher.... For the same Gilson who ardently espouses the cause of Thomistic existentialism has refused ... to separate the philosophy of St. Thomas from the theology within which it came into existence.... And this refusal is the decision of a historian who has aimed at being faithful to the historical personality of St. Thomas in all its concreteness and individuality." But the 1942–1944 *Thomisme* is a little depersonalized: the spiritual biography of the Christian Doctor with which the 1927 *Thomisme* commenced has been abbreviated. The 1927 edition had gone on from this prologue to the description of Thomas's arguments for the existence of God. The 1942–1944 edition is "substantially refounded." The first chapter, "Dieu," launches straight into "existence and reality." The barely penetrable examinations of the difference between *entity* and its act of existing developed in Aquinas's *De Ente et Essentia* now "become the preamble to all other considerations, and sustain a reinterpretation of the *Summa Theologiae*."[68]

Gilson and Marie-Dominique Chenu were both great historians, in different ways. Carmelo Conticello finds Chenu to be the truly *historical* thinker of the two. "Chenu's theological research was," he says, "an effort to understand sacred history and the concrete effects of the Incarnation, whereas ... Gilson preferred to direct his efforts into the process of the rigorous rationalization of Thomist thought."[69] Whereas Chenu, the theologian, looked to the point at which eternity meets *time,* Gilson, the anti-extrinsicist philosopher, has been seeking the point where the historical human mind meets *eternity*. Bergson had set him off on this quest for a philosophical truth that could be conceived as a *dynamic* eternity. Why was Gilson not satisfied with the *essence,* since a Thomist believes that, as definitions of the universal, essences transcend the fluctuations of time? He says that the Thomist philosophy of existence is a humanism. It does not deny or diminish natures, the intelligible side of reality: philosophy has always

67. FitzGerald, "Étienne Gilson: From Historian to Philosopher," 49.

68. Pegis, "Gilson and Thomism," 437; Prouvost, "Les relations entre philosophie et théologie chez É. Gilson," 424.

69. Conticello "Métaphysique de l'être et théologie de la grâce," 434.

been a "hunt for essences." "But," he goes on, "the great question is to know whether we will capture them and bring them in dead or alive. The dead essence is the residue left in the understanding under the form of a concept, which has lost its contact with its act of existing. Dead essences are certainly much easier to handle." Essences are not sufficiently living to mark what Gilson was looking for. Bergson's student had been worried by Loisy's distinction between the "living development" of doctrine and its "purely logical elaboration."[70] With his discovery of *esse*, Gilson has found his point of continuity, at which time touches an electrically vital eternity. Gilson says Maritain is right to speak of Thomism as an "existential philosophy." For Gilson himself, the significance of calling Thomism an existential philosophy is that it goes one further than those disciples of Thomas who insisted on his use of the real distinction between essence and existence, but nonetheless "essentialized" what Saint Thomas meant by existence.[71]

In *Reason and Revelation in the Middle Ages,* Gilson had wished to show how, for a Thomist, faith and reason are distinct, for Thomism alone keeps clear of conceiving divine revelation as a product of human philosophy. He also had to show that Thomism steers clear of Tertullianism. So, he had said, once offered it by divine revelation, reason can tear off a portion of the *revelabile* and assimilate it into itself. In this process, belief turns into knowledge. Here, a Thomist is one who "does not like to believe what he can know";[72] the *reveable* section of Christian beliefs *can* be assimilated into knowledge. But knowledge cannot be assimilated into belief, or else we marry into the "Augustinian family." Conceiving them as psychological acts, Gilson weights the Thomist harmony between belief and knowledge on the extrinsicist side.

In the 1942–1944 *Thomisme,* the prologue has been renamed. *Le Thomisme*'s new prologue, "Révélabile," has a different emphasis than the 1937 lectures, a less psychological focus. Gilson points out that the psychological distinction between reason and belief is not the same as the metaphysical distinction between the *orders* of philosophy and theology. The psychological impossibility of knowing and believing at the same time does not amount to the metaphysical impossibility of the coexistence of the two orders of philosophy and theology. A philosopher's thinking mind cannot be assimilated into his faith, but his science can be elevated into a revealed

70. Gilson, *Le Thomisme* (5th ed.), 513; Gouhier, *Études sur l'histoire des idées en France,* 134–36.

71. Gilson, *Le Thomisme* (5th ed.), 505, 512. Gilson is referring to Maritain's *Sept leçons.*

72. Gilson, *Reason and Revelation in the Middle Ages,* 83–84.

order. Although the psychological acts of knowing and believing cannot be sustained concurrently, philosophy can exist within theology. A theologian's philosophy is elevated into eternity: "This human knowledge, assumed by theology for its own ends, is what St. Thomas calls the 'revealable.'" The question of who Saint Thomas was and how he philosophized is an empirical matter, which translates faith into natural human knowledge. God's revealed light of faith touches, not the who nor the how, but what Saint Thomas knew, in his philosophy, and retains its supernatural agency. While the act of knowing is extrinsic to faith, *what* is known can inhere in faith. The "pure act-of-being which St. Thomas the philosopher met at the end of metaphysics, St. Thomas the theologian had met too in Holy Scripture . . . two beams of light so converging that they fused into each other," out of which came an "overwhelming truth blazing forth from their point of fusion." Why insist that "St. Thomas thought that God had revealed that it is his essence to exist"?[73] Because, having seen the Burning Bush on holy ground, Moses's human insight was sealed with the sign of eternity, and is no longer just an empirical presupposition to faith.

God is undefinable because his essence is pure *exist*ence, or act of being. An existential Thomism is above all a negative theology. When we proceed to "remove" creaturely attributes from God, in order to name him by "negative differences," each of the divine attributes is a pillar of sheer existence. To be a pure act of being is to be simple; it is to have being *perfect*ly; a pure act is immutable; eternity is "the uniformity of the existing itself which God is."[74] It is being that confers unity; the convertibility of the transcendentals turns on the fact that *being* is one, just as it is true and beautiful.

As a Sorbonne student, Gilson "was passionate about all the arts, but . . . it appears, he had a predilection for music; he was present at every performance" of Debussy's "*Pelléas [et Mélisande]*." During World War I, he had written two articles on philosophy of art, which drew on the aesthetic theory, and the experience of Wagner's Operas; the first of these, "Art et métaphysique," begins from D'Annunzio's observation on hearing of Wagner's death: "The death of an artist is a diminution of the value of the world."[75]

Gilson had written in his notes for his 1917 lectures on Bergson, "Freedom, spirituality of the soul; creative power immanent in the world and which is what religion calls God. Difference from Catholicism." Thomas's

73. Gilson, *Le Thomisme* (5th ed.), 18, 136.
74. Ibid., 141, 148–49.
75. Gouhier, "Post-Face: Etienne Gilson," 156. "Ah, Stelio, t'aspettavo! Riccardo Wagner è morto. Il mondo parve diminuito di valore." G. D'Annunzio, *Il fuoco*, cited in Gilson, "Art et métaphysique," 241.

God is not "immanent in the world," but Gilson wanted to draw out what was true in Bergson's philosophy. He said in 1949 that Bergson "was not mistaken in situating at the bottom and as the root of being, a beyond of contemplation."[76] Gilson's intellectual pilgrimage was a search for a Thomist analogue to Bergson's ever energetic, creative "beyond" of contemplation.

In his 1924 biography of Bonaventure, Gilson contrasted the Franciscan's idea of God with that of Thomas. He "sounded" the Bonaventurian God as sheer, self-expressive creative energy. He had designated the God of Bonaventure, and not that of Thomas, as an Artist. The comparison was tinged with regret for the man whose rationality impelled him to Thomism but whose aesthetic experience led him toward the "fairy-tale" expressionism of Bonaventure.[77] Metaphysicians have feelings, and now as he uncovers the *existentiality* of Thomas's conception of God, Gilson is able to feel Thomas's *actus purus* as musical energy per se. He has learned that the experience at the heart of Bonaventure's theology is present in Thomas, also. The ways of "Saint Francis and Saint Dominic" are drawing together.

To cause is to give of, or reproduce, one's essence. When this Aristotelian thesis is transposed to the key of the Thomist conception of divine creation, one enters an "enchanted universe" in which that which is caused is existence itself. If creation is the production of the "act of to be" of each form, then only God, whose essence is to be, can create. God makes an *en*tity to be by conjoining its matter and form; to give a thing existence is to create this conjunction of matter and form. Whereas the God of Aristotle makes things move, the God of Aquinas is the cause of the existence of their movement, and therefore immediately present to substances. The "resemblance" (Gilson rarely says analogy) of creatures to God is expressed by their act-of-being.[78]

## French History (and Geography) as Common Ground for Catholics and Republicans

At the Liberation, all Vichy legislation was declared null. Through its involvement in the Résistance, Sangnier's *Sillon* movement had evolved into the Mouvement Républicain Populaire. Henri Frenay believed the creation of this political party "a serious mistake": "the war and the Resistance"

76. Gilson, notes on 1917 Bergson lectures, Gilson Papers; Gilson, "Compagnons de route," 284–85.
77. See ch. 4.
78. Gilson, *Le Thomisme* (5th ed.), 147, 116–18, 516.

ought to have buried the problem of "'established religion.'" The MRP was debarred from the lists of the first, local elections through a reawakened abomination of the "clerical peril." From the spring of 1944, the Teacher's Union demanded the abolition of the Catholic "free" schools. Monsignor Théas called for a "new resistance" against the municipal council of Montauban, which suppressed the state subvention to the Catholic schools. After a furious debate in the Assembly, the state's assistance to the free schools was "provisionally" retained. *Esprit* entered the fray against the "divisive" private schools.[79]

In "Pour une éducation nationale," composed in February 1945, Gilson concedes that church education, intended to make pupils citizens of the City of God, and republican education, intended to put children at the service of the republic, are two "universals" that do not appear to mix. Must the two vital parts of France once again go their separate ways? Gilson finds that inconceivable after their common "experience" of "subjected misery": "the French who, for four years, resisted side by side the German peril did not do so primarily for the 'Republic' or for the 'Church,' they did it first of all for France and it was for the same France that they died. . . . But this is not the most beautiful thing. What is most beautiful is that . . . in dying for France those who believed in God poured out their blood for Democracy . . . and . . . those who gave their blood for Democracy died, in their absolute purity of their sacrifice, for the God in whom they did not believe." With a Gilsonian prosaic poetry, the writer finds common ground in French geography, taught with the help of pictures, slide projections and films, and in French history. Free, Catholic schools must "freely assume responsibility for a French public service." The secular *instituteurs* and their religious counterparts must both teach "that our history up to the Revolution was not a tissue of intellectual and moral turpitude, and that our history since the Revolution is not a grotesque decadence."[80] They may take in this respect the example of the Catholic schools of the United States, "over which the national flag . . . floats, the manifest symbol of its will to work, for the Church, in and through the nation." Gilson's note on his transcript indicates that the essay was passed on to General de Gaulle.

79. Frenay, *The Night Will End*, 366; Cointet, *L'église sous Vichy*, 360.
80. Gilson, "Pour une éducation nationale," 123, 129, 126.

# 10

# Gilson's Theological Existentialism

## The Metaphysics of the Exodus

In the new *Thomisme,* Gilson marked out a line of theologians, from Augustine, through Boethius, Richard of Saint Victor, to Bonaventure, whose definitions of God are enclosed in an *essence.* God's essence can be named as "deitas," or divinity. The lectures he gave first at the Collège de France and then in Toronto, in 1946–1947, take the story of the pursuit and capture of stuffed animals up to the present. They were published as *L'être et l'essence. Being and Some Philosophers* (1948) is a version, rather than a translation, of half of the French text. Just before it appeared, Gilson told Canon Van Steenberghen that his book argues that Avicenna was "the predecessor of Duns Scotus more than of Saint Thomas: Scotus qui genuit Suarezium, qui genuit Wolffium, qui genuit Kantium."[1]

## Being a Christian Philosopher Is Not Enough

As Gilson's reliance on the theological mystery of being increased, so it was felt that his use of philosophical demonstrations within the order of nature decreased. "At times," says Vernon Bourke, "those of us who had studied with Gilson in Toronto wondered whether we should go back and study theology, for its handmaid was obviously becoming second rate." *L'être et l'essence* states that the question of the difference between substance and being is "a purely philosophical problem." The distinction of essence and existence is "not a dictate of revelation." Although all Christian philosophers concur in distinguishing creature and Creator, few have referred this fact to the distinction between existence and essence in crea-

---

1. Gilson to Fernand Van Steenberghen, March 23, 1948, in Van Steenberghen, ed., "Correspondance avec Étienne Gilson," 613.

tures.[2] Gilson is belaboring Siger of Brabant for commenting that Albertus Magnus distinguished entity and existence *because* Albertus believed that "things have their being from the first principle," that is, exist as *creatures*. One can, Gilson notes, believe that all things are created by God without finding in them the real distinction. An unwary reader might conceive these remarks as an effort to disengage oneself from the taint of theologism, or as a concession that Christian philosophy does not deliver the goods.

In his initial attempts to legitimate Christian philosophy, Gilson paired the doctrine of God's free creation, as an article of faith, with the principle of sufficient reason, as a proof of the existence of God. In the era of *The Spirit of Mediaeval Philosophy,* he had found that mediaeval theology as a whole had been invigorated by the revealed truth of creation; even Descartes is a Christian philosopher, to that extent. Now Gilson wants to say that a doctrine of creation is not enough. Nor is the "real distinction," to which one can "pay lip service," so as to steer clear of pantheism, but "ignore ... in practice, ... treat[ing] essences as if they were existents."[3] That trap is open for those for whom Thomism is a Christian Aristotelianism. Gilson now sees the revealed truth on which Christian philosophy works, not simply as creation, but as existence. In and of itself, the principle of sufficient reason will not permit us to achieve the fact of existence.

Gilson points to the "rupture" within the scholastic philosophical tradition that uprooted "natural theology" from its soil in "actually existent being." Gilson wants to replant metaphysics, "the science of Being qua Being," in that soil. Can this be a purely philosophical venture? He points the finger back: "It is true that to begin from existence is to suspend the whole of philosophy from an absolute position, but to seek a philosophy which begins without such a position is to pursue a chimera." Not everyone makes "the conceivable rely on the inconceivable": but those who refuse to concede, with Karl Jaspers, that "all philosophy is philosophy in virtue of a source which, as a source, never becomes its adequate object," do so because they "make believe that this ultimate source does not exist or that, if it exists, we have no reason to concern ourselves about it." *L'être et l'essence* intends to make the choice to do philosophy on revealed grounds less than "arbitrary," that is, to give that "option" the fullest mustering of "empirical" support Gilson was ever to supply.[4]

Having traced the essentialist philosophies from Suarez to Hegel, and

2. Bourke, "'Aeterni Patris,'" 7; Étienne Gilson, *Being and Some Philosophers,* 63.
3. Noonan, "The Existentialism of Etienne Gilson," 425.
4. Gilson, *L'être et l'essence,* 141, 318, 308, 319.

found modern existentialism to rest in a nauseatingly "pure sensation of existing which is experienced by a sensibility which is . . . cut off from its intellect," Gilson concludes that "philosophies without existence, existence without philosophy, such are finally the options to which we are today condemned." That is, unless we turn to a position "not formulated by a professional philosopher, but by a theologian," who lived in the thirteenth century. Apparently cutting his alliance with all but one of the "Christian philosophers" and bypassing the "onto-theology" of Aristotelian philosophical tradition, Gilson now develops a "theo-onto-logy." Christian philosophy only holds water as Thomistic existentialism. When Gilson says that "what deeply alters the Aristotelian notion of metaphysics in the doctrine of Thomas Aquinas is the presence, above natural theology, of a higher theology, which is the science of God as known through revelation,"[5] we know that he is still making his case for Christian philosophy.

A final clue that Gilson is still seeking to present a Christian philosophy is found in a scantily veiled discussion of Bergson. A certain metaphysics, he says, avoided essentialism, with its "immobile and static" idea of being, by taking *becoming* for reality. With the whole Thomist family, Gilson recognizes that this is to abandon the human power to know. Just as the concept is the partner to the essence, so "a sort of intuitionism, much closer to instinct than intelligence," is the epistemic spouse of the metaphysic of "pure duration." But Gilson presents the Thomist *esse* as the "beyond" that Bergson was seeking:

> That which this metaphysics has always sought, under the name of duration, is the existence which is the act of being, but it did not know this. How can one not see a certain sign of this in that slow evolution, foreseen from the beginning by the pitiless clairvoyance of more than one adversary, which continually approaches the metaphysics of the Exodus? In its true name, creative evolution calls itself Yahweh. Only, 'I am' is a creator who creates creators, a being whose essence, identical to its own existence, is life, fecundity and movement of such depths that he is the being in which everything has movement and life from the very fact that they owe their existence to him.

The book intends to do equal justice to human knowledge, through essences, and to existence. Gilson says he would have liked to call it "'*l'étant et l'essence*,'" but it "appears to us that we have elsewhere read a book

---

5. Ibid., 297, 320–21; Floucat, "Gilson et la métaphysique thomiste de l'acte d'être," 365; Gilson, *Being and Some Philosophers*, 157.

which bears this title," and he was therefore restrained, "perhaps" by a "false timidity."[6] *L'être et l'essence* is a suitable stable-mate to Aquinas's *De Ente et Essentia.*

*L'être et l'essence* takes up where *The Unity of Philosophical Experience* left off: why has human thought perpetually substituted *a particular science,* an ensemble of related essences, for being? Why, despite the fact that our *existence* in an *existing* world is ever available to us, does philosophy usually bracket existence in order to flounder upon essences? The fact that metaphysics repeatedly drives into dead-ends, in essence analysis, rather than look at its *existential* map, present in every act of knowledge, is, Gilson says, "a paradox."[7] It is not as if people did not know that they existed, until the prophet Moses came along to advise them of that fact; Gilson wants to find out "how it is that what men so infallibly know *qua* men, they so often overlook *qua* philosophers." The map becomes invisible to philosophy, even when it is before its eyes. What Siger of Brabant "does is to ask Brother Thomas: '*What* is existence?' and, of course, Brother Thomas cannot answer.... unable as he was to say what existence is, he had at least tried to point it out, that is, to call our attention to it, so that we might at least realize *that* it is." As *God and Philosophy* puts it, "The human mind feels shy before a reality of which it can form no proper concept."[8] The "science of God as known through revelation" gave Saint Thomas a thematic clue as to how to proceed, with philosophical and human reason, into a mystery; the Spirit that "blows where it listeth" led him to characterize that enigmatic and shadowy figure which slides into every act of human understanding, or to examine what he already *knew,* that is, existence. Thomas saw, therefore, that "being" is not a static noun-concept but a dynamic and causative verb, an act.

## Being as a Noun

If we take "being" in its noun sense, the object it brings to mind is *this being,* or "a being": a horse, a lion, a unicorn. We can *conceive* such things with or without actual existence. We can have as good a concept of "a being" who does not exist, a unicorn, as of "a being" that does, like a lion. Some objects, such as those of mathematics, are more perfectly instantiated, and thus defined, in their concepts than in reality.

6. Gilson, *L'être et l'essence,* 290–91, 20.
7. Ibid., 7.
8. Gilson, *Being and Some Philosophers,* ix, 67; Gilson, *God and Philosophy,* 69.

When philosophy first achieved analytic rigor, with the Greeks, it took the fateful decision to be "existentially neutral" with respect to its objects, that is, to define "being" as subtracted from actual existence. Parmenides equated being with identity. Plato elaborates on the truth that a total re-making of a thing is equivalent to its annihilation: if the tree ceases to be it*self* and becomes a table, it has ceased to be *this* being and become an-other. A *being* is thus the *what* of the thing we can know and name, and if it alters sufficiently to require a new name, it is a new and different being. If one loses one's being in the proportion that one changes, then to have being perfectly is not to change at all, but to remain forever identical with oneself. An object that eternally retains the same identity is most securely identifiable. As mathematical objects are instantiated perfectly in the realm of theory, so being is most appropriately attributed to the Idea, and the Idea is happily the state in which being is most knowable: "conceptual thought" is the progenitor of being thus defined. Plotinus takes the next step: "if being is because it is one," that is, identical with itself, "the ulti-mate principle of being is bound to be the One."[9]

Aristotle seems to make a better start, eschewing Plato's immobilism and defining being as "energy and efficacy." Aristotelian substance is an act, a continuous movement of actualizing form; the oak is an oak by acting out its potential to oak, the potential dog an actual dog by its dogging form. But the determination that the world be knowable got the better both of Aristotle's dynamic metaphysics *and* of his vast empirical curiosity about natural life. Aristotle the zoologist, who wrote treatises about bees and sharks, and Aristotle the metaphysician who wondered at the actuation of form, is also, Gilson claims, Aristotle the epistemologist, who "bungled the whole question" of universals.[10] In answer to the question What is common to all members of a species? he said *the form*. When called to answer the question *What* is that particular thing? we respond by reference to the form, oak. This *same* answer can be given with reference to every other member of the species. What is real in the thing, for Aristotle no less than for Plato, is the form. As that which all members of the species hold in common, the form is indifferent to *particularity*, that is, neutral with respect to *existence*. Take away the matter which individuates them, and all trees are the same act of treeing, all humans the same act of humanizing, and because it can be conceived without individuality, the act of substance can be conceived

9. Gilson, *Being and Some Philosophers*, 6, 14, 21.
10. Ibid., 44, 49.

without existence. Gilson attributes the origin of idealism to the Greeks, as Père Laberthonnière had done.

When Gilson was writing his Giffords, Maritain had encouraged him to recognize that Avicenna is also an heir of the Mosaic revelation. Utilizing the Aristotelian distinction of substance and accident, and the revealed datum that God created the world *ex nihilo*, Avicenna says that existence is an "accident" of essence, that is, not built by necessity into the substance of each thing. He introduced the notion of a beginning and an end, that is, of temporal "might-not-have-been," into the world of substance. History brings with it "novelty," the unexpected variant, which makes any explanation less than complete. Averroës preferred perfection of philosophical explanation to Genesis. Arguing furiously against Avicenna, he seeks to close and seal the world of substances by defining it as *eternal*. If something new could happen to substance, a bit of its story would be left open and unknown to us, and the world would not present a "solid block of intelligible necessity."[11]

The question of whether the world's origin in time is rationally demonstrable or purely a matter of revelation was the axis of the debate between the Christian Averroists and their Augustinian foes. The brief day of the Christian Averroists was cut short by the sword of authority in the hand of Bishop Étienne Tempier. Condemnations do not always have foreseeable consequences, and least of all when they are written in the defense of divine and created *freedom*. Taking Tempier's "charter" as their manifesto, "fourteenth century Christian speculation" wanted "to blow up the solid block of Graeco-Arabic determinism." Ockham put his powder kegs under essences and did his work thoroughly, by "annihilating them first in God." In the story that Gilson is tracing in this book, it is Duns Scotus who is the more influential actor: he had the same Franciscan agenda, which he achieved, not by exploding Aristotelian-Avicennian substances, but "by taking fullest advantage of their existential neutrality."[12]

One can picture the Scotist metaphysics as a conveyor belt along which essences travel, entering upon various "conditions." The first stage is eternal presence in the frozen store-cabinet of the divine mind. Present and intelligible in God's mind, natures have "being of object." They are not present *to* the divine mind: "Their existence in him is His own existence," and in opposition to Averroës's necessary world, "there is in Him no law which

11. Maritain to Étienne Gilson, May 5, 1931, *Deux approches*, 64; Gilson, *Being and Some Philosophers*, 60.

12. Gilson, *Being and Some Philosophers*, 84.

binds Him to create anything."[13] The second stage is the selection of *creabilia* from among the essences: once the divine will is directed upon an essence, with exit from the store-cabinet into creation in view, it enters the condition of a *potential* essence. The third stage is that in which the essence enters fully fledged into the created realm, as *this* essence. The process is defined throughout by the transitional stages in the life of *essences,* as manipulated by the divine will. Essences always exist, whether as the divine mind, as potential "creables," or as this existing thing. *En*tity is intrinsically *exis*tent, the existent being variously conditioned by its position on a trajectory driven forward by the Divine will.

Just as Avicenna had said that existence is an accident of substance, so for Duns Scotus existence is conditioned by essence, as an accidental determination, or fixing, of the location of the essence. All really existing things are individual. Where Thomas ascribed that fact to their act of existence, Duns Scotus attributed the individuality of things to their *haecceitas,* or thisness. In a doctrine in which nothing changes in itself, as it travels the trajectory from divine reality to worldly reality, heccitas, or "thisness" "is not a cause of existence, but . . . the unmistakable sign that the essence . . . is now fit to exist." For Scotus, being is a univocal concept, the same everywhere and in everything. There is no communication of being, through God's existential causality, but a univocal transfer of essences from one condition to another. The divine mind qua horsey object, the horsey object qua potential creabilia, the existent horse, are all one and the same horse. Duns Scotus's metaphysical "horse is still the same as that of Avicenna, only it has been broken in."[14] The Muslim philosopher made existence "accidental" so as to express its created contingency and novelty; Scotus makes existence cave in under the pressure of its accidentiality.

The same logic that applies to finite essences applies to God. The marks of His existence are, first, that He is an essence, second, that He is infinite, and third, that He is "this one." Scotus's God exists, Gilson says, because He is a unified, infinite essence. Scotus practiced Christian philosophy in the broad sense that Gilson had employed in the 1930s, but his faith in God's free creation did not save him from forgetfulness of existence.

Francesco Suarez nearly identifies an *en*tity with its existence. He writes that "used as a noun, *ens* signifies what has a real essence *(essentia realis),*

13. Ibid., 85.
14. Ibid., 94, 90.

prescinding from actual existence, that is to say, neither excluding it nor denying it, but merely leaving it out of account by mode of abstraction *(praecisive tantum abstrahendo);* on the contrary, taken as a participle (namely, as a verb) *ens* signifies real being itself, that is, such a being as has both real essence and actual existence, and, in this sense, it signifies being as more contracted." Suarez defines being, not by the tangential fact *that* it is, but by *what* it is. A dog has its being through its actual dogginess; the essence is the cause of *what* is there. Suarez thinks in terms of an already-there-world. Because his intellectual imagination is taken up in the what-ness of things, when he raises the question of the "real distinction" between *ens* and *esse,* he cannot see what *esse* could add to the fact that the essence is *there,* present in the dog, or what-ever, that it actualizes. As a Christian philosopher, Suarez believes that created nature is dependent upon God, so he knows that essences need not have been actual. But he conceives the Divine creative act as the actualization of essences. Suarez's already-there-world would not have been, without the performance described in Genesis. But he interprets the Divine fiat as a command to the potential essences of earth, sky, sea, fish, birds of the air, beasts of the ground, and so forth, to jump out of the boxes in which they are already there in the divine mind, and to spring into actuality: the conversion of potential fish, birds, and beasts into actualized ones. Suarez is not existence blind, says Gilson, but his "philosophical essentialism . . . forbids" the Jesuit philosopher to observe that "Creation . . . actualizes . . . essence in another order than that of essence, by granting it existence."[15]

Gilson gleefully exhibits the nineteenth-century Roman Thomist Joseph Kleutgen as a super-Suarezian who explicitly excluded existence from metaphysics. For Kleutgen, metaphysical reason is employed, not on contingent and actual essences, but purely on possible ones: "among *the Scholastics,*" he said,

> the *real* is not confused with what is *actual* or existing, nor is it opposed to the possible. The real may be possible as well as existence; and this, Kleutgen adds, "is what Suarez has expressly stated." God save us from our disciples, for, even though this be more or less what Suarez has said, he had at least common sense enough not to say it in that way. . . . Kleutgen . . . not only says it, he emphasizes it: "When we conceive a being as real, we do not think of it as merely possible, by excluding existence, nor yet do we think of it as existing, but we leave existence out of consideration." Whereupon he triumphantly

15. Ibid., 98, 102.

concludes: "Thus, and only thus, can those finite and created things, to which existence is not essential, become objects of science."[16]

Secularized Suarezianism makes its appearance as the new science of ontology, which is "a metaphysics without natural theology, because it is *a metaphysics without existence.*" Taught how to be a Christian philosopher by Suarezian Jesuits, Descartes does not see the distinction between essence and existence as following from the doctrine of creation. The seventeenth-century metaphysicians had the philosophy of their a-theology: "because they have lost sight of Him Who Is, philosophers have also lost sight of the fact that finite things themselves are. The times are now ripe for some systematic science of 'being qua being,'" that is, for the birth of *ontology.*[17] Ontology is metaphysics qua essence analysis.

Drawing on his Jesuit formation, Descartes attributes to each substance one "principle property," its essence. His "worthy interpreter" Clauberg defines the "'root and foundation'" of a thing, its "'principle'" as its essence.[18] That epigone is memorable for having discovered the *word* for metaphysics as essence analysis, publishing the *Elementa philosophiae sive Ontosophiae* in 1647. The form is actualized in Christian Wolff's *Ontologia* (1729).

The contemporary exemplars of *common sense* realism had caught Gilson's attention in *Réalisme thomiste.* In *L'être et l'essence,* Gilson traces the origin of this supposed *philosophia perennis* to Wolff. This "divided spirit" yearned to be a Scholastic but was kept in the closet for fear of Descartes. It seemed to Wolff that Descartes' critique of Scholasticism was most destructively successful on the point of the Schoolmen's failure to define their terms. He therefore claimed that human beings possess a subphilosophical awareness of "general notions" and that Scholasticism was the endeavor to clarify these "obscure" notions. The Scholastics' efforts resulted in a "natural ontology." The "common use of reason" can rise above Descartes' criticisms by methodological rigor, hanging upon an exact use of definitions. This will result in a truly "scientific ontology."[19]

Why should the effort to be verbally precise give rise to the first "*ontology without theology,* that is, a science of being taken abstractly in itself, independent of all question of knowing whether it actually exists or not"?

16. Ibid., 106.
17. Ibid., 119, 112.
18. Gilson, *L'être et l'essence,* 174.
19. Ibid., 163, 166–67.

Ontology "is the science of being as integrally deexistentialized."[20] This is because, for the benefit of the Cartesian objections to defective precision, Wolff founds it upon the a priori deduction of *what could possibly exist.* Gilson's analysis of Wolff results from his digging deeper into the flaws in "Cartesian-Thomism." This questioning follows from the problem of why his Thomist contemporaries denied any influence of Christianity on philosophy other than the ethical.

Taking as his logical criterion the principle of non-contradiction, Wolff works backward into existence from the impossible—the contradictory. He moves thence to the possible, the non-contradictory association of essences. The *reality* of the essence, for Wolff, is its logical possibility: "*quod possible est, ens est,*" he says. Wolff thinks out clearly what could exist and produces a landscape of essences to which there are no logical objections, in the form of internal contradiction. He defines the non-contradictory and primary elements of a being as its "essentialia." What is essential in a being is thus its internal logic; extrinsic to its potentiality, its existence is a side-effect of its reality. Existence enters the landscape as "'the compliment of possibility.'"[21] As an "accidental" or contingent addition to essence, existence does not belong to ontological science. Wolff farms it out to the various sciences, psychology, cosmology, and natural theology.

One can see how such an ontology resurfaces in the neo-Thomist tradition. To defend the intelligibility of being, Kleutgen will look to an *ideal* world of pure possibles, without which "'all our sciences and thoughts are false'"; he can withdraw "science" from the "'realm of concrete realities,'" because "existence is not an object of science, for it is contingent and depends upon the free will of God."[22] For Wolff, in the avant-garde of Roman Thomism, it is essence, as the sheet anchor of necessity, and not contingent existence, which is the object of science.

Leibniz had explained the order of essences by reference to the principle of non-contradiction, while referring the rational legitimization of the order of existence to the principle of sufficient reason. That principle will underwrite the Wolffian ontology. A Wolffian being is thus, first, an undetermined "something," whose essence, second, harbors no self-contradiction; third, this essence must be self-explanatory. Its real existence caused by its rationality, Wolffian ontology is founded not only in the principle of non-contradiction but in the principle of sufficient reason: "every being has a sufficient reason for its own existence." If it fails in this respect, that being

20. Ibid., 169.
21. Ibid., 171, 175.
22. Riet, *Thomistic Epistemology,* 1:66.

"must have it in another, until one attains to a being which contains in itself the sufficient reason for its own existence." Such a being will be necessary. God's existence is necessary, in the Wolffian system, because his *essence* "contains in itself" the cause of his existence. The divine existence is thus also a complement to his essence, which equals itself with so great an ardor of rationality that it *must* exist; "the sufficient reason for the existence of the necessary being" is "its essential determinations." Since it is possible that a supreme perfection exists, and since being logically possible is the prerequisite of the existence of any Wolffian "being," God exists. It would be a lack of perfection in the Supreme Potentiality not to have this complement to his essentiality. As Gilson puts it: "Since the essence of the necessary being founds its existence, and the essence of every being is identified with its possibility, it is inevitably in its own possibility that the necessary being finds the sufficient reason for its existence: *Ens a se existit ideo, quia possibile.*"[23]

Wolff was not alone is applying to such a proof: "all of the representatives of Cartesianism," from its originator to Malebranche, Fénelon, Spinoza, and Leibniz made use of what Kant will call the ontological proof of God's existence, and that because the "Thomist *esse* is absent from the Cartesian world." This "theology of essence" is unable to depart from the circle of "ontology."[24] Gilson had been patiently prowling around the mouse hole of the ontological argument since 1913; now he pounces.

Perhaps his animosity goes back even to a decade before that. In a book much denounced by Catholic social conservatives, but adored by the adolescent Gilson, Lucien Lévy-Bruhl had defended the right of sociology to consider how people actually behave instead of allowing a priori ethical schemas the privilege of "determining 'what ought to be.'" For Lévy-Bruhl, the flaw in Leibniz's effort to develop a mathematical science of ethics was that "the propositions they establish are only of worth in a social system" which puts them into actual effect.[25] For Lévy-Bruhl, a society's ethical theory is derived from its behavioral practices and not vice-versa. Gilson's Thomist conviction that actuality precedes and causes all possibilities has some roots in his reductionist professor's critique of a priori ethics.

One may hazard the guess that when Père Chenu spoke of a Scholasticism that surmounts its philosophical difficulties "without struggles and without problems" he had in mind such formulae as "If being is not the primary and formal object of the intellect, the intellect will never acquire any knowledge of being"; so it is. For Garrigou, the principle of non-

23. Gilson, *L'être et l'essence*, 173, 177–78.
24. Ibid., 159, 180.
25. Lévy-Bruhl, *Ethics and Moral Science*, 26, 16.

contradiction, as "viewed" by Saint Thomas, "following as usual, the teaching of Aristotle," has the task of slaying the monster of Hegelian pantheism. The distinction between nature and supernature, he says, depends upon the principle of noncontradiction.[26]

For Garrigou, the formal objects of the intellect are the first principles, the principle of identity, the principle of contradiction, the principle of *raison d'être*, that everything is intelligible, having its reason for being in itself or in another; these principles are "analytic." Being-as-first-principle must be the object of an intelligence that is not confined to sensation: the human mind as such knows "Ideas which express not sensible qualities, but something which is in itself intelligible and...have ontological validity."[27] Because the Roman Thomist's gravest preoccupation was to portray the "abstract principles" as the expression of the "stability of being, the *identity* of being with itself, the *substantial* character of being,"[28] he takes "being is being" as our first object of knowledge. This truth is perennial to philosophy: "we must be grateful to Parmenides for so resolutely affirming the supreme law of thought and reality, i.e., the principle of identity, which is the basis of every proof of the existence of God." Gilson turns aside, in a footnote to indicate the importance of the principles of identity and sufficient reason in *Dieu, son existence et sa nature:* "Those who reason otherwise, he assures us...separate themselves from 'the traditional philosophy.' Yes, from that which it has become since the time of Leibniz and Wolff, but which is the negation of that of Saint Thomas Aquinas."[29]

Gilson concluded his chapter on the origins of ontology with the statement that this best of all possible worlds is sufficiently reasonable in the eyes of the Wolffian God for that rational Essence to have no choice but to create it. That is, this philosophy is so rational as logically to terminate in the denial of the doctrine of God's free creation. Having permitted what Chenu had called "the philosophy of the clerical functionaries of Joseph II" to run between his paws for long enough, Gilson playfully convicts the contemporary defenders of Christian orthodoxy of, *horrible dictu,* pantheism.[30]

Wolff's ontology was studied by Franz Albert Schulz, professor at Koenigsberg, whose best-known pupil taught that "existence is not a pred-

---

26. Chenu, *Une école de théologie,* 152; Garrigou-Lagrange, *God: His Existence and Nature,* 124 and 159.
27. Garrigou-Lagrange, *Le sens commun,* 115; Garrigou-Lagrange, *God: His Existence and Nature,* 128.
28. Riet, *Thomistic Epistemology,* 1:307.
29. Garrigou-Lagrange, *God: His Existence and Nature,* 197; Gilson, *L'être et l'essence,* 176.
30. Chenu, *Une école de théologie,* 157; Gilson, *L'être et l'essence,* 182–83.

icate." The slumbers from which Hume awoke him were thoroughly Wolffian. Having dreamed so deeply of logically compatible essences, Kant was puzzled by what the actual existence of the triangle could add to the triangle's potential for existence: "Can I well say," he asked, "that in existence *(im Dasein)* there is more than pure possibility?" He found the "added factor" in the forceful style by which I ascribe existence to things: "what" is posited remains the same, whether I posit the existence of Julius Caesar or of God, but "how" I posit the two essences is different. Although existence adds no logical determination to the compossibles of the divine essence, we posit God differently than we do Caesar. Even before Hume woke him up, existence is for Kant a quality of the mental act of signification. In what sense did Hume's "existential explosive" shatter Kant's Wolffian ontology? By making his "philosophical problem": "what are we to do with existence, if all our perceptions are distinct existences, and if the mind never perceives any real connection between them?" Kant's answer would be: "The mind does not perceive such connections, it *prescribes* them."[31]

Kant has a Wolffian left brain and a Humean right brain. Having translated the Wolffian essences into a constituent feature of the self-organization of the understanding, Kant hands the realm of which philosophy can speak over to the calculation of logical compatibles. The aspect of cognition which, in deference to his rowdy awakening by the Scotsman, does justice to the fact that one is alive in a real world, is the sensibility. The lesson the *existentialist* David Hume teaches Kant is that an uncontainable ingredient of existence hammers its way through the window of our sensations. Kant retains one of his shocks from Humean empiricism in the passive, existence-responsive faculty of "sense intuition." Metaphysical realism thus enters his system. The entry is not gained by any law known to philosophy. Hume had shocked Kant's system so badly that existence is, for him, a noisy and incoherent intruder to the faculty of philosophy. Kant makes existence "a necessary condition for real knowledge . . . of which nothing is or can be known."[32]

In Hegel's system, a Wolffian abstract being and a Humean empirical being construct that dialectical synthesis that is reality itself: ontology has the first and the last word in a philosophy for which "the self-movement of the concrete logical notion is the common principle of nature and of mind." One might have imagined that Gilson would be sympathetic to Kierke-

31. Cited in Gilson, *Being and Some Philosophers,* 125; ibid., 122.
32. Ibid., 131.

gaard's efforts to retrieve "existence" from its disappearance into Hegelian logic. Could one not expect this anti-rationalist Christian philosopher to express an affinity with Kierkegaard's deepest question, which is whether religion transcends, or, conversely, is swallowed up by, its rational explanation?[33] Gilson turned ferociously on William Barrett's *Irrational Man* (1958), which describes *Being and Some Philosophers* as a Kierkegaardian solution for the problems faced by Thomas Aquinas: "Our own Thomism," he asserts, "would be exactly what it is, even if modern existentialism had never existed."[34]

"Le christianisme et la tradition philosophique" (1943) was an exercise in taking one's distance from modern existentialism. Gilson's critique of Kierkegaard leads out of this lecture. Kierkegaard's ideal is the identification of the subject-philosopher with the objects of his reflection: "Socrates did not *have* a philosophy, he *was* one." It is only as an *existent* individual subject, with all of his own "infinite passion for beatitude," that the Dane can escape the coils of Hegelian logic. If Hume was a sort of existentialist, Kierkegaard is an empiricist: what matters to him is not *that* we know but *how* we know. Truth then becomes a mode of subjective existence. Existence as faith becomes truth, in Kierkegaard's holy war against rationalism. Gilson turns back to the psychological arguments that served him at the Christian philosophy debate: no human being, he says, has a pure faith that prescinds from any trace of rational proof: "the believer is not a category, he is a man."[35] The spirit of abstraction is not exorcised by religious existentialism. By defining the existent as an absolute act of faith, Kierkegaard abstracts from what concrete human beings are like.

Kierkegaard makes another antithesis, that between existence and eternity. Where, for Kierkegaard, the existent is "that of which the being is strung out . . . , moment by moment," the twentieth-century existentialists take as their object the "essence . . . of being in its becoming in time." Existentialism is simply a descriptive phenomenology. "The true metaphysics of existence," Gilson says, "has never had the phenomenology to which it had the right, and modern phenomenology is not the metaphysics which can found it. . . . It is thus desirable that the two philosophical methods come to completion by uniting with one another."[36] For Gilson, the subject matter of phenomenology is temporality. "Those who want to know who really influenced our metaphysics of being," he said, "should read *Le*

33. Gilson, *L'être et l'essence*, 222, 225.
34. Gilson, *L'être et l'essence* (2nd ed.), 352–57.
35. Ibid.; Gilson, *L'être et l'essence* (1st ed.), 231, 226, 241.
36. Ibid., 243, 20.

*philosophe et la théologie,* where they will find that Kierkegaard played no role in it, it was much more a question of Bergson."[37]

## Existence as a Verb

Gilson habitually sat in cafés, offices, and his sitting-room, silently perusing his *Summa,* until he disturbed his neighbors by "spontaneously exclaiming 'How intelligent that man was!'"[38] It is only Aquinas, he says, who maintains an "equilibrium" between existentialism and essentialism. The equilibrium is less of a tightrope walker's balancing act than a fire-swallowing; the fire being plunged into the damp regions of the throat, how can it come out again as fire, and the performer survive the ordeal with tongue and vocal chords intact? The fire is not extinguished, and the watery throat survives, because they belong to different orders of reality, or *causality.* For Aquinas, "being" is created in two ways, both in its act of substancing and its act of existing. His Creator causes "being" both in respect of the noun-substance, or *ens,* the entity, and in respect of the verb-that, *esse,* or "to be." God creates the "to be," or *esse,* in an act of efficient causality; He creates the substance in an act of formal, that is, forming, causality. A mental cartoon of balloons filling out with the water of existence is misleading, for there is *no* thing there to be filled, unless there is existence. Gilson says that to "posit substance as the proper receiver of existence . . . is not to posit it as a 'container' into which existence has but to flow in order to make it be. So long as there is no existence, there is no receptacle to receive it."[39] How can a world of empirical individuals also be a world of rational universals? The empiricists stop at the specificity of this particular cat. When the rationalists absolutize the rational universal, the individual cat disappears into the realm of conceptual essences. As existential-substantialist, Aquinas can say that what demands my attention is the individual *exist-*ence of the cat, its "to be" hurling itself at knees and lap, whereas the universal essence of "cat," which can be conceptually relegated to suspended animation, or neutralized existence, is its substance or *ens.*

What does it mean to call the energetic verb "to be" a substrate, and even a *particularizing* substrate? Lifting an analogy from Gilson's *Painting and Reality,* we can say that existence creates the squared canvas upon which essence paints and that this rectangle is in itself the cause of the thisness or

37. Gilson, *L'être et l'essence* (2nd ed.), 378.
38. D'Alverny, "Nécrologie Étienne Gilson," 428.
39. Gilson, *Being and Some Philosophers,* 169.

individuality of the painting, the boarded boundaries upon which the painting takes shape. No canvas, no painting, and thus existence itself individuates substance. As the oils are brushed on to it, the painting makes its canvas into *what* it is, so that the substance "colors" its existence, formal and efficient causality acting "reciprocally" upon one another. Although it be a mere "habens esse," created reality is no *thing* without its substance.

The effort to define reality by the principle of non-contradiction has to withdraw from the concrete before it begins, because reality allies contradictory essences; Thomas's embodied thinker is Pascal's "abyss of contradictions." The principle of identity fares no better, for as Kant learned from Hume, we cannot explain one thing by another; no essence can explain another, because essences "retrench" upon themselves alone. Nor can we explain anything by itself. Illogical, unreasonable, and therefore unforeseeable and improbable, nature finds a limited analogy in the unpredictability of art. The actual existence given to the *Saint John Passion* by Bach is what makes that oratorio possible; it has no "potential" reality in limbo prior to its creation. The "possibility" of the work's existence is measured by the "existence of the artist," as its first cause. The existence of a fourth choral for organ by César Franck is impossible because the composer did not create it. The possible is a product of the actual, because only actuality is creative and sufficiently productive to unify "the 'other' in a 'same' which is transcendent to the order of essences and capable of making them coexist."[40]

## A Wagnerian Epistemology

Gilson's "quantum leap" into *L'être et l'essence* was assisted by the freshly clarified epistemology of the 1942–1944 *Le Thomisme*. Aquinas distinguishes the act of the apprehension of a single essence, as a simple or undivided act, from the judgment of existence, as a complex act in which two objects are combined. Like the existence it intends, judgment is a "dynamic" act. It focuses on the "copula," the "is"; it affirms that the known essence really exists.[41] Apprehension of essence, or *ens,* is the first noetic act. The intellect assimilates the specific form of an object, through which it knows the *entity.*

Unless we know whether a thing exists, our mental exercises about its "whatness" are futile. The act of conceiving *what* an essence is leads to a final act, in which we judge *that* the essence exists. Judgment is a process of

40. Gilson, *L'être et l'essence* (1st ed.), 301–4.
41. FitzGerald, "Étienne Gilson: From Historian to Philosopher," 52; Gilson, *Le Thomisme* (5th ed.), 62.

uniting or separation: one either unites *what* one knows to existence, to its being in the thing, or separates the quiddity from existence, finding in it no pairing with reality. Judgment bears upon truth: is our known "whatness" actualized by an existing counterpart? Judgment is the act of a concretely existing and embodied human being: "An organic chain of mental operations links the sense perception of what is known as being to the abstraction and to the judgment through which one knows it as being. . . . [I]t is sensible concreteness itself which is known as a being. The whole cycle of operations which begins in sensible intuition ends in the very same sensible intuition, and at no moment . . . does it get out of it."[42] Gilson materializes the act of knowledge, but he does not rest in a simple "empiricism" of apprehension: in perception, we experience existence; in judgment, we say that our experience is true.

Why should it be useful to say that "sensory perception is the vital exchange which constantly takes place between existing intellectual souls and actually existing things. It is . . . the meeting point between distinct acts of existing"?The old Thomist dictum that "truth is the adequation of mind and reality" can be shot to pieces by any "candidate for the Baccalaureate," when it is conceived as a mind taking "photographs" of reality. No such mental "transfer" or copy ever duplicates its object in its entirety; knowledge of the object becomes an unapproachable goal. Both Garrigou and Maritain had answered these criticisms of the representative theory of perception by reference to the epistemological fact that we do not know the concept, we know the object *through* the concept. Gilson takes this one step further. He puts the point that knowledge is a *relation* into the framework of the dynamics of existence: "intellectual knowledge 'conceives' existence, but the fruit of that conception," judgment, "is not an 'objective concept' of some essence, it is an act which corresponds to an act." Act touches upon act; it is because, in the Thomist metaphysical anthropology, "our intellects are existents that they can grasp existence."[43]

In Gilson's philosophy of art, it is by dint of communion with the artist's expressed intentions that we are brought to appreciate what a work of art is doing. Wagner's operas, he had said in 1915, prepare us to "model our psychic 'I' on the will of the artist expressed in the work of art."[44] He seemed to picture aesthetic experience more as a direct encounter with an artist's

---

42. Gilson, *Being and Some Philosophers,* 206–7.
43. Ibid., 207; Gilson, *L'être et l'essence* (1st ed.), 291–93; Maritain, *The Degrees of Knowledge,* 145–46; Garrigou-Lagrange, *God: His Existence and Nature,* 140–141; Noonan, "The Existentialism of Etienne Gilson," 437.
44. Gilson, "Art et métaphysique," 257.

creative energy than as engagement with the "essence" of their works. It is likewise in the newly minted "Thomist" theory of judgment. Judgment is creative energy meeting creative energy. Everything that attracted Gilson to the individual artistic personality is now sublimated into the existent.

Chenu had said, "Pity the intellect which, because it has *explained* everything, no longer *sees* anything: dialectic has become the solvent of contemplation." Gilson concludes, "There are philosophies, William Ernest Hocking aptly says, which rest *on assumption,* while some others rest *on seeing.* The philosophy which naturally follows from the above-defined conception of being definitely rests on seeing. And it does not do so in virtue of any assumption. The only excuse there is for a philosopher to make an assumption is that he does not see. He who assumes *thinks,* but he who sees *knows.*" "Sight" is the most obvious metaphor for what Gilson is getting at, but it *is* a metaphor. He uses it to convey the fact, simultaneously blunt and mysterious, of the presence of existence to us. The act of knowledge "escapes representation"; we must not try to picture it: but being is nonetheless "included in all intelligible enunciation."[45] We maneuver around existence, through essences.

## L'être et l'essence: A Work of Philosophy, Not of History

In 1915 Gilson had defined art as "a *poesis,* that is, an activity that produces new realities." He had claimed for the artist the power of bringing about "the existing of beings which other men can know but which they do not have the power to create; if he himself had not existed, they would not have existed." As we have several times remarked, he went on in 1924 to distinguish the philosophies of Thomas and of Bonaventure on the ground that the Franciscan, but not the Dominican, saint portrayed God as an artist. Now, in *L'être et l'essence,* Gilson confidently affirms that God is the "supreme Artist."[46]

This alteration can be interpreted variously. One could say that Gilson no longer sees Thomas's God as a "static" act of existence[47] but rather realizes that Thomas's God has all of that liveliness and vitality he had once discovered in Bonaventure's expressive God. Another view is that the Gilson

45. Chenu, *Une école de théologie,* 164; Gilson, *Being and Some Philosophers,* 212; Gilson, *L'être et l'essence* (1st ed.), 299.
46. Gilson, "Art et métaphysique," 254; Gilson, *Bonaventure,* 158–59; Gilson, *L'être et l'essence* (1st ed.), 304.
47. Gilson, *Bonaventure,* 158. The French is cited in ch. 4 n116.

of 1947 is not such a pure Thomist as he claims but has imaginatively identified the God of Thomas with the God of Bonaventure. Twenty years later, pricked by his empirical, *chosiste* conscience, Gilson will abandon the claim that God is an artist. Neither Saint Francis nor Saint Dominic ever got the upper hand in his thought.

Gilson commented in 1925 that no philosopher has just one idea. A philosopher employs numerous building blocks, each balanced against the other's weight: "The work of the philosopher is precisely to ensure that equilibrium by adjusting and organizing the theses."[48] Perhaps that analogy lodged in his mind because it is not only architectural but aesthetic; one may picture this equilibrium as the balance between blocks of color in a painting by Paul Klee. In his "Remarques sur l'expérience en métaphysique," a paper given in Brussels in 1953, Gilson ascribes this insight to one of his Sorbonne professors: "Victor Delbos used to say that every philosophical doctrine is the result not of one principle, but of a compromise among a number of principles, some of which serve to prevent any of the others from developing the whole train of its consequences."[49]

If each principle stands for an "essential" idea, and an "idea," like a gene cell, will, if left to its own automatism, perpetually reproduce itself, an individual philosopher can limit or modify this reproduction by cross-fertilizing it with different cells. Thus, Kant uses the active understanding to show how we organize the "logical compossibles" in which our experience of the world is given and the passive sensibility and the noumenal realm to express his intuition that a world beyond us exists. The primitive cells retain their integrity within the synthesis. So the German idealists can clone from Kant's construction a new monster, using only the cell containing the idea of the active understanding.

The task of the philosopher is to examine such ideas *independently of their place in history and of their historical sequence.* Once he does that, "the observer loses the right to attach proper names to them"[50]: "occasionalism" generates theologism, whether in the mind of Al Ashari or of Père Malebranche, and not because the latter was influenced by the former. When one speaks of "theologism," or "Suarezian onto-theology," one is not referring to what Gilson understands as the *history* of philosophy. Once having extracted one idea from the personal bundle in which it had been a single stick, a writer departs from historical biography, and enters the realm

48. Lefèvre, *Une heure avec... Étienne Gilson,* 71–72.
49. Gilson, "Remarks on Experience in Metaphysics," 40–41.
50. Ibid., 42.

of philosophy. The experimentalist who cuts a single cell from the rounded synthesis formed by a philosoph*er,* and describes the "dialectic" whereby the *x* cell becomes *a,* then *b,* and then *c,* is discerning the necessary chain of growth of philosoph*ies.*

The "Remarques sur l'expérience en métaphysique" are an apologia for Gilson's impersonal works, *The Unity of Philosophical Experience, God and Philosophy,* and *L'être et l'essence,* in which he turns aside from the architectonic balance of ideas within an individual philosopher to theoretical patterns. He achieved in these works a kind of philosophical cubism. Just as the cubist painters attempted to make space show a Bergsonian, musical "duration" by painting an object's many movements collectively on a single canvas, so Gilson's "cubist texts" cut out blocks of ideas from their varying historical contexts in order to re-present them in an almost a-chronological simultaneity. If *L'être et l'essence* is a work of "cubist historiography," that is, an aesthetic realignment of the historical tradition of philosophy, then, whether the God it portrays is "Bonaventurian" or "Thomistic" in inspiration, the book issued from the "Franciscan," not the "Dominican" side of Gilson's mind.

Géry Prouvost considers that Gilson gradually became a "more 'exclusive Thomist.'" He dates the "primacy of Thomas Aquinas" to the early 1940s, and especially to "the fourth edition of *Le thomisme,*" which, he says, "decided the birth of Gilsonism." But "Gilsonism" may have seen daylight by 1936, for as its parent ruefully remarked to Henri Gouhier, "I never conceived *The Unity of Philosophical Experience* as a book of the history of philosophy. Many have mistaken it for that. . . . I believe in the possibility of an experience of metaphysics, where the doctrine serves only to verify *in concreto* the abstract necessity of certain intelligible relations. I spoke of it one day, in Brussels, I believe, but it must be an absurd idea, for it had no come back whatsoever. R.I.P."[51]

Gilson claimed that he wrote two types of book, *histories* of philosophy and *philosophical* works. His philosophies, based in experimental play with the "essence" of an idea, discover "common systems." In *Reason and Revelation,* all the "Augustinians" are convicted of Platonist error. In *L'être et l'essence* the "Aristotelians" stand for essentialism. A rough calculation among Gilson's notable books numbers those dedicated to descriptive history, in-

---

51. Prouvost, "Postface," in *Deux approches,* 278, 280; Gilson to Henri Gouhier, June 6, 1966, in "Lettres d'Étienne Gilson à Henri Gouhier," 478.

cluding vast tomes such as the eight-hundred-page *History of Christian Philosophy in the Middle Ages* (1955) and biographical studies like *Héloïse et Abélard* (1938) at thirty-two,[52] and those devoted to philosophy at twenty-three. Someone who has read a few of each may retain the impression that Gilson was the author of a slippery slope argument: "*once* you have Scotus, you get Kant; with Suarez, Kleutgen looms on the horizon: these figures are what the authors of *1066 and All That* designate as 'Bad Things.'" Henri Bars asks, "Is it historicism to oppose a philosophy with the lessons given by the history of philosophy?" Gilson's response was that his philosophical analyses are not intended to be *historical*. By the time he published the second edition of *Being and Some Philosophers*, in 1952, he was seeking to make this clear: this is "not a book in the history of philosophy," he says in the preface, "it is a philosophical book, and a dogmatically philosophical one at that."[53] As a Thomist, he believed that essences are indifferent to temporal position.

The disclaimer leaves some questions open. If "Plato," "Aristotle," "Suarez," "Leibniz," "Hegel," are not historical labels, then what Gilson says about them is outside historical refutation or verification. If these philosopher's names *are* intended to have some historical reference, then the "internal necessity of metaphysical essences" must have evolved through a process of *historical* causation, given that they do not exist prior to their creation in the limbo of potentiality.

A further question is whether it is circular to state, as Gilson so often does, that his subjects have *failed*. The test seems to be subscription to Gilson's existential realism. He was aware that neither the history of philosophy nor experimenting on essences can show us truth. Metaphysics, he says, "rests on the intellectual intuition of first principles and the direct perception of their truth." This "metaphysical experience alone gives us direct access to the truth." What then, is the purpose of his philosophical laboratory experiments? It directs us to a decision: "Leading in every case to an intellectual choice,... experimentation... leaves to the philosopher the discernment of truth, the vision of which will of necessity determine his choice." Gilson's meta-historical test "does not make us see; it leads us to the point from where we see."[54] Although he steadily resisted the identification

---

52. The indispensable bibliographical guide to Gilson's published writings is Mc-Grath, *Etienne Gilson: A Bibliography/Une Bibliographie*. I say a rough calculation because one cannot distinguish a notable book on one's fingers.

53. Bars, "Gilson et Maritain," 269; Gilson, *Being and Some Philosophers*, ix.

54. Gilson, "Remarks on Experience in Metaphysics," 43–44, 46.

of truth with beauty, the purpose of Gilson's "cubist" philosophical works is to make the truth of his essential insights about the philosophers beautiful, so that it can be clearly seen.

It is felt that it was as a literal-minded historian that Gilson objected to developments of Thomas's thought. Géry Prouvost contends that Maritain was "more open than Gilson to the principle and the possibility of using Thomistic philosophy to tackle living, contemporary problems, unknown to St. Thomas: that is the sense of Maritain's formula 'apostle for our times.' The divergences between Gilson and Maritain about the 'commentators,' and that concerning the difference between 'critical realism' and 'methodical realism' originate here." *L'être et l'essence* concludes with an exhortation to carry on where Saint Thomas left off. Thomas did not work out a metaphysics of being in full, and the lacunae has not been made good, for Thomas has had many commentators but "few imitators": "The only genuine way to do so would be to redo his work as he himself would do it today beginning from the same principles and going further than him in the same way which he already opened up. If these principles are true, their fecundity has certainly not been exhausted. . . . The history of philosophy has not come to an end; to the contrary, the story of so many adventures run by thought invites us to run them anew, and the best moment for it has perhaps arrived."[55] As we shall see in the next chapter, these remarks were not well received by a Roman Thomist, but this is no good reason for historians or philosophers to neglect them today.

But why did Gilson himself not insist that he had as good a claim to be a contemporary Thomist philosopher as, for example, Maritain? It may have been because *L'être et l'essence* had no serious come back among the secular philosophers. As Gilson told a Thomist friend in 1950, "I have remained, as an *historian,* but, as a philosopher, I have long since ceased to appear at the Société française de philosophie, where I would have the effect of a dinosaur. The last time that I brought Jacques Maritain there, his speech lifted me off my feet. After the meeting, the excellent Bouglé said to me, 'He is mad.' Scholastics and 'moderns' form two separate worlds: the first is peopled by priests and monks, with their disciples; the second, more mixed, but in which, in every way, a priest, a religious, or a Catholic can only belong if he is 'antischolastic.'"[56] If the project of promoting Christian philosophy had initially been a mission to the Gentiles and Jews,

55. Prouvost, "Les relations entre philosophie et théologie chez É. Gilson," 430; Gilson, *L'être et l'essence* (1st ed.), 321–22, 328.
56. Gilson to M. M. Labourdette, September 26, 1950, in Donneaud, ed., "Correspondance Étienne Gilson-Michel Labourdette," 515.

Gilson largely withdrew from full-frontal attack. He had half a dozen great works of philosophy yet to create, all of them deepened excursions into the mountain he had climbed in *L'être et l'essence.* Although the author does not resist sideswipes at "separated philosophy," none of these books is explicitly set out as a defense of Christian philosophy. The exception to that rule, *Elements of Christian Metaphysics,* is an enchanted manual for Catholic college students. Gilson fell back on calling himself a historian partly out of misplaced modesty and also because he considered that those who made a direct attempt to "work" Thomism creatively had missed Thomas's greatest insight.

Thus, and this is where he derives his reputation for refusing to go beyond the letter of the *Summa Theologiae,* Gilson continued to put his philosophical perspective to his fellow Thomists, disguising a quest for metaphysical truth as an insistence upon a historically accurate interpretation of Saint Thomas. He conceded that "to reflect philosophically on the givens of history is certainly not the most direct method, nor the best, but one seeks the truth as one can."[57] One always knows truth mediately, and Gilson saw the truth through history.

Gilson had been taught by the "Erasmian" Lévy-Bruhl. In his obituary tribute to him, Gilson recalled his teacher's intellectual generosity; he once found his professor marveling over *L'evolution créatrice,* which he pronounced admirable and without a word of truth in it.[58] One feature of the public speaker that made the secular universities respect this "dogmatic realist" is the unfailing respect with which he speaks of Abelard, Kant, Comte. One can make "Gilson Thomism" into an easily memorable system, a pure position that requires no correlation with historical facts, only by eliminating the Erasmian building block and traducing the Bergsonian one. Gilson loved philosophy, and history also. A contrite Erasmian historian, who had disagreed with Van Steenberghen about the authenticity of some of the texts attributed to Siger of Brabant, told the canon in 1949 that "it seems to me that we mix up philosophy with history, and that, starting with my own, our classifications are often more doctrinal than historical.... Not one single 'ism' fits all of the facts. Irenicism is the only one with which we should concern ourselves and do not doubt that I will address myself to this lesson."[59] The beauty of history, as Gilson knew full well, was of a different, rather more opaque, order to that of philosophy.

57. Gilson, *L'être et l'essence* (1st ed.), 20.
58. Gilson, "Mon ami Lévy-Bruhl, philosophe, sociologue, analyste des mentalités," 1.
59. Gilson to Fernand Van Steenberghen, March 23, 1949, in Van Steenberghen, "Correspondance avec Étienne Gilson," 616.

Gilson observed, with ironic courtesy, that "whatever one may think of its intrinsic value," the philosophy of Wolff was "well-made for teaching."[60] He had pressed himself to greater clarity about what he was doing as a teacher and decided that he was pointing to something he could not describe. He had said in his inaugural lecture at the Collège de France that his great forerunner had taught him to go beyond the documentation of historical facts to the eternal message taught by the philosophers; no one stated with greater care than Bergson that this message is known by "sight" alone and is unvoicable. Nonetheless, that further step to existence is, not beyond metaphysics, but the final step metaphysics is compelled to take. The "conclusion" of *L'être et l'essence*, Gilson said, is "that the metaphysics of all times has wanted to take the essence of the entity as its object, but that, by the force of things, it has found itself continually constrained to surpass the entity in order to seek its root beyond itself."[61]

60. Gilson, *L'être et l'essence* (1st ed.), 163.
61. Gilson, *L'être et l'essence* (2nd ed.), 371.

# 11

# Ecclesial Cold War

## Return to the Sources at Fourvière: The Nouvelle Théologie

Victor Fontoynant, the prefect of studies at Fourvière, loved the Greek Fathers. He developed two schemes to give modern people access to them. The first initiative to make headway, in 1942, was the series *Sources chrétiennes,* in which the Greek texts of the fathers were printed alongside French translations. *Sources chrétiennes* was overseen by de Lubac, in Lyons, and Père Jean Daniélou, in Paris; Daniélou eventually took over sole directorship. Père Henri Bouillard looked after the second series, *Théologie,* whose first titles included Daniélou's *Platonisme et théologie mystique: Essai sur la doctrine spirituelle de Grégoire de Nysse,* Bouillard's doctoral thesis, *Conversion et grâce chez saint Thomas d'Aquin* (1944), and Henri de Lubac's *Surnaturel* (1946).

The Jesuits of Fourvière conceived these projects as works of intellectual evangelization to their European contemporaries, many of whom, as they took it, were unlikely to be converted from agnosticism by Scholastic dialectics. If *Sources chrétiennes* and *Théologie* floated on a shared love for the Greek sources of Christian thought, they carried, as a negative ballast, a conception of neo-Scholastic Thomism as evangelically inexpedient. A Dominican who was still at Saulchoir, Père Yves Congar, told Marie-Dominique Chenu in 1946 that "'baroque theology'" was daily being liquidated, and the Jesuits were in the avant-garde of its "liquidators." Others, some of them in positions of ecclesial authority, shared this perception, conceiving the *Sources chrétiennes* as an "instrument of warfare against classical, more particularly, Thomistic, philosophy and theology."[1]

The Fourvièrists did not publicly indicate that Greek patrology was being selected *in preference* to Thomism. It was Daniélou who broke the strategic

---

1. Congar, *Journal d'un théologien,* 59, see also 24; de Lubac, *At the Service of the Church,* 310.

silence, in "Les orientations présentes de la pensée religieuse," published in the spring of 1946. The editor of *Sources chrétiennes* rounded up an advertisement for patristic theology by denouncing contemporary Scholasticism as a stagnant pool within "the immobile world of Greek thought," which missed the opening for Christianity located in modern people's attachment to "history," and in the "dramatic world of persons," those "concrete universals" distinguished by existence, not "intellection." Daniélou's piece was a "red rag" to the Roman bull.[2]

In August 1946 Pius XII told a gathering of Jesuits at Castel Gandolfo that "there has been too much talk for some time about new theology." In September, the Pope warned the Jesuits that a church founded on changeless dogma must examine with caution anything calling itself a "new theology." By the end of the month, Daniélou had been formally denounced and the seminarians at the *Angelicum* had learned that Père Bouillard was a modernist.[3]

The French Jesuits did not name their work a "new theology": it was through Père Garrigou-Lagrange that Fourvièrisme acquired that connotation. In the same year, Père Reginald published a piece that assesses the Lyons project from a negative perspective. "La nouvelle théologie où va-t-elle?" finds in Bouillard's *Conversion et grâce chez saint Thomas d'Aquin* a noxious mixture of Blondelianism and evolutionism, theories which had little novelty for the Roman Thomist. Blondelianism leads the new theologians to imagine that theology must be *"actuel,"* that is, have living relevance. The evolutionism causes Bouillard to distinguish theological forms from the philosophical notions in which they were originally cast, updating the notion at the cost of the truth of the theological form. The answer to the question Where is the New Theology going? is, obviously, "to modernism."[4] The Fourvièristes thought they were giving the liturgy and apologetics a fresh existential concreteness; for the Roman Thomists the Nouvelle Théologie stood for the promotion of doctrinal relativism.

## Surnaturel

When the Gestapo entered Lyon in late 1942 de Lubac seized three completed chapters of a book and fled into hiding, where he wrote the bulk

---

2. Daniélou, "Les orientations présentes de la pensée religieuse," 14; Fouilloux, *Une église en quête de liberté,* 280.
   3. De Lubac, *At the Service of the Church,* 60, 194; Fouilloux, *Une église en quête de liberté,* 193; de Lubac, *At the Service of the Church,* 194.
   4. Garrigou-Lagrange, "La nouvelle théologie où va-t-elle?" 143–44.

of his masterpiece. *Surnaturel* would not have made so many waves if it had not been delightfully *surfaite*. De Lubac's book observes that Augustine's anti-Pelagian writings do not set off from speculation about what "Adam" could, might, or should have been like in theory; instead, they are based on his own personal experience of grace in the light of scripture and tradition.[5] Aquinas was deemed safer than Augustine because it was believed that Augustinianism had fomented the sixteenth-century aberrations of Baianism and Jansenism. De Lubac argues that neither Baius nor Jansénius were true heirs of Augustine; they were, rather, early modern Pelagians. Setting off, not from God, but from a theory about fallen humanity, Baius taught that human beings have a legal right to divine grace.

To counter Baianism, the Baroque Thomists developed a hypothesis depicting what would have happened to human beings if they had been left in a "state of pure nature": Cajetan, Bellarmine, and Suarez argued that this potential-hypothetical human nature would only have achieved a *natural* beatitude. These men considered that if we say that people have a natural desire, not just for natural happiness but for the *supernatural* vision, we will oblige God to fulfill this desire. Pantheism looms if we say that the Creator *must* respond to the creature's natural desire. Where, according to de Lubac, Thomas had taught that "the soul is naturally capable of grace," Cajetan claimed that Thomas taught that we have only an "obediential potential" to receive it: the happiness to which "pure nature" destines us is not supernatural but natural. The Baroque theologians' belief that human beings inhabit a "state of pure nature" removed the supernatural from nature as securely as Descartes had done; this purely natural *state* became a complete natural *order*, self-regulating in its own domain.[6]

Garrigou-Lagrange noted among the vagaries of the Nouvelle Théologie that de Lubac asserts, in *Surnaturel,* that Aquinas had no notion of a "double finality" for human nature, one natural, and the other superadded by grace. After a citation from Blondel, de Lubac had concluded by describing the human orientation in his own words: we do not desire a God who turns to us by obligation, but a God who gives Himself to us as a "gift"; the natural desire for the supernatural vision is a "call" inscribed in our nature through the grace of God; written into our being, its "pull" commands us, not our Creator. De Lubac hardly needed to tell Blondel that *Surnaturel* was written against "extrinsicism." Pères Garrigou-Lagrange and Boyer interpreted the book as teaching that grace is intrinsic to human nature.

5. De Lubac, *Surnaturel,* 47.
6. Ibid., 104–14, 137, 175, 291.

Garrigou's 1946 article became known as his *"bombe atomique."*[7] The strike was launched against the "natural desire" and the Blondelian equation of truth with life, seen to endanger transubstantiation, monogenesis, and original sin. The attack was conceived as a defense of a Thomism whose philosophy was the inseparable expression of its theology.

De Lubac argued that, where Thomas used the doctrine of the natural desire for God to establish a bridge between philosophy and theology, his baroque "interpreters, conversely, set themselves to consummating a rupture" between them, "by permanently enclosing philosophy in the tunnel vision of the Philosopher who had never heard of creation. They had no wish to know the 'natural desire' which emerges from beginning in divine revelation and the contemplation of the effects of grace. What a surprise to find no desire to see God in a being who is from the outset cut off from all relation to God!"[8] De Lubac ascribed this to the Baroque theology of grace:

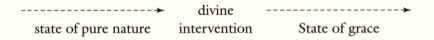

state of pure nature    intervention    State of grace
                        divine

This schema was analogous to that which Gilson had combated under the guise of the neo-Thomist interpretation of Aquinas's writings as containing, first, philosophy and, in addition, revealed theology.

From the early days of their friendship, Gilson had disagreed with Maritain on the issue of the natural desire for God. On the question of finality, he falls closer to de Lubac. The statement in *Surnaturel* that, for Augustine, there is not "opposition but inclusion, not conflict, but union," between nature and grace is matched by the assertion in *Le Thomisme* that supernatural "beatitude, which transcends man and nature, is no adventitious term trumped up to bring morality and religion into accord. There is . . . almost a continuity of order between the earthly beatitude accessible here below and the heavenly beatitude to which we are called. The last end is not the negation of our human ends, rather it gathers them together, sublimates and refines them, because human ends are but partial intuitions of our last end and imperfect substitutes for it." Gilson's formulas are more cautious than de Lubac's. We tend to beatitude, he says, without grasping what it is, because our knowledge of God is bound to that of sensible reality.[9] "The

7. Garrigou-Lagrange, "La nouvelle théologie où va-t-elle?" 132; de Lubac, *Surnaturel,* 483–87 ("son propre appel," 487); Fouilloux, *Une église en quête de liberté,* 189, 283.

8. De Lubac, *Surnaturel,* 132–33.

9. Ibid., 69; Gilson, *The Christian Philosophy of St. Thomas Aquinas,* 355.

historian" adds that we read the "natural desire" out of Thomas by the way of negation: "St. Thomas leaves questions only partially settled, like the projecting stones of an unfinished wall awaiting the hand of a second builder. The very gaps in St. Thomas's work suggest that nature awaits the finishing touches of grace."

From 1932 Congar and Chenu had agreed that one way of responding to the genuine questions raised by modernism was to redress the unilaterally objectivist focus of theology, that is, by recalling that God addresses a human *subject*. On his way back from Rome in 1946 Congar told Gaston Fessard that "it is forbidden to talk about 'religious experience' as the foundation of dogma and of the Church." For both the outspoken Dominicans at Saulchoir and for the Jesuits of Fourvière, the problem facing the French church in the postwar years was the pastoral one of evangelizing their countrymen. Their superiors were still addressing the concern of 1903, the doctrinal requirement of maintaining the objectivity of Christian dogma. It was because he spoke of the *concrete* basis of Christian doctrine in religious experience that de Lubac was perceived at Rome as a "Crypto-Modernist."[10] How was one to convert nonbelievers when mentioning religious experience was off-limits, in case one jeopardized the objectivity of doctrine?

Gilson saw the consequences of such a failure of imagination. He told Maritain in 1947 that "French Catholics and their hierarchy" have "become strangers to one another": this is "not a matter of schism but of the disappearance of Catholicism in our country." Gilson linked the beatific vision to religious experience: "What lies back of" Thomas's "ideas," he says, "is a deep religious life, the interior warmth of a soul in search of God."[11] But for Gilson, the route to the renewal of the concreteness of philosophical theology lay in the rediscovery of existence, taken as an objective event.

De Lubac's critique of the commentators cannot have fallen foul of the Erasmian Étienne. On the other hand, whereas de Lubac includes Dominico Banez amongst the "pure naturists," Gilson had found a Sancho in this Spanish Dominican. The Louvain Thomist Monsignor de Raeymaeker had called his attention to the sixteenth-century commentator's "existentialism."[12] For Gilson, Banez's existentialism outshone his "pure naturism."

It was Père Chenu, and not Gilson, who first appreciated the debt of the

10. Congar, *Journal d'un théologien*, 24, 59; Fessard to Henri de Lubac, June 22, 1946, cited ibid., 132 n359; ibid., 213–14.

11. Gilson to Jacques Maritain, January 12, 1947, in *Deux approches*, 156–57; Gilson, *The Christian Philosophy of St. Thomas Aquinas*, 375.

12. Bonino, "Historiographie de l'école thomiste," 311.

mediaevals to Dionysius the Areopagite, and to the Greek fathers. The Sorbonne-trained Gilson, uniformly described by Frenchmen with the untranslatable adjective *universitaire,* was temperamentally of the Latin persuasion in Christian theology. In his *Corpus Mysticum* (1941) de Lubac described the transition from the fathers' "'ontological symbolism'" to the "Christian rationalism" of Saint Thomas with an evident sense of "regret." The Nouvelle Théologie was united around a preference for "symbolism" over "dialectics."[13] Gilson never grasped what the "Grecophilia" of the Nouvelle Théologie was *for.* As (literally) a *lay*-Thomist, Gilson's belief in the dynamic quality of existence was confirmed though secular experiences, especially those he had in concert halls and museums.

## Political Adventures

Charles Maurras was tried for treason in January 1945: when he was given the verdict of life imprisonment, he shouted "C'est la revanche de Dreyfus!" His newspaper had from 1940 given its support to the marshall, had in time called for the guillotine to fall upon Gaullists and Free French "'terrorists'" and had opposed Pétain's anti-Semitic laws for their "laxity": "The venom poured out by . . . Calzant and Maurras . . . on the Jewish people does not bear detail in its repetitiousness." Maurras had objected equally to "collaboration" and to "resistance" because neither fit this utopian intellectual's "model" of French political cohesion: De Gaulle remarked that "Maurras was so right that it would drive him mad."[14] His conception of politics was woven out of a series of logical steps that gave their author a conception of how history ought to have transpired, perfect but for its lack of foundation in the world in which practical choices are made. He was able to believe that he had neither collaborated nor resisted, because neither belonged to his theory.

In May 1947 Gilson received the highest prize France offers its intellectuals, reception into the Académie Française. He was nominated by Louis Pasteur Vallery Radot on the grounds of his resistance to collaboration and his prompt rallying to France libre. His friends gave the model French citizen a ceremonial sword, in tribute to his success. Daniélou saluted Gilson's triumph in *Études.* The Jesuit celebrated Gilson's work as a proof that the

13. Conticello "Métaphysique de l'être et théologie de la grâce," 455–56; Komonchak, "Theology and Culture at Mid-Century," 589–90, 587.

14. Weber, *Action Française,* 475 ("This is the revenge of Dreyfus"), 470–71, 462–63, 456.

theologies of Augustine, Bernard, Bonaventure, and Thomas are all "equally orthodox."[15] The salutation was published in the same issue of *Études* as Daniélou's "red rag" to the Roman bull.

The Mouvement Républicain Populaire appointed Gilson to the Conseil de la République between 1947 and 1949; he became, as he told Phelan, "senateur malgré lui." "But he liked the idea too, particularly if it placed him in a position of influence at a time when reform of the national education system seemed likely to arise. If the future of Catholic schools was at issue, Gilson would, he warned Pegis, miss a fall term in Toronto: 'If there is a fight, I should be among the fighters.'"[16]

The year 1949 opens the curtain on the worst years of Étienne's life. Thérèse Gilson died of leukemia. "Like so many men before and since," Gilson said of Petrarch, "he had experienced the total and sudden absorption of the one who lives by the one who had just gone. It is a presence lived all the more intensely, a reality all the more overwhelming because it is unexpected: the soul of it is love and its physical form is grief."[17] Without his wife's mediation, the father and son had a bad falling out. A man who lectured relentlessly at the Collège de France and in Toronto, who stubbornly pursued a "wandering quest of truth" which deviated so little that his colleagues at the Institute of Mediaeval Studies heard him enter his office each day as the minute hand reached 9.00 a.m., perhaps exercised his paternity more directly upon his students than upon his children. He had been in Toronto, and Bernard in France, in the years when the institute was created. Although the girls, especially Cécile, remained close to him, Gilson "blamed his own shortcomings as a father for the fact that his daughters, now nearing forty, were not married—as a Frenchman he considered unmarried daughters to represent a parental failure."[18]

On January 14, 1950, he published a short piece which teased the question of whether Maurras had been a "traitor": "After Montoire," Gilson wrote, Maurras had advised his countrymen to "collaborate without discussion"; and although "at this distance" Maurras' "exhortation to march on London" sounds comical, it might not have raised a laugh with Déat and Laval in 1941.[19] On January 15, Gilson gave the Paris branch of the Mouvement Républicain Populaire a paper outlining its objectives: "The

15. Shook, *Gilson*, 270–71; Daniélou, "Étienne Gilson à l'Académie," 264.

16. Shook, *Gilson*, 272–73.

17. Gilson, *Choir of Muses*, 52. Shook says that *L'école des muses* "had been largely written in France since the war's end, . . . and includ[ed] three items previously published." *Gilson*, 312.

18. Gilson, *Being and Some Philosophers*, x; Shook, *Gilson*, 293.

19. Gilson, "1940–1950," 1.

MRP would only nationalize industry where normal production and distribution called for it, never on principle. . . . It would treat every French citizen as a moral individual. . . . [T]here would be no state religion, no official philosophy or science, and no discrimination in the realm of teaching." When he had finished, there was an uproar from the floor: "'Why did M. Gilson call monarchists "historical paleontologists?" and Charles Maurras a "traitor?"'" Georges Calzant had arrived "armed with the previous day's *Le Monde*": he was "enraged" by Gilson's suggestion that the Action Française had advised "collaboration." There was a heated textual analysis of the meaning of Maurras' statement in *La seule France* (1941): "The Marshall [Pétain] decided he had to collaborate with Germany. Do we refuse him? No. Do we accept? No. We do it *without discussion*."[20] This absurd episode had lasting repercussions in Gilson's life.

## *Humani Generis* (1950)

It was, de Lubac thinks, as a compensation for his failure to obtain a condemnation for Bouillard's *Conversion et grâce* that Père Garrigou-Lagrange sought to achieve that end with respect to *Surnaturel*. His comments about Fourvière in 1947 were "'a declaration of war'"; "'We will have them!'" he told his friends at the Angelicum. In the same year, Gilson wrote to Monsignor Montini to "insist that little good could be achieved by a condemnation, at the price of the ill which will be caused by its exploitation by the tribe for whom the Christian faith is the least concern," a well-intentioned but less than fulsome recommendation of the Blondelians. In 1948 the Jesuit Gregorian University lined up a "spectacular offensive" against the Nouvelle Théologie, directing a series of lectures against polygenism, for original sin and against the natural desire for the supernatural vision—Charles Boyer and Guy de Broglie were the speakers—and on method in theology.[21] In June 1950 the ranks of Fourvière were dispersed, Bouillard and de Lubac both being extricated and dispatched to Paris.

The Gregorian's orchestration of anxieties was a prelude to the encyclical *Humani Generis,* published in August 1950. Van Steenberghen describes

20. Shook, *Gilson*, 293–94.
21. De Lubac, *At the Service of the Church*, 252–54; Gilson to Michel Labourdette, August 12, 1950, in Donneaud, ed., "Correspondance Étienne Gilson-Michel Labourdette," 499, in which Gilson reports the comments he had made two years earlier to Msgr. Montin; Fouilloux, *Une église en quête de liberté*, 289.

*Humani Generis* as the "peak" of the "conservative reaction in theology and of the power of the Holy Office."[22] Pius XII's encyclical notes that some theologians "destroy the gratuity of the supernatural order, since God, they say, cannot create intellectual beings without ordering and calling them to the beatific vision" (para. 26). De Lubac had ten years of imposed silence ahead of him.

Meantime, Gilson decided to use the *force frappé* against the Roman Thomists. He was planning to attend two conferences in Rome in September 1950: first, the International Scholastic Congress, which had been organized by the Scotist scholar Father Carlo Balic, and second, the International Thomistic Congress. Gilson was interrupted in the construction of his weaponry by Canon Van Steenberghen, who had been invited to spend a semester at the Institute of Mediaeval Studies and wanted to find out how a French-speaker got by on a lecture-tour of America. Gilson wrote to Phelan in May 1950, "Van Steenberghen is a saintly priest, a hard worker and a very great scholar. He has a literal mind . . . out for scientific demonstrations and clarifications in a field where they don't work. The main trouble is that the Lovanienses have turned the formal distinction between philosophy *(in divinis)* and theology into a practical separation." In June he told Anton Pegis that it was good to hear that the tour had been successful, but "as for his own philosophical ideas, they are indeed fantastic. Tony, let me tell you something, the *only* chance for a Catholic to be a great philosopher is to be, above all, a theologian. This is what I am going to tell them in Rome; and very few will like it." As he modestly remarked to Phelan in June, his lecture for the Scholastic Congress is "'an H-bomb, but it came to me.'"[23]

Gilson had always withheld his articles from Saint Maximin, conceiving that French Dominican school as an outpost of Garrigou-Lagrange's dominions; the priory had associations with the Action Française dating back to the turn of the century.[24] But when his duties as an MRP senator took him there in 1948, he found a like mind in Père Michel Labourdette. Daniélou's "Les orientations présentes" was seen as a critique of Saint Maximin. Père Reginald asked the editors of the *Revue Thomiste* to defend orthodoxy against novelty. Labourdette refused, fearing that Saint Maximin would

22. Van Steenberghen, "Un incident révélateur," 380–81.
23. Shook, *Gilson*, 297; Gilson to Anton C. Pegis, June 1,1950, ibid., 299.
24. See Donneaud's note, in Donneaud, ed., "Correspondance Étienne Gilson-Michel Labourdette," 479–80, and Laudouze, *Dominicains Français et Action Française: 1899–1940*.

acquire the tincture of integrism; such accusations were well within earshot. When he heard of the fracas, Gilson rode to the defense of a Thomist in distress. In July and August 1950 he assured Labourdette that he was no ally of Daniélou's. Gilson responded to the Jesuit with the same reflexes he had turned on Laberthonnière, as a man with "a sort of religious hatred of Saint Thomas." He had evidently not been flattered by Daniélou's recruitment of himself in *Études*. On the day that *Humani Generis* was published, Gilson told Père Michel that "I truly regret what has affected P. de Lubac, who is in a totally different class from his confrères, but my remarks about whether the measures are 'politically opportune' do not at all signify that I find their attitude justifiable."[25]

Garrigou accused Bouillard of treating Thomas's philosophical "notions" as "contingent," thus exposing the theological formulae they explained to the same perishability. It was the charge of which Loisy had been convicted and seems to have been among the philosophical objections to Chenu's *Une école de théologie*. In the summer of 1950 Gilson was working on *Jean Duns Scot: Introduction à ses positions fondamentales* (1952). He confessed to Labourdette that he could neither prove Scotus false on philosophical grounds nor discover any fault in his doctrinal orthodoxy. The reason was that Gilson did not have a "noncircular" philosophical means of *demonstrating* that "being is not *essentia realis* but *habens esse*": "I believe that the notion is included in that of *ens* as a principle. One sees this principle or one does not see it. . . . [M]y personal experience of forty years is not communicable." It is because they can find no philosophical way of refuting Scotus's idea of the univocity of being that "fake criticisms" are dreamed up against his religious or "doctrinal" position (pantheism, spinozism, etc.)."[26] Scotist theology provides as full an account of the articles of faith as does Thomism.

In July 1950 Gilson was probing the "factual relativity of theology" and calling himself an "old *enfant terrible*" for suggesting that the use of philosophy introduces a certain "contingency" into theology. By August he was arguing for a mutual illumination, by the light of faith, of philosophy and theology, creating a "sort of symbiosis" between the two: "that is what I am going to Rome to say," Gilson announced, and, on fire for martyrdom,

25. Donneaud's note, in "Correspondance Étienne Gilson-Michel Labourdette," 499; Gilson to Michel Labourdette, letters of July 28, August 12, 1950, ibid., 482, 499.

26. Garrigou-Lagrange, "La nouvelle théologie où va-t-elle?" 126, 128; Gilson to Michel Labourdette, July 28, 1950, in Donneaud, ed., "Correspondance Étienne Gilson-Michel Labourdette," 482–83.

"some will surely accuse me of fideism" for it. "I would have preferred it," he remarked to Chenu, "if the publication of a new Syllabus had taken place after the two conferences."[27]

Pères Garrigou-Lagrange and Boyer, commonly considered to have written *Humani Generis,*[28] treated the two Roman congresses as a triumphal celebration of their victory against the Nouvelle Théologie. Gilson seems not to have endeared himself to Garrigou-Lagrange by numbering the Roman Thomist among the essentialists, in *L'être et l'essence*. Shook, de Lubac, and Canon Van Steenberghen have all given accounts of these highly charged events. Gilson's reports, in outraged letters to Labourdette and Chenu, contain the best wording of Garrigou's conversation with him. On the penultimate day of the first, Scotist conference, the Roman Thomist walked up to Gilson and said, "'In *L'être et l'essence,* you speak of the great adventure *[grande aventure]* of metaphysics...'...I replied, 'Yes, and what of that?' Then, he went on, 'you take metaphysics for an adventure, that it is a story told for fun?'...I am still flabbergasted."[29] Garrigou threatened to criticize Gilson's heresies from the podium "'on Monday at the Thomist Congress.'" Gilson shot back, "'Mon père, if you do that, I will leave Rome immediately.'" Confronted by an enemy who could resist, the champion withdrew. After the Dominican's retreat, a "fearful and angry" Gilson inquired whether his friends would "visit me in Paris with one of my books on the Index?"[30]

Delivered the next day, his paper trots off innocuously to describe the history of research into mediaeval thought. Mediaeval researchers began by talking about the philosophy of their period, rather than its theology. The nineteenth-century historians shared this interest with the early modern Scholastics. When Scholasticism was criticized as a philosophy, it retaliated on the same ground. "Then as today," Scotists and Thomists "oppose a philosophy to a philosophy; and that is why the theologians of the Middle Ages, who never wrote a philosophy while they were alive, have composed

27. Gilson to Labourdette, July 28, 1950, in Donneaud, ed., "Correspondance Étienne Gilson-Michel Labourdette," 484; Gilson to Michel Labourdette, August 12, 1950, ibid., 501–2; Gilson to Marie-Dominique Chenu, August 21, 1950, in Gilson Correspondence.
28. Shook, *Gilson,* 299.
29. Gilson to Michel Labourdette, September 26, 1950, in Donneaud, ed., "Correspondance Étienne Gilson-Michel Labourdette," 512. Gilson gives the same account in a letter to Chenu: Gilson to Marie-Dominique Chenu, September 25, 1950, in Chenu Papers.
30. Van Steenberghen, "Un incident révélateur," 381–82.

so many after their death." Since the neo-Scholastics were Aristotelians before they were Thomists, "it is no wonder that the historians who are the most anxious to extract from medieval texts a philosophy that is entirely free of theology are usually the same historians who insist upon . . . the existence of a Scholastic 'synthesis,' of which it is possible to say that it was the common philosophy of the thirteenth century in its entirety."[31] The next step was dropping the collective term *Scholastics*. Mediaeval thought did not repackage shriveled Aristotelian formulae. If we reintegrate the philosophies with the theologies, we shall find that each mediaeval "master" was a unique, creative thinker.

Aristotle is "healthy but that is thanks to the Bible," Gilson had told Maritain in 1931, and grace stimulates rational invention. In the Giffords, Gilson had contended, as a historian, that there has been a Christian philosophy, and he described it in order to prove it. Now, in 1950, he tells his co-religionists, prescriptively, that their philosophies *ought* to be Christian: "Scholastic philosophy must return to theology!" Gilson illustrated the "symbiosis" of philosophy and theology thus: "There are certain fish that live only in warm water. To say that they will die in cold water is not to deny that they are fish. As for the fish that, as some insist at all costs, must be made to live in cold water in order to maintain the purity of their essences, they do not become true fish, but dead fish." In an autobiographical piece of 1949, Gilson had written that "through music, we were already in" the "fluid, continuous, moving" reality that Bergson described, "like fish in the sea."[32] Scholastic-fish are a species of the genus fish; Gilson is not laying down the law for non-Christian thinkers. Those fish who have sunk into the warm water of Baptism think in a particular medium. Gilson is not asking Scholastic philosophers to set aside their generically fishy (philosophical) penchant for reasoned argument. The fish are not the warm water. Gilson is not prescribing that the Christian philosopher must *be* a theologian, but affirming that his fins or reason must dart to the kinetic melodies of a theological *Le Mer,* that is, the watery ambiance of existence. Theology enables us to swim (reason about) the currents of the existence in which we bathe so habitually that we are oblivious to it.

*Humani Generis* criticized the notion that Christian dogmas evolve without retaining any substantial identity: "They" say "that the history of dogmas consists in the reporting of the various forms in which revealed truth

---

31. Gilson, "Historical Research and the Future of Scholasticism," 3, 5–6.
32. Ibid., 9–10; Gilson, "Compagnons de route," 283.

has been clothed, forms that have succeeded one another in accordance with the different teachings and opinions that have arisen over the course of the centuries" (*Humani Generis,* para. 15). Gilson argues, further, that not all of the Scholastic rationalists are Aristotelians: some are happy to meet their secular opponents on any philosophical ground they chose. Pius XII would not have shaken his head over Gilson's affirmation that theological truths are a permanent acquisition:

> The decisive achievement of the masters of the Middle Ages was perhaps this, that, because they were theologians, they did not think *on the basis of* any science or *on the basis of* any philosophy. We are therefore interpreting history in a misleading way if we say that Scholasticism tied the Christian faith to the ancient philosophy of Aristotle, and, consequently, that we are invited by its example to do the same thing with the philosophy of our age. What Scholastic theology did was rather to create…a new metaphysics, whose truth, being independent of the state of science at any given historical moment, remains as permanent as the light of faith within which it was born.[33]

Gilson had been claiming since the Giffords that Christian philosophy is a "new metaphysics," which is not implicit in Aristotle. Maritain had been astute enough to perceive it, for he had lived through the modernist controversy. Gilson's catholic veering, from 1913, toward *faith* in order to include what the anti-modernists had excommunicated and silenced makes him insist, from 1950, on the foundation of Christian philosophy in unalterable theological verities. He had begun to sense that the "conservative" anti-modernists, who taught that one must get one's philosophy right *in order to* maintain the articles of faith, had therefore given philosophy the task of preparing the essential foundations, upon whose structure faith is shaped. These rationalists would unwittingly produce "progressive" heirs who, sharing their teachers' rationalism but setting out from different philosophies, would proceed to redesign the articles of faith.

For Gilson, the fact that faith is not dependent on any particular philosophy is a charter of freedom for the Christian philosopher. Since revealed doctrine requires no specific philosophical basis, a philosopher who bases herself in the order of faith is as free as a bird, or a fish, with respect to her reasoned arguments. Since 1905 many people had behaved as if one had to get one's philosophy straight *as a condition* of keeping one's theology out of modernist error. In his own "fideist" way, Gilson sets out a manifesto for

---

33. Gilson, "Historical Research and the Future of Scholasticism," 8.

philosophical pluralism. Cardinal Pizzardo, who was presiding over Gilson's session, was impressed: he "advanced toward the speaker, took his hands in his and, obviously moved, said, 'Monsieur Gilson, you are a genius!' ... The specter of the Index retreated." Van Steenberghen saw Gilson's move as a concession to authoritarianism: "putting the Christian philosophers under the tutelage of the theologians would guarantee their perfect orthodoxy!"[34]

Gilson's paper at the Thomistic Congress argued that Thomas's notion of a "real composition" of essence and existence in creatures is not a proof of the existence of God.[35] Van Steenberghen gave a paper in which he distinguished between the language and the truth of the Thomistic proofs for the existence of God, arguing that in their original formulation the five ways do not deliver the existence of a single God. Objecting to Steenberghen's proposal for a transliteration of Thomistic metaphysics, Charles Boyer responded with a "Latin oration," which concluded "Ergo obiectiones clarissimi Domini Professoris nihil valent" (Therefore the most clear objections of the Reverend Professor do not stand). Canon Raeymaeker, president of the Louvain Institut Supérieur de Philosophie, remonstrated with Boyer *after* the event—he did not, as Shook and de Lubac imagine, march onto the platform and interrupt the Jesuit's speech.[36]

When Van Steenberghen made his "peace" with the most vocal members of the "dangerous tribe," he found Boyer sweetly apologetic; Père Pecksniff-Lagrange was as confraternal as ever: "I prayed for you to Saint Thomas last night," he said. Boyer spent some time at the congress trying to persuade Pegis that *Humani Generis* was directed against de Lubac. Gilson would assure the latter that: "all of this, Boyer included, is ... a manifestation of the superficial philosophizing endemic to the Church from the beginning but which has infested Scholasticism since the thirteenth century. For every Saint Thomas and others like him, who magnificently destroyed the obstacle, or even hoisted ... themselves over it, there have been hundreds of low-grade 'rationalists' who foundered on it." Van Steenberghen considered that Boyer, Garrigou, and their emulators "had seriously compromised the future of the Thomistic renaissance." Gilson told Labourdette in September that, even "from a merely apologetic view-point, neoscholastic philosophy" has been a "failure. It has never convinced anyone." From the "experience of a lifetime, I am persuaded that some have taken a false route. ... The faith has converted more philosophers to Thomism than

34. Van Steenberghen, "Un incident révélateur," 382.
35. Gilson, "La Preuve du *De Ente et Essentia*," 257–60; Van Steenberghen, "Correspondance avec Étienne Gilson," 617–18.
36. Van Steenberghen, "Un incident révélateur," 386–87; Shook, *Gilson*, 299–300.

'Thomist philosophy' has converted philosophers to faith." Étienne nonetheless considered it a "pity" that de Lubac was not a Thomist.[37]

He notes in 1960 that, precisely because Catholic dogmas are not philosophical propositions, the church's "invincible opposition" to a philosophical "reform" of doctrinal language is legitimate. He also records the occasion upon which he turned over in his hands a Thomist manual belonging to Lucien Paulet, the *Elementa philosophiae scholasticae* of Sébastien Reinstadler (1904), and was surprised by the rudeness with the author barked out his Latin dismissals of the modern philosophers: "He was not content to condemn the crime, he had to insult it....[T]he Kantian critique was rejected as an insanity....During their 17th century controversies with their worst enemies, the humanists, modern scholasticism had picked up some bad manners: Every conclusion that Sanseverino rejects is absurd: *absurdus est modo quo Kantius criticam suam confirmare studet*," as are the doctrines of Rosmini and the German idealists. If "a theologian has the right to condemn Kantianism as contrary to the faith" he "should not pretend he is speaking as a mere philosopher."[38] Gilson's memoir was written after a decade in which he made a survey of such texts as Sanseverino's.

## Gilson Undergoes Reprisals for "Neutralism"

President Roosevelt's war strategy had done all too much to control the French resistance. This marked those who had remained in France with a different sentiment about American power than that of European refugees in the United States. During 1950 Gilson several times argued in print that France should remain neutral in the event of a hot war between Russia and the United States.[39] Lecturing at Notre Dame in November, he expressed the same opinion on some social occasions. Having labored within the French education system since 1907, on December 12, 1950, he dropped the news of his retirement on the Collège de France. On December 15, in *Commonweal,* a Russian-German professor of political philosophy at Notre Dame, Waldemar Gurian, rounded on the "neutralist defeatist." On the basis of academic "gossip," Gurian said in his "Open Letter to Étienne Gilson"

---

37. Van Steenberghen, "Un incident révélateur," 387; Gilson to Henri de Lubac, June 21 1965, in de Lubac, ed., *Letters of Gilson to de Lubac,* 94; Van Steenberghen, "Un incident révélateur," 390; Gilson to Michel Labourdette, September 26, 1950, in Donneaud, ed., "Correspondance Étienne Gilson-Michel Labourdette," 512, 515.

38. Gilson, *Le philosophe et la théologie,* 19, 55–57.

39. Gilson, "Neutrality for France?" 203–5.

that "you have stunned those whom you have met with your prophecy that France will be occupied by the Red Army without much resistance and that the United States will not do much about it."[40] Seeing an opportunity to revenge the incident of January 1950, the French paleoconservatives accused the "traitor to France" of retiring because he preferred teaching in Canada to working in the Collège de France. The "neo-Maurrassian" *Aspects de la France* led the assault and was imitated by the Gaullist *Carrefour,* and then by *Figaro.* Louis Pasteur Vallery Radot decided that Gilson was not such a good French citizen after all.

In mid-February, with Gilson under heavy journalistic bombardment, the Collège de France voted to deny the "fugitive" a retirement pension. After a year's exile by the French intellectual establishment, *Esprit* came to his defense. The editor, Albert Beguin, wrote to Gilson to commiserate about "'the hurtful campaign waged against you by the A.F. [Action Française] press.'" Gilson's academic prizes were important to him, and one gauges that he spent a bit of time nursing the wound of his dishonorable discharge from the Collège de France and tracing the lineage of his opponents back to 1905. A sign of the rankling pride will be the use of faux-Latin tags, such as *ex nihilo Thomismi* (Maritain) or "We have a *De ente et essentia,* we are lacking a *De causa et causato*" (Garrigou-Lagrange).[41]

---

40. FitzGerald, "Maritain and Gilson on the Challenge of Political Democracy," 61–72, 69.
41. Beguin, "L'affair Gilson," 590, and see 591 for the vote on Gilson's retirement pension; Shook, *Gilson,* 308; Gilson, *Matières et formes,* 17; Gilson, "Prolégomènes a la Prima Via," in *Autour de Saint Thomas,* 55. Subsequent citations hereinafter are to the pages in *Autour de Saint Thomas.*

# 12

# Between the Temporal and the Eternal Cities

## Maritain's Case for World Government

During the Second World War, Maritain began to argue that, whereas the individual is just an instrumental "part" within the "whole" of the state, the person is an autonomous whole, an absolute value. When France was under occupation, some Catholics had felt that democracy and Thomism are ill-fitted. In its initial stages, Maritain's "personalism" belonged to a Thomist defense of democracy. Charles de Koninck was an Aristotelian-Thomist who taught philosophy at Laval, in Quebec. Between 1943 and 1945 he composed a hard-hitting and well-informed indictment of Maritain's personalism, arguing that it departed from Aristotelian-Thomist premises in political ethics, and that it gave the game away to totalitarianism by undermining the centrality of the "common good" as the medium through which individuals are related to God. De Koninck's text carried a preface by the cardinal archbishop of Quebec. The cardinal saw personalism as an invitation to humanity to worship itself. Maritain told Gilson that while the world is in ruins, "the integrists of Quebec raise the cry of alarm in the presbyteries of the New World against Neo-Liberalism, Neo-Individualism, and, as our good friends at the *Tablet* call it, Neo-Pelagianism."[1]

Speaking to political scientists in Toronto in 1947, Gilson had set up a much simpler distinction between "person" and "individual" than Maritain's. He said that everyone knows a tree is an individual, but not a person, whereas a human being, as rational and social, merits treatment by others as a person, under the "moral law." Gilson claimed that "the proper

1. Maritain, *The Rights of Man and Natural Law;* Koninck, *De la primauté du bien commun contre les personnalistes,* 3, 11, 15–18, and then, in response to a defense of Maritain, de Koninck, "In Defence of Saint Thomas: A Reply to Father Eschmann's Attack on the Primacy of the Common Good," 89; J. M. Rodrigue Villeneuve, Preface to Koninck, *De la primauté du bien commun contre les personnalistes;* Maritain to Étienne Gilson, November 15, 1945, in *Deux approches,* 141.

function of the modern State is to ensure the common good of all, by putting at the disposal of various social groups all the legal and technical means which they need in order to achieve themselves their own ends. Neither the direct management of loose individuals by some totalitarian State, nor the economic and social anarchy of a purely political democracy, but the State as protector and helper of those social groups outside of which there can be no personal liberty."[2]

In March 1945 Gilson traveled to San Francisco as one of the French delegates to the first UNESCO conference, where he helped to write the United Nations charter. The ministry of foreign affairs sent him to London in the autumn. Étienne spent October and November seated on a committee composing the United Nations' constitution. The interlude focused his attention on globalization: "Henceforth," he told the readers of *Le Monde,* "the United Nations exists and the destiny of France is indissolubly bound to it. The time of isolation is past for every country in the world."[3] At the November 1947 UNESCO conference, in Mexico, Maritain urged all the countries of the world to seek a common good. The idea bore fruit in *Man and the State* (1951), a philosophical justification of world government, replacing sovereign nations.

According to Van Steenberghen, Gilson was not, as de Lubac suggested, invited to Louvain to inaugurate the Cardinal Mercier chair of philosophy in 1952 as a "reward" for allying with the Louvain school at the Rome Congress of 1950. Rather, he was chosen because the president of the Institut regarded him as a "great personality and brilliant conference speaker."[4] His lectures became *Les métamorphoses de la cité de Dieu.*

Henri Bars was surprised to discover that *Les métamorphoses* carries no explicit reference to Maritain's political writings. He believed he might have lighted upon one allusion to Maritain in it: the discussion of the "idea of a 'supra-national' authority...appears to relate to [Maritain's] *Man and the State,* published in America the preceding year."[5] It is more than likely that *Les métamorphoses* is, in its entirety, a parody of *Man and the State.*

2. Gilson, "The Principles of a Democratic State," Address to the Political Science Society, University of Toronto, November 1947, pp. 13–14, 19, in Gilson Papers, Articles and Lectures, Separated Pieces, On Social and Political Subjects, Pontifical Institute of Mediaeval Studies Records, University of St. Michael's College Archives.

3. Gilson, "L'éducation des Nations Unies," 1.

4. De Lubac's footnote in *Letters of Gilson to de Lubac,* 225; Van Steenberghen, "Les lettres d'Étienne Gilson au P. de Lubac," 330.

5. Bars, "Gilson et Maritain," 247–48.

The Parti de l'intelligence had stood for rationalist internationalism: its manifesto affirmed belief in "the intellectual federation of Europe and of the world under the aegis of a victorious France." Taking the opposite tack to de Koninck, Gilson arrived at the same conclusion: by founding his political argument on Aristotelian premises, Maritain was unwittingly giving ground to secularism. In *Man and the State,* Maritain had inadvertently retreated into the presuppositions about the relation of nature and grace that had marked the "Maurrassian" era of French Catholic political thinking, in the 1920s. On his trip to Mexico in 1948 Maritain impressed the South American Christian Democrats; this organization was denounced by the Chilean bishops as "enemies of Christ." Maritain told Yves Simon that "there is around me in the whole of Latin America an ideological (and political) battle . . . comparable to that which at this moment surrounds Maurras."[6] There may have been an unconscious irony in that remark, or at least Gilson might have thought so. His most touchy negative political trigger was Maurrassianism, especially in 1952, immediately after the episode that led to his unpensioned retirement from the Collège de France.

Maritain had taken up with the Aristotelians of the University of Chicago, and this filtered through into *Man and the State.* He was attempting to conform his politics to the Chicago school's canon of rationality at the precise moment when the notion of Thomism as an avatar of Aristotelianism had become a singular bugbear for Étienne Gilson. Maritain's project for a world government grew out of his attempt to find common ground in ethics with agnostic Aristotelians. Gilson would have none of it.

The *Métamorphoses de la cité de Dieu* "exhibited, not without amusement, a series of grandiose utopias."[7] Its purpose is to show the castles that moral philosophers build when they found their constructions, not in the secret places within human nature that grace creates, but on the extrinsic shell of "natural morality."

Maritain appreciated that all of the peoples of the world are unlikely to achieve theoretical or "speculative" agreement about the common good. But his experience with UNESCO, which brought people of different cultural, religious, and philosophical presuppositions together in a common project, inclined him to consider that, even where there are no shared metaphysical goals, there can still be concord as to what must be done in practice. A future world civilization must found itself, he says in *Man and*

6. Prévotat, "Autour du parti de l'intelligence," 174; Maritain to Yves Simon, April 28, 1947, cited in Barré, *Jacques et Raïssa Maritain,* 530.
7. D'Alverny, "Nécrologie Étienne Gilson," 428.

*the State,* on a shared "faith," and that, not *religious* faith, but a practical faith, in democracy. Maritain therefore speaks of a *"temporal or secular faith,* bearing on the essential tenets of life in common in the earthly city" and which is "in no way a religious faith." The future world democracy will, Maritain affirms, be united by a *"creed of freedom."*[8]

This devout Thomist believed that democracy itself is the fruit of Christianity, citing Henri Bergson's *Les deux sources de la morale et de la religion* to that effect. He hoped that the "new civilization" would be "inspired by the Christian spirit." This would not be on the basis of compulsion, but "because Christians will have been able, as free men speaking to free men, . . . to persuade . . . the majority of the people, of the truth of Christian faith, or at least of the validity of Christian social and political philosophy."[9] Maritain's "democratic secular faith" must be detachable from Christian spirituality if the world project is to gain universal assent without coercion. This

> renewed democracy will not ignore religion, . . . and . . . this renewed, 'personalist' democracy will be of a *pluralist* type. Thus—supposing that the people have regained their Christian faith, or at least recognized the value and good sense of Christian conceptions of freedom, social progress and political order—we would have . . . a body politic inspired by Christian principles in its own political life. . . . [T]his personalist body politic would recognize that men belonging to . . . different philosophical or religious creeds . . . should co-operate in the common task . . . , provided they likewise assent to the basic tenets of a society of free men.[10]

The devil is in the "at leasts," or so Gilson may have thought.

## Gilson: Christendom Begins in Abraham's Faith

In the 1930s Gilson had held his debates with the Louvainistes about "Christianisme" and philosophy. He inaugurated the Cardinal Mercier chair by discussing *Chrétienté,* that is, Christendom. Can we have a global Christendom without a global Christianity, a Christendom based on a secular philosophy such as democracy, when, as Gilson told the Louvain Thomists, "the content of faith is not a knowledge which is universally rationalizable"? All of the efforts of apologetics cannot alter the fact that "the act of

---

8. Maritain, *Man and the State,* 99–101.
9. For the citation from Bergson, ibid., 56; for the religious basis of the world state, ibid., 152.
10. Ibid., 99.

faith in the word of God is always irreducibly distinguished from the simple assent to the evidence of a rational proposition."[11] The Gospel, which is open to universal humanity, requires assent to particular doctrines of faith, which we have no reason to think that all humanity will make.

The Stoics, Gilson said, were the first philosophers who saw themselves as citizens of a universal city. They gained its keys by self-subjection to the laws of nature. Such a "cosmic order" is an equivocal metaphor for a city. "When Marcus Aurelius tells us, 'As Anthony, I have Rome for a fatherland; as man, the world,' he wrote a noble phrase, but did he use the word 'fatherland' twice with the same meaning? It is open to doubt. Rome is a society of men, the world is an order of things."[12] One cannot be a fellow citizen to laws of nature; societies are not made up of things. The notion of a universal *society* had its birth in God's promise to Abraham: "I will be your God and you will be my people." It was born from Abraham's *faith*.

Several times in 1952 Gilson gave a lecture entitled "The Breakdown of Morals and Christian Education" in which he urged that "'the real trouble of our times is not the multiplication of sinners, it is the disappearance of sin.'" Thomas Aquinas believed that if one takes away grace, one does not go back "to a state of nature, but to the state of fallen nature." So *"there is no sense in pretending to arrive at natural virtues by separating them from grace, in a doctrine in which grace, by healing nature, actually makes nature capable of having virtues."* As Gilson sees it, in *Les métamorphoses*, Augustine holds the natural and the supernatural virtues together by a kind of paradox: "Since the world could prosper without the [supernatural virtues], this is because they are not there in view of the world: 'In showing, through the opulence and the glory of the Roman empire, that all this could be produced by the civic virtues without true religion, God gave us to understand that religion makes men citizens of another city, in which truth is the Queen, Charity is the law, and whose duration is eternity.' The self-sufficiency, in their own order, of the political virtues, attests to the supernatural specificity of the Christian virtues in their essence and their final end."[13] Like Augustine, Gilson reaches the cardinal virtues by way of the theological ones.

Bars wonders whether "Gilson's Thomism did not have a more Augustinian side than that of Maritain." Gilson claims that Augustine took a step

11. Gilson, *Les métamorphoses de la cité de Dieu*, 19.
12. Ibid., 6.
13. Shook, *Gilson*, 314–15; Gilson, *The Christian Philosophy of St. Thomas Aquinas*, 347, 343, Gilson's italics; Gilson, *Les métamorphoses de la cité de Dieu*, 34–35.

beyond the Stoics when he claimed that "love for the same things" is the basis of any society. Reasonable beings, or persons, *love* the same objects: "when" Augustine "speaks of a 'city,' he doesn't mean an order of things, but a true society." The *civitas terrena* uses its gods in order to enjoy the world; the *Civitas Dei* uses the world in order to enjoy God. Augustine not only failed to speak of a *single* society: he ruled it out as an impossibility. On Augustine's account, there are from eternity two societies, the one predestined to salvation, the other to damnation. His conception is thus "wider" and "narrower" than a philosophy of history. It is wider because its notion of "universality" is not an inference from "empirical history" but founded in theology; it is narrower because Augustine's dualism requires a schism between "the city of the devil and the city of God." Bars finds that Gilson's "definition of the two cities by two loves, of which one is essentially perverse, seems . . . to reject the sacrality of the profane world as such, and I do not see how certain hard positions in the *City of God* . . . can be accommodated to the naturally religious universe of Thomism, as Gilson describes it." Maurice Nédoncelle goes rather further. He gives as a reason for Gilson's having been a defender of Christian philosophy the fact that, "as a psychologist and a historian," Gilson "points to the fumblings and the follies of the human mind," which ensure that reason is helpless without religion. "Fundamentally," Gilson "has little confidence in the autonomous powers of the intellect. I would almost say (but this might be an exaggeration) that he is in that respect a Jansenist."[14] Blaise Pascal, defender of Port-Royal against the Jesuits, is noted for his political pessimism, adhering in the most literal sense to Augustine's teaching on the "two cities."

Gilson had recommended to French Catholics to study the models of the free universities of England and America, such as Chicago, Harvard, or Cambridge, paid for by "generations of men who, wanting a certain education for themselves and their children, have decided to . . . maintain it," instead of "hoping for a new Charlemagne to provide them with the schools they need." But when in 1946 Pius XII advised France not to nationalize its major industries, Gilson found against the Pope: Does "the formula 'nationalize the mines' have a meaning? To whom does the carbon contained in the French-sub-soil actually belong? One cannot nationalize that which is intrinsically national." One reason for the suspicions directed by Rome at Saulchoir was that the curia, increasingly cognizant of the danger posed by

---

14. Bars, "Gilson et Maritain," 244; Gilson, *Les métamorphoses de la cité de Dieu,* 68, 71–72; Bars, "Gilson et Maritain," 248; Nédoncelle, *Is There a Christian Philosophy?* 87. Nédoncelle's observations are directed at the "Christian philosophy" debate of the 1930s; in that context they are anachronistic and, as he says himself, exaggerated.

Soviet communism, tended to conflate the Saulchoir "program" with the French worker-priest movement.[15] Having been barred from teaching, and expelled from Saulchoir to Paris, Chenu had taken his apostolate to the working class. A letter written by Gilson in 1947 shrewdly points out to the French Dominican provincial, Antonin Motte, that if Chenu "is diverted from . . . the history of *Sacra doctrina,* he will turn elsewhere. I particularly fear . . . to see him throw himself into the study of contemporary social problems, where he will no longer be protected by the strict doctrinal discipline which he always imposes on himself in his historical research." Some feel that Gilson's letter to Motte is a token of his political conservativism; but in the same month that he wrote to Motte, Gilson expressed delight in a pastoral letter by Cardinal Suhard that called worker priests the missionaries of our time. It spoke to his feeling, expressed two months earlier, that if French Catholics continue to be governed by bishops "who have no access to their deep aspirations . . . in social, political and national matters, an unimaginable religious catastrophe is in the making."[16]

In a speech to the University of Toronto's Political Science Society, given in November 1947, Gilson described the "principle" upon which a genuinely democratic state should be founded. He disavowed both "pure political democracy," or "exclusively political liberalism," as concentrating economic—and thus political—liberty in the hands of a new "nobility," a wealthy minority, and Marxism as "State capitalism," in which the state becomes the "solitary capitalist left . . . to which all so-called citizens are both politically and economically subjugated." He said that "political liberty is not an end in itself, but a means to ensure all other liberties. . . . Whatever country I might happen to be a citizen of, I personally would enlist in the party whose main program it was to use political democracy with a view to achieving social and economic democracy. What is wrong with Marxism is not that it wants to do it—quite the reverse, that is what is right with Marxism."[17] Gilson's political temperament was that of a Pascalian Thomist, Thomistic in the priority it gives to the common good, Pascalian in its negative evaluation of what can in practice be achieved by earthly cities. The

---

15. Gilson, "Un enseignement catholique," in *Pour un ordre catholique,* 171–79, 173–74; Gilson, "Le Vatican et les nationalisations," 1–2; Congar, *Journal d'un théologien,* 223–24, 233, 240–41, 252–55, 260–64, 311, 318. It was in particular from the early 1950s that Roman authorities began to look askance at the French worker-priest movement and to object to Congar and Chenu's relations with it.

16. Gilson to Père Antonin Motte, January 7, 1947, cited in Fouilloux, *Une église en quête de liberté,* 137; Fouilloux's note, in Congar, *Journal d'un théologien,* 191 n53; Gilson to Jacques Maritain, March 24, January 12, 1947, in *Deux approches,* 162, 157.

17. Gilson, "The Principles of a Democratic State," 6, 9, 2, 8.

Augustinian demarcation between the two cities does not cut across time and eternity. One can, Gilson affirmed, belong to the *Civitas Dei* while participating in the temporal order.

By assigning a common ancestor to the human race and by "consider[ing] all men as a single man, whose history unfolds without a break from beginning to end," Augustine indicated "the notion of a universal history." Although Augustine had no philosophy of history, but a "Christian wisdom of history," his writings made "the notion of universal history" possible: it is not logically "contradictory" to conceive of "all men as a collective being." Once Augustine had defined the theological notion of a universal society, its philosophical progress was inevitable: "In order to inspire princes to desire to organize a single society on earth made in its image ... it was sufficient for the City of God to exist."[18]

Maritain's temporal "City of God," his putative world government, is achieved, in *Man and the State*, through Aristotelian themes, which are made to operate for a post-Cartesian perspective. He distinguishes "community" and "society" as, respectively, "biological" and "rational" social groupings. The "nation," Maritain says, belongs to the former, as a self-conscious community. The nation depends ontologically upon political society as the body depends upon the mind. The state should be confused with neither of these entities. As the organizational apparatus within political society, the state is founded on political society, as an Aristotelian "part" is founded upon a "whole." Just as the Aristotelian part is inferior to the whole on which it is dependent, so the state is a subordinate or "inferior" part of political society. According to Aristotle, a "whole" in the realm of politics is marked by its self-sufficiency: only self-sufficient political bodies are autonomous, and therefore "perfect." As Maritain sees it, the "first element" of political *sovereignty* is independence. Because it is a "part" and "instrumental agency of the body politic," the state lacks this most basic feature that logic requires of a sovereign entity.[19]

In the modern world, the various "bodies politic"—countries—suffer the imperfection of economically or political interdependence: it would thus be preferable if the body politic "recognizes that it is no longer a perfect society and decides to enter a larger, and truly 'perfect' political society." Maritain concludes that "if we place ourselves in the perspective of rational necessities (neglecting for a moment the factual entanglements of history), and if we look at the final conclusions of logic in relation to the issue, we

18. Gilson, *Les métamorphoses de la cité de Dieu*, 69, 73.
19. Ibid.; Maritain, *Man and the State*, 4–5, 10–11, 37–38.

shall see how cogently the advocates of World Government, or of one political organization of the world, make out their case." Chancellor Robert
Hutchins of the University of Chicago had, Maritain believed, demonstrated that the "concept of a pluralist world-wide political society perfectly
squares"[20] with Aquinas's political principles.

Gilson observed in *Les métamorphoses* that Roger Bacon had got there
before Hutchins's Aquinas. Roger Bacon invented the notion of the *respub-
lica fidelium,* or *Christianitas,* the Christian people pursuing their temporal
goods in time. The thirteenth-century Franciscan beat the United Nations
to the notion of "One World": it is not only laudable for the peoples of the
world to unite but necessary, because "'the whole Wisdom has been given
by a single God, to a single world and for a single end.'" How shall we ensure that *all* of the peoples in the world are united by a bond of love to the
Christian God? Bacon's idea of Wisdom is theological, but his practical
means for universalizing it are less securely founded in the Gospel: "our
reformer counts less upon experimental science to convert" the Muslims "than
to exterminate them."[21]

In Gilson's mind, Dante's politics paved the way to modern secularism
through its double-track theory of beatitude: "Saint Thomas repeatedly
said that the end of man is dual *(finis duplex);* Dante repeatedly said that
man has two ends *(fines duo).* This is not the same thing, but it is what permitted him to subordinate the Church to God through the Pope and the
Empire directly to God through the emperor." For Dante, the emperor
stands for the earthly paradise, the Pope for heavenly beatitude. Dante's
empire could not be universal unless it treated faith and grace as extrinsic
to its rational procedures. Dante's "Roman Empire is . . . a properly political
city, co-extensive with the whole human race, and for that reason doubly
alien to the City of God" as Augustine understood it. The progress of
Dante's universal empire does not require the conversion of the heathen
since it is founded in natural reason. Such a solution is unworkable today,
Gilson told the Louvain Thomists, because Dante's "natural reason" is actually Aristotelian "reason." Gilson asks, "Is it certain that the triumph of Aristotle in the Middle Ages was purely philosophical and rational, and that
faith and theology did nothing towards it? However it goes with that point,
the situation is not the same today. None of the known candidates for universal monarchy lay claim to either the *Ethics* or the *Politics* of Aristotle in
order to administer their world empire." Gilson discusses the notion of

20. Maritain, *Man and the State,* 179, 181.
21. Gilson, *Les métamorphoses de la cité de Dieu,* 95, citing Roger Bacon, *Opus Ter-
tium,* c. XXIII, 73; ibid., 106.

world government as he finds it in Dante's *De Monarchia,* noting that "we are very familiar with it today." The flaws he detects in the program are that of persuading each state to abandon its sovereignty; the practical difficulty of ensuring that this world authority will be just; Dante's lack of attention to the legal basis of this authority; and that "universal justice" is deduced by a syllogism: "all B is A; only C is B; so C alone is B": "This is why the whole world ought to obey a single ruler."[22]

Maritain's argument to world government combined logic and ethics. He considered that "it is at the price of patient self-contradiction that Sovereign states reluctantly allow the least measure of autonomy for particular agencies and associations born of freedom. Through the inner logic of the idea of Sovereignty, they tend to totalitarianism." Mortimer Adler having shown that it is the "anarchy" of independent states that leads to war, Maritain called for the world to become "*One* body politic," in a "pluralistic unity" in which "the sense of the common good of that *one* people should develop."[23]

Gilson reminded the Louvain Thomists that Dante's empire was to be pluralist and its emperor was to protect the people against their princes. Or putting it "in modern language," as Gilson said, Dante considered that "the universal monarch is, for the peoples, the only conceivable recourse against the totalitarianism of particular States."[24]

Such a detailed caricature was not achieved by accident. Gilson was speaking the truth when he told Maritain in 1953, "Outside our shared love of the same truth, we do not resemble one another very much."[25] But if the critique is this extensive, why should it have been so veiled as to raise no shadow in the correspondence between the two friends?

Since his espousal of democracy in the 1930s Maritain's politics had gained many enemies within the church. Maritain's most accomplished statement of the contemporary meaning of Christian political philosophy was *True Humanism*. The book reflects a serene Catholic devotion to political freedom. *True Humanism* was the object of multiple maneuvers for placement on the Index of Forbidden Books; these moves continued until they were finally checkmated by the Second Vatican Council.

Gilson shared his friend's commitment to political freedom and, if Maritain was right to define it as a "rational organization of freedom founded upon law," to democracy. He did not want his own reservations regarding

22. Ibid., 152, 146, 151, 119–21.
23. Maritain, *Man and the State,* 46, 180, 191.
24. Gilson, *Les métamorphoses de la cité de Dieu,* 125–26.
25. Gilson to Jacques Maritain, January 29, 1953, in *Deux approches,* 183.

Maritain's politics to be conflated with those of Maritain's reactionary opponents, such as the Argentinean priest Julio Meinveille, who accused Maritain of liberalism, in his *De Lamennais à Maritain* (1945). "Had Maritain and I been monks or priests," Gilson would one day tell de Lubac, "we'd have been, as they say here, *crucified*. But I've nothing to teach you on that score, have I? Nonetheless, there will have to be a new edition of *Surnaturel*."[26] The remark is evidence of his sympathy for both of his friends. This is why he shrouded the source of the inspiration for his Louvain lectures.

Just before Gilson set off for Louvain, Labourdette had told him that he was receiving anonymous attacks on Maritain, "fed by the ... abbé Meinville's book, ... and the campaign created in Canada ... by de Koninck. ... [A] great majority of the South American episcopate wants a condemnation of Maritain."[27] Gilson was fierce in his personal loyalty to Maritain. "It would take us a hundred years," he told Joseph Vrin in 1939, "to say how much we owe to that man!"[28] A year after his trip to Louvain, Gilson thought to console Maritain about his many enemies within the church, writing: "Whether you know it or not, you are great, and this is what will never be forgiven you."[29]

The *Métamorphoses* is the longest of the many pseudo-historical sallies at the expense of modern Aristotelian-Thomism that marked Gilson's output in the 1950s. These skirmishes against Thomist rationalism pick out the weak points in its armor. They target historical characters, such as "Dante" or "Cajetan," as stand-ins for living individuals. It was because it went to one side that Gilson's lunge against *Man and the State* drew so little blood.

In *Surnaturel,* de Lubac posited an unwitting or inadvertent univocalism as the root of the objection to the "natural desire" for God. If one pictures God and humanity as two of the same kind of object, as "two beings *facing* one another," God must be literally external to humanity in order to be free. From 1950 until 1960, Henri de Lubac was forbidden to teach, to

26. Maritain, *Man and the State,* 54; Gilson to Henri de Lubac, April 1, 1964, in de Lubac, ed., *Letters of Gilson to de Lubac,* 69.

27. Labourdette to Étienne Gilson, March 12, 1952, in Donneaud, "Correspondance Étienne Gilson-Michel Labourdette," 523.

28. Père L. J. Bondy, an old friend of both Maritain and Gilson, recounted this story to Shook: "Un jour de juin 1939, l'Éditeur Vrin invita Gilson et moi à déjeuner au Café d'Harcourt. ... La conversation tourna sur Bergson qui était de l'Académie et était très âgé. 'Moi,' dit Vrin, 'je crois connaître son successeur.' Gilson se sentit visé et dit, 'Non, son successeur, c'est Maritain.' 'Oh, Maritain!' dit Vrin, que le connaissait mal. 'Écoutez, Vrin,' dit Gilson. 'Nous mettrons cent ans à nous rendre compte de ce que Maritain a fait pour nous.'" Cited by Prouvost, in *Deux approches,* 152. Prouvost picked up the story from Shook's notes, in the archive at St. Michael's College, Toronto.

29. Gilson to Jacques Maritain, January 29, 1953, in *Deux approches,* 183.

write, or to respond to the objections to *Surnaturel* which poured forth from around the Scholastic globe. He was driven into "complete isolation" by this "silent ostracism," his "books were banned, removed from the libraries of the Society of Jesus and impounded from the market." In his first letter to de Lubac of 1956, Gilson told him that he was writing because "I have just read . . . *Sur les chemins de Dieu* with so much pleasure that I can't keep from writing to tell you. The theological anthropomorphism of which you speak seems to me to be one of the main obstacles to belief in God, especially among intellectuals"; but it has "patronage in very high places," because it "panders to the kind of deism that most" neo-Thomists "deep down, really prefer to teach."[30]

Gilson was anti-Deist because he envisaged nature from the perspective of the supernatural final end placed within it at creation. For Gilson, Thomas's universe is naturally religious because God is the cause of its being: "*'being* (esse) *is innermost in each thing and most fundamentally present within all things,'*" Saint Thomas said, since being "*'is formal with respect of everything found in a thing . . . Hence it must be that God is in all things, and innermostly.'*" *Les métamorphoses* sketches the outline of an anti-Deist ethics. Their author would tell Chenu that the ethics of the *Summa* "owes nothing to Aristotle."[31]

The Louvain lectures recall that Campanella composed his utopian novel, the *City of the Sun,* in order to show that Christianity "adds nothing to the law of nature except the sacraments." Obedient to a Platonic moral law, the Solarians live perfectly without the Christian revelation. The seventeenth-century Dominican cardinal conceives of Christianity as universalizable and its revealed faith as an extrinsic refinement of its morality. Leibniz will propose a "Christian Republic," whose "common bond is a dechristianised deism." The Stoic "universal city" is rehabilitated in Leibniz's conception of nature as a web of monadic souls, "each spirit like a little divinity in its department."[32]

Others, such as the eighteenth-century abbé Charles Francois Castel, devised a localized variant of Christendom, as a Union of European States. During the controversy of 1951 about his patriotism, Gilson had pointed out that "the secret of my public life, if there is one, is to be found in the dedi-

---

30. De Lubac, *Surnaturel,* 485; Balthasar, *The Theology of Henri de Lubac,* 17–18; Gilson to Henri de Lubac, July 8, 1956, in de Lubac, ed., *Letters of Gilson to de Lubac,* 23.

31. Gilson, *The Elements of Christian Philosophy,* 196, citing *S.T.* I, q. 8, a. 1; Gilson to Marie-Dominique Chenu, September 21, 1959, in Gilson Correspondence.

32. Gilson, *Les métamorphoses de la cité de Dieu,* 196, citing *Città del Sole,* 59; ibid., 243, 241.

cation of my book *La philosophie au moyen âge*. At the height of the German occupation, I dedicated it to an Englishman, Alcuin, tutor of France. He is the hero of my story, a man without genius or even great talent, who nonetheless 'abandoned' England at the invitation of Charlemagne, because he immediately saw the importance of the immense civilizing task which he had been asked to take upon himself." Now he treacherously observes that "Jesus Christ is not a European. Bethlehem is not in Europe; and nor is Tarsus.... In identifying the two notions of Europe and the Christian Republic, the Abbé de Saint-Pierre gave an example of an error, so common today, which consists in justifying a line of frontier by a universal principle. If the essence of Europe is to be a Christian society, it ceases to be Europe; it founds itself in Christianity."[33]

Auguste Comte's "Cité des Savants" exhibits a "perfect experience" of the secularized City of God. That is because the positivist saw the whole problem for what it is. If "the word could be purged of all derisory implications, one could say that Comte's Humanity is a parody of Saint Augustine's City of God.... Comte also posits 'love for principle' at the origin of the universal society of tomorrow.... [I]n Augustine's Christian city the object of that love would be given by supernatural faith; we will have henceforth a natural faith which ... will furnish the common truth by which Humanity must live." Comte's Great Being could feasibly "'occupy the whole planet,'" since no mysteries of faith exclude any portion of humanity from self-worship. Comte was not a telescopic philanthropist, for he "loved humanity concretely" in Clotilde de Vaux. He composed for this goddess not only the *Système politique positive* but prayers intended for the use of the entire positivist cult. Christian realism is hindered from universalization by the intractable particularity of its faith, as also by the *irrationality* of the faith that "calls" human beings "to scorn the world and love invisible things" and "to suffer persecution for the truth," requirements unknown to the natural law, perhaps, but which, Gilson reminded his audience, are listed in the *Summa Contra Gentiles* I, chapter 6. We may hope that a universal society is in the making, but it will only be so if humanity "accepts from the Church the perfect unity towards which it tends and which it is incapable of giving itself."[34]

This Pascalian interpreter of Aquinas believed that "the only universal society is not the republic of believers, or Christendom, but the Church."

---

33. Gilson's appendix to Beguin, "L'affair Gilson," 596; Gilson, *Les métamorphoses de la cité de Dieu*, 218.

34. Gilson, *Les métamorphoses de la cité de Dieu*, 248, 258; Gilson, *Choir of Muses*, 117; Gilson, *Les métamorphoses de la cité de Dieu*, 272–73, 285.

In 1954 Gilson's notion of world unity based in faith seemed to Hannah Arendt to "jeopardize political freedom."[35] She was no more impressed by the Pascalian Christian than by the Aristotelians ones.

The curious boundary notion of Christendom fascinated Étienne as neither separable from the church nor identical with it. Christendom was not an abstraction for Gilson. When he asks where it is, he responds that he has met it in churches the world over, and describes them. He had found it in a church near the railway station in Chicago, in which nothing "disturbed the silence, save for a thin trickle of water from Lake Michigan that fell drop by drop in a grotto of Lourdes. Where was I? Neither in America nor in France, nor at any geographical point on earth. Yet I had surely reached a journey's end, since I was at home: I was in Christendom." He had met it as an alien visitor to the church in Bloomington, Indiana, where an altar boy had approached him with a threat of excommunication from the pastor "if you do not take breakfast with him," and learned that *the Christian is not a stranger in any parish, for wherever there is a parish he stands on Christian soil.* It fascinated him particularly, perhaps, as a layman, as being a third human society, between the church and the state, to which "all disciples of Christ" belong.[36]

35. Gilson, *Les métamorphoses de la cité de Dieu,* 274; Courtine-Denamy, *Three Women in Dark Times,* 28, citing Arendt's "Concern with Politics in Recent European Political Thought."

36. "Where Is Christendom," in *A Gilson Reader,* 342–46, first published in *Temoignage,* January 1, 1956.

# 13

# "Facts Are for Cretins"

## Tilting against Baroque Windmills

"The Scholastic method," Étienne Fouilloux suggests, "sign-posted it-self by its speculative character. '*Les faits, c'est pour les crétins,*'" Père Régi-nald Garrigou-Lagrange was heard to say. In 1954, Garrigou was promoted from Qualifier to Consultor at the Holy Office. The same year, a second purge of Saulchoir uprooted Père Congar. "You want an article? You shall have one," Gilson told Père Labourdette in the September after the Rome Congresses of 1950, even if Garrigou-Lagrange would rather "see me as a gallows bird."[1] His renewed attack on neo-Thomism turned to its rather abstract doctrine of God.

Van Steenberghen received an admonitory letter in 1952: "The well in-tentioned tribe, by whom we are surrounded, will not fail to say that you invent Thomist proofs for the pleasure of refuting them.... The more we believe in intellectual freedom, the more we must be on guard about how we use it, and not play its adversaries' game, for they are more numerous than its defenders."[2] Gilson chose to pelt Roman Thomism under the cover of a continuous peppering of its predecessors. His offensive against his Thomist contemporaries took a roundabout turn, through Baroque scholas-ticism, perhaps as one-sidedly conceived.

This "anti-Cajetanian offensive, which dates from the beginning of the 1950s,"[3] has been faulted for a lack of attention to the prosaic in our Don Quixote. When Gilson set out to rebut the Roman Thomists, he had just buried his wife of forty years. If "the knight serves a lady that he may fight

1. Fouilloux, *Une église en quête de liberté,* 51 ("Facts are for cretins"); Gilson to Michel Labourdette, September 26, 1950, in Donneaud, ed., "Correspondance Éti-enne Gilson-Michel Labourdette," 517.

2. Gilson to Fernand Van Steenberghen, January 4, 1952, in Van Steenberghen, "Correspondance avec Étienne Gilson," 618–19.

3. Bonino, "Historiographie de l'école thomiste," 303.

the better," it may have been something beyond Clio, his historical muse, in whose service Gilson worked: "if the poet meets so many disappointments in daily life, it is because he is aiming above it. His 'mighty wings' get in his way when he walks."[4]

Gilson associated the idea that the "real distinction" functions as a proof of God's existence with Roman Thomism. Before the Thomist congress of 1950, he told Père Chenu: "I have chosen the section presided over by R.P. Garrigou-Lagrange to explain that saint Thomas does not introduce the proof of the existence of God into the *Summa* through the distinction between *esse* and *essentia* because, since the notion of *esse* is a principle, it cannot be demonstrated."[5] Was his argument strictly a matter of fidelity to the *Summa*?

For Garrigou, the first principles are fonts of intelligibility. Each of the first principles implies the others. He read in Aquinas and Aristotle that the first principle that enters our intellect is being; he took this to mean that the first principle, on which all human intellectual operations work, is the analytic proposition, or judgment, "Being is Being." Nonbeing follows from being, so the second principle is that of contradiction: a thing cannot both be and not be at the same time. The "ontological validity of our intellect, and of its first ideas, and its first principles, cannot be directly demonstrated," Garrigou says; but "it admits of a sort of indirect proof, by the logical process of *reductio ad absurdum*, by a recourse to the principle of contradiction."[6] It can be shown that the empiricists, idealists, and agnostics are led into absurdity, or contradiction, by their denial of the first principle "Being is Being."

Garrigou-Lagrange used the principle of sufficient reason to establish the existence of God. Because everything is intelligible, everything has a sufficient reason, whether in itself or in another. We can only make the process of *becoming* intelligible by asking about its sufficient reason. To ask about the rationale of things that change is to seek their efficient cause: "We are . . . certain that *every being which is indifferent to existence requires an efficient cause*, . . . because the intellect knows intuitively that this being does not exist as something which has existence intrinsically and primarily as its own *(per se primo)*, but as something which gets this existence from another *(ab alio* or *per aliud)*." It is "certain" or *necessary* that this "principle

4. Gilson, *Choir of Muses,* 25, 28.
5. Gilson to Marie-Dominique Chenu, August 21, 1950, in Gilson Correspondence.
6. Garrigou-Lagrange, *God: His Existence and Nature,* 118.

of causality" is "universally true"; "Reason" and not "experience" establishes the "fact of universal causality."[7]

The article Gilson gave Père Labourdette, "Les principes et les causes" (1952), is ostensibly concerned with the use of the principles of noncontradiction and of sufficient reason in the writings of the nineteenth-century Roman Thomist Gaetano Sanseverino. With the fundamentalist fixation upon what Saint Thomas Aquinas actually wrote for which he was later to be distinguished, Étienne points out that, unlike Sanseverino, Thomas never says things like "A is A, from which results the second [principle], A is not not-A." What does this narrow-minded scrutiny of Thomas's language tell us about Thomas's understanding of principles and causes? Gilson says that the reason the neo-Scholastics take the principle of contradiction as the axiom from which all other principles can be "indirectly" demonstrated is that it is *certain*. According to Sanseverino, after the first principle has dropped into it, the mind can form judgments, such as "being is being," or the principle of contradiction, "B is not not B." Saint Thomas differs from this neo-Scholastic tradition, Gilson says, because, for him, the first principle is not immediately related to judgment but to apprehension: and because apprehension "is not a judgment, it is not expressed under the form of a proposition, which today we would call the 'principle of identity.'" The first principle is *ens,* or entity, the object of simple apprehension. To say that entity is the first principle of knowledge is not to say anything about formal principles, the rules which make human thought intelligible, or rational. It is to say that the first constraint upon human thought is the nature of entities, the rules that govern reality. Every *ens* has being, is a *habens esse.* When Thomas says *impossibile est esse et non esse simul,* "the accent bears on being itself; it is the intrinsic impossibility for being not to be which is directly targeted, and this is probably why Saint Thomas did not experience the need to call the principle by the name which we give it today, which displaces the accent on the thing onto knowledge, and translates a fundamental exigency of being into the terms of non-contradiction within judgment." Sanseverino-Garrigou substitute conceptualization for the judgment of existence, or identify the two. When Sanseverino makes "the first principle of demonstration into the first principle of knowledge" he has bound himself to making conceptual principles *causes* of knowledge. Thomas does describe rules like that of noncontradiction as first principles, but for him, they are first principles of demonstration, not of knowledge. For Saint

7. Ibid., 193, 119.

Thomas the principle of knowledge is being: one has to be within reality, and know it, before one has anything to demonstrate; "if there is no knowledge, there is no matter for demonstrations." The "illusion shared by Descartes and his critics" is to imagine that formal principles yield knowledge of reality because they are formal principles, and not because being is anterior to thought.[8] All causes are principles, Gilson's article suggests, but if we take all principles as causes, we charge intelligibility, the rules of demonstration, with fabricating reality.

## There Is No Intuition of Being

After the publication of *L'être et l'essence* Maritain sent the author a letter thanking him for writing "in the perspective of the intuition on which all else depends." Although *L'être et l'essence* may have jolted Maritain's memory, one need not imagine that Maritain needed Gilson's assistance to construct his own version of existential Thomism. As in *Sept leçons* (1934), Maritain's *Existence and the Existent* (1947) founds metaphysics in an intuition of being. Designating himself a "palaeothomist," Maritain once again speaks of a unique form of judgment, "eidetic . . . visualization." He claims that this is the most abstract and active form of human knowledge, which is the counterpart of the act of being in things.[9]

*Existence and the Existent* is a metaphysical forest of symbols. It is rudely unpoetic to say that existence is unintelligible, as if it had no symbolic offshoots in the concepts it creates. So, says Maritain, if existence is not literally intelligible, as concepts are, it is nonetheless "superintelligible," as the "source" of the intelligibility of concepts. Metaphysics begins in "the third degree of abstraction," reaching above matter, above essences, and directly into existence. Maritain pictures essences as particular "shades," which flow from the darkest blue of existence. Without an intuitive abstraction of the act of being within things, we will not be able to know the essences, for "all other concepts are variations or determinations of this primary one."[10] The judgment of essence is an analogue of the judgment of existence.

8. Gilson, "Les principes et les causes" (1952), rev. version in the posthumous *Constantes philosophiques de l'être*, ch. 2, 53–84, 59, 62–64, 54.

9. Maritain to Étienne Gilson, May 15, 1948, in *Deux approches*, 168; McInerny, "Maritain, Jacques, (1882–1973)," 103; Maritain, *Existence and the Existent*, 1, 20. The frontmatter calls the book a "version," not, for instance, a "translation."

10. Maritain, *Existence and the Existent*, 25.

*L'être et l'essence* could appear to posit a new proof of the existence of God, from existence. In order to sidestep such a move, Gilson revised the fifth edition of *Le Thomisme* while Lawrence Shook was translating it. The translation, *The Christian Philosophy of Thomas Aquinas,* is said by Gilson, in the introductory notes, to derive from the "fifth, 1948" edition of *Le Thomisme,* although none of the other bibliographical material marks a new edition in that year. The French 1948 reprint of *Le Thomisme* and the English *Christian Philosophy of Thomas Aquinas* is, as it were, edition number 5½. No one should ever have to consider such matters, were it not for the significant fact that Gilson now apologizes for having described the distinction of essence and existence as a "sixth way," that is, for having made it sound like an additional argument for the existence of God over and above the "five ways" Thomas sets out. That distinction cannot be a demonstration of the existence of God because it "presupposes the very notion of the pure act of being," which a proof of the existence of God is supposed to discover. Gilson denies the possibility of a direct "intuition" of the act of being itself; existence is continuously "staring" us in the face; but we cannot "see" it, we can only "locate" it through judgment, "as the hidden root of what we can see and of what we can attempt to define."[11]

At the Thomistic congress of August 1950 he observed that Thomas never refers to the "real distinction" when proving the existence of God, not even in the Third Way, which may seem "irresistibly to invite" a reference to it. Gilson vigorously denied that the "five ways" rely upon a distinction between essence and existence in creatures. The fact that caused things require an Uncaused Cause, or that beings are generated and corrupted, proves neither that essence and existence is not identical within them nor that there is a being Whose Essence is Existing. "The contingency of finite being implies that one can attribute it to an uncaused cause; it does not demand that one draws out of it a composition of essence and existence": one cannot prove that sensible things contingently *exist* by proving that they are caused, moved, or corruptible. For existence, or being, is not the object of demonstration, or proof. Being is the principle, in the light of which we understand everything else. Any attempt to investigate it must be carried out in the light that being itself gives us: one cannot "make this principle seen" because its "light is that in which the eye sees everything else." The revealed "Ego sum qui sum" is at the threshold of the five ways, just as "being" is the threshold through which we must pass in speaking about

11. Gilson, *The Christian Philosophy of St. Thomas Aquinas,* 82, 368, 374.

empirical facts. But "the distinction of essence and existence is not something which we observe with our senses."[12] The five arguments for the existence of God each come back to sense experiences, not to an intuition of being, whether existentially contingent or existentially necessary.

Gilson tended (he was, to his regret, not scientific in the matter[13]) to write *être* rather than *exist,* because, he said, the existentialists had "property rights" in the word *existence.*[14] He was as careful a writer as he was a reader, and there may have been another thought at the back of his mind, which is that the word *existence* has a more generalizable (or less empirical) feel to it than "*a* being." He will take care to point out, in "Principes et causes," that "common being is an abstraction," not a real object but a logical construct. For Gilson, the act of being is an individual act within each concrete fact. The nonconceivability of being is due to its case-by-caseness. He says that "Being...is...first in the order of the concepts, and since our judgments are made up of concepts, it is also first in the order of judgment. Nevertheless, the concept of being always registers in the same manner an infinity of acts of existing, all different. It represents what St. Thomas has called...*ens commune:* the abstract notion of being, understood in its universal and pure indetermination."[15] *Ens commune* designates, not a universal, uniform object, but a plurality of unique acts. It is not doubled by a universal "substance" of existence. Gilson was as close to nominalism with respect to being*s* as a Thomist could properly be.

## Distinguishing Causes and Causality

Step by step from the early 1950s to the mid-1960s, Gilson brought his emphasis on facticity, and sense experience, into line with his stress on being. Philosophers like to work from an analytic table of contents in the first principles, he said, because that frees knowledge from the taint of sense experience. "I was in my seventy-eighth year," that is, in 1962, Gilson told Maritain, "when I perceived for the first time" that Thomas never uses "the word 'causa' in setting out the *prima via,*" that is, the argument from "movement" ("That doesn't prevent Garrigou-Lagrange from resting the

12. Gilson, "La Preuve du *De Ente et Essentia,*" 258–60, 258.
13. Gilson, *L'être et l'essence* (2nd ed.), 350–51.
14. Gilson, *L'être et l'essence* (1st ed.), 20.
15. Gilson, "Les principes et les causes," in *Constantes,* 68; Gilson, *The Christian Philosophy of St. Thomas Aquinas,* 44.

whole proof on the 'principle of causality.'")[16] The first principles are themselves modes of being, so that if "one concedes that causality is a first principle, it becomes inseparable from being: thus every being has a cause, even God." For Gilson, a cause is an active sort of fact, whereas causality is an interpretative intellectual category, or a concept. One still has to explain change by reference to a cause, "but the necessity of assigning" a cause "to it is an induction beginning from experience." Thomas gets the "content" or the "constraining force" of "causal inference," not out of a principle, "but from the intrinsic evidence of causality in each given case."[17]

The objects of each of the five arguments for the existence of God, motion, causes, and so on, are each energized by being, but one begins to work toward the existence of God by noticing the objects, observing them with sense perception, not by intuiting existence. Thus, the contingency of finite existents as such, that is, the "ontological difference" between finite essences and their acts of existing, does not function for the mature Gilson as a *proof* of the existence of God. From 1913 to 1940, Gilson simply assumed the facticity of Thomas's arguments for God's existence; after 1948, he highlighted their prosaic basis in sensed objects.

The point that principles or rules are not a hose out of which knowledge of facts sprinkles is also relevant in ethics. Jacques Maritain had noted in *Man and the State* that ethics had become "essentialized" since the seventeenth century, when "people had begun to think of Nature with a capital N": "natural law was thus conceived after the pattern of a *written* code... of which any just law should be a transcription, and which should determine a priori... the norms of human behavior through ordinances supposed prescribed by Nature." Taking the example of "genocide," a "new" crime for which, as ambassador to the Vatican, he had been fruitlessly attempting to extract a public condemnation,[18] Maritain argued that knowledge of particular moral laws emerges when human, "existential" situations "pose questions" to human nature. This "does not imply that such a prohibition was eternally inscribed as a kind of metaphysical feature in the essence of man."[19]

Gilson agreed with his friend that the natural law is an "unwritten law."[20] In this respect, their thinking was growing in the same, empirical direction.

16. Gilson, "Les principes et les causes," in *Constantes*, 53; Gilson to Jacques Maritain, November 28, 1963, in *Deux Approches*, 217.
17. Gilson, "Prolégomènes à la *Prima Via*," 54; Gilson, "Les principes et les causes," in *Constantes*, 81.
18. Maritain, *Man and the State*, 74–75; Barré, *Jacques et Raïssa Maritain*, 525–26.
19. Maritain, *Man and the State*, 80.
20. Ibid., 78.

Gilson recalls the "apparently paradoxical formula of Lucien Lévy-Bruhl: to the question 'what must one do' there is no reply." The Erasmian moralist continued:

> It is not possible to deduce the rules of morality from the first principle of practical reason, for no one doubts that he must pursue the good and avoid evil: the will essentially desires the good, but the principle does not tell us what is good and what is evil. One cannot deduce it analytically, for moral action bears on the particular case, whose circumstances no universal rule can foresee and because the virtue of prudence, which is the only thing capable of finding the suitable response to questions of this type, must at the end of the day resolve them by a sort of divination, certainly rational, but very different in its enterprise from that of deductive reason.... [T]here is a discontinuity between the order of the abstract universal to which the first principle applies in all its forms, and that of the concrete singular which is the domain of real objects of knowledge and of action.[21]

These lines, from "De la nature du principe," which follows "Les principes et les causes" in Gilson's posthumous *Constantes philosophiques de l'être,* are undatable. In a long, shrewd, and affectionate letter to "mon cher ami," Jacques, of January 1953, Gilson asked, "Why the devil do you say that your conclusions touching the natural law of the practical intellect don't count for the first principles of the speculative intellect? Don't you see that it is identically the same problem? You are not afraid of that blockhead Garrigaldo-Lagrangéen are you? Or is it that you really do not see the double-door of your liberating discovery? The grasp of the *content* of the first principle is as progressive as that of the content of the principles of practical reason." The rationalist's nonempirical way of understanding the principles "are the delight of professors of the history of philosophy, because they 'teach well.'"[22] They give all the appearance of working in the classroom because they are so easily memorized—and forgotten, after the test.

## Did Gilson Become a Single-Minded Thomist— or More of a Franciscan?

It has seemed to many readers that, after *L'être et l'essence,* the only thinker Gilson was willing to identify as a Christian philosopher was Saint Thomas.

21. Gilson, *Constantes,* 90.
22. Gilson to Jacques Maritain, January 29, 1953, in *Deux approches,* 184; Gilson, *Constantes,* 50.

It is natural "to ask whether (at the level of argumentative discourse proper to philosophy) a single rationalization is possible in order to be faithful to revelation." My opinion is that Gilson did not throw overboard "the concluding sentence of *La philosophie de saint Bonaventure* (1924): 'The philosophy of Saint Thomas and that of Saint Bonaventure complement one another as the two most universal interpretations of Christianity.'"[23] If I am right to imagine that there are traces of the Bonaventurian God in the *Thomisme* of 1944 and in *L'être et l'essence,* then it is likely that from 1950 Gilson further retraced his steps to where he had made his adult, intellectual entrance into the church, under what he had in 1924 called the "ensign of Saint-Francois-Saint-Dominique."[24]

In the first article of the first question of the *Summa Theologiae,* Thomas asks if theology can learn sufficient truths from philosophy, or whether it requires divine revelation. The *revelatum* consists of those facts that would be entirely unknown to us if God had not revealed them to us, such as the Trinity. The *revelabile* is whatever it is possible for God to reveal, the "revealable." Saint Thomas taught, Gilson claims in the 1942–1944 *Le Thomisme,* that God has revealed, not only *revelata,* theological data, such as the Trinity, but also *philosophical* truths, thus placing the latter among the *revelabile,* as a matter of concrete historical fact. In the course of his analysis of the *revelabile* and the *revelatum,* Gilson remarks that Saint Thomas "always speaks concretely about the concrete. Because we have forgotten this we have . . . changed into a logic of pure essences a doctrine which its author had conceived as an explanation of facts."[25]

In 1953 Gilson argues that Thomas looks at the question of revelation from a practical perspective, that of the salvation of the whole human race.

---

23. In the "postface" of his edition of the Maritain-Gilson letters, Prouvost argues that Gilson's conception of Christian philosophy narrowed from the pluralistic perspective of *The Spirit of Mediaeval Philosophy* toward Thomistic tunnel-vision. He feels that this entropic progression played false to the insight that Gilson had when he wrote his biography of Bonaventure, in the 1920s. Prouvost remarks that "la question que se pose est de savoir si (au niveau du discours argumentatif propre à la philosophie) une seule rationalisation est possible pour être fidèle à la présupposition révélée. Une des déclarations les plus nettes en faveur d'un pluralisme philosophique se trouve sans doute dans cette phrase conclusive de *La Philosophie de saint Bonaventure* (1924): 'La philosophie de saint Thomas et celle de saint Bonaventure se complètent comme les deux interprétations les plus universelles du christianisme, et c'est parce qu'elles se complètent qu'elles ne peuvent ni s'exclure ni coïncider.'" *Deux Approches,* 279. Prouvost's notes provide a goldmine of information about both Maritain and Gilson; readers can judge for themselves how much we owe to his edition of their letters, but not all will realize how few of today's scholars are capable of his achievement.

24. Gilson, cited in Gouhier, "Post-Face: Etienne Gilson," 153.

25. Gilson, *Le Thomisme* (5th ed.), 19–20.

Gilson's "Note sur le revelabile selon Cajetan" claims that, for Thomas, God considered, not whether, in theory, He was "*knowable*," but what had, necessarily, to be *done*—what concrete measures had to be taken—in order to save the human race. With this concrete finality in view, God did not procrastinate over the formal question of what might be knowable about himself "to a few, after a long time, and with an admixture of errors." Holding a microscope up to his sitter's book, Gilson paints these defects as cumulative, picturing Thomas's question as concluding that, without revelation, an elite band of philosophers would take eons to reach partially false conclusions about God's existence and nature. This is a reading of Thomas that would not have displeased that eighteenth-century anti-rationalist David Hume.

With his psychological addiction to subtlety, Thomas's Baroque commentator obscured this plain truth. Cajetan finds in the same passage in the *Summa* a distinction between *revelabilia* and *demonstrabilia*. The *demonstrabilia* are those things God must have left for philosophers to discern for themselves, because they are, in principle, knowable to human reason. With the division of human knowledge into the conceptual principles of *revelabile* and *demonstrabilia*, Cajetan has made the necessary bifurcation for the new division of theology into "natural" and "revealed." Just as, de Lubac had argued, Cajetan had assisted at the birth of the "state of pure nature," which achieves its final end within nature, so, as Gilson has it, the man who "loved distinctions" invented natural theology, as distinct from the revealed branch of the discipline. Like the state of pure nature, the notion of *demonstrabilia* is "demanding": once the distinction is made "it is necessary to deny that the demonstrables can also be revealables in the full sense of the word."[26]

Gilson's "denunciation of the errors of the" Dominican "school would not have been so vigorous if there had not been, behind Cajetan, the profiles of contemporary neo-Thomism. . . . At its origins the neo-Thomist project is tainted by a kind of well intentioned rationalism, linked to the hardening of the formal distinction between the natural and the supernatural order." Gilson understood contemporary Catholic Aristotelianism as the petrified expression of this rationalism. As he joked to Maritain in 1953, "The worst enemy of Thomas in the Dominican order was Aristotle, of whom Cajetan is the prophet."[27]

26. Gilson, "Note sur le *revelabile* selon Cajetan," 202; de Lubac, *Surnaturel,* 174; Gilson, "Note sur le *revelabile* selon Cajetan," 203.

27. Bonino, "Historiographie de l'école thomiste," 308; Gilson to Jacques Maritain, April 6, 1953, in *Deux approches,* 188.

But did Cajetan take the steps toward a separated philosophy that Gilson ascribes to him? Henri Donneaud says he did not: his commentary is merely distinguishing between the *revelabile tantum,* the revealable *as such,* from the demonstrable, the one being known by the formal light of revelation and the other by the natural light of reason. He does not say that the *revelabile tantum* contains the entire *revelabile.* Moreover, the 1953 "Note" turns a blind eye to the *revelatum,* those things that are intrinsically inaccessible to human reason, such as that God is Triune and became Incarnate. It does so, Donneaud argues, because it tacitly turns *everything, in its relation to God,* into a possible object of revelation: "In order to criticize Cajetan for having retracted the notion of revelabile so as to exclude the *demonstrabilia* from it, Gilson has himself enlarged his own conception of *revelabile* in order to include the *revelatum* in it."[28]

The *revelatum*—our knowledge that, for example, God became Incarnate in Palestine and is a Trinity of Persons—was revealed to us in history. Without that 'saving history' which the Bible describes, these doctrines would be unknown to us. What Gilson does is to consider the question of *natural knowledge of God* in a historical context. The question then becomes what, as the history of human civilization tells us, our ethics and metaphysics have been like in the concrete: an opaque mixture of genuine insight and culturally relative aberrations. Gilson considers "natural" knowledge of God in a "practical" rather than "speculative" light: this is the mediaevalist's way of bringing the issue down from a question about "philosophy" in the abstract, to one about philosophers, in their factual historicity. Donneaud is unjust, I think, to complain that in later editions of *Le Thomisme* Gilson went back to his customary distinction of the *revelatum* and the *revelabile.*[29] He does not so much identify *revelatum* and *revelabile,* in the "Note" on Cajetan, as consider them both in the same practical, human, and historical light.

Gilson's philosophical manipulation of Cajetan and his play upon the notion of the *revelabile* have two facets. The first is that historical facts are contingent. Someone could say to the defender of Christian philosophy that it may *in fact* be the case that belief in Christian revelation has altered the way some philosophies work, but that is just a fact. We can in principle prescind from it: one always sets out, toward God, from the same position. If the status of Christian philosophy depends on a fact, it depends on something accidental, something that does not *have* to be taken into account.

28. Donneaud, "Note sur le *revelabile* selon Étienne Gilson," 646, 643.
29. Ibid., 643–44.

Both the reactions to *L'être et l'essence* and the controversy over the Nouvelle Théologie had acutely raised the issue of historicity. Gilson makes it impossible to escape into thinking about God "in principle," outside of history by saying that the "whole show" is *revelabile;* from eternity, God decided that the "economy of salvation" should thus proceed.

In the second place, the question on which Gilson joined ranks with Fourvière, the "natural desire," had made him very articulate on the subject of the "final cause," for which humanity has been created by God. In this article, he is picturing the relation of Creator to creature from one particular angle, that of finality.

It was Bonaventure who had "suborned" philosophy for theology on the grounds, Gilson said, that the *purpose* of philosophical wisdom is to lead to the vision of God. There is something of "Bonaventure" in the Thomas whose purity Gilson defends against the Baroque commentators. "Le christianisme et la tradition philosophique" (1943) had distinguished Bonaventure and Thomas on the grounds that the former was preoccupied with the practical question of personal salvation, whereas for Thomas theology is a speculative science dealing with the salvation of the whole human race. Intermittently, from 1952, Gilson will redefine Thomistic theology as taking its cue from the practical question of the salvation of humanity—he never took the last, existentialist step to "individual salvation."

When I suggest that there is a hint of Bonaventure in Gilson's later thought, we may bear in mind what he said of Laura: "It was to Petrarch alone that a dazzling golden-haired girl appeared that morning in the church at Avignon. Everyone could see *her,* but only he could see the Muse of a *Canzoniere.*"[30] I am speaking here of what Bonaventure meant within the special alchemy of Gilson's mind. Against the Roman Thomists, he wants to begin from a "fact," and the one he selects is *salvation,* as the concrete purpose of God in creating humanity. With that final end in view, Gilson's version of "philosophy" sometimes appeared to be brusquely functionalized or instrumentalized, in the service of theology.

In December 1954 Père Yves Congar discussed Chenu's case with Michael Browne, who had been elected Master of the Dominican Order a few months later. Browne read Congar the passage in "*Une école de théologie...* where P. Chenu said that a theology worthy of the name is a spirituality which has found its instruments of conceptualization; that the grandeur and the truth of Scotism derive from how it transmits the spiritual life of Saint Francis... P. Browne saw in this a relativism in doctrinal matters.

---

30. Gilson, *Choir of Muses,* 14.

To say that a theology is not driven by the rigor of its systematisation and the content of its conclusions, but from the spiritual life which it transmits, is seriously to misunderstand the absolute value of metaphysics . . . [H]e relativizes Saint Thomas."[31] Chenu's understanding of how theology works was indebted to Gilson's exposition of the theology of Bonaventure. It may have been frustrating to see a friend so hardily penalized for having generalized one's insights. Chenu's case may have kept his allegiance to Saint Dominic *and* Saint Francis in the foreground of Gilson's attention; but the kernel he was now drawing out of Bonaventure was perhaps more "factual" than experiential or phenomenological. It is the functional or practical quality of Bonaventure's idea of philosophy that made sense to the draper's son.

## The Human Soul as Existent

It was, Gilson argued in 1955, Cajetan's fondness for Aristotle that barred him from *certainty* of the immortality of the soul.[32] Cognition transcends materiality. Working from the soul's operations, that is, from cognition, Cajetan tried to show that the soul must be immortal because it is functionally immaterial. This argument falls at the fence of the Aristotelian dictum that we cannot think without images. Cajetan's commentary on the *De Anima* claims that Aristotle intended to say that the obstacle is an accident: the use of imagination by thought is not inherent in the soul as such. Abandoning this circular eisegesis, Cajetan later said that Aristotle made a mistake; still later, he kicked in trying to demonstrate the immortality of the soul.

For Thomas, on the other hand, the soul-body conjunction is *one* act of existence, in which the soul performs the existence making act of individuation upon the material body: "As an ontological block, man is made truly one by the unity of its existential act."[33] Each soul is a pure subsistent form, a block of *esse* that does not depend upon matter for its existence. It prefers not to perform its essential function of reasoning without its body; but within the conjunction of the human, the act of being or *esse* belongs necessarily to the soul. It is because he focuses on the soul as an *existent* that Thomas is *certain* that it survives death, and not, as some mediaeval

31. Congar, *Journal d'un théologie*, 330–31.
32. Gilson, "Cajetan et l'humanisme théologique," 120.
33. Gilson, *The Christian Philosophy of St. Thomas Aquinas*, 196–98; Gilson, *Elements of Christian Philosophy*, 229.

Aristotelians legitimately read in the Philosopher, as a collective mind, but as an individual.

These latter were points Gilson could and did make without reference to any commentators; here he makes them against Cajetan, denounced as a poor humanist for having failed to notice that, "in order for an incorruptible substance to continue to exist, it must first exist." Gilson concludes that "today certain people hold Cajetan's commentary as the most efficacious *corruptorium Sancti Thomae* which has ever been composed; whilst others . . . print it alongside the *Summae* in order to read the text in its light."[34]

In his first letter to de Lubac of July 1956, he told the Jesuit that Cajetan's "famous commentary is . . . the consummate example of a *corruptorium Thomae*. . . . [F]rom the viewpoint of the final cause, which is the highest of causes, every evidence . . . *in mankind as God created them,* points to the supernatural end for which God destined us. In short, according to the *Contra Gentiles,* the structure and nature of created man are those of a being called to eternal bliss. But who cares, these days, about the final cause? It's only the formal cause that counts."[35]

## Is Gilson's "Baroque Scholasticism" a Strawman?

After a quarter of century, in which Baroque Thomism had been put to flight, it has begun to find defenders, who inquire whether "fidelity" to the "existential understanding of *esse* by itself . . . constitute[s] a sufficient *historiographical* hypothesis" by which to test the "history of Thomism."[36] Gilson's deprecation of the neo-Thomist conflation of Aristotle with Thomas reached a new height in *L'être et l'essence,* in which he discovered a tradition of nonrealism, flowing from Aristotle to Avicenna to Scotus, who squeezed the "accidentiality" of existence flat, to Suarez, to a Kleutgen for whom metaphysical "science" has Nothing as its object. Or does he not so much discover as invent it? Did he invent the Cajetan of his "offensive"? Brunschvicg felt that Gilson's weak spot was his choice of strawmen. And

34. Gilson, "Cajetan et l'humanisme théologique," 127, 136.

35. Gilson to Henri de Lubac, July 8, 1956, in de Lubac, ed., *Letters of Gilson to de Lubac,* 24–25.

36. Bonino, "Historiographie de l'école thomiste," 312–13. My italics. An admirer of Gilson's thought need have no quarrel with Bonino's objection, insofar as it entails that it would be inane to write off *everything* in the Thomism of Cajetan (say, his interpretation of Aquinas on the Trinity), or Suarez (as for instance, his Mariology), because "it's bound to be tainted with essentialism."

not only strawmen, or targets; Donneaud considers that the historical Saint Thomas did not write the first question of the *Summa* to defend Christian philosophy.

Gilson was aware that there are other elements in Aristotle than the part he has cut out of him; historians may argue that he has taken a mere slice out of Scotus, Cajetan, or Suarez. This was a consequence of his philosophical method, which could be called "perspectival." Plato observes, in the *Theaetetus:* "We are in a critical situation where it is a necessity for us to turn the objects on all sides in order to probe the truth." When he is thinking philosophically, Gilson cuts his philosophers down to their finest particles and rearranges the pieces. He presents his object as a cubist painting does, from a variety of different angles. Historians make use of naturalistic portraiture, but it would be unwise to draw conclusions about contingent facts from works in the style of Picasso. Gilson fixes Saint Thomas in a single glance. It is, as Jason West says, "unclear that St. Thomas really discovered" his "theory of esse" "through sustained reflection upon the 'qui est' of Exodus 3.13–14." Gilson makes Exodus 3:13–14 into a pure symbol of the scriptural basis of Thomas's theology. A philosopher has, he says, to make "cuts": objections to the lost unity of reality resemble the "chagrin of the tailor at the moment when he cuts a beautiful piece of stuff. Without that mutilation, no potential clothes." The draper's son wielded his scissors not only on the philosophers, but on metaphysical objects, such as the transcendentals. When he conducted a debate with Maritain about whether art is a kind of knowledge, that is, whether beauty *is* truth, he insisted that "in order not to wound truth . . . it is . . . suitable to define each transcendental, not in its relation to the others, but such as it is in itself, when it is alone."[37]

But Gilson was not merely an inexorable *analyst*. One can, he turns around to say, only make the principles *clear* by treating them like mathematical notions, that is, as strictly definable within an order of numerical equivalents. This clarity cannot last, because "the first glance at a metaphysical notion loses itself in an impenetrable thicket, as if the exigent notion of being were seized in its totality and refused to allow itself to be analyzed." Being *is* a unity, so that when one tries to seize one of its modes, "all of them want to come along together." This is why Parmenides saw all of the aspects of Being, its eternity, immutability, necessity, identity with itself, and simplicity, "in one single blow." The laws of human discourse constrained

---

37. West, "The Thomistic Debate Concerning the Existence and Nature of Christian Philosophy," 52–53; Gilson, *Constantes,* 124; Gilson, *Matières et formes,* 222.

the first philosopher to "enumerate" the modes of being one at a time. But the metaphysician's work is not "deduction, nor even cataloguing or classifying, but rather habituating itself to living in the primary notion," being.[38] Thus, in his philosophy, Gilson cuts out blocks of essence in order to lay them against a background of being, as refractions from it, positive and negative. His cubist portrait of Cajetan is not intended to be naturalistic; it tests history from the dynamic center of eternity within history, and that is *esse*. Modernist art contains some visual jokes.

## Radical Contingency

In 1956 Gilson was again noting that philosophical judgments of existence cannot say *what* it is they perceive; they only achieve a positive name for this insight with the revelation to Moses. The positive revelation of the name of the object of our judgments leaves us with a negative knowledge of God. Gilson said, "Even in the theology of Thomas Aquinas, . . . it is specified that . . . we do not know the meaning of the verb *is* when applied to God."[39] God's act of being cannot be circumscribed in any concept.

The efforts of Henry of Ghent, Duns Scotus, and Descartes to elucidate the nature of God more positively than Aquinas had done, by reference to the concept of divine *infinitude,* hit upon a notion which has no proportion to human *finitude.* Humanity out of proportion to God finds itself out of proportion to everything. Pascal turned the hourglass upside down and perceived infinitude within the contingent universe: "Man loses himself in the smallest thing as in a maze and he becomes to himself the most inextricable of mazes."[40]

Once dislodged from its secure tenure in the existential act, the world of essences has lost its hold upon us: "We have even ceased to imagine that what is best and deepest in any finite part" of the cosmos "can be expressed in terms of quiddities and exhaustively expressed by abstract definitions." Those Christian metaphysicians who base their enterprise in the intuition of essences rather than the revelation of being have thereby positioned themselves in a radically contingent universe, whose ordering principles are unknowable. Non-Christian existentialists have seen the point: the seeming

38. Gilson, *Constantes,* 29–30.
39. Gilson, "Theology and the Unity of Knowledge," in *The Unity of Knowledge,* ed. Lewis Leary (New York: Doubleday, 1955), 35–46, reprinted in *A Gilson Reader,* 141–55, 144.
40. Ibid., 151.

*philosophies* of Karl Jaspers and Heidegger "could be understood as . . . attempts to provide a non-Christian answer for the questions raised by a Christian universe . . . and the condition of man in such a universe."[41]

## Some Americans Are Not Amused: Living in Two Worlds

Thérèse D'Alverny remarks that the European students who first heard Gilson speak about the *Métamorphoses de la cité de Dieu* enjoyed his sense of humor. But, she says, "Canadian and American students seemed to have more austere tastes. It was there that a friend of Gilson, a professor at the 'Pontifical Institute' in Toronto . . . assembled . . . *A Gilson Reader*, . . . [1957]. The selection brought together, above all, articles or extracts concerning the 'Christian philosophy' of Thomas Aquinas, and education, a subject more relevant in America than in Europe. Our jovial professor from the Hautes Études and the Collège de France seemed to be transformed into a doctor of the Church."[42]

The New World harbored the possibility of creating Catholic universities. This cultural context is partly responsible for the reception of Gilson's "Franciscan" turn: the theologizing educationalist appealed to some, and they regarded his aims as achievable, whereas other professors of philosophy in the financially independent and ever so highly Catholic schools of America were unexcited by the prospect of founding their discipline in theology. Finding him in Washington in 1955, Monsignor Hart invited Gilson to speak at Catholic University of America. The lecture was housed in a minor auditorium, so as not to spark the wrath of the dean of philosophy, Fr. Ignatius Smith. Hart took the precaution of inviting the dean to open the meeting: he "introduced Gilson, carefully pointing out that he personally held no brief for Christian philosophy and citing texts from Thomas in his own support." The 750 students who squeezed into the room thanked Gilson with "rousing cheers." Vernon Bourke recalls that "at the time that his North American students issued *An Etienne Gilson Tribute* (1959), I wrote and told Gilson that some Catholic colleges and universities were . . . abandoning the teaching of philosophy and substituting something that they called theology—and they were labeling this a Gilson program." In an essay of 1962, James Collins approaches Gilson's "proposal" not as a *theory* about the relation of philosophy to theology, but as a *program* to be

41. Ibid., 153–54.
42. D'Alverny, "Nécrologie Étienne Gilson," 428.

pursued in philosophy departments, and with results likely to stunt the inventiveness of philosophers.[43] It did not help matters that while tilting against the notion of Thomas's Aristotle commentaries as a Philosophical *Summa,* one had discovered that Thomas and Aristotle both said that a young person should not engage upon the study of metaphysics before the age of fifty; Quixote conceded that "it could be that young people today are more intelligent than they were in the 13th century." As Gilson's close friend Henri Gouhier remarked, "A life spent between two worlds poses its problems."[44] A philosophical debate that had been stimulated by ecclesial ruptures in Europe had serious consequences in the United States; his anti-Cajetanian provocations were not taken as a joke on the other side of the Atlantic. And of course, Gilson was not innocent of the intention for them to be taken seriously; he had always looked to America as the place where one could achieve what appeared to be impracticable in Europe. Finally, in 1956, the Collège de France processed his pension, after five years of penury for a fiscally inept widower whose wife had balanced the books. By then, Gilson had taken his decisive step into aesthetics. The deepest thread by which Saint Bonaventure was tied to his heart was not ecclesial-political, but artistic.

43. Shook, *Gilson,* 328; Bourke, "'Aeterni Patris,'" 8; Collins, *Three Paths in Philosophy,* 281.
44. Gilson, "Note sur un texte de S. Thomas" (1954), in *Autour de saint Thomas,* 35–40, 39; "Une vie entre deux mondes pose des problèmes," Gouhier, "Post-Face: Etienne Gilson," 149.

# 14

# A "Pictorial Approach to Philosophy"

## A Modernist Aesthetic

Gilson regarded himself as a Burgundian. Although his paternal family tree tends against that supposition, he had planted himself in the maternal soil by acquiring a home in Yonne. The priest who presided over his musical education, at the Petit Séminaire Notre Dame Des Champs, Abbé Victor Thorelle, came from Pont-sur-Yonne and had "said his first mass" in the Cathedral of Auxerre. These mediaeval villages "became shrines to Étienne as he grew older and he loved to tell his friends how and why to visit them, even as he sent them to Vézelay and La Cordelle."[1] During his years at the Petit Séminaire, the Parisian made a ritual visit to the Louvre each week. So as not to divide the *conjunctum,* we may say that Romanesque Vézelay and Paris each contributed to his aesthetic tastes.

A lifelong friend recalled that the "most demanding forms of art did not displease him; to visit an exhibition of Picasso's designs and engravings in his company was a great privilege." Gilson's aesthetic sensibility was modernist. He was something of an artistic puritan both in his preference for the purely formal beauty of "ancient Greek temples, primitive Roman churches or Cistercian chapels" and in his admiration for the "geometrical painting" of Mondrian, which has "form without content." So austere was his conception of each specific art that he recommended a silent ballet—Jerome Robbin's *Moves,* of 1961.[2]

## Formalism—and the Muse

Gilson had spent 1915 to 1918 in a prison officer's camp, writing articles in defense of anti-naturalism in aesthetics and reading Bonaventure's

1. Shook, *Gilson,* 7–8.
2. D'Alverny, "Nécrologie Étienne Gilson," 429; Gilson, *Matières et formes,* 73, 137, 200.

*Commentary on the Sentences.* In 1920 he was writing that those who perpetually experience the presence of God "consider the universe as a transparent veil beyond which one can divine the creator everywhere in it; as a mirror in which...we perceive the reflection of his face."[3] The germ of Gilson's aesthetics was the conviction that the world which artists evoke is not a photo-realistic copy of physical objects or the reduplication of an idea.

A few green leaves of this notion emerge in *Dante the Philosopher* (1939), in which Gilson argues that we cannot assess *The Divine Comedy* by correlating its characters with historical facts: Dante's "Beatrice" was "born of the genius of Dante, not the marriage of Folco Portinari and Cilia Caponsacchi."[4] The physical beauty of Beatrice releases Dante's poetic genius to take flight and sing because the desire which she arouses in him *exceeds* anything which a corporeal body can give.

The bud begins to flower in *Choir of Muses* (1951), in which the physical beauty of the artist's muse is taken as a promissory note of a "beauty which transcends her." It is the muse's fate to disappear into the artist's work, whose end she serves. Wagner's Mathilde "was merely Isolde's understudy." Few are the artists who realize that Isolde, too, is a "vision" of "something above art," sent by God.[5]

Gilson the historian, whose muse was Clio, the "endless gossip," was filled with interest in the conspirations between artists and women. He considered the relationship an irreplaceable one: "The poet himself, in the concrete fact of his personality, must make himself into the man who can give birth to the work." For this he needs a feminine alter ego: "To create life, a man needs a woman. To create the perfection of beauty...the man must also *be* the woman." The *Commedia* would be drier and emptier if Dante "had not so deeply absorbed the femininity of Beatrice" and with it "that *Mundus Muliebris* of which Baudelaire wrote." Duccio's Madonna contains a churchfull of human types. Gilson has been called a "Thomists' Thomist." That is true if we think of Saint Thomas Aquinas as engrossing the troubadours Francis, Villon, Dante, and Baudelaire, whose "latent Platonism" is revealed in the "preface of *Paradise artificiels,*" which "affirms... the existential primacy of the dream over reality."[6]

To the extent that his muse was the access which his senses gave him to

3. Gilson, "Essai sur la vie intérieure," 32.
4. Gilson, *Dante the Philosopher,* 53.
5. Ibid.; Gilson, *Choir of Muses,* 54, 176, 29.
6. Ibid., 9, 26, 81–80; Jaki, *Lord Gifford and His Lectures,* 28; Gilson, *Choir of Muses,* 78.

the existence of the world, Gilson did not keep her on a pedestal. By 1953 the philosopher who had admired Chesterton's *Thomas Aquinas* had grown so fat that Maurice Gilson ordered him to diet. Étienne was so far from complying with his doctor brother's instructions that, visiting Belgium for the conference at which he gave his paper on metaphysical experience, he "got stuck in his bathtub and had to ring for emergency assistance."[7]

## Maritain and Gilson Give the Mellon Lectures

In the 1920s and 1930s Gilson's contemporaries had delighted in artistic mediaevalism. Maritain wrote *Art and Scholasticism;* Eric Gill forged pastiche Romanesque lithographs and composed *Beauty Looks After Herself,* a vernacular exposition of Maritain's ideas. In 1952 Maritain gave the Mellon lectures on the fine arts in Washington, published as *Creative Intuition in Art and Poetry.* Gilson was invited the following year, presenting his Mellon lectures in March and April 1955. He would fall out severely with Jacques Maritain on the question of whether aesthetic intuition is sensible or intellectual.

Gilson told his audience at the outset that he would not give them a philosopher's interpretation of *paintings.* Rather, he would meditate aloud upon a "pictorial approach to philosophy" in order to show how paintings express the *philosopher's* problem.[8] The philosopher's problem is "Why is there something rather than nothing?" How far was Gilson's expression of that problem conditioned by his aesthetic experiences? He might not have seized on the notion of existence as *dynamic and actual form,* were it not for his musical sensibility. He owes his conceptualization of the experience to Bergson. He rarely mentions music without naming Bergson within a sentence or two. In *Painting and Reality,* the Thomist gives pictures, rather than music, as an analogy of what a philosopher understands by "existence."

An *anima naturaliter Aristotelicae* would be tempted to exhibit *Painting and Reality* in the reverse order to that in which the lectures were given. Gilson's text must be taken literally, however, because the order he chooses is theological. Although this exegete refused to call his philosophy of art "Thomistic," because the author of the *Summa Theologiae* said nothing about the abbey church at Saint-Denis and had never seen a painting,

---

7. Shook, *Gilson,* 319.
8. Gilson, *Painting and Reality,* 7.

Gilson follows the order he attributes to Thomas. He begins with the two ways of existing: the eternal God *is existence,* whereas all things that endure in time *have existence.*

Gilson continues with an analysis of temporality familiar to readers of Augustine's *Confessions.* The art form that most fully exhibits the temporal condition is music. In music, the tempo of contingency is, as it were, speeded up, because its material bases are *sounds,* which rapidly come into being and pass away. The written score which the performers use is not music. Music only actually exists when it is being performed. On the other hand, paintings are *things.* Things endure much more slowly than sounds: it is unusual to see a thing melting into nothingness.

The topic of art has two sides: one, the objective, which Gilson calls *philosophy of art,* and the other, having to do with the human experience of works of art, which he calls *aesthetics.* It is only as the objects of aesthetic experience that paintings exist as paintings. When the Louvre is closed, and the lights dark, the *Mona Lisa* subsides into simple thingliness; when the night porter passes by, and glances at her, she becomes a painting. And so it might seem that the painting as such comes and goes almost as rapidly as music does. Not quite so, for the slow enduringness of the *thing* objectively conditions our *experience* of the work of art. Gilson concludes that "in the case of music, we have a fleeting apprehension of a fleeting and always incompletely existing thing; in the case of painting, we have a changing, fleeting, and always incomplete experience of a stable, complete, and enduring entity." We cannot, except in memory, when its actual existence is past, experience a complete symphony, but we can contemplate a whole painting: "The powerful shock, sometimes amounting to a blow, inflicted by certain paintings upon our sensibilities is due to the fact that, being solid bodies, they are totally given at once."[9]

The artist utilizes the expressiveness of a particular material. Because they *are* oil on canvas or wood, set fast forever, once dry, paintings are best suited to depict *motionless* images. Because of the manner of their material existence, paintings do best at capturing, not the transitory, but the immobile. Debussy could "do" the sea, and Wagner could represent musical battles, but "dynamic action" does not work well in paintings. Rather, "painting is best equipped to depict" the "still life." As the Dutch masters extend the still-life, from bowls of fruit, to churches, houses, and streets, their game plan remains that of capturing a motionless quality. Even the people

9. Ibid., 41, 61.

shown in the Dutch still-lives are frozen for a quiet moment of bare activity: Jan Vermeer's "famous View of Delft shares in the same qualities of quiet presence and *actionless existentiality* that characterize his little street." The seventeenth-century masters did not seek to rival the as yet uninvented art of photography. The Dutch still-life painters sought something more than an imitation of the substance of things. No less than its modern counterpart, the still-life is an "abstract painting": it has "no subject."[10]

Paintings get back to the silent act of existing, before the narrative of definition begins. For "the things that a still life represents exercise only one single act, but it is the simplest and most primitive of all acts, namely, to be." Painting is not an entirely nonrepresentative art-form, but what it best represents is not the essence of natural objects but their primitive "act of existing"; thus, "the true work of art is 'the one which *is*.'" The painter has his own way of perceiving the force of the metaphysician's question "Why is there something rather than nothing": he unwraps the envelope of words, meanings, and doings from things and, having found out their secret "act of being," "provides us with a visible image of it that corresponds, in the order of sensible appearances, to what its intuition is in the mind of the metaphysician."[11]

The painter is a creator, bringing a little world into existence. Although the painter does not work ex nihilo, as God does, in breathing existence into contingent things, she can pass on her own "communicated existence" to her work. If, as Saint Thomas said in the *De potentia*, "To act is nothing else than to communicate that by which the acting being is in act . . . to the extent that it is possible," then painters can transfer their own act of existing to their works. Such a communication of existence is, Gilson says, "the least imperfect image there is of what theologians call creation." God's creativity has two consequences: it lends existence and it divides those existents into classes. The painter who invents a little world on oil and canvas creates a thing that is so far incarnate in its material that it has only one existence: paintings are absolute individuals; the reproduction (which loses the material texture) is not the painting. Thus blocked out as a singular existent by the artist, the painting both exercises and expresses the act of existence: "An etching done from a pen drawing of Pieter Bruegel succeeds in educing the most complex landscape from the blank surface of a plate. The mere interplay of the lines, ordered as they are by a supremely lucid imagination,

10. Ibid., 46, 48–50. My italics.
11. Ibid., 50, 135, 50.

even permits him to pretend that the very Journey to Emmaus . . . is included in this creation of his hand."[12] Bruegel *reinvents* the journey to Emmaus by giving it actual existence as an image.

Thomas's cool definition of the communicated act, in the *De potentia*, has its coarser aspect in Gilson's conception of artistic making as a naturally communicated *energy:* "the troubadours," he said in *Choir of Muses*, "saw their delight as intimately linked with the delight of nature bursting into new life in springtime." If, for the troubadours, "the fullest well-spring of delight is man's love for woman," the "Scholastics used to define the beautiful *(pulchrum):* that which pleases when seen." This is why the poet can only become a maker by "absorbing the spiritual essence of a woman."[13]

From his infancy, the draper's son had the good fortune of having observed a great artist at work: his mother Caroline "possessed" an attribute that was useful in the dry goods business: "with deft twists of her hands and fingers she could transform remnants of fabric into hats, kerchiefs and other pleasing and useful objects." Perhaps the image of his mother's creative hands, plucking and stitching her toile, remained with Étienne all his life. Cécile Gilson was a professional painter, and she advised her father about his lectures. *Painting and Reality* claims that the artist does not impart her act of existence out of her mind, but rather gives it through her hands (as God does in scripture). The painter must teach her hands to think, for it is they who will exercise her creativity. The idea for the work floats vaguely in her mind, as the creative process begins, like the shadow of the thing it will become, but the painter cannot contemplate such "indistinct" possibilities: to "enable him to see his own images, the hand of the painter must give them actual being."[14]

The painter imparts existence and essence to his little world, so that it lives from its own center: "still more than it is an individual, each painting . . . is a completely self-sufficient system of internal relations regulated by its own laws." Like all human beings, painters live through their senses, but their inspiration requires the play of *imagination* upon sense perception: "His starting point is fantasy," and any element of the sensed object to be depicted that does not accord with the "fiction" is "ruthlessly eliminated." The art object is related to a given world, but through "abstraction" rather than pictorial or literal representation. When we visit Siena, in

12. Ibid., 347–48, 127.
13. Gilson, *Choir of Muses*, 172; Gilson, *Painting and Reality*, 175; Gilson, *Choir of Muses*, 79.
14. Shook, *Gilson*, 4; Gilson, *Painting and Reality*, 153.

order to observe works of art, *we* will see lives of Christ and his Mother; what mattered to the painter was how to set up these life scenes as relationships of lines. The painter does not invent out of thin air, but her visual object is the "plastic forms" that can be made out of the life-scene.[15]

Artistic creation illuminates the philosophy of nature; the two are more immediately analogous to one another than either is to divine creativity. The "pictorial approach to philosophy" deviously makes a way to restate some Aristotelian theses. Aristotle found in nature three things: matter, privation, and form. If we have long ago had the habit of constructing dollhouse furniture, we notice the materials for little tables and chairs on a visit to a hardware store: when a seamstress sees a bit of cloth, or the carpenter a plank of wood, he or she notices what *could be* made out of them. Makers have the gift of perceiving privation. They see that a material is asking to be cut and sewn into the form of a dress, or sawn and hammered into a table. The fabric *could be* twisted into the form of a hat; this *could be* is the positive privation of a form. Gilson comments that "the aesthetic inspiration of Aristotle's philosophy of nature is clearly felt in . . . this curious notion of privation. . . . [T]he notion of privation points out the non-being of something that ought to be or . . . the absence of something that should be there. . . . [T]he becoming of every work of art consists in substituting the presence of a certain form for the privation of that form in a certain matter."[16]

The painter gives the requisite material a "separate existence" by giving it a *form:* only that which "is endowed with determinate size, shape, and position in space" is capable of its own act of existence. Nature is not an artist; no organism emerges from her whose function is simply to give aesthetic delight. Nature creates art by the roundabout route of producing artists, who sense in the whole realm of organic things just this positive privation: where is that "earthly paradise" in which objects *could* exist only "in order to please the perceiving powers by which they are apprehended"?[17]

Aesthetics looks to the qualities of a work of an art that please a subject. The objective philosophy of art locates the beauty of a work in the fact of its having integrity, as an individual, harmony, as a "world" functioning according to its own pictorial laws, and clarity. All three, but especially clarity, or "radiance," make the object pleasing by making it intelligible. In the "terrestrial paradise" of the work of art, intelligibility is matter made mean-

15. Gilson, *Painting and Reality,* 135, 133, 241, 143.
16. Ibid., 115–16.
17. Ibid., 118, 178.

ingful: the work of art "glorifies" matter, Gilson says. In a painting, "the qualities of matter develop an intelligibility perceptible to sense." Gilson differs from Maritain in finding, at the back of this, not logical, but *mathematical* intelligibility.[18] Nonfigurative artists such as Mondrian have achieved a pure representation of such mathematical intelligibility.

Étienne Gilson is not slow to point out that, according to Descartes, material qualities have no such intelligibility. Descartes relegated Aristotle's qualitative physics to the nursery, by noting that color, taste, tangibility, smell, sound, are not to be found in nature "in the form of unperceived perceptions." The existence of qualities is *aesthetic,* requiring both an object and a perceiver. Aristotle had not, Gilson claims, failed to recognize that "both subject and object are necessary for a perception." That is why Aristotle's philosophy is aesthetic: painters appreciate the fact that there "are sensible qualities so long as there are perceptions," because art deals in the qualities of sense made intelligible in a network of lines on wood or canvas. What Aristotle did forget, according to Gilson, was to give "quality" an objective base, in *quantities.* If we are liable, common-sensically, to mark off a thing by its color, that observation of essential difference is founded in the fact that colors are "qualities of numbers."[19] Quantities yield quality on the moment of their aesthetic observation.

Quantity does not produce quality in an empty laboratory. Nor will just any quantities do. Quantitative "wholes," quantities as little circumscribed fields of regularity, enter the realm or state of quality when they are aesthetically perceived:

> Nature is abundantly provided with such wholes. What child has not found himself unconsciously fascinated by the perfect geometrical beauty of certain pebbles, sea shells, crystals, tree leaves, etc.? Why are most people so fond of flowers, not always for their colors, but often enough for the amazing perfection of their forms? The only reason for their admiration is that they are apprehending by sight the presence of a certain order among parts within a whole. Certain sea shells are so perfectly regular that their shape could be expressed by the algebraic formulas applicable to similar curves, but even such formulas do not make us see the curve; they only let us know why each one of the points of the curve ... has to be found where it is. And just as the law of a geometrical curve is intelligible only to a mind, so also the order of its parts within their whole is perceptible only to such a sense as human sight. The

18. Ibid., 187; Maritain, *Art and Scholasticism,* 185, 51 n; Gilson, *Painting and Reality,* 181.

19. Gilson, *Painting and Reality,* 251–53.

order proper to each quantitative whole apprehended by sense perception is its quality. Modern painters have been the explorers of this universe of qualities, just as modern musicians have been . . . the explorers of the universe of audible qualities.[20]

The work of art is *radiant* because it reveals the intelligibility of the act of being, in the "order of," or in its relation to, sensible human perception.

## Maritain and Gilson Disagree about Aesthetics

The two sets of Mellon lectures gave rise to a rupture between the two Thomists. Raïssa Maritain was a poet, and her beliefs about the process of composition influenced her husband's aesthetic philosophy. The disagreement between the two men was exacerbated to the breaking point by a visit from Gilson to Princeton, on which she misheard him tell her, "You are not a poet."[21] Raïssa's poetry was not widely admired among the critics and writers who gathered around the Maritains in Princeton,[22] and she may have been tacitly aware of this. Gilson believed that his position stood firmly on Aquinas, who said no such things as Maritain did about art and poetry; Jacques believed that the disagreement was planted firmly on Raïssa's toes. In vain did Gilson protest that "I still distinctly remember telling her 'you *are* a poet,'" for Raïssa had placed him "on the Index." That was because she "was pained by the critique"[23] of *Creative Intuition* that she discerned in *Painting and Reality*.

What was the debate really about? One *casus belli* can be found in various steps which Maritain makes beyond Saint Thomas. It is one thing to know a thing passively, to read French, for example, and another thing to be able to communicate with a Frenchman: "with John of St. Thomas and his school it must be said that we really have the idea of a thing only when we are capable of producing it." Such a capacity does not belong to the mind alone: Maritain distinguishes between intellectual knowledge, whose object is an already existent truth, and practical knowledge, which comes about in the doing. Maritain distinguishes further, within practical knowledge, ethical

20. Ibid., 254.
21. Maritain to Étienne Gilson, February 2, 1958, in *Deux approches*, 198.
22. Francis Fergusson said that "Raïssa's poetry was 'too personal, self-indulgent. Tate also took a dim view of it.'" Cited in Dunaway, ed., *Exiles and Fugitives*, 108.
23. Gilson to Laurence Shook, November 25, 1963, in *Deux approches*, 201; Bars, "Gilson et Maritain," 262.

action, which improves the doer, and making, which improves upon an object by "impregnating" it with an idea. If knowing is driven by the mind, making is propelled by the will: art is the congruence between the object, which the mind knows as an idea, and the will to reproduce it, which is effected by voluntative and habitual "connaturality" with one's object. One has to become like the object that one seeks to reproduce: only then will one see perfectly, or "infallibly." Maritain writes that "the work to be done is merely the matter of art, the form of it is undeviating reason. *Recta ratio factibilium:* I will try to translate into English this vigorous Aristotelian and Scholastic definition and define Art as the undeviating determination of work to be done."[24]

No such "undeviating determination" can exist unless the artist has the "habit" of connaturality with her object. The artist's object is the beautiful, understood as a transcendental property of being. If we are connatural to beauty, we will want it so much that our minds will be able to create it: the desire, for this lovely, transcendental perfection, enables the "intellect . . . to engender in beauty." If "beauty" is for Maritain "essentially the object of the intelligence," nonetheless, the "artist must be in love with what he is doing, so that . . . beauty becomes connatural to him, bedded in his being through affection." According to Maritain, what the artist *is* enables her to intuit transcendent beauty; making a beautiful poem or vase follows after this. Poetry flows from what an artist *is;* art is the product of what he or she does. Maritain distinguishes becoming spiritually at one with beauty from *making* beautiful things. The first is *poetry,* the act which reaches through finite things to infinite beauty. Historically, art comes first; but poetry reaches higher, deep into "the things of sense": "in the historical evolution of mankind, the *homo faber* carries on his shoulders the *homo poeta.*"[25] We first have a "poetic intuition" of sensible beauty, and then reproduce it in the object we make, and so poetry takes formal if not historical precedence over art.

Gilson told Maritain that he admired the way that he discussed the transcendental of beauty; but he feared that his friend was disembodying aesthetic intuition and told him that poetry is not just a matter of the soul.[26] Gilson speaks, not of how the artist *knows,* but of how the artist *makes,* and that is, with her hands. There are not two acts, a *knowing* of the transcendentally beautiful, followed by the making of a beautiful object, but only one act: homo poeta *is* homo faber, for Gilson.

24. Maritain, *Art and Scholasticism,* 89, 8.
25. Maritain, *Creative Intuition in Art and Poetry,* 55; Maritain, *Art and Scholasticism,* 23, 49, 96; Maritain, *Creative Intuition in Art and Poetry,* 45.
26. Gilson to Jacques Maritain, April 6, 1953, in *Deux approches,* 187.

Both philosophers say that the artist's *object* is sensible. Maritain claims that "Poetry" "glimpses" the spiritual "in the flesh, by the point of the sense sharpened by the mind."[27] But, for Gilson, the artist, grasping beauty with her senses, knows it *as* her hands bring it into reality, and not in an intuition of beauty as a transcendental analogue of being, which precedes artistic making.

Could the debate have been about Bergson? In 1914 Maritain had written that "unforgivable" book, adversely comparing Bergson with Thomas. But that little bit of "Platonism" that Gilson so disliked in Maritain's philosophy of art comes from Bergson. Bergson had defined intuition as that "effort of imagination" by which I insert myself in things or as the "intellectual sympathy by which one places oneself within the object in order to coincide with what is unique in it." The intuition moves with the dynamism of its object, experiencing the "direction" of its movement.[28]

Maritain says that such a coincidence between "Self" and "Thing" *is* "poetry" or "creative intuition." The "Platonic muse" is not above the soul but within it, working *behind* the "Illuminating intellect." The agent or illuminating intellect is filled with images, and some do not reach the light of day, remaining in a cognitively preconscious state. The "spiritual unconscious" is the realm of the mind in which images and even concepts are present, without achieving conceptual clarity. It is *because* the poet's knowledge of things flows through this source that he produces poetry, and not philosophy: "poetic knowledge...expresses itself through images—or through concepts which are not carried to the state of rational thought, but are still steeped in images, being used in that nascent state when they are emerging from images as Venus from the sea. And the thought of the poet...escapes to a certain extent the sunlit regime of the logos, and participates...in the nocturnal regime of the imagination, in which the principle of non-contradiction does not come into force and things are at the same time themselves and another." The poet first realizes that she knows the beautiful through a "musical stir," which is not "the musicality of the words" she will later write but an emotion "linked with poetic intuition itself...in which words play no part."[29] Maritain was impaled upon no logical contradiction but upon the horns of a Burgundian bull at whom he had waved the red rag of the commentators and on which was emblazoned a Bergsonian epistemology of art.

Where Maritain envelops the reader like a "many-eyed cloud," Gilson

27. Maritain, *Art and Scholasticism*, 97.
28. Bergson, *An Introduction to Metaphysics*, 2, 6, 77.
29. Maritain, *Creative Intuition in Art and Poetry*, 231, 300.

charges at his readers like a bull, hitting them with the insight that all human activity is embodied and existent. He complained of Maritain to Phelan that had Saint Thomas ever "thought about that art...he would have connected art to being, to the entire man, and not to some form of knowledge—to take art for knowledge is to indulge in the sophism of misplaced intellectualism."[30]

Where Maritain placed what he had learned from Bergson in the artist's preconscious faculties, Gilson projected his Bergsonism into reality. In a paper describing a ceremony of 1947 "in the Amphitheatre of the Sorbonne...which paid 'national homage'" to Bergson, Gilson records that "César Franck and Claude Debussy poured into our hearts music that was closer to his profound philosophy than anything words could express." At the Sorbonne in 1904 "our teacher held us under the...spell that only the music of pure intellect can create." If Bergson's "musicality" led him "astray" into the "mystical belief in an intuition that knows no middle ground between the concept and the ineffable," he had by the end of his life realized that "pure duration is not the ultimate source from which we draw life, movement and being."[31] Gilson would later say that music is the most "striking image of that creative élan whose material, as Bergson said, is deposited in its wake like radioactive fallout from the spirit."[32]

From another angle, the debate could be said to be about the *commentators*. As de Lubac sternly computes, Maritain cites Cajetan seven times and John of Saint Thomas eleven times in *Art and Scholasticism* alone; this romantic thinker is more casual than a historian would be in supplying collective "definitions of the schoolmen"; somewhat mythological "Scholastics" abound in both of his great works on the philosophy of art. Maritain had developed a contemporary Thom*istic* philosophy, "abstracted" from what Gilson saw as the strictly "theological works of Thomas."[33]

A modest person, and a public speaker, Gilson took on roles with respect to his friends. With Maritain, he was the historian, and the other French Thomist was the philosopher. But *Painting and Reality* is a work of philosophy, not history. Gilson disliked some commentators, not because they were commentators, but because he believed them to be intellectualists.

30. Ibid., 99; Gilson to Gerard Phelan, November 16, 1957, in Shook, *Gilson,* 338.
31. Gilson, "The Glory of Bergson," 581–83.
32. One of the few untranslatable phrases that Gilson wrote: "image plus saisissante de cet élan créateur dont Bergson disait que la matière se dépose dans son sillage, comme une retombée de l'esprit." Gilson, *Matières et formes,* 182.
33. De Lubac, ed., *Letters of Gilson to de Lubac,* 235; Prouvost, "Les relations entre philosophie et théologie chez É. Gilson," 430.

*Art and Scholasticism* had inflamed Gilson by defining art as *knowledge* and anachronistically calling that "Thomism"; Maritain's Mellon lectures annoyed his friend by elaborating the subjective instrumentality of artistic knowing as "creative intuition." Gilson complained to Phelan that "Maritain's use of the expression 'creative intuition' is in error; an intuition cannot be creative in the order of material things because it has no hands."[34]

Ralph McInerny says of Gilson's *Introduction aux arts de beau* (1963) that if the author was a "fundamentalist" when he was "writing about Thomas," "when he philosophized his method was anything but catechetical." No catechism demolishes strawmen in order to make the reader think through the explanatory steps leading to its doctrines. McInerny cannot conceive "who is guilty of the error Gilson would refute" in this book. Perhaps he was unfamiliar with Pierre Lasserre's *Le romanticisme Française* (1917). Although Gilson thought he was indicating where Maritain's philosophy of art errs, his true opponent is artistic rationalism; the ghost of Lasserre, wearing neo-classical dress, has been replaced in Gilson's mind by the figure of Maritain. Art is not, the author insists, a kind of *knowledge*. Those "visionaries" who say that it is maintain that the artist gains his information through an "intuition."[35] Such intuitionism is blind to existence.

Gilson would tell Henri Bars that the "'intuitive notion of understanding' as Maritain defined it 'described very well his own way of understanding, his personal manner of thinking.' But as an historian he found nothing like it in the letter of Saint Thomas, and it is too exceptional a gift to enter into a general theory of knowledge." In relation to the theory of art, the problem went deeper than that. It was not just that only an elite have poetic intuitions. For Gilson, artistic knowledge is energized knowledge, knowledge born of action within existence. Gilson declares that art is making, and that the artist's manufacturing is caused by, or flows from, his exercise of existence: "Man as capable of making *(homo faber)*, is first a making being *(ens faber)*, because his activity as a craftsman is like an outer manifestation of his act of existing."[36] No intuited *idea* of beauty could *cause* the artist to create. The artifact is caused, rather, by the energetic overflow of the artist's act of existence into a new essence, whose end is beauty, and not truth.

34. Gilson to Gerard Phelan, November 16, 1957, in Shook, *Gilson*, 337.
35. McInerny, "Gilson's Theory of Art," 350, 348; Gilson, *The Arts of the Beautiful*, 56.
36. Bars, "Gilson et Maritain," 254; Gilson, *The Arts of the Beautiful*, 19.

## The Institute of Mediaeval Studies Can
## Exist without Its Progenitor

In his teaching at the Collège de France Gilson had kept rigorously to his historical brief. Having set up the *Archives d'histoire doctrinale et littéraire du moyen âge* and the series *Études de philosophie médiévale*, he continued to edit them throughout his life. He was also one of the great intellectual stage performers of his generation. For his platform in Toronto, he took the role of the mediaeval historian. He was an artist in words, and one who could woo an audience with laughter. The man of many obligations knew very well the dangers of playing to an audience: "it is . . . in the hour of his first success, that the most subtle temptation comes to the artist, to let the genius that created his public be directed by that public. Once he has won them, they always keep asking for the identical pleasure they experienced the first time. So the painter sells himself to the dealer who is certain he can place any number of copies of the same work with his customers. . . . The novelist rewrites the same novel. The musician repeats the same songs. The artist . . . becomes his own disciple and calls upon his talent to exploit the creations of his genius."[37] This modest man devoted an immense energy to perfecting his technique as a historian. And yet his very artistry was a signal to him that he too had had the genius's glimpse of eternity.

Gerald Phelan, who had told Étienne in 1951 that "I do not like what you have written in *The Modern Schoolman*" about the future of Scholasticism, sided with Maritain in the quarrel about *Creative Intuition*. From 1957, Gilson began to withdraw from teaching at the Institute of Mediaeval Studies. His finances had entered irremediable confusion after the death of Thérèse, and the misery of paying both Canadian and French income tax entered the equation. He was seventy-three years old: he was becoming reliant "while his colleagues grew more independent; this proved that his mission had been successful, but was nonetheless difficult to accept." In the *Choir of Muses*, written around the time of the loss of Thérèse, Gilson asks: "does not every great work of art involve to some degree a renunciation of God? The question arises even for *Le Partage de Midi*, even for the *Divina Commedia*. . . . Buonarotti in his old age sometimes smashed his statues: art satisfied him no longer, he was athirst for the infinite: 'Neither painting nor sculpture,' he said, 'can thrill the soul that has turned towards that divine love who opened his arms to us upon the Cross.' Rodin, who quotes this

37. Gilson, *Choir of Muses*, 183.

saying of Michelangelo, adds that the words are those of the *Imitation of Christ*." Maritain had told him that "you have created a lasting and admirable work in Toronto, which is intimately bound in with your writings and lives through it."[38] What is the artist to do when his work can exist without him?

38. Phelan to Étienne Gilson, December 12, 1951, in Shook, *Gilson,* 299; on the dispute between Phelan and Gilson over Maritain's philosophy of art, *Étienne Gilson,* 337–38; Gilson, *Choir of Muses,* 192–94; Maritain to Étienne Gilson, February 2, 1958, in *Deux approches,* 199.

# 15

# Gilson's Grumpy Years

## Change and Continuity

Étienne Gilson was a man of many parts. Many of his Canadian and North American contemporaries received the disconcerting impression that, from the time of his 1950 "H-bomb" lecture, he began to overplay the theologian. By contrast, Gilson's countrymen have sensed the continuity in Gilson's thinking. Yves Floucat observes that the "greater importance which is attached to theological reflection as the source of the most perfect expression of philosophical wisdom, and to the return to theology, so ardently desired in *The Philosopher and Theology* [1960], is already contained in germ" in the "primordial affirmation of the Judaeo-Christian root of the metaphysic of existence,"[1] which one can find as far back as *The Spirit of Mediaeval Philosophy*.

One way of interpreting this divergent perception is to say that the priority of grace was at some times more central than at others, for Gilson. He seldom dropped a theme, and this makes it impossible to construct an empirical division of his thought into phases. One can only demarcate phases in his life by marking a particular period by the production of a classical text. Gilson never forgot that religious dogmas enable us to articulate our "natural" realism. Even so, there are certain eras when what Canon Van Steenberghen called Gilson's "electric pen" was more alight than at others, in the respective fields of nature and of grace.

Theology is there at the beginning: Gilson inadvertently let slip at the trial of his doctorate, in 1913, that "metaphysics stems from theology." In the same year, he exhibited Thomas's thought in a theological order. He could not take this much further than the commonplace Scholastic assertion that Thomas recognized the ontological difference. In the 1927 *Thomisme*, Gilson relates the existentiality of Aquinas's thought to the doctrine of cre-

---

1. Floucat, "Gilson et la métaphysique thomiste de l'acte d'être," 361–62.

ation. This will be one of the means by which he characterizes the spirit of mediaeval, Christian philosophy as a whole. Stanley Jaki indicates that the Giffords were a wasted opportunity for Gilson: he would have made better use of his stage if he had displayed his realistic epistemology.[2] He was just about to do so.

*The Unity of Philosophical Experience,* said Anton Pegis, "preaches to men the lesson that only the pure of intellect shall possess philosophical truth adequately"; a French friend said the book was not only written in English but "thought in that language." Gilson and Maritain were companions in arms in the 1930s under the banner of Christian humanism. That campaign made the Christian in Maritain more evident, and the humanist in Gilson. *The Unity* brings Gilson as close to Maritain as he ever was, perhaps, to some extent, under his influence, for the Maritain who spoke about the intuition of being, in *Sept leçons sur l'être,* had made some progress on *The Degrees of Knowledge. The Unity* and *Thomist Realism* created for Gilson a reputation among American and Canadian Thomists of a man who could take on the moderns and defeat them on sound philosophical grounds. They were alive to those of his arguments that touched on *nature,* such as the observation, in *Christianisme et philosophie,* that "Catholics, who profess the eminent value of nature, because it is the work of God, show their respect for it in positing as their first rule of action, that *piety does not dispense with technique.*"[3] The neo-Thomist revival had prepared the ground for the view that the key to Catholicism is its openness to philosophy, nature, and the analogy of being. His American audiences thrilled to the Christian humanist in Gilson. We could count the 1930s as his period of "exclusive" Thomism.

With its discovery of being, *God and Philosophy* led Gilson back to an explicit concern for theology, in the *Thomisme* of the war years and in *L'être et l'essence.* His sense of the dependence of Christian philosophy on theology had affective roots in the youthful observation of the anti-modernist campaign. The theological cold wars of the late 1940s and early 1950s, the "anti-Protestant" bullying to which friends such as Chenu and de Lubac were subjected, pushed the septuagenarian into a historical reconstruction of bygone battles. When he sat down to write an autobiography in 1959, he churned out, in three weeks, a book, interspersed with factual errors, about the modernist crisis. And here he said that "fideism is the inbuilt

---

temptation of Protestantism," but because they respect the order of nature, "a certain rationalism is that of Catholicism in every age."[4]

From across the Atlantic, the turbulent horizon of France, circa 1907, was cut off by the fogs of time and distance, and American and Canadian Catholics received Gilson's sharpened expressions of impatience with neo-Thomism, and his concomitant accent upon the priority of theology, as a new intellectual departure. Many had become accustomed to conceiving Gilson and Maritain as a double act, the philosophical apologist boosted by the historian. It was these in particular who, having benevolently absorbed the Thomist critic of Kantianism, would not be delighted to learn from him that the neo-Thomists had brought the modernist crisis on themselves, by their forgetfulness of faith.

Gilson had not just altered in the eyes of his beholders. In his most loved and most beautiful books, *The Spirit of Mediaeval Philosophy* and *The Unity,* he was writing for an audience and giving back to them what it was good for them to hear. Those interlocutors, his dear friends and enemies, Maritain, the neo-Thomists, Brunschvicg, and the rest, are living actors within these works. As he lectured less intensely, from the late 1950s, Gilson's writings acquire the feel of monologues, meditations on his own, idiosyncratic questions. An unanswerable question of personal identity lies behind the problem of which gives us the *real* Gilson, the sociable books or the personal ones. At least we can say that Gilson's remark that Raïssa had placed him "on the Index" tells us as much about his own preoccupations, in 1963, as it does about the Maritains' past predilections.

At a "ceremony" held in honor of Bergson's memory, in 1947, Gilson "evoked that extraordinarily frail-looking figure whose appearance twice a week in his chair at the Collège de France marked the beginning of the most memorable hours of our intellectual life." *Painting and Reality* led Gilson back to the place upon which he had taken his first stand for Bergson, aesthetics. The subject continued to hold his attention during his last years. Gilson told Gouhier in 1959 that he could never read Bergson's *Two Sources of Religion and Morality,* "for fear" of a "parricide." As the germ unfolded, so Gilson was increasingly grateful to his author. In the same year, de Lubac "wrote to Father Bouillard" that "'Gilson is becoming more independent in his language in his old age.'"[5]

---

4. For instance, Laberthonnière, dead in 1932, is said to have criticized *Christianisme et philosophie,* printed in 1936. Gilson, *Le philosophe et la théologie,* 90; the comment about fideism and rationalism is on the same page.

5. Gilson, "The Glory of Bergson," 582; Gilson to Henri Gouhier, 1959, in "Lettres d'Étienne Gilson à Henri Gouhier," 469. Géry Prouvost quotes this statement in

Ever since 1950 he had made it ever clearer that his "Thomas" was no enemy of "Bonaventure"; these pranks seldom failed to infuriate. Perhaps his learned American and Canadian friends were the genuine "exclusive Thomists," and Gilson put himself beyond the pale with that Bonaventurian tinge. For others, the underlying difficulty was perhaps the belief that "for Gilson, the idea of a development of the Thomist doctrine is neither possible nor desirable. In fact, his tendency to reduce philosophy to metaphysics alone and to a metaphysics which is avowedly bound to a revelation which cannot be altered by scientific developments prevents him from considering a genuine philosophical progress."[6]

## Gilson's Loyalties

In 1957 Gilson was asked to edit a four-volume Catholic textbook on the *History of Philosophy,* and he dutifully accepted. He commanded his authors to "let your philosophers speak for themselves as often as can be done. . . . Do not substitute philosophical continuity for historical continuity. . . . Never write anything about a philosopher without having one of his books in front of you." If Gilson found his task wearisome, some of his authors found him an exacting taskmaster. Some of the authors dropped out, unable to live up to his expectations. Like many editors, Gilson was left to do much of the writing himself. His biographer considers that "in many ways the fault was his own. His stipulations had been forbidding, and his comments on proffered work had been harsh, offering such judgments as 'philosophically weak,' 'less clear than the original,' 'still unregenerated,' and 'in need of perambulatory metanoia,' to mention but a few."[7] Gilson was a good teacher, if a harsh one, and the pedagogue was delighted with the achievement of his pupils in the finished *History.*

Gilson's editing for Vrin was still a source of pleasures and of learning. This year also saw the publication of Père Chenu's *La théologie au douzième siècle*. With its many chapters on the illumination of the Latin West by the Greek Fathers, the book is a triumphant exposition of nouvelle théologie.[8]

---

his commentary on the Gilson-Gouhier letters but does not exhibit the letter from which he draws it. Very similar remarks can be seen in Gilson's letter to Gouhier of June 4, 1958, ibid., 469–70; de Lubac to Henri Bouillard, 1959, in *At the Service of the Church,* 363–64.

6. Bonino, "Historiographie de l'école thomiste," 310.

7. Shook, *Gilson,* 336.

8. Conticello, "Métaphysique de l'être et théologie de la grâce," 456–57.

When Gabriel Thèry retired as co-editor of the *Archives d'histoire doctrinale et littéraire du moyen âge* in 1959, Chenu took his place.

Visiting Freiburg in 1958, Gilson heard Martin Heidegger lecture. The experience induced tears. He told Pegis, who had brushed off any similarity between Gilson's existentialism and that of the Germans, that Heidegger "is taking us to the only real metaphysical problems. I believe he could . . . help us not only to deeper insights into his own thought, but even into that of your own dear Thomas Aquinas. His thought is different. . . . But it is where it is [and it is] a good exercise for the mind to be taken there in a new and unfamiliar way." Gilson suggested that Heidegger's "Anguish in the face of pure being is perhaps just another name for fear of God."[9]

In 1959, at a Sorbonne centenary celebration of the birth of Henri Bergson, Fr. Joseph de Tonquédec launched a "diatribe" against Bergson from the podium. When the question period opened, Gilson leapt to his feet in defense of his teacher. Afterward, before a steadily accumulating audience, he declaimed Bergson's praises and, looking at de Lubac, ridiculed "a certain kind of Scholasticism" for its "out-of-date methods, its lack of historical sense," and its "need to create heretics to cut up."[10]

That audience was perhaps the largest in the face of which Gilson had criticized the curial policy which had favored "a certain kind of Scholasticism." The critical attitude to the Holy Office that he expressed in private letters to friends could never have been exposed by Gilson in public. Catholics of his generation were taught not to give scandal, and this required verbal loyalty to the church as an institution. One might curse in private but not blaspheme in public. Gilson never shut his mouth on behalf of a sect, as is evident from his forays against the neo-Thomist club. But he was spontaneously and trenchantly faithful to the church; he loved it.

The discipline of fidelity to the institutional church went side by side with loyalty to personal friends. "I have never tolerated a verbal or epistolary attack upon you without responding to it," he had told Jacques in 1953. His acclamatory tributes to Maritain flowed as much from his generosity as from intellectual kinship. Their metaphysics were less in unison than Maritain believed and Gilson made out in public—until the last decade of his writing life. One of the novelties in his writings of the 1960s is Gilson's sense of loneliness, a thinning of the bonds of loyalty, expressed in a certain acerbity in his theological apologetic. Love, Gilson said, sometimes must

9. Pegis, "Gilson and Thomism," 451; Gilson to Anton Pegis, January 26, 1958, in Shook, *Gilson*, 335; Gilson, *L'être et l'essence* (2nd ed.), 375.

10. De Lubac, in *Letters of Gilson to de Lubac*, 10–11.

take precedence over understanding, because God, the object of our desire, exceeds our knowledge. The virtue of loyalty to human friends is founded in this truth, and if we forget it, we risk subsisting what Maritain called the *object* of intelligence, the mental construct, for the *thing* itself; for human beings are also mysteries.[11]

In November 1959 Gilson chaired a meeting of La Semaine des Intellectuels Catholiques, at which the speakers were Chenu and Jean Lacroix, the one beginning from faith, the other from reason. The chair was at his most flamboyant, summing up his concurrence with Chenu in the words:

> Christian mystery... does not follow reason, it precedes it, accompanies it as it moves along; it wraps it round and eventually shows it salutary perspectives which reason left to itself would never suspect possible. While Père Chenu was speaking I remembered a passage in... Thomas' *Commentary on the De Trinitate of Boethius*. St. Thomas was (even then) being accused of pouring the water of philosophy into the wine of Holy Scripture. He replied simply that theology was not a mixture in which a constituent kept its own nature. A theologian doesn't mix water with wine, he changes water into wine. We ought not to be disturbed by this manifest allusion to the miracle at Cana. St. Thomas is speaking for all theologians conscious of the supernatural function they are performing. A discipline founded on faith in God's word must share the privileges of divinity. It would be surprising if its operation had nothing of the miraculous about it.

Shook is not alone in considering that Gilson "came very near to saying that, for the believer, philosophy in the generally accepted sense of the word is an impossibility." He says that much of "Gilson's loneliness lay in his unique perception of Thomas' philosophy as a philosophy of being";[12] the idea of the miracle of the revelation of being is at the heart of Gilson's reputation for fideism.

But one could suggest that Gilson has, so to speak, colored the water by a Bonaventurian "reducere" of philosophy to theology. On occasions like this, Gilson makes philosophical knowledge represent mere information, as it did for the Seraphic Doctor, for Bergson, and, indeed, for Loisy. If Saint Thomas was also among the Franciscans, it was Gilson's vocation to notice this affiliation.

When, in December 1959, Gilson begin to cogitate his memoir, *La philosophe et la théologie,* he wrote to Pegis, "*Re* Jacques Maritain, the truth

11. Gilson to Jacques Maritain, January 29, 1953, in *Deux approches,* 184; Gilson, *The Christian Philosophy of St. Thomas Aquinas,* 275–76; Maritain, *The Degrees of Knowledge,* 110.

12. Shook, *Gilson,* 349, 338.

is that what he has written has played no part at all in my intellectual history." Gilson told Pegis that, "were I to get started on him, for whom I have a brotherly affection, I would have to raise problems better left untouched. . . . Still, there is one thing that cannot be done: to condone his book on Bergson. . . . There would be no problem if Maritain didn't wield Thomism like a bludgeon. . . . I have never had to take Maritain's positions into account until recently in *Painting and Reality*. The result is that I have been expelled from the earthly paradise by an angel of wrath [Raïssa] who is especially charged to protect by flame and sword the truth about poetry." He evaded the difficulty by devoting one and a half pages to his friend, assaulting Maritain's enemies, defining him as "a great mind who is also a great heart," whose work creates a "delicious complicity between metaphysics and poetry," and omitting a description of the content of his philosophy. Henri Bars considers that Gilson's lengthy discussion of Thomists who "in rejecting the Bergsonian conception of intelligence . . . disarmed their ally in a fight which he alone conducted on the same ground as his adversaries" is about Maritain. Van Steenberghen observed that *La philosophe et la théologie* "was filled with verve and humor, but also with passion."[13] It is a generous repayment of Gilson's debt to his philosophical father.

## On Using Philosophy *within* Theology

If "the pains of existence often sobered him, and if his thought often took on a somber hue, he never lost his verve" or his love of an "outrageous assertion." Delighted by the reception of his Wedding at Cana metaphor by the Catholic intellectuals, Gilson used the image of water and wine again in *La philosophe et la théologie* (1960) and in *The Elements of Christian Philosophy* (1960).[14] Since the resultant wine is not *watery*, not a "mixture," but "homogeneous," wine throughout, philosophy does indeed lose its "essence": for the unity or homogeneity of theology consists in the theologian's faithful borrowing of the mind of God, her interpretation of creatures from divine and omniscient eyes. Gilson casts a poet's glance over what this divine vision permitted Aquinas to see:

13. Gilson to Anton Pegis, December 7, 1959, ibid., 346; Gilson, *Le philosophe et la théologie*, 219–20, 158; Bars "Gilson et Maritain," 256; Van Steenberghen, "In Memoriam Étienne Gilson," 541.
14. D'Alverny, "Nécrologie Étienne Gilson," 428–29; McInerny, "Gilson's Theory of Art," 349; Gilson, *Elements of Christian Philosophy*, 316, 14 n.

the work of the Saint is a world. It is even many worlds, one within the other. It is the world of the word of God: Scripture which, to him, alone is infinite. It is the world of the Fathers. . . . It is the world of Aristotle and of philosophy, whose frontiers recede in the measure that one believes that one is on the point of reaching them. It is finally the personal world of Saint Thomas himself, situated at the heart of the rest and opening upon all of them, but discreet, almost effaced, . . . so that one is at risk of crossing it without recognizing it. But one sign advises one of its presence, not always but often. This is that after having enumerated two, ten, or twenty reasons in favor of a certain conclusion, and sometimes included within the series, Saint Thomas writes the word *esse*, which belongs to the whole world, but of which he made a use which belongs to him alone. This notion is for him a light which, above all in metaphysics and theology, illuminates all the rest.

It *is* possible, Gilson says, to combine knowledge of the existence of God with faith in God's reality, because the biblical God includes the gods attained by rational demonstration, such as the Prime Mover, and infinitely exceeds them.[15] Even the language by which Gilson maintains the "formal distinction" between the objects of philosophy and theology can make us think that he conceived of philosophy as a wizened and lifeless thing, alongside the existential and eternal theological verities

It is with another dash of stylistic brilliance, and a Bonaventurian metaphor, that Gilson describes how Thomas used the "cumulative" "philosophical progress" of his forerunners: he did so by getting *inside* the philosophers' arguments, judging that he must "recapitulate . . . by accompanying it from within, the pilgrimage of the human mind in quest of the true notion of God." It was to the discredit of the neo-Thomists that they never tried to do this with Bergson's philosophy. They knew in advance what their philosophy was setting out to prove, but as a genuine philosopher, Bergson did not: approaching his open-ended thought from the outside, they "devoted themselves to forcing him to accept a completely preformed system of concepts, *en bloc*."[16]

Because he knew that he was writing, not philosophy, but theology, Thomas could have appropriated Bergson's "Egyptian gold," bringing all that was fine in it to perfection. The theme of Bergson's *Creative Evolution* is life, conceived as a "current passing from germ to germ," a "continuous progress" that is sufficiently indeterminate to encourage the free transfor-

15. Gilson, *Le philosophe et la théologie*, 112, 225, 163–65.
16. Gilson, *Elements of Christian Philosophy*, 98; Gilson, *Le philosophe et la théologie*, 176.

mations of organisms. Thomas would not have made nervous attacks on Bergson's *élan vital,* because he would have known that the Unmoved mover is no more identical to the biblical God than is creativity. Confident in that theological assurance, Thomas could have developed Bergson's conception to enhance his own understanding of God's immobility. For the Bible is not monolithic; it tells us both that God is unchanging (Mal. 3:6) and changing (Wisdom 7:24): a genuinely theological Thomism could have used the Jewish agnostic's sense of movement in God to deepen its elucidation of divine actuality.[17] Thomas could, in other words, have achieved that energetic-expressive idea of God which, in 1924, Gilson had found in Saint Bonaventure.

For Gilson the aesthetician, the most striking gift of the artist is *poesis,* the invention of new imaginative worlds. If, he says, Bergson's evolving universe was a creature of the late nineteenth century, the same theological task will have to be performed for the world of Einstein. It is because it is not a *philosophy,* with invisible strings to Rome attached, that Thomism is open to new philosophical developments: "A Thomist is a free spirit," Gilson writes. "This liberty surely does not consist in having neither God nor man for master, but rather in having no other master than God, who enfranchises all the others. For God is the sole protector of man against human tyrannies.... the disciple of Saint Thomas can say...: 'believe and think what you like. Like charity, faith is liberating.'"[18]

Consciously agnostic philosophies, like Bergson's, can be alive, and according to Gilson, there is also a vitality in the use of philosophical reason within theology. It is only if we saw off a branch from theology that we find ourselves holding a lifeless stick: it was thus that the neo-Thomists "administered" to Bergson "a volley of dead wood." Such Catholic rationalism was not, in the early twentieth century, founded on a genuine love of reason: it always had a "Roman collar": "Their type of rationalism is recognized by this sign: priest or lay-man, theologian or philosopher, the Christian who defends the rights of reason against you will never take long before accusing you of heresy."[19]

Once at a meeting of Catholic philosophers, and again in a Catholic university, when Gilson said that he *believed* in the existence of God, and that Aquinas was a theologian, the "fideist" was thumped with the *Constitutio dogmatica de fide catholica* of Vatican I; if they "happen to have it to hand," the rationalists will also apply Pius X's *Proprio Motu* of September 1, 1910,

17. Bergson, *Creative Evolution,* 27; Gilson, *Le philosophe et la théologie,* 163, 168–69.
18. Gilson, *Le philosophe et la théologie,* 145–46, 221.
19. Ibid., 139, 92.

*Sacrorum Antistitum.*[20] Their martyr was indefatigable on the subject of Leo XIII's *pontifical* recommendation of Christian philosophy, refusing ever to relinquish that field to Canon Van Steenberghen.

## Vatican II (1962–1965)

In January 1959 Pope John XXIII mentioned that he wanted to call an Ecumenical Council. By July 1960 Henri de Lubac and Yves Congar had been appointed to the Theological Commission set up to work on the texts for the Second Vatican Council.[21] De Lubac was engaged by the document on the church in the modern world, *Gaudium et Spes.* The Pope intended Vatican II (1962–1965) to be a pastoral—rather than a dogmatic—council. He described its purpose as *aggiornamento.*

Gilson would feel increasingly out of sorts with his times. He never missed an opportunity to deploy the word *aggiornamento* sarcastically, using this preemptive strike against anyone who adapted their metaphysics to the thought of their day.[22] Like the French "new theologians" who came home to roost at the council, John XXIII "thought in images." Gilson's bête noire of this era was Teilhard de Chardin, of whose literary style he said, "I have a horror of imprecision and fluff in matters of intellectual knowledge." He recorded the day when "our beloved Holy Father John XXIII said to me... 'For me, you know, theology is '*Our Father, who art in heaven....* '"[23] This evinced precision.

## Philosophy of Art

As he disengaged himself from teaching, Gilson's writings followed their own chosen currents. The first fruits was the *Introduction aux arts de beau,* of 1963. The book is critical of the notion of a poetic *intuition* of transcendental beauty. There is such a thing as "poetic *cognition,*" Gilson says, but in the first place, it places "truth at the service of... art," and in the second, it is turned "to a concrete object endowed with actual existence and there-

---

20. Ibid., 94.
21. Komonchak, "A Hero of Vatican II."
22. Gilson, *Linguistics and Philosophy,* 10; Gilson, *Les tribulations de Sophie,* 27; *Constantes,* 71; Gilson, "L'Esse du Verbe incarné" (1968), 23–37, and in *Autour de Saint Thomas,* 84.
23. Peter Hebblethwaite, "John XXIII," 28; Gilson, *Les tribulations de Sophie,* 76, 30.

fore singular, like all real beings."[24] Poetic cognition is based in the sensing of particular facts, affecting imagination, and guiding to form. In *Matières et formes: poiétiques particulières des arts majeurs* (1964), Gilson cites "Maritain's formulas . . . without references or the author's name; . . . Eric Gill, rendered unfortunate by his admiration for the author of *Art and Scholasticism*, is discussed in detail." Well . . . , the preface makes fun of the *sculptor* who obediently swallowed the tenet that physical skill has no part in the making of beautiful objects, and of "jeandesainthomisme," but the seventeenth-century origination of these aberrations is clearly marked down.[25] Thereafter, *Matières et formes* drops the quarrel.

In the *Introduction aux arts de beau,* Gilson created a sister for ethics, epistemology, and metaphysics: "calology," the objective science of the transcendental of beauty. He now had a triolet of *calology,* belonging to metaphysics, *philosophy of art,* which deals in artistic making, and *aesthetics,* concerned with judgments of beautiful objects. Philosophy of art and aesthetics differ because the artist-maker does not have the form of his work before his eyes, is not the "spectator of his work."[26]

In "Du fondement des jugements esthétiques" (1917), Gilson had argued that aesthetic judgments are irredeemably subjective. Sixty years had not altered his opinion, perhaps because the French educational system had solidly dyed him with elitism. He freely admits that most people do not share his formalist aesthetic tastes, preferring narrative or figuration in painting, sculpture, and music: "Few men," he writes, "are endowed with a sufficiently delicate sensibility to be satisfied by a mere agreement of tones." One cannot expect the same aesthetic judgments from the tone-deaf as from those who have an ear for music: "some experience a vivid pleasure at the sight of pictures uniquely calculated to give the eye the type of pleasures it prefers. One cannot blame those who do not experience it for expressing their disapproval of painting of this type." Unlike judgments about truth, aesthetic judgments are "not universalizable," because what is related to beauty is, according to Gilson, "the *particular sensibility* of the subject."[27]

*Matières et formes* will be about philosophy of art, for the author has "never found an opening" into aesthetics. The text journeys through the "temples of Art" analyzing each of the arts of the beautiful in relation to its

24. D'Alverny, "Nécrologie Étienne Gilson," 429; Gilson, *The Arts of the Beautiful,* 15, 82.

25. Bars, "Gilson et Maritain," 261–62; Gilson, *Matières et formes,* 18.

26. Gilson, *The Arts of the Beautiful,* 22; Gilson, *Matières et formes,* 32.

27. Gilson, *Matières et formes,* 128–29; Diodato, "Note Sull' Ontologia dell' Arte di Étienne Gilson," 613.

matter. Painting, sculpture, and architecture have an immobile matter; the matter of dance is the human body, that of theater, human life; the matter of poetry and music is sound. The bracketing of aesthetic *judgment* does not entail ignoring the way in which the matter of each particular art controls our subjective *apprehension*. So, for example, as "a series of sonic events," music is an art of the fluent medium of time. We never hear more than a single tone at once; picking out a single tone as marked off from others requires an intelligent memory, a musical memory trained to hear the intervals between notes. "The possibility," Gilson writes, "of a sort of sonorous space, where successive sounds coexist in a certain way, is thus due to the imagination which is itself the most immediate form of the memory of sounds."[28] He says more about musical apprehension than about composition; the philosophy of art includes a Bergsonian phenomenology of perception.

Imagination is important in this philosophy of making: sculptors and architects require "imagination of volumes"; the dancer uses a "plastic imagination" on the shapes that can be made by her body.[29] The word *plastic* recurs in connection with imagination. All of the arts are "plastic," some, like music, by extension. "Plastic" has the connotation of malleable "stuff." When Gilson speaks of "plastic qualities" he means "formed" or "trans-formed": whether it works on organic or inorganic matter, art-making is the transformation of some physical "stuff." It does not just rearrange given materials; musical sounds, for instance, are of a different *kind* to physical and brute sounds.

If a sculptor must imagine volumes, and dancers imagine what can be done with their bodies, do they not begin with some pre-given knowledge? Gilson uses the words *imagination* and *imagerie* in different senses. *Imagerie* is the photographic copying of some reality, and preferably, as the eighteenth-century classicist the Abbé du Bos said, the "imitation" of a refined and not a "low-life" subject. *Imagerie* gives us photo-realistic art, art which literally re-produces reality: that is, art as a universal "language" of "natural signs." Gilson clearly considers that those of "delicate" pictorial sensibilities will not take this for the perfection of art; he is grateful that "one cannot be mistaken about music, because it has no *imagerie* with which one could confuse it."[30]

Moreover, "music 'says' nothing; because it does not speak and it is not

---

28. Gilson, *Matières et formes,* 10; Gilson, *Choir of Muses,* 190 ("temples of Art"); Gilson, *Matières et formes,* 147, 157.
29. Gilson, *Matières et formes,* 98, 189.
30. Ibid., 125–26, 110–11, 130, 144.

a language." But if Gilson is to deprecate language, which is the most common expression of human reasoning, and to insist on the formal character of the highest art, how is he to defend his philosophy of art against artistic formlessness, one-note symphonies and monochrome canvases? Gilson himself observed, with a trace of *froideur,* that "we live in a time in which many painters think that it is enough for a painting to have no subject to be a good painting." His answer is that "the knowledge of artistic beauty is always essentially a perception, but to be an apprehension of beauty that perception must necessarily be of a matter which has been deliberately packed with intelligibility. Without form and order, art and its proper beauty disappear."[31] Art has nothing to do with knowledge and is closely connected to intelligibility. *Imagerie* is the representation or reproduction of the world as understood, in conceptual definition; the plastic *imagination,* on the other hand, aims at "intelligibility," which is a kind of acted existential judgment.

Gilson had a predilection for artistic styles requiring hands-on production. He admired "African art," because it "puts us in the presence of a *technique,* that of pure sculpture," in which "the imagination of the artist informs matter without any other intermediary than the utensil in his hand." He was ambivalent about post-Renaissance sculptural "modelage." Having repeatedly returned to the Paris Opera in the effort to "understand Debussy's key work, *Pelléas et Mélisande,*" Gilson claims that "some would say" that the music which works with the instrument of the human voice alone is the most beautiful. But plastic imagination is not identical to unmediated production; its outstanding feature is, rather, the communication of the intelligibility of existence. People want to be novelists before they have a subject; we want to make something before we ask ourselves "What am I going to make?" Existence is ready to impart itself "*before*" we have in mind a "knowable object."[32]

## Dionysian Calology

Those who believe that the modernist move toward nonfigurative art was a wise one have a historical question to answer. Excepting music, all the arts of beauty have been imitative since the dawn of human artifacture,

31. Ibid., 169; Gilson, "Delacroix et Dante," in *Dante et Béatrice: Études dantesques,* 46. Most of the essays in *Dante et Béatrice* were first published in 1965. Gilson, *Matières et formes,* 138.

32. Gilson, *Matières et formes,* 85; D'Alverny, "Nécrologie Étienne Gilson," 429; Gilson, *Matières et formes,* 148; Gilson, *The Arts of the Beautiful,* 74.

on the caves of Lascaux. Does not its history show that imitation is the norm for art? Gilson responds that the imitative feature in the arts is part of their *matter*. The artist is using "material" just as much when he copies an object from life, or draws "life-like" sounds into music, as when he carves a block of stone or wrestles with clay: both the "copied" objects and the clay are equally transformed by him into a formally new, plastic design. Once absorbed into the new, artistic design, the matter is no longer what it once was: musical sounds belong on a different planet from extra-artistic noises. Gilson says that "sculpture, like painting, works . . . on a double matter," that of pigments and that of "natural forms." So, yes, art is imitative, but the artist does not make in order to imitate, but imitates, draws on matter, in order to create forms.[33]

Poetry also uses a double matter, straining against two poles. On the one side, as Mallarmé rightly said, its true aim is to create a pure "'verbal euphony,'" and on the other, words are representative by their nature. By its use of language, poetry is weighed down to the signification of concepts, images, and sentiments: nonetheless, "its own unique aim is not to do so" but to "create beauty with words." Novels seldom achieve such formal beauty. Because he concentrated, not on description, but on the poetic *shaping* of events, Flaubert came nearer the mark than Balzac. Seeking the imaginative evocation of life, Balzac was the better novelist, but the worse artist: in his realistic usage, "the novel . . . is not an art of the beautiful."[34]

One has a sense that Gilson's philosophy of art is directed beyond any comprehensible "aboutness"; he robustly denied that it was Thomistic, because Thomas had no philosophy of art but only "the elements of a calology which the reading of the platonising Dionysius the Areopagite suggested to him."[35] Perhaps, just as it contains not a little aesthetics, so too Gilson's philosophy of art is tipped toward a Dionysian calology.

Ever the apologist, Gilson wanted to show that Heidegger's quest to transcend "onto-theology" is fulfilled in Thomist theology, in which God is not an entity. In these last years, Gilson brings out what Thomas learned from Dionysius the Areopagite, his appreciation for the beautiful and for the unsayable. Gilson's taste for the tactile, the audible, and the visual, his belief that Fra Angelico "prayed with his hands," was correlated by the conviction of the "fundamentalist" historian that Thomas's anthropology requires that our intellect knows by entering into sensible facts. He had pointed this out

---

33. Gilson, *Matières et formes,* 119; Gilson, *The Arts of the Beautiful,* 81.
34. Gilson, *Matières et formes,* citing Mallarmé's *Lettre à Edmund Gosse,* 226, 221, 42.
35. Ibid., 16.

in the 1913–1919 *Thomisme;* the contrast between Descartes and Thomas, in "L'innéisme Cartésien et la théologie" (1914), turns on their varying attitudes to the phantasm. Gilson suggests that Heidegger's stalled effort to get beyond entity *(Dasein)* to being *(Sein)* could have been avoided if one started "from the simplest possible experience of the entity, which is that given in pure and simple sensation, provided it is the sensation of an intelligent being."[36]

In his last years, Gilson expended much energy in contending that Thomas was, first and foremost, a *negative* theologian. His argument begins from the human senses. For Thomas, the "proper object of the human intellect is neither the data of sense perception nor some pure intelligible apprehended by intuition; it is the intelligible essence whose concept it abstracts from the data of sense experience."[37] The way from sense experience to God goes by way of the perception that existing things cannot answer for their own existence. The only being who can answer for himself will *be* his own act of existing. His essence is simply existing, so there is no question "why" to ask. This gives us the bare conviction *that* God *is*.

It may seem to follow from this that there is no *essence* in God for the embodied human mind to know. Thomas did not follow Avicenna to the logical hilt in this matter. If we say that God has no quiddity, no whatness, then when we ask "what is God?" the correct answer is "nothing"—God's *what* is nothing. Human language about God requires moorings in facts and their essences, even if there is, properly speaking, no essence in God. When we set out to sea, our ship casts the land behind, but we must still navigate by reference to it, as when we say we are "forty miles from the coast." When we "attempt to describe God by removing from Him what is proper to the being of creatures, we must give up essence in order to reach the open sea of pure actual existence, but we must also keep the notion of essence present to the mind so as not to leave it without any object."[38] We have to use the language of quiddities, or whats, about God, because we think by tossing ropes out to essences. For the human mind, the existential judgment is, necessarily, a judgment *that* this individual *"what"* exists.

In the case of God, there is, for us, no known *"what"* to insert. We are perpetually in danger of putting one in, of imagining God as the supreme Essence: negative "theology is a fight" against the "recurring illusion" of dry land in the midst of God. Although the biblical God includes them, the

36. Gilson, *L'être et l'essence* (2nd ed.), 272; Gilson, *Choir of Muses,* 194; Gilson, *Constantes,* 144.
37. Gilson, *Elements of Christian Philosophy,* 249.
38. Ibid., 145–47.

sailor must not mistake such philosophical, conceptual horizons as the Un-moved Mover, or the élan vital for a bit of coastline. Thomas "accepts without any reservation the most extreme conclusions of the Greek theologian" Dionysius about the addition of the negation sign to everything we say about God, because human concepts drawn from created quiddities have no counterpart in the Being whose quiddity is existing. "One would," Gilson writes, "like to know how to tell Martin Heidegger how many unknown companions he has with him on his way, on which he has often said that he believes himself alone. And perhaps on those lost frontiers of high philosophical thought, the most perspicacious foresters often delude themselves in believing that they know where they are."[39]

## Beatific Vision: Round Four

The debate between Gilson and de Lubac on the one side, and Maritain and his Roman teachers on the other, was not about whether creatures desire God. They all agreed that creatures do. It concerned whether a rational creature's desire to know God is *natural* or, as the commentary tradition said, *supernaturally* added to a bare "obediential potential" in human beings or angels.

In 1963 Gilson engaged Maritain in a friendly match about the "natural desire."[40] He used the texts from the *Summa Contra Gentiles*, which he put before Maritain into an article, the "Problématique thomiste de la *vision béatifique*" (1964). Gilson takes us through the steps in the third volume of the *Contra Gentiles*. Every created substance desires its good in accordance with its own nature, that is, not simply by being itself, but by seeking what its own nature lacks, in order to fulfill itself, achieve its end or good. Intellectual substances, that is, human beings and angels, desire to know, seeking an object of knowledge that fulfills their intellectual appetite. *SCG* III, chapter 50, states that even the natural knowledge of God achieved by angels is insufficient to fulfill their *natural appetite*. If Thomas, ignorant of later controversies, did not italicize the last two words, Gilson did. "It thus follows, that man experiences a *natural* desire to know God which he cannot satisfy naturally, which is to see God through his essence." The negative theologian goes on: "From this moment the perspective is enlarged and deepened: it is not simply a question of knowing God but of seeing

39. Ibid., 119, 155; Gilson, *L'être et l'essence* (2nd ed.), 376.
40. Letters between Gilson and Maritain, November 28, December 16, 18, 1963, in *Deux approches,* 214–24.

Him." The commentators thought that the insufficiency entails a super-added *desire;* but what Thomas's God adds to nature is not the *desire* but the ability to achieve it. "In good Thomist theology," the divine act that creates and fulfills its chosen potentialities within nature "is a grace." The most gratuitous of Thomistic graces leads nature to its perfection: "the grace of the beatific vision . . . far from suppressing the natural character of the desire to see God, supernaturally fulfills this desire."[41]

But if we find in *SCG* III, 50.1, the contention that "intellectual substances" *must* have a God-given potential for the vision of God, because a "natural desire" cannot be in vain, are we not, in the words used in the recent ecclesial disturbances, "destroy[ing] the gratuity of the supernatural order," saying that God "cannot create intellectual beings without ordering and calling them to the beatific vision"? Gilson answers that "Scripture" made Thomas envisage a "nature-willed-by-God-in-view-of-grace."[42]

In 1965 de Lubac published *Le mystère du surnaturel.* Gilson told him that "you are right to insist on the natural vocation of the intellect to a vision of God of which it is naturally incapable. Your Thomistic texts are conclusive." He wrote an article about *Le mystère,* commending de Lubac's work for standing outside the "falsifying interpretations" that "turned Saint Augustine's elegant system into Jansen's mutant that shied away from nature, and Thomism into the Aristotelian naturalism that hid itself from grace." While Augustine emphasized grace and Thomas underlined nature, both recognized that human desire is oriented to a *mystery.* Because both theologians realized that their object was not a system of words but "the highest reality," de Lubac has shown that they "grow together, for the simple reason that they come into contact with theological reality itself."[43]

Gilson believed that the "whole thought of Saint Thomas is at stake" in the matter of the "natural desire": "Risk just this one proposition in good theological company, and you will see what happens. I do not say: risk this proposition as true, but merely as expressing the authentic thought of Saint Thomas. However, that is what he said: '*Omnis intellectus naturaliter desiderat divinae substantiae visionem*' (Cont. Gent. III, 57, 4)." Sharing the same "heterodox" side, Gilson and de Lubac grew together in the be-

---

41. Gilson, "Sur la problématique thomiste de la vision béatifique" (1964), in *Autour de Saint Thomas,* 63–66.

42. Pope Pius XII, *Humani Generis,* para. 26; Gilson, "Sur la problématique thomiste de la vision béatifique," 66–67.

43. Gilson to Henri de Lubac, June 19, 1965, in de Lubac, ed., *Letters of Gilson to de Lubac,* 76; Gilson (1965), reprinted ibid., 181–82.

lief that in the Christian universe everything acts in view of God and therefore implicitly desires God.[44]

## Le Thomisme (1965)

The 1942–1944 edition of *Le Thomisme* had begun with an investigation of the distinction between *ens* and *esse, id quod est* and *id quo est*. The sixth edition of 1965 takes the text back to the place at which it had begun, in 1919, with the existence of God: "Did Gilson fear he had gone too far from Thomas? He wanted to return to the analysis given in *La Philosophie au Moyen Age* [1956]: 'The first things which we know,' says Gilson in the chapter about St. Thomas, 'are sensible things, but the first thing that God reveals to us is his existence; one begins theologically where one arrives philosophically, after a long preparation.'" Gilson was a teacher, and the fact that the 1942 entrée is rather mind-numbing for beginner Thomists will have entered his considerations. He had observed in 1960 that it is an "error to systematize" Thomas's theology "on the basis of his own notion of God and of being."[45] He must have decided it would be a good idea to get that straight at the outset.

The book's explication of Thomas's epistemology and existential metaphysics is directly critical of Maritain. Gilson states in his final elucidation of *Le Thomisme:*

> To will to attain to existence through an intellectual intuition which directly knows it, and knows it alone, is impossible. To think, is first of all to conceive. And the object of the concept is always an essence, or something which offers itself to thought like an essence, in short, an object. And existence is an act. One can therefore only know it in and through the essence whose act it is. A pure *est* is unthinkable, but one can think an *id quod est*. And every *id quod est* is first of all a being, and because no other concept is anterior to it, being is indeed the first principle of knowledge. It is in reality, and it is in the doctrine of Saint Thomas.[46]

44. Gilson, *Les tribulations de Sophie*, 23; Gilson, *Elements of Christian Philosophy*, 271.

45. Prouvost, "Les relations entre philosophie et théologie chez É Gilson," 425; Gilson, *Elements of Christian Philosophy*, 132.

46. Bars, "Gilson et Maritain," 253; Gilson, *Le Thomisme* (6th ed.), 448 ff., cited ibid., 254.

For Gilson's Thomas, our understanding of *esse* or being is limited by the fact that each act of knowing travels through the sensing, imagining, and ultimately, cognition of an actual *entity*. Gilson increasingly "affirmed the central significance of the judgment of existence—in this he is close to Maritain—but he refused to separate the judgment of the concept of the existent ... from the 'concrete substances whose sensible qualities affect our senses'" and if, as he says in *Thomisme* VI, "'to think is first of all to conceive,' to conceive is always to conceive a *quid* abstracted from the sensible."[47]

Gilson is quite willing to write "intuition" of being for "judgment of being." Commiserating with Jacques on the demise of the Thomist revival, he commented that the "insoluble problem" is the "professors." "The Church can recommend or prescribe his doctrine to its teachers," but "it is necessary to *see* the truth of Thomism"—and how many have the "fundamental intuition" to do so? It is not the analogy of sight to which he objects, but the notion of vision unbounded by particular, substantial forms. For if one could have an undelimited conceptual vision of *esse*, one would "be able to conceive God."[48]


## Paul VI Commends Theological Pluralism (1965)

Gilson enjoyed the sixth Thomistic Conference, of 1965, more than that of 1950. He gave his paper entitled "De la notion d'être divin dans la philosophie de saint Thomas d'Aquin." He notes that both Thomists, with an analogical notion of being, and Scotists, deploying a univocal notion, are equally led to negative theology, because infinitude is just as inconceivable as being: "Christians have different theologies, but the same God," whose essence is unknowable. Desperate to ingratiate himself, Charles Boyer had invited de Lubac. Gilson groused to Pegis, "Ah, that I could cure our friend Father de Lubac of his acute 'Teilhard-de-Chardinism.' Teilhard is a gnostic." The Thomists were bused out to Castel Gandolfo, where Pope Paul VI gave a lecture that impressed Gilson better than that of his Jesuit friend. "The pope spoke in French," which, as we know from his previous avatar as Mgr. Montini, Gilson considered impeccable. Moreover, "he was obviously laying down the law for the council [about to begin its final ses-

47. Floucat, "Étienne Gilson et la métaphysique thomiste de l'acte d'être," 383.
48. Gilson to Jacques Maritain, November 23, 1963, in *Deux approches*, 225; Floucat, "Étienne Gilson et la métaphysique thomiste de l'acte d'être," 384, citing Gilson's *Introduction à la philosophie chrétienne*, 189.

sion].... Thomas is, was, and always will be the Doctor Communis.... Then [the Pope] said what I have always been waiting for: that by making him the Common Doctor, the church did not intend to exclude other doctors whose teachings are theologically sound.... I was living through a historical moment in the development of Thomism. At that moment the devil got so angry he unleashed one more diabolical storm; a soaked congress returned to its buses." Gilson often came back to this statement, which, as he believed, would "one day...be acclaimed as the best thing ever to have happened to Thomism," for it meant that Thomism was no longer what Chenu had called the church's "authoritarian arm against modernism," the recognition of the "factual relativity" of a theology that must stand or fall with the professors' *seeing* its truth. Étienne could not resist pointing out to his Scotist friends that God's reply to Moses was not "my name is *ens infinitum*."[49]

## Orthodoxy in the Hands of Its Destroyers

The first conciliar document to be promulgated, *Sacrosanctum Concilium* (1963), set the tone for the Vatican Council. It intended to reform the liturgy and led rapidly to the translation of the Latin rites into everyday language. The post-conciliar liberties did not consistently delight Gilson. In 1965 he published in a popular journal his objections to the new French translation of the creed, which states that the Son "*est de même nature que le Père*"; his article is entitled "Suis-je schismatique?" Maritain sent his encouragement, in a letter that, Gilson told him, made him feel less alone in his "melancholy."[50]

The next year saw the appearance of Maritain's *Le Paysan de la Garonne*, which earned him the obloquy of progressive Catholics. In 1967 Gilson published *Les tribulations de Sophie*, in which he disparages the religious fashions arising in immediate response to the Second Vatican Council, jokes sardonically about the flight of priests to the altar, quoting press references about these lately married individuals, and lets fly his own objurgations about the transformation of the Magnificat into a drinking song. Gilson

49. Gilson, "De la notion d'être divin dans la philosophie de saint Thomas d'Aquin," 126; Gilson to Anton Pegis, July 20, 1965, in Shook, *Gilson*, 370; Gilson to Anton Pegis, September 17, 1965, quoted in Shook, *Gilson*, 370; Gilson, "De la notion d'être divin dans la philosophie de saint Thomas d'Aquin," 126.

50. Kavanah, "The Conciliar Documents (Sacrosanctum Concilium)," 68–73; Gilson to Jacques Maritain, December 1, 1965, in *Deux approches*, 227.

thereby attained permanent heroic status with those Catholics who would have preferred their church to remain the way it had been in 1950. Having taken a life-long stand against political Gallicanism, the universality of the church's liturgical language had a great symbolic and indeed spiritual significance to him; the anecdotes with which he records its loss do not quite rise to the occasion.[51]

Gilson realized that his own negative reactions to the council would be taken as "grist to the mill of the conservatives" and that he would "doubtless be considered as an integrist" for having been persuaded by Cardinal Pizzardo to clarify his objections to Teilhard de Chardin (these were reprinted in *Les Tribulations*). "This is what is frightening," Gilson told de Lubac in 1965, "orthodoxy in the hands of her destroyers. The tragedy of modernism was that the rotten theology promulgated by its opponents was in large part responsible for modernism's errors. Modernism was wrong, but its repression was undertaken by men who were also wrong, *whose pseudo-theology made a modernist reaction inevitable.*"[52] He may have intended his correspondent to take that as applying, not only to the events of sixty years before, but also to the present.

Seminarians were still learning, Gilson said in 1965, "to *recite by heart* the responses in their manuals," so as to prevent them from inclining to subjectivism, in theology. The council opened the door to a vociferous reaction against Thomism, to be carried through by clerics who had themselves been trained in Aristotelian rationalism. "After having taught their own Thomisms instead of Saint Thomas Aquinas, now they want to exclude the teaching of genuine Thomism in order to deliver themselves from the false one which they themselves set up in its place." The "99%" of clergy who are built to be "pastorals" ought to be given something better to do with their time than philosophy.[53]

In his memoir, Gilson describes Christianity as a fact so cretinous that a week-old baby can engage in it: the infant who is held in the baptismal font passively receives a sacrament that decides for him his eternal future. When the child begins to study his faith, he would do better to learn it from a catechism which bluntly tells him what to believe, without trying to justify the articles of faith by a "pseudo-philosophy." By this criterion, we learn

51. Gilson, *Les tribulations de Sophie*, 11, 144–47, 140–41.

52. Gilson to Stefan Sweizawski, August 14, 1965, in Georges Kalinowski, *L'impossible métaphysique*, 247; Gilson to Henri de Lubac, June 21, 1965, in *Letters of Gilson to de Lubac*, 94–95. My italics.

53. Gilson to Stefan Seizawski, August 14, 1965, in Kalinowski, *L'impossible métaphysique*, 248.

that French catechisms have steadily deteriorated since 1885, each new one padding out the articles with philosophical explanations. Gilson's sense of where the wind was blowing could only reinforce his "Bonaventurian" intuition about the preferability of "salvific"[54] knowledge to philosophical explanations.

As a demonstration of the priority of faith over reason, infant baptism has a fine graphite objectivity. But Gilson's use of the biographical medium invites one to ask whether it always works that way. The particular architectonic balance of ideas and experiences which made up Gilson's own orientation upon faith and reason is not universal. Someone could even have been pointed toward faith by reading *The Unity of Philosophical Experience*. An adult convert like Maritain naturally saw conversion to Catholicism through intellectual conviction as a possibility, and he may have been less robust than Gilson in feeling that Bergson ought never to have been urged to rethink the foundations of his thought because "not to have the faith is not a personal fault, it is a misfortune."[55]

On receipt of Maritain's *De la grace et humanité de Jesus* (1967), which argues that the human and the divine natures of Christ each have their own *esse*, he employed the tactic of humility: "I'm not enough of a theologian to follow you," Gilson said. The philosopher did not let go of his strategic mission: "if the human nature has a distinct esse from the divine person," he told the author, "it becomes another being from the divine being. . . . He is true man through his nature, but he is true God through his being which is the divine *esse* common to the three persons of the blessed Trinity." A letter to Chenu is more emotive: "Discussing such a question with Maritain gives me the impression of playing in a Molièrian scene. I don't like to feel in disagreement with Jacques on a point where, for me, anyway, the whole of Thomism is at stake. If there can be a single being that has two existences, I understand nothing of St. Thomas." That missive did not see the light of day. But another letter, to Antonio Livi, from 1968, which states that "the whole historical perspective of Canon Van Steenberghen is falsified by the notion" of Christian philosophy, "making him invent works by Siger which he never wrote, all to prove that there have been Christian philosophers who philosophized as if they were not Christians," was printed, with Gilson's knowledge, and wounded its subject.[56]

54. Gilson, *Le philosophe et la théologie*, 13, 82, 75.
55. Ibid., 176.
56. Gilson to Maritain, June 16, 1967, in *Deux approches,* 242; Gilson to Marie-Dominique Chenu, September 11, 1968, ibid., 243; Gilson to Antonio Livi, May 5, 1968, cited in Van Steenberghen, "Étienne Gilson et l'université de Louvain," 20.

## The Mystery of Language

"'Mystery speaking through mysteries. Isn't that the conscious or un-conscious purpose of the compulsive urge to create?' Kandinsky had asked in 1910." Picasso's humorous, surrealistic symbolism often alerted his audi-ence to the *estrangement* between a person and the universe. He remarked that "we tried to get rid of '*trompe l'oeil*' to find a '*trompe l'esprit.*'" Gilson's autumnal probings of the philosophy of art led him back to the artistic springtime of his Parisian youth. Armand Maurer saw that *Linguistics and Philosophy* (1969) was about "the heart of the mystery of language" and was "intended as an acknowledgment rather than as an unveiling of this mystery." The mystery of language is its surreal "incommensurability" with "the things signified" and with thought itself.[57]

Gilson had said in his memoir that the neo-Thomists' negative verdict upon Bergson was dishonorable because his epistemology "had the immense merit of facing the problem *in the terms in which it is posed today,*" that is, criticizing scientific determinism by way of asking *why* human intelligence tends to mechanism. Bergson's answer to the "problem" of idealism, as a continuous philosophical temptation, was that science needs to "cut out" immobile little squares which are intellectually manageable, and it calls the spatial mosaic which it thus constructs "reality." The intellect's "unlimited power of decomposing" disorients it from the whole and moving fabric of life.[58] Idealism is avoidable only if we realize that where "science" gives us parts, intuition sees the whole.

In the first chapter of *Linguistics and Philosophy,* "The Decomposition of Thought," Gilson says that the error of the linguists begins in Condillac's *Grammaire,* which contains a word-equivalent for every thought. The identification fails because, whereas words are things of parts, thought is indivisible. A professor's thought must be communicated in one hour; the thought and the time that words take to convey it belong to different uni-verses. The extraterrestrial relation of thought to language is indicated by the difficulty of knowing where to begin expressing a thought: Americans begin serious orations by telling jokes, because that "deaden[s] the shock" of the transition from a planet of simultaneity to the planet of language-users, in which the law of temporal duration pertains. Words are mouthed in time and in sound, but both of these material media are alien to thought. "One cuts" words "out of thought," Gilson says, "in the process of utter-

57. Dube, *The Expressionists,* 112; Golding, "Cubism," 66; Maurer, "Gilson on Lin-guistics and Philosophy of Art," 335; Gilson, *Linguistics and Philosophy,* 14.
58. Gilson, *Le philosophe et la théologie,* 159; Bergson, *Creative Evolution,* 17, 157.

ing them, their intelligible vitality there being replaced by the flux of the discourse.... [M]oreover, since there is no resemblance between the meaning and the sounds which signify it,... when the meaning is important... thought no longer recognizes itself in the sound.... Thought... refuses to recognize itself in that which detaches itself from it, just as an animal refuses to recognize itself in its stillborn offspring."[59]

For Bergson, the wholeness of life is the spiritual creativity behind the material variations evidenced in the evolution of species. When that process reached beyond animals, whose biological systems are automatically adjusted to their habitat, to human beings, whose biological shortcomings require them to recreate their environment by the invention of tools, a society emerged in which "each individual must learn his part, because he is not preordained to its structure. So a language is required which makes it possible to be always passing from what is known to what is yet to be known. There must be a language whose signs... are extensible to an infinity of objects.... The word, made to pass from one thing to another, is... by nature transferable and free."[60]

Gilson knew that the linguist's efforts to find precise correlations between thought and words break down under the uncontainable growth of real language. If language governs thought, how do we continually change the meanings of words and invent new ones? The linguistic positivists refused to acknowledge that the explanatory tool which they need is *quality,* which as we know from their reception of the *Données immediates de la conscience* is a "suspect" notion "to holders of a truly scientific attitude." Thomas had at hand the notion of the "Divine Word" as "creator," and still better, Bonaventure's "expressionism could easily develop" in the direction of an analysis of human linguistic creativity. It was not these theologians but Wilhelm von Humboldt who "recognized in language a poetic activity, or... a creative activity." Von Humboldt and, today, Noam Chomsky have rediscovered the creative power in language, the fact that "language is not a product *(Erzeugtes)* but primarily a production *(Erzeugnung)."* The creative power of language gives us our "'human ability to express new thoughts within the framework of an 'instituted language.'"[61]

That babies have silent "thinks" before they speak is evident to anyone who has watched one performing this feat. We experience thoughts that are "anterior" even to inner language. It is the artists who have best articulated this fact, says Gilson. By the practice of such deliberate absurdities as

59. Gilson, *Linguistics and Philosophy,* 90–91.
60. Bergson, *Creative Evolution,* 158–59.
61. Gilson, *Linguistics and Philosophy,* 54–56.

automatic writing, attempting to shake off the grip of the grammarians, the Dadaists and the surrealists performed "exceptionally lucid experiments" on language, attempting to find out what lies behind it. The surrealist André Breton spoke of the "'torpedoing of the idea' by the sentence that enunciates it": language blows thought up into fragments. It took a sur-realist to realize that there is "something beyond the physically real"; although "Breton professed to be an atheist,... when it came to pure thought, he did not hesitate to speak the language of grace."[62]

Henri Bergson remarked in 1905, "From this ocean of life in which we are immersed, we are continually drawing something"; Gilson's comeback was that "words are sorts of floating buoys...to which thought fastens itself."[63] The artist is Gilson's emblem of the useless outsider to positivist culture, but as he had always emphasized in reference to *esse,* so he reminds us here that trying to *imagine* thought is the first step toward identifying it with a material *thing.*

Ferdinand de Saussure's linguistics did in fact recognize the duality of language: he called it a "two-fold object." The precise phonic material one uses in a particular language to designate a particular thing is arbitrary. One way to disarm the duality of "signs" or words, and "signified" or meanings, is to treat the latter as being likewise arbitrary. De Saussure neutralized the meaning, by calling it a "value." He analyzes linguistic "value" by analogy to monetary values, the socially arbitrated attribution of "values" to particular amounts of cash, which enables us to exchange it for things. Linguistic "values" are therefore as arbitrary, or "pure," as monetary ones, where *purity* means unbound by reference. Against this, the brilliant orator, whose only insuperable adversary was his overdraft, noted that the linguist's analogy falters on the fact that when we exchange words, our wallets encounter no loss, for both thought and its words remain our own property.[64]

People are often convinced of the identity of thought and language by the argument that it is impossible to translate from one language into another. Having "often had to transpose into English for an American audience a lecture he had originally prepared in French,"[65] Gilson considered that the case was not fully demonstrated. In fact, having participated for two decades in the Académie Française's deliberations on the perfect French dictionary, he thought the situation was rather grimmer than the argument

62. Ibid., 64, 98.
63. Bergson, *Creative Evolution,* 191; Gilson, *Linguistics and Philosophy,* 65.
64. Gilson, *Linguistics and Philosophy,* 2, 27.
65. Maurer, "Gilson on Linguistics and Philosophy of Art," 341.

from two "heterogeneous" languages supposes: no language can even be translated into itself. No dictionary can find the words which perfectly pin down a "dog," let alone such abstractions as "love," for someone who has not experienced these things *beyond the dictionary.* Dictionary definitions are almost self-deductive, presupposing readers who have experiences outside of the circle. Dictionaries are the last stronghold of extreme realism, but in the world of things, there are no universals, but only individual dogs, horses, and loves. When, in chapter 14, I used an animal metaphor instead of "Gilson," no reader projected an "uncastrated male ox" (OED). The meaning of words seems arbitrary to linguistic analysts because each individual word has a vast, perhaps infinite, range of meanings, shifting each time it is creatively deployed in a different sentence. "Bull" means different things in different linguistic contexts; coming upon this word in sentences about canon law, one takes it to mean one thing, encountering it in an enticement to the arena, another, and still another when one meets it as an exclamatory objection to one's thesis. Gilson's explanation of this is that it is not the word which means, but the sentence. If language is a referential tool, then "one could even say that language is not composed of words but of what the poet [Mallarmé] called . . . 'understandable mouthfuls.' Every 'mouthful' is uttered all together, and as legitimate as it might be to try to analyze it, the elements which one distinguishes in it do not possess really distinct existence."[66]

Gilson thought that poetic cognition grapples, not with the reproduction of *imagerie,* but with the invention of plastic forms. He was sympathetic to Mallarmé's wish to create a poetry purified of all "reportage," all reference to things. Mallarmé's statement that "every thought sets in action a throw of the dice" is the epigraph to *Linguistics and Philosophy:* the hazard the poet endeavored to avoid was the jump from pure thought to the contingent names for things. The knowledge that the "lexicographical use of words designed to communicate information is radically foreign to the end that poetry pursues" is the artist's elliptical access to a theological insight: Saint Thomas finds that, before spoken words, and before the "interior word," the thought spoken to oneself, is a silent "word of the heart." The "poetic passion and death of Mallarmé" prove "the transcendence of pure thought, the *verbum cordis* without which there would have been no language": like every "mystery . . . this one is, in a sense, silence." Mallarmé's great project, THE BOOK, defeated the poet because he sought silence, but did not perceive its orientation: and likewise,

66. Gilson, *Linguistics and Philosophy,* 31–33, 13.

Bergson was right to look for metaphysics, not in the philosophies, but in the philosophers. One must add...that it cannot be by chance that so many philosophers should have yielded to the need to express themselves in a philosophy. That which cannot be said is at the same time an irresistible urge to express itself....What is this secret seething of thoughts, which rumbles with a confused din of a crowd but which can only issue one word at a time? And why is it absolutely necessary to speak, so much so that the Divine Word Himself desired to become flesh and lived among us? Meditating on the lesson of Plotinus...Bergson regretted that this Greek mistook a bubbling spring for a waterfall, as if a waterfall could not be a bubbling spring. But Plotinus was not wrong either to see in the manifold an inferior image of the One,...the unmoved source of the many. How else can we explain within us this inexhaustible spring which gushes forth in a cascade of words incapable of drying it up? All the great metaphysicians come to a standstill with Plato at the end of this source.[67]

The task of the philosophy of language is to balance the theological intuition of silence against the claims of rationality, directed at things and enfleshed in arbitrary words. It is made possible by finding the potential for living growth within the silence.

In his inaugural lecture at the Collège de France, Gilson had presented mediaeval humanism as the attempt to keep Greek and Roman thought alive, as evidenced in the unclassical "dog" Latin used as a working tongue by the Scholastics; he had slyly exhibited himself as a successor to the mediaevals in this, on the ground of having learned the trick from Bergson. Forty years later, with help from the linguist Émile Benveniste, Gilson distinguishes physical time from linguistic time. Every human person, Benveniste argued, lives in his own subjective time, which is neither the same as physical time or chronological time. Living acts of speech bring into play a fourth form of temporality, in which two subjective times meet in a concreated and shared temporality. Phenomenologically, speech acts do not bring together two or more biological times, or chronological times, but experiential or subjective times.

Spontaneous spoken discourse is thus, for Gilson, the most living form of language. Anyone can tell the difference between an impromptu lecture and one read from a text. This is because an improvised talk puts an audience in contact with a personality, whereas a lecturer who reads from a prepared script hands over his ideas. Gilson concurs with Wittgenstein in

67. Ibid., 101, 74–75, 104, 142–43.

this at least, that lectures read from notes have a "cadaverous appearance": "sentences, alive when written, are dead when read." What writing kills is, not the author, but the author's *personality*. Here Gilson refers to Alain Robbe-Grillet's dictum that "the highest ambition of every writer" is to create an "object so perfect that it should wipe out our imprints." Gilson equates impersonality with eternity. The characteristic of writing, of "immobilizing thought in time in conferring upon it the ... possibility of an indefinitely renewable present," enables written thought to create an inter-subjective temporality which is the highest human analogy to eternity. When I read a Platonic dialogue, there emerges a "linguistic time" in which "I become a contemporary of Plato's Socrates, who invites me to sit down with him in the shade of the Ilissus."[68] The materiality of the medium be-lies the nonmateriality of the message. In the aesthetics of language, the music of living speech is a less perfect impress of eternity than the book, with its lapidary expression of thought.

History and philosophy thus constitute two separate orders. In 1963, Gilson read Gouhier's essay in which Loisy's thought is defined as an effort to describe doctrine as living or vital and yet simultaneously to separate its empirical from its unchanging elements. He told Gouhier that "everything that you say about Loisy makes me see him objectively (dead) for the first time."[69] I believe that Gouhier killed Loisy for Gilson by putting his own life-long problem clearly before his eyes.

The year before, against the contention that methodological atheism is a condition of a specifically *modern* philosophy, Gilson noted that "it is sadly impossible to introduce history into philosophy without rupturing its con-tinuity. The one order is not the continuation of the other." Gilson told his former pupil that "I am far from contesting" "your radical historical con-tingentism. ... I ceaselessly teach it. I have often told my students that if Kant had died at the same age as Descartes, we could not talk about the *Critique of Pure Reason*. Naturally, you are going to verify the dates and wreck my fine example! But, when it is a matter of philosophy, a necessity inscribes itself in this contingence. ... The great difference between our manners of writing history is that you are interested above all in philoso-phers, whereas I am interested above all in philosophy. Since Parmenides, a world of concepts and conceptual relations floats (in what?); let's just say, floats; it is enough to accept any one of them to find oneself engaged in de-

68. Ibid., 113, 126, 86.
69. Gilson to Henri Gouhier, July 19, 1963, in "Lettres d'Étienne Gilson à Henri Gouhier," 473–74.

terminations . . . from which thought cannot extract itself. . . . I believe in the *(sui generis)* existence of philosophical thought. The philosophers themselves and their doctrines are contingent, as you say; I have proved it in my own life; but I believe that there are necessities of thought."[70] Among Gilson's readers it has been Gouhier who accentuated this search for the eternal as being the heart of Gilson's thinking. His interpretation of his close friend's writing, which he loved, has the merit of explaining why, on going through his papers, Gilson's biographer found so many expressions of sympathy for Loisy. The "Loisy problem" was contiguous with the Bergson problem, in Gilson's mind.

"Here below," Gilson says in *Linguistics and Philosophy,* we live in time. Dialogue creates a "pluri-personal temporality in the present": language is the handmaiden of sociality. Sociality is, as both Bergson and Thomas noted, the condition of the use of tools: "It is difficult for an isolated individual to prepare alone all those things he requires for himself and his family." Bergson distinguished animal instinct, as the "faculty of using and even of constructing organized instruments," from human intelligence, as "the faculty of making and using unorganized instruments." The linguist Edward Sapir pointed out that human beings have no precise organ of speech: the closest approximation, the vocal chords, are not themselves an "organized instrument" of speech. If the creative drive behind language is thought, then we may say, not that language is the tool by which we create society, but rather that society is the *end for which* language is used. In order to find out a philosopher able to digest such finalism, "swallowing all sense of shame, we have to go back . . . to that scoundrel Aristotle." The human species has created language to enable itself to fulfill its "vocation as a political animal."[71]

Gilson enjoyed sharing his grumpiness with the tranquil Maritain, and their correspondence of these years often concludes with a verbal embrace. If they did not fully agree as to the causes of modernism past, they spontaneously concurred about what they saw as its current manifestation. Gilson felt able to tell the *Paysanne* that he objected to *Populorum Progressio,* a papal encyclical that contradicts Péguy's insight that Christianity is not a

---

70. Gilson, "L'Être et Dieu" (1962), in *Constantes,* 215; Gilson to Henri Gouhier, June 9, 1966, in "Lettres d'Étienne Gilson à Henri Gouhier," 476–78. My italics.
71. Gilson, *Linguistics and Philosophy,* 86; Gilson, *The Christian Philosophy of St. Thomas Aquinas,* 327; Bergson, *Creative Evolution,* 140; Gilson, *Linguistics and Philosophy,* 46–47, 57, 61.

religion of progress. In the thick of the completion of the "Bergson" chapter of one of his last books, Gilson told Gouhier that Bergson had "put his faith in a *progressive* evolution which, through Spencer, relied on Lamarck, on Condorcet, and the optimistic guillotiners of the 18th century."[72]

Gilson, now aged eighty-six, had long ago abandoned the belief in progress which he had espoused in his Gifford lectures. The answer to Loisy was, in the end, just the priority of eternity over time.

## From Aristotle to Darwin and Back

Since 1951, Gilson had published six books about poetics, art, and beauty. *De Aristote à Darwin et retour,* published in 1970, may be a seventh. Ralph McInerny is not idiosyncratic in considering that, in *Being and Some Philosophers,* Gilson caricatured the historical Aristotle: he feels that the "fact that he could later write *From Aristotle to Darwin and Back,* a book suffused with respect to Aristotle, suggests that" in the earlier book, "Gilson was being artfully anti-Aristotelian."[73] In 1970 Gilson is leaning on a different building block, both in Aristotle and in his own mind.

Gilson notices that Aristotle's aesthetic is found not only in the *Poetics* but in the *Parts of Animals,* which states that "we should venture on the study of every kind of animal without distaste; for each and all will reveal to us something natural and something beautiful. Absence of haphazard and conduciveness of everything to an end are found in Nature's works in the highest degree, and the resultant end of her generations and combinations is a form of the beautiful." Aristotle was unlike most contemporary philosophers in lecturing on "the teeth of dogs, horses, men, and elephants," and the reason for his omnivorous interest was that he admired the "intelligible beauty" of nature, the discovery of an artistic or ordered structure; his natural science was actually a calology that exhibited the "truth of nature." An open-minded person could also have noted that *Creative Evolution* is daunting to those who are untrained in the observation of wasps, "monera," insects, and hymenoptera. It is evidently the work, not of the idealist for which the neo-Thomists took him, but of a man of his generation, who revered natural science: "no philosopher resembled" Aristotle "more than Bergson in his taste for empirical knowledge, the care...which he took to

72. Gilson to Jacques Maritain, June 9, 1967, in *Deux approches,* 235; Gilson to Henri Gouhier, September 12, 1970, in "Lettres d'Étienne Gilson à Henri Gouhier," 471.
73. McInerny, "Gilson's Theory of Art," 350.

confront his conclusions with the concrete facts."[74] It is thus in part from Bergsonian or Aristotelian calological realism that Gilson sets out to refute philosophical evolutionism. Human reason can see the intelligible beauty of nature because it is there. It is in the reality of artistic forms in nature that he founds his argument for a return from the Darwinian dissolution of natural forms to an Aristotelian "biophilosophy."

The students who "heard Bergson lecture on Spencer's *First Principles* at the Collège de France...took away the impression that it was all over with this kind of evolutionism." In "reviving a true Aristotelianism," Bergson "put an end to the...conflict of mechanism and finalism,...precisely because he developed a metaphysics of 'quality' against every type of quantitative determinism."[75] But using the "tactic...at which he excelled, Bergson initially imagines two adversaries between whom he himself will define the proper position on the question," that is, the "strawmen" of absolute mechanism and absolute finalism. Although Bergson placed his position closer to finalism than to mechanism, Gilson notes that Bergson rejected absolute finalism, or the idea that every species is present from the outset, because he confused the scientific notion of evolution with philosophical evolution*ism*, believing the latter to have been scientifically demonstrated.[76] Bergson was unconscious of his achievement in restoring Aristotelian forms to nature.

In Gilson's book, Charles Darwin was a "fixist" who lost his rationally ungrounded scriptural faith in the divine "creation of beings such as we know them at the present time" in the course of his unfortunate voyage on the *Beagle*. Although Darwin was thus converted from fixed species to "transformism," the latter is not identical to evolution*ism*. The word *evolution* does not occur in the *Origin of the Species* until the fifth edition, thirteen years after the composition of the first. Darwin picked the term up, as the buzzword of the anti-creationists, but what he saw as his own discovery was the modification of species through *natural selection*. Natural selection appears to require a selector, as with Darwin's own exemplary cases, of stockbreeding and horticulture.[77] Darwin found a motor for the process of

74. Gilson, *From Aristotle to Darwin and Back,* citing Aristotle, *Parts of Animals* 1.5, 645a, 20–21, 1, 19; Bergson, *Creative Evolution,* e.g., 134, 142–47, 173–74, and, effectively, passim; Gilson, *Le philosophe et la théologie,* 128.

75. Gilson, *From Aristotle to Darwin and Back,* 92; Conticello "Métaphysique de l'être et théologie de la grâce," 443–44.

76. Gilson, *From Aristotle to Darwin and Back,* 91, 96; Bergson, *Creative Evolution,* 50.

77. Gilson, *From Aristotle to Darwin and Back,* 34, 75.

selection in Malthus's "law of political economy," that is, the deliberate attempt by societies to restrict growth in the human population. Although it lacks a mind to drive it, Darwin's nature is no less teleologically "anthropomorphic" than Aristotle's.

It is this unacknowledged weaving of an aiming mind into the empirical evidence that makes the theory of evolution "a philosophical notion... introduced from outside of science." The notion was not Darwin's; in 1895, Herbert Spencer rightly claimed it as his own. It was Thomas Huxley and James Scully, who, in their item on "Evolution" in the 1878 *Encyclopedia Brittanica*, fused Darwinian modification through selection with Spencerian evolution, creating the "new unicorn, *evolutionismus darwinianus.*" As a "hybrid" of philosophy and science, with the "generality of the one and the demonstrative certitude of the other," it can adapt to any climate and survive against the onslaughts of every species of evidence.[78]

In *L'être et l'essence,* Gilson said that God is the "supreme Artist," but in *The Arts of the Beautiful* we learn that God is not an artist. Coming in between, Gilson's offensive against the Roman Thomist's abuse of "pseudo-principle[s]" had led him to examine the demonstrations of the existence of God more closely. Now, taking the sympathy for Hume that he showed in *L'être et l'essence* a bit further, he finds that the so-called "skeptic" was right to deny that causality is a principle. The Scottish philosopher "never placed in doubt that effects come from causes, he simply recognized that the relation of causality does not correspond to any clear idea in the mind, which is something different." We do not know, a priori, that "every change has a cause" but rather obtain that generalization through "spontaneous inference." If it were *necessary* that every change has a cause, that is, if causality was a transcendental, then the child who asks "Who made God?" would legitimately put a stop to this line in argument for His existence. If causality is not a principle, then one has to retreat from deduction to the more solid ground of "empirical observation."[79]

In *Matières et formes,* Gilson discussed why sculptors like to imitate, not just nature, but living nature: "nothing interests man more than life and the movement which is the sign of it, which resembles him. When one's glance travels across the expanse of an immense plain, it is enough for something to move to arrest one's gaze. Animals feel the same." In his defense of teleology in nature, Gilson applies to "spontaneous inference" to indicate

78. Ibid., 89, 70.
79. Gilson, *L'être et l'essence* (1st ed.), 304; Gilson, *The Arts of the Beautiful,* 25; Gilson, *Constantes,* 95–96, 99.

the presence of purpose in nature: arising, not from a "logical operation composed of explicit judgments," but from "psychology," its "foundation is the perception of beings capable of self-movement."[80] As with aesthetics, based in perception, the observation of natural movement comes back to an *individual's sensing*.

The first rationally ungrounded, scriptural "fixists" were Descartes and Francis Bacon, in their philosophical elimination of formal causality from nature and their endeavor to explain the natural world by way of mechanical, or efficient, causation. If *From Aristotle to Darwin* is an attempt to rescue nature from a complete explanation in terms of *efficient* causality, then Gilson's analysis of the First Way seems to help us to understand it. Gilson told Georges Kalinowski that "I have never been anything other than a professor. It was in preparing for the hundredth time a lesson on the *prima via*, at the age of 79, that I perceived for the first time that Saint Thomas did not pronounce the word *causa* in any of the three major expositions which he devoted to it. I had taught throughout my life the *cause through movement*, which he had deliberately avoided speaking of. One has to be modest."[81]

In his reinterpretation of the way from movement, Gilson lays out the Latin texts of Thomas's three versions of this argument in order to show that the word *cause* never appears; the way from *movement* is not a "particular case" of Thomas's second way, from an efficient cause of movement. Thomas's First Way is concerned with the relation of instrumental movers to principal movers. Whereas physical beings can be instrumental movers, only spiritual entities can be principal movers. The First Way begins from a fact of experience, that things are moving, to *metaphysics*, for physical science cannot observe a principal mover:

> A chain reaction can involve literally innumerable terms, in which each one is principal in relation to the instrumental term which follows it, and always requires an absolutely principal term at the origin of the series, without which it would not take place. A modern would doubtless object that, precisely, experience never allows one to encounter an absolutely first and principal term. The person who presses a button in order to trigger an atomic explosion is far from being the first mover or the first cause. This is true, but it is also why the problem of the first origin of movement, even as regards the data of physics, is essentially metaphysical. The principal origin of experience

80. Gilson, *Matières et formes*, 119; Gilson, *From Aristotle to Darwin and Back*, 123.
81. Gilson to Georges Kalinowski, January 12, 1964, in Kalinowski, *L'impossible métaphysique*, 246.

is not given in experience. In order to have the right to affirm it, it is required that, in the sensible experience which is the origin of our rational knowledge, any observable fact authorizes the reason to conceive a causal primacy of this type.[82]

*From Aristotle to Darwin and Back* distinguishes homogeneous and heterogeneous beings. A homogeneous being is one that does not move of its own accord; the stone rolls because someone kicks it. A being that can move itself is heterogeneous, in Gilson's sense, because it is made of two elements, a "motor" part and passively moved parts. We see in nature the welding together of otherwise inanimate parts into living, that is, self-moving, beings. Animate movement can be spotted by its orientatedness. That heterogeneous parts should become wholes may be explained in terms of "final ends," or, as Aristotle puts it, an "in view of which," an "end," or a "why." To perceive organic and living beings is to perceive species: "There is no essential difference between seeing a being that is organic *[organisé]* and seeing that it is a dog." Human artists put heterogeneous materials to an end in which they cohere, but these artifacts still have a homogeneous base in that the principle of self-causality cannot be transferred to inanimate things; they cannot generate their successors or move themselves. Aristotle sees the artisan as doing what nature does, although less proficiently; lucky the artist who could do exactly as he conceives, as does the "spider weaving its web or a bird making its nest."[83] There is more design and a greater beauty in nature's living artifacts than in their inanimate counterparts.

Bergson had a "philosophy made to measure for theological experience"; the theologian leaves Kant and Comte for a better air on entering the territory of *Creative Evolution:* this is because Bergson's realism compelled him to acquiesce in the existence of mystery.[84] "The biophilosopher is not," Gilson says, "a theologian"; for what he perceives is not a directive Mind behind or within nature but, simply, nature functioning teleologically. That a nature which has no mind or "consciousness" should attempt to achieve ends is ultimately inexplicable, or "mysterious" to the philosopher: Aristotle was aware "of the difficulty, but, unlike some of our contemporaries, a fact remained a fact for him even when he realized that he was incapable of explaining it." Aristotle's analogy of the artist who begins from an idea, which Gilson demurely cites at the inception of his book, cannot ultimately be applied to a God whose intentions, as Descartes rightly saw, are unknown

82. Gilson, "Prolégomènes à la *Prima Via*," 44, 49–50.
83. Gilson, *From Aristotle to Darwin and Back*, 2, 123–24, 10.
84. Gilson, *Le philosophe et la théologie*, 131; ibid., 149.

to us.[85] Gilson's argument from movement in *From Aristotle to Darwin and Back* takes us not to the Christian God but to a mystery.

Gilson had claimed that Thomas differentiates his First Way from his Second in order that those Aristotelian necessitarians who were his colleagues in the Paris Faculty of Arts, and who rejected the proof from efficient causality, should still have a proof for the existence of God: "The Aristotle of Averroes had the right to be taken into account." Gilson's motives for writing this book were twofold and did not include a mixture of philosophical water with theological wine. On the one hand, he wanted to suggest that the inference to teleology is not withheld from those who have the misfortune not to believe in the revealed doctrine of creation. On the other hand, Gilson deplored the current popularity of Teilhard de Chardin, and when he finally got around to reading Bergson's *Two Sources of Religion and Morality,* his "worst fears were confirmed" by the author's failure to distinguish nature and grace. Gilson believed that Teilhard's all-too-imaginative "theology-fiction" depicts, not Christ as evolution, but evolution as Christ. One gets a hint of the negative stimulant to his rehabilitation of Aristotelian biophilosophy when he told Maritain that "the passion with which our *progressive* theologians throw themselves" at evolution "is enough to convince one of its falsity. In these matters, most theologians have an infallible flair for error."[86]

## The Last Debate with Maritain: The Intuition of Being

Maritain issued a final conciliatory statement in "Réflexions sur la nature blessée et sur l'intuition de l'être" (1968): it was perhaps not a good idea, by this juncture, to state that Gilson is completely correct about Aristotle's notionalism.[87] It would be difficult to conceive a concoction of ideas better designed to enrage his epistolary companion of forty years. It seems to exhibit nearly all the differences between them, and as I recite them, I shall tell Gilson's side of the story, not because Maritain's perspectives are illegitimate, but because it is Gilson's intellectual personality we are making one last effort to comprehend.

85. Gilson, *From Aristotle to Darwin and Back,* 121, 10, 7–8, 121.
86. Gilson, "Prolégomènes à la *Prima Via*," 46; Gilson, *Le philosophe et la théologie,* 181; Gilson, *Les tribulations de Sophie,* 68, 91; Gilson to Jacques Maritain, September 8, 1972, in *Deux approches,* 251.
87. Maritain, "Réflexions sur la nature blessée" (1968), in *Approches sans entraves,* 249–90, 284.

The "Réflexions" spring off from Thomas's definition of the wound to humanity brought about by original sin. Although Thomas described original sin as affecting our appetites, or *will*, it is easy, Maritain says, to shift the discussion to the effects of the Fall upon our *reason*. Thomas conceived of the effects of the Fall within the realm of the good: this can be translated into a description of how fallen human beings are related to truth.[88]

Although *odium philosophicum* and *theologicum* were not unknown to him, it is rare for Gilson to discuss a person's moral stature. He questions his opponents' reasoning but not their ethical standing. He refers to personalities in his letters, and sometimes cruelly, but the boundaries between public, reasoned debate and private feeling are kept clear. So he responds to Maritain in the persona of the fundamentalist Thomist historian: "Thomas," for whom a wound to our reason "does not exist," "appears to be more struck by the intellectual luminosity amongst the pagans...above all his dear Aristotle."[89]

Thomas described the effect of the Fall as the loss of the gift of "original justice," a disequilibrium within our willing powers, in which the lower desires tend to get the upper hand. Translating this from ethical into epistemological terms, Maritain explains it as a discoordination between imagination and reason. Fallen reason is more weighed down by imagination than it should be, he says, and this can work out either as a "*solidifying impact of the image on the idea*" or as a "*notionalizing impact on the exercise of intelligence.*"[90]

Gilson would not have interpreted the aberrations of idealism, phenomenology, or of Aristotle by reference to a wound to our fallen nature, because he had an acute ear for what could rationally convince an audience, and who was that going to convince who did not already *believe* the articles of faith regarding the Fall? In relation to Maritain, the foot-soldiering "historian" had once ceded place while the mounted knight took up the philosophical charge. At the Christian philosophy debate, Gilson was trying to prove, not that Christianity is a good moral influence on philosophers, but that Christian philosophy *exists*. Maritain had re-routed his *objective* arguments in the defense of Christian philosophy into moral psychology. Maritain repeats the same point in the "Réflexions": "it is in the climate of grace and of contemplation that the metaphysics of Saint Thomas has broken" the "barriers" of notionalism.[91]

88. Ibid., 249–53.
89. Gilson, "Propos sur l'être et sa notion," 7.
90. Maritain, "Réflexions sur la nature blessée," 260.
91. Ibid., 261.

Our debater had not the mellifluous intellectual charity that led Maritain to say that "Étienne Gilson appears to be so fascinated by the intuition of existence that he writes, if I recall correctly, that there is no *concept* of existence. In reality there are two" or even three: the concept of a rose's *thereness,* that of its particular *existence,* and the analogous concept of being that flows from this. Gilson interrupts to object that it is "scandalous" that Thomists can disagree on a "point of such importance as the notion of being."[92]

Maritain begins in sense perception. He sees a rose. From this sensible perception there emerges the knowledge that I am seeing a rose, that the flower is present to my senses. I know that this *implies* that the rose exists, but I do not go beyond the phenomenological "rose" experience: this is the level of knowledge of felt presence, to *me.* I know at this "first level of abstraction" from matter that the rose is there; this is the "register of *Dasein.*" Knowing that I sense renders an existent *implicitly* or intentionally present to the mind. One rises to a second order of abstraction by actualizing this implication. Now one can say, not just that the rose is *there,* for my experience, but that it exists in *actuality,* in the domain of *Sein.* I do not just see that a rose is there, I see the rose's being. It is because I can *see being,* conceptually, that there is an order of objective, trans-phenomenological judgments.[93] Such judgments of being are analogical, one to another, in that each judgment sees *being,* under a different form. Maritain has worked from the implicit knowledge of the thereness of things, to the explicit knowledge of their existence, and from there to that of existence as such. This argumentation requires a pure concept of existence, taken not as a verbal happening, but, so to speak, as a solidified noun.

Gilson interjects that we do not see the rose's existence, we see a rose, existing. The verb is the prosaic *have,* the rose-entity's having its being. One constantly sees the event of existing, but never as detached from the particular havings of being by entities: "we only apprehend" *esse* as the being-of-this-entity, which is for us the object of a "sensible perception." So "it will not do to take a sensible intuition of the entity for the intellectual intuition of its being."[94]

Maritain replies that, for Gilson, the intuition of being designates "an intelligible—the esse or the existence—which is not derived from phantasms by abstractive operation, in the manner of all other conceptual objects." Gilson pushes in to ask whether we can "say that there is a concept of being

92. Ibid., 265; Gilson, "Propos sur l'être et sa notion," 8.
93. Maritain, "Réflexions sur la nature blessée," 269–71.
94. Gilson, "Propos sur l'être et sa notion," 10.

*(esse),* and even two, not to say three . . . [T]here are many who believe themselves to be in agreement with Thomas Aquinas, who do not recognize themselves as being endowed with this intelligible intuition of esse." For Gilson, being is not an intelligible concept but a principle by which we make judgments concerning entities: "the intellect cannot think without affirming it,"[95] but neither can the intellect define it. This is why any reasoning that begins from the concept of being, rather than from sensed causation, is circular.

Where Maritain pictures being as acting analogically in all things, and uniting them, Gilson has before him a world of individuals, each an exciting, sharp note of existing. He notes that the concept-noun *ens commune,* common being, is an intellectual tool that has no real existence outside our minds. *Exist*ence is the verb-event of making to be, and to make to be is to bring about an individual. We can see that the event of being is happening *to* entities, that they have an "immanent cause"; we cannot abstract the cause from them and view it in itself as a concept. If "being were perceptible in itself, it would be that of God, and only thus could it be an object of intellectual intuition." This, said the literally minded man, is "palaeothomism."[96]

Like Debussy, Gilson liked discordant notes, sudden novelties: he had written in 1919, in defense of *La Mer,* "All chords and tones are legitimate if they . . . satisfy the ear and stir the imagination." "Judging from the numerous articles, papers and volumes devoted" to the topic of analogy in Thomas, Gilson said in 1948, with a footnote to *The Degrees of Knowledge,* "we might easily think that St. Thomas had explained himself at some length. But this is not so." Thomas's conception of analogy is the meager "not altogether equivocal."[97] Because he was a philosopher of the analogy of being, the transcendentals play a significant role in Maritain's thought. As he honed his focus down to *esse,* Gilson came to see the transcendentals as "superfluous" in relation to that primary metaphysical object. Each of the transcendentals, he says, is a way in which being is related to human subjects: "Being is one for the concept, true for the judgment, good for the desire, and beautiful for the sensibility or the intellect whose powers of apprehension it satisfies." The transcendentals are "real relations" in the "multiple powers which the unity of being refracts from itself." Although each of them is "founded in being," it is "only in knowledge that the transcendental is given." One cannot make one's way from "known being" to

95. Maritain, "Réflexions sur la nature blessée," 267; Gilson, "Propos sur l'être et sa notion," 15–16.
96. Gilson, "Propos sur l'être et sa notion," 11.
97. Shook, *Gilson,* 101; Gilson, *The Christian Philosophy of St. Thomas Aquinas,* 105.

being. Gilson bypassed Maritain's conception of the analogical imagination like a ship in the night, on the way to an invisible God, remarking on "the great texts of Thomas Aquinas, detested by so many Thomists, on the unknowability of the divine being in this life."[98] One of his gifts was a sort of narrowness, which saw its truth and refused to compromise it by expanding into analogical conjunction with his opponent.

It was not that Gilson had no psychological sensitivity. He was shrewd. In a letter to Gouhier written shortly after Maritain's death, in 1973, Gilson said, "But this holy man (this devil of a holy man!) is at the cross-roads of all the roads of his time, running all the risks and winning all the prizes." Still smarting from the "Réflexions," Gilson told Gouhier that having become "Thomist without having studied Saint Thomas, and by a sort of act of faith," Maritain "began by believing he had to be anti-Bergsonian in order to be Thomist": this "fighter" took as his patch the "primacy of noetics over ontology." The maneuver left him high and dry in epistemology. Critical realism was ever an attempt to analyze being into existence: "Many Thomists," Gilson writes, "have fought the evil" of idealism "by opposing to it the Thomistic doctrine of knowledge, but that is to put the cart before the horse."[99]

In a letter in English to Armand Maurer in 1974, a very grumpy old man said that "ontology has not been Maritain's initial preoccupation. . . . I only *remember* that the philosophical party he founded was [French] *le parti de l'intelligence,* it was not the 'party of being.'"[100] The below belt, private outburst, written half a century after Maritain had detached himself from the *Action Française,* shows the depth at which republican political loyalties were engaged in Gilson's trenchant metaphysical battle for the "party of being."

The "party of being" was not hostile to the idea of personality. Quite the reverse, for Maurras was a collectivist, and there was a determined anti-Maurrassianism in Gilson's initial focus on the individual personalities of artists, philosophers, and theologians. That lasted from the early 1920s until the late 1930s. But once he finds the center of his theological apologetics in the act of *existing,* the individual personality no longer has so

98. Gilson, *Constantes,* 116–17; Gilson, "Propos sur l'être et sa notion," 12.

99. Gilson to Henri Gouhier, May 2, 1973, in "Lettres d'Étienne Gilson à Henri Gouhier," 476, 474–75. In this letter, Gilson argues that much of Maritain's thought, especially his aesthetics, derives from his wife, Raïssa; that which was peculiar to Maritain himself, Gilson says, is his noetic focus. Gilson, "Propos sur l'être et sa notion," 13.

100. Gilson to Armand Maurer, March 18, 1974, in *Deux approches,* 275–76. Gilson's letter was written in English; Prouvost cites the original, and his own French translation.

much purchase in Gilson's philosophy. Nonetheless, the fact of his beginning his research in the history of ideas, writing historical biographies, marked his understanding of reality. Like people, being contains a mass of almost unresolvable contradictions; simply being logical is no more help in understanding a person than in the "inductive science" of metaphysics.[101]

## An Old Apprentice Tries to Return to Pascal

In 1968 Gilson completed *Constantes philosophiques de l'être,* leaving it for posthumous publication. He states in the introduction (which everyone writes last), that "when I was young, I often thought that the historian of philosophy is the guardian of a cemetery. Age and reflection have taught me that there are no dead truths in metaphysics; there are only inexhaustible ones; in rediscovering them for himself, each person takes his place in an immense family of knowns and unknowns, who are inspired by the desire, always partially frustrated, of reliving the ideas which one does not genuinely understand in the measure that one is content to speak of them by hearsay. But he who once allows himself to be seduced by this study is sure of much later playing the role, always slightly comic, of an old apprentice." Put at the service of eternity, Gilson's sense of humor turns to self-deprecation. His polemicism was never egotism, and this has allowed us to take him at his word, for less than he was. The last book that he published was *Dante et Béatrice: Études dantesques* (1974), made available "by subscription, on the occasion of the author's ninetieth birthday."[102]

He had the texts of Bonaventure before him when, in November 1972, he wrote an introduction for a centenary volume on that theologian: as he handed his piece over to the editor, he told him, "My dear Father, from now on the only book in my library will be the Bible." Gilson's introduction stated: "The centre of every thing is Jesus Christ. That is why I shall not undertake to prove the existence of God through natural reason, or the Trinity, or the immortality of the soul, or anything else of that nature, because this knowledge is useless and sterile without Jesus Christ. It was thus that Blaise Pascal spoke, more faithful in this to the true spirit of Saint Bonaventure than an apprentice philosopher, for whom it was not enough to be a good historian." Still protesting his booklessness, and the cessation of his mental life, two years later, he assured Canon Van Steenberghen that

---

101. Gilson, *Constantes,* 120.
102. Ibid., 14; Van Steenberghen, "In Memoriam Étienne Gilson," 542.

Duns Scotus, and not Thomas, is a philosopher of *praxis:* the "*Ordinatio* abounds in explicit texts on this question."[103]

In 1975 Paul VI sent Gilson a personal letter, praising him for finding Thomas's "originality" in his discovery of the "metaphysics of the Exodus" and for his outstanding use of an "idea . . . that is particularly dear to Us," that faith is "a light and a stimulant" to human thought and culture. The Pope concluded his letter: "Above all, dear Professor—this is one of the points that impresses Us most at the present time—you have spent your efforts and shown your Christian Faith in the bosom of the Catholic Church, whom you have always regarded as a mother." Canon Van Steenberghen tells us that on September 19, 1978, "Étienne Gilson ended his long existence a long way from Paris, in the peace of the Burgundian countryside, not far from the old mediaeval town of Auxerre."[104]

103. Bougerol, "Quand Étienne Gilson rencontre Saint Bonaventure," 42; Gilson to Van Steenbeergen, March 3, 1974, in Van Steenberghen, "Correspondance avec Étienne Gilson," 625.

104. Appendix 4, "Autograph Letter from Paul VI 'To the Esteemed Professor É. Gilson, Our Son in Jesus Christ,'" *Letters of Gilson to de Lubac,* 204–6. The Pope's letter was published in *L'Osservatore romano,* September 11, 1975. Van Steenberghen, "In Memoriam Étienne Gilson," 542.

# *Afterword*

## The Miracle of Being

### Gilson's Presence in Contemporary Theology

Gilson has not lacked philosophical exponents since his death. But the sociological structure of Anglo-American universities and colleges requires a separation between philosophy and theology within which Gilson's own thought cannot fully blossom. Bonaventure saw that, rather than literally adhering to the primitive ideal of the Master, the *spirit* must overwrite the *letter*.[1] Gilsonianism has been most creative, and influential, when set within the work of contemporary theologians. Gilson's "L'Esse du Verbe incarné" is a unique example of his moving beyond natural theology into revealed theology. He left it to others to take his thought beyond the doctrine of creation, to the Trinity, Christology, and the Sacraments. This afterword will show how Gilsonianism has borne fruit in the theology of the Dominican Herbert McCabe, and the Franciscan Tom Weinandy and in the genius of Hans Urs von Balthasar. Anyone who today is attracted by these writers' thought is perhaps an anonymous Gilsonian. But the secret influence of Gilson in theology is not the point at issue: what matters is that Gilsonian ideas have been exercised very fruitfully in contemporary theology and could still be put to further, creative development. I will contrast the notions of the Creator-God, the Trinity, the Eucharist, and the Incarnation found in McCabe, Weinandy, and von Balthasar with those of some of our contemporaries. I have gratefully abandoned my task as a biographer so as to extract "pure principles" from these theologians' thought. Nor will I envisage them as a *team*.

The English Dominican Herbert McCabe, who disliked being called a "Thomist," let alone a "Gilson-Thomist," created a Christian philosophy inculturated within the thought of Ludwig Wittgenstein. Thomas Weinandy has said that it "was through the work of E. Gilson that I saw the philo-

---

1. Gilson, *Bonaventure*, 45, 68.

sophical importance of Thomas, his insistence on 'esse is act,' on God as pure act."[2] This Franciscan friar has applied Gilsonian principles to the issue of God's impassibility and to Christology.

In 1987 Hans Urs von Balthasar told an importunate Ph.D. student, writing about theological aesthetics, that, in his interpretation of Thomas, "I have followed Gilson's route." There spoke the adversary of Karl Rahner. Thomas mattered in his *aesthetics* because "the kingdom of beauty (of the Thomist *esse non subsistens*) is . . . as being, transparent to the divine *esse subsistens* . . . which is, as a hidden primordial ground, radiant glory. The elevation of God over against being, . . . established by Thomas (over against all pantheism), secures at the same time for the concept of glory a place in metaphysics." Von Balthasar updates the narrative of the decline of metaphysics into essentialism in the Baroque era, which Gilson supplied in *L'etre et l'essence*.[3] Throughout *The Glory of the Lord,* von Balthasar is standing on Gilson's shoulders.

Both Gilson's admirers and his denigrators have sometimes imagined that being a Gilson-Thomist requires being a hatchet-headed Thomist fundamentalist. Von Balthasar saw that this is not true to Gilson's method, for von Balthasar also "followed Gilson's route" in his *exegesis* of Saint Thomas. Gilson's aesthetic-cubist approach to Aquinas meant turning Thomas's questions inside out. Likewise, von Balthasar threaded his way through Thomas's replies to objections, the grains of truth Thomas finds in ideas whose major thrust he does not accept. Before he gives his demonstrations of the existence of God in the *Summa Theologiae*, Thomas deals with John of Damascus's claim that the existence of God is not susceptible of demonstration because it is *self-evident*. Thomas obviously denies this, but in his reply, Thomas accepts that it is true that everyone has an "inchoate idea" of God: "To know that God exists in a general and confused way is implanted in us by nature, in as much as God is man's beatitude. For man naturally desires happiness, and what is naturally desired by man must be naturally known to him. This, however, is not to know absolutely that God exists; just as to know someone is approaching is not to know that Peter is approaching."[4] By making use of this idea, von Balthasar is able, not just to

2. McCabe, "Obituary," *Times* (London), July 11, 2001; Weinandy interview, "There Is a Connection between Holiness and Doing Theology," May 1999, Thomas Institut Utrecht, http://www.thomasinstituut.org/thomasinstituut/scripts/.

3. Hans Urs von Balthasar to the author, November 13 1987; Balthasar, *The Glory of the Lord: A Theological Aesthetics,* Vol. 4, *The Realm of Metaphysics in Antiquity,* 375; Balthasar, *The Glory of the Lord: A Theological Aesthetics,* Vol. 5, *The Realm of Metaphysics in the Modern Age,* 13–29.

4. Thomas Aquinas, *Summa Theologiae* I, q. 2, a. 2 ad 1.

give a more rounded picture of Thomas, but to draw the Augustinian insight into his own theology.

That Augustinian intuition lay behind the twentieth-century phenomenologists' efforts to prove the existence of God through a sense of the holy. Von Balthasar's work is indebted to existential phenomenologists, such as Marcel and Max Scheler, so much so that it is possible to mistake his own arguments for God's existence for ontological arguments, such as Scheler gave.[5] It is especially in his theological aesthetics that he draws on Gilson and on phenomenology. The design of *The Glory of the Lord* requires a fusion of "Saint Francis and Saint Dominic," Bonaventurian expressivist-experientialism with Thomist "ontology," as an "elemental, historical experience of Being."[6] Gilson had ever tried to make "Saint Francis and Saint Dominic" *one* door into Christianity. *The Glory* is closer to the genetic roots of Gilsonianism than a purely Thomist theology could have been.

## Trinity

Contemporary theology so far accentuates the *tri*-unity of persons within God that it treats the word *monotheist* as a term of abuse. Theologians such as Colin Gunton and Jürgen Moltmann have popularized the conception of God as relational, a society of persons, not a unitary "essence."[7] The danger is that of elevating "relationality" or tri-personality into a category above that of "God."[8] Can one simultaneously foreground the relationality within God, avoid essentialism, and steer clear of implying *numerical* difference within God? Some contemporary theologians evidently feel that the Triunity of God comes only at the expense of God's unity.

In Weinandy's Trinitarian theology, God is *one* as *actus purus* of divine *esse*. God's "to be" *is* the Trinity of persons. Echoing the distinction, in *God and Philosophy*, between conceiving substance as noun and conceiving it as verb, Weinandy reminds us that "the terms 'Father,' 'Son,' and 'Holy Spirit' are *verbs*": they designate "the *interrelated acts* by which all three

5. See for example my "The Sound of the Analogia Entis: An Essay on the Philosophical Context of Hans Urs von Balthasar's Theology, Part I and Part II," *New Blackfriars* (November 1993): 508–21 (pt. 1), ibid. (December 1993): 557–65 (pt. 2).
6. Balthasar, *The Glory of the Lord*, 5:9.
7. In *Trinity and the Kingdom: The Doctrine of God*, trans. Margaret Kohl (San Francisco: Harper and Row, 1981), 1, 63, Jürgen Moltmann claims that Barth "really" has "a monotheistic conception of the Trinity." See also Colin Gunton, *The Promise of Trinitarian Theology* (Edinburgh: T&T Clark, 1991).
8. Fr. Richard Conrad, OP, pointed this out to me.

persons are who they are." Neither *esse* nor relations have priority over the other, since both are Pure Act. There is "a reciprocal constitutive ontological oneness, between being *ipsum esse* and being subsistent relations . . . for both express 'being' as actus purus. . . . to be fully 'to-be' . . . is 'to be fully relational.'"[9]

## God the Creator

Roger Haight is typical of many contemporary theologians in his conviction that Christian faith needs "transcendental" rather than "extrinsic" criteria. So as not to rest faith on anything conceived as external to the believing subject, he gives an "anthropological" definition of faith. It is based in "experience" in general, as implicitly containing "religious experience." "The 'religious' as a category," he writes, "should not be understood in the first place on the level of content, as though religious experience began with a religious object."[10] Haight relates faith to the *subject,* and not the *object* of experience, so as not to make it an extrinsic imposition upon the human believer. Can the theological objectivity that Haight sets aside be regained, without obscuring that important concern?

Herbert McCabe begins his argument for the existence of God by asking "'How come Fido?'"; he proceeds to "'How come dogs anyway?'" and from there to "'How come everything?'" The last question is effectively asking "how come Fido exists instead of nothing?" If "God is whatever answers"[11] the question of why there are existents, then God is not one existent among others, not "an existent" at all. He is *outside* the ballgame in which autonomy and heteronomy bat against one another.

Only an *existent* can be external to, or over against another existent, rubbing up against it as, for instance, one would in relation to untoward objective "authority." God as *Esse* is not a celestial Essence, whose "appearances" are interferences. God as "creator, as source of esse," cannot be conceived as "interfering" in creation: "If God is the cause of everything, there is nothing that he is alongside."[12] Aquinas's God creates through his *esse:* only a God who *is* his very existing can confer existing on others.[13] Our existing is *intrinsically* dependent on God; we are related to God's be-

---

9. Weinandy, *Does God Suffer?* 118, 127.
10. Haight, *Jesus: Symbol of God,* 17–18, 30, 192.
11. McCabe, *God Matters,* 3–6.
12. Ibid., 59, 6.
13. Gilson, *Elements of Christian Philosophy,* 190–91.

ing through the act of existing that *makes us ourselves.* "Every action in the world is an action of God; not because it is not an action of a creature but because it is by God's action that the creature is *itself.*"[14]

If, as von Balthasar points out, we "know all existents" in the light of "Being," we know those objective realities in a light that is interior to ourselves. The "*lumen fidei* as Origen, Augustine and Thomas understood it" is *already* present in our knowledge of this world, because "through grace eternal life has already begun"—a de Lubacian twist. The "infused"—objective—"*lumen fidei* . . . is not any more 'heteronomous' than the light of rational nature, which is innate" in the believer: for even "this light . . . is not properly speaking man's own light, but rather his openness to the light of Being itself." God's 'immanent-*because*-transcendent' *Esse* is the light through which we are given both natural and revealed knowledge. It speaks in our own act of existing. The doctrine of God as *Esse* bypasses the dichotomy of external authority versus subjective or anthropological criteria for faith.

The experience of the *contingency* of entities need not necessarily carry us to the Christian God. Heidegger raised the question of whether the fact that we experience entities as contingent, as containing no necessary bond between essence and existence, leads to the experience of entities as created. John Milbank imagines this shows that "Gilson's" use of the ontological distinction as a proof of the Christian God is circular. I put "Gilson" in quotation marks since a cursory survey of his writings indicates that, from 1948, he revoked the use of the "distinction" as a "Sixth Proof" of God's existence, returning to arguments that begin from sensation.[15] Gilson drew down Garrigou's wrath at the 1950 Thomistic conference by claiming: "The contingency of finite being implies that one can attribute it to an uncaused cause; it does not demand that one draws out of it a composition of essence and existence. One cannot denounce too much the practically ineradicable illusion that makes the composition of essence and existence a mere translation, into metaphysical terms, of the relation of creature to Creator." For Gilson, the notion of finite, existentially "composite" beings as related to the Pure Being of God is a "consequence, not a precondition" of the Five Ways.[16]

14. McCabe, *God Matters,* 7.
15. See above, ch. 13. The misunderstanding would be easier to understand as natural if authors referred their complaint to the 1942 or 1944 editions of *Le Thomisme;* but since it is the 1948 *Christian Philosophy of Thomas Aquinas* to which Milbank refers in his bibliography, it's hard to see where he found this argument: see Milbank and Pickstock, *Truth in Aquinas,* 49–50.
16. Gilson, "La Preuve du *De Ente et Essentia,*" 259, 258.

Milbank feels that "Marion is perfectly right to say, against Etienne Gilson, that appeal to the ontological difference will not secure transcendence, since it can well be construed nihilistically, as by Heidegger." On the other hand, F. X. Knasas has argued that Maritain's version of the ontological distinction, but not Gilson's, is liable to Heidegger's critique. The reason is that Maritain claimed that we have direct, intuitive knowledge of *esse*, whereas for Gilson we always "grasp . . . esse as the most profound principle in the sensible existents before us." That indicates why, on the one hand, one needs to have been moved by sensible things to posit the existence of God before one can see the "real distinction" and why, on the other hand, "ens commune" is a logical, not a real notion. As McCabe remarks, "The Aristotelian is . . . right to deny that any sense can be made of 'existence' as a detachable or abstract quality or element common to things that exist."[17] We do not see existence but existents. So our human discussion of *existence* has to pass through analysis of concrete and particular *natures*, such as that of Fido.

Von Balthasar treats the "Gilsonian" argument from the real distinction as containing the Five Ways to God, from the facts that sensible objects are moved, caused, contingent, designed, and better or worse. He divides it into four meditations on concrete experience. The first is the child's experience of being *given* shelter, *receiving* existence, *as* a "nourishing kiss" from its mother. The second is the later realization that, not only "I," but all "existents partake in Being, yet . . . never exhaust it." Now "my wonder is directed at both sides of the Ontological Difference, whether this is construed in Thomist or Heideggerian terms": that is, I wonder both about "natures" and about their "existence."[18]

In his third meditation, von Balthasar distinguishes the Heideggerian ontological difference from Thomas's version. Taken in itself, "Being" or existence does not design essences. It is "impossible to attribute to Being the responsibility for the essential forms of entities" because "the 'plans' lie in the entity, not in Being." We can "read" in sensible natures the truth that "the 'ground' of a living entity—be it a plant, animal or person"—is the product of *freely* creative Being. If Being creates freely, it need not produce *this* particular sensible nature. Heidegger cannot, von Balthasar says, give us any "information" about how to get from Being to essential form, or vice versa. Natures "bear the mark of an imaginative power to which one

---

17. Milbank and Pickstock, *Truth in Aquinas,* 49; Knasas, "A Heideggerian Critique of Aquinas and a Gilsonian Reply," 432; McCabe, *God Matters,* 150.
18. McCabe, *God Matters,* 150; Balthasar, *The Glory of the Lord,* 5:616, 618–19.

must be blind if one . . . explains them" wholly through "their position within the process."[19] It is both true and false that the "ontological distinction" does not point, by itself, to the Christian God. It is the contingent beauty of natures that impels us to the question of God. One has to see natures both as contingent and as formally beautiful for either the Five Ways or the "distinction" to work as arguments.

In the fourth experience, one recognizes "the distinction between God and the world, in which God is the sole sufficient ground for both Being and the existent in its possession of form." Being, as sheer existence, is only creative because the Creator-Esse acts through it. The "grounding in God of this Being . . . points to an *ultimate freedom* which neither Being (as non-subsistent) could have, nor the existent entity (since it always finds itself as already constituted in its own essentiality)."[20]

## The Eucharist

The idea of transubstantiation is supposed by some to make sense only in an "Aristotelian" thought-world, in which God can substitute one nature, that of bread, for another, that of Christ. And yet, many Thomists who have been reared in Aristotelianism cannot make any sense of it, precisely because the idea of one nature's being substituted for another within the "same" entity could not have had any meaning for a Greek philosopher.

Herbert McCabe agrees that "Aristotle would have been able to make nothing of the idea of transubstantiation, but, as Etienne Gilson has frequently pointed out, he would have had the same trouble with the notion of creation." Aristotle conceived substantial *changes,* but not creation, because it is "not a matter of transition from one kind of thing to another kind of thing." Transubstantiation and creation are cousins in Aquinas's theology, kin because neither is an alteration of something that is already there. Both are *mysteries:* "in doing theology," McCabe claims, "as in any other kind of prayer, we are reaching out into a mystery for which our language is inadequate." Language falters when it speaks of a new, divinely created *existence:* "we do not know what we are talking about when we speak of transubstantiation; it is a change which, . . . like creation, takes place . . . at the level of existence itself."[21]

19. Balthasar, *The Glory of the Lord,* 5:620–22.
20. Ibid., 624–25.
21. McCabe, *God Matters,* 131, 147–49.

## Christology: "Nothing Is Less Naive Than the Faith of a True Metaphysician"[22]

The sticking point of modern Christology is "How can a God who is almighty, all-knowing, and all-powerful become man, and so take on human limitations—weakness, lack of knowledge, etc.?" As thus conceived in the mind of John Hick, the conundrum issued in the dictum that to say "the historical Jesus of Nazareth was also God is as devoid of meaning as to say that this circle drawn with a pencil on paper is also a square." As Weinandy observes, modern Christology has been plagued by essentialism, the thankless task of "uniting two contradictory natures or essences (divine and human) containing . . . contradictory attributes" such as "omniscience and limited knowledge."[23] It is not too much to say that all of the problems of modern Christology stem from conceiving God as a Super-Essence.

The Chalcedonian Formula stated that Christ was "made known in two natures," both "concurring into one Person (prosopon) and one hypostasis . . . the divine Logos, the Lord Jesus Christ." As Gilson observed, the idea of a divine and a human nature coming together in one Christ is "a point of faith" in the face of which "the theologian" must "incline his reason before a mystery."[24] What did Chalcedon mean in 451, and what does it mean for us today?

It is a commonplace opinion that the formula is a "compromise" between the Antiochenes, who drew out the significance of Christ's humanity, and the Alexandrians, focusing on the divinity. As Haight sees it, the protagonist of Alexandrianism at Chalcedon, Cyril, considered that Jesus was "really the heavenly Logos," the divine essence, dropping down from heaven into earth-space. Weinandy reads Cyril differently. He thinks that through the phrase "mia phusis" [Greek, "one nature"] Cyril was attesting to the fact that Christ was one single divine *existent*. If, as Weinandy believes, Cyril had a "personal/existential conception" of Incarnation, then Chalcedon is no compromise, which gives equal credit to the divine and the human *natures* of Christ, not primarily a statement about the two *whats* in Christ but an assertion of *who* he was, that is, the Son as divine *Esse*.[25]

---

22. Gilson, "L'Esse du Verbe incarné," 91.

23. Weinandy, *Does God Suffer?* 35; Hick, *The Metaphor of God Incarnate*, 3. Hick originally used this phrase in *The Myth of God Incarnate* (London: SCM Press, 1977), 178. Weinandy, *In the Likeness of Sinful Flesh*, 10.

24. Gilson, "L'Esse du Verbe incarné," 81.

25. Haight, *Jesus: Symbol of God*, 285, 288; Weinandy, *Does God Suffer?* 197.

On Haight's view, Chalcedon failed as a compromise between humanist-Antiochene essentialism and Alexandrian theistic-essentialism. Because it finds the principle of unity in the Logos, Chalcedon led to the modern situation in which as "Rahner as pointed out ... many Christians are really monophysites in practice." For Thomas, according to Gilson, the issue was the "unum esse personae divinae," the "one divine personal *esse*." In his theology, it is the divine *esse* that makes "the human nature be there." If, as for Haight, what matters about Christ is his "distinctive character of a historical human being," *one particular* historical event surpasses all the rest, and we have to answer the question of why Christianity is historically more important than, say, Hinduism, either by aggrandizement, as in the colonial past, or by diminution, as is correct today. On the other hand, never fearful of grasping the bull by the horns, Catherine Pickstock observes that "Aquinas' near monophysitism is much less *fetishistic* of the particular" than theologies that have to account for him as in terms of outstanding human importance. For those who see in Christ a "unity of esse," she says, the "Incarnation sacralizes no one site." As Weinandy puts it, "The one ontological entity that Jesus is, is the person of the divine Son of God existing as ... man."[26]

According to von Balthasar, from the nineteenth century fundamental theology shifted from asking the question "'How does God's revelation confront man in history'" to asking how the claim of a man to be God can be rationally verified. The upshot was an "apologetics that distinguishes a *content* to be believed ... and the '*signs*' that plead for the rightness of this content, signs which ... prove too much or too little." Haight finds both that "Jesus is the concrete symbol of God" and that a "symbol makes present something else." We cannot simply say Jesus *is* God, on this account, because a "symbol is that through which something other than itself is known."[27] The historical man Jesus is the "medium" through which "something other than" himself, namely, God, is known.

One can, Haight affirms "see the grounds for the normativity of Jesus in the foundations of knowing itself." Human knowledge is based in concrete facts and events. Transcendence is always known symbolically. To know the transcendent is to articulate an idea that is already implicitly present to us.

26. Haight, *Jesus: Symbol of God*, 290; Gilson, "L'Esse du Verbe incarné," 83–84; Pickstock, *Truth in Aquinas*, 69; Haight, *Jesus: Symbol of God*, 291; Weinandy, *Does God Suffer?* 174.

27. Balthasar, *The Glory of the Lord: A Theological Aesthetics*, Vol. 1, *Seeing the Form*, 173; Haight, Jesus: *Symbol of God*, 14, 197, 8.

As Haight notes, one "needs the symbolic mediation of an external event or an objective and specifying medium to given an otherwise vague awareness a practical name." It follows that Jesus as symbol of God "reveals God as already present and active in human existence." His function is the psychological one of making us conscious of our awareness of God: "symbolic . . . causality effects by bringing to consciousness something that is . . . present within, but latent and not an object of clear and focused recognition." How does Jesus *cause* us to refer ourselves to the God concealed within our consciousness? When Haight tells us that we "know" that Jesus symbolizes God "because people encountered God in him and still do," we seem to be locked into circularity. This is an anthropological Christology for which "the interpreter" "approaches" Jesus "with the religious question, looking for salvation that comes from . . . God."[28]

Conversely, von Balthasar names Christ as transcendent beauty because, in "the luminous form of the beautiful the being of the existent becomes perceivable as nowhere else." Christ, *the* form of beauty, is the medium through which the divine light of faith approaches the believing subject. In this realist Christology, the "light of faith stems from the object . . . revealing itself to the subject."[29]

Von Balthasar reads the Gospels with a realistic imagination. He does not find that the story of the Synoptics or John is about human beings putting their existential questions to Jesus. In their peasant simplicity, the Gospel stories about Jesus's encounters in Galilee picture Jesus making "the decision about the man." In *his* eyes, and before his sometimes baleful countenance, "in virtue of the light that falls on them from Jesus," people are made to be who they really are. Like Haight, von Balthasar is interested in what Christ *does:* "because the original situation of *being seen through* by Jesus . . . is wholly integrated with Jesus' commission to salvation . . . the theological explication of the eschatological judgment of Christ as a sovereign act of decision is," von Balthasar believes, "unavoidable."[30]

Historical-critical study of the New Testament has, John Hick says, "led . . . historians to conclude, with an impressive degree of unanimity, that Jesus did not claim to be God incarnate." Chalcedon raises the question of how the divine or the human nature can really be itself, within the Incarnate Christ. "The idea that," in his personal-divine *Existence* in Galilee, Jesus "constructed some special divinely authorized set of propositions as

28. Haight, *Jesus: Symbol of God*, 30, 12–13, 359, 198, 203.
29. Balthasar, *The Glory of the Lord*, 1:153, 181.
30. Balthasar, *The Glory of the Lord: A Theological Aesthetics*, Vol. 7, *Theology, the New Covenant*, 117, 121–23.

the Christian creed is as anthropomorphic as the idea that God has a white beard." For McCabe, "Jesus' knowledge of history, as Son of God, was . . . not in the same ball-game with what he learnt as man." Jesus's divine "omniscience and his human ignorance" do not "exclude each other in the way that two created natures would"; we can only say metaphorically that they belong to different universes, since "the divine does not occupy any universe."[31]

Although, *absolutely* speaking, *one,* "relatively speaking," Christ is "two by reason of his two natures." It follows, for Weinandy, that, as "incarnate, the eternal Son never said or did anything *qua* God, always *qua* man." The divine Esse acted *in* a human nature: if and when Jesus ate carrots, it was, Weinandy writes, the *man* who ate the carrots. This is not just because divine nature does not permit this experience, but also—since Jesus no less raised Lazarus as man—because, as Christian doctrine teaches, "the eternal Word, . . . through the human nature which he assumes . . . becomes this particular being, Jesus Christ." It is, as McCabe says, the man Jesus who "*has*" the divine nature. And yet, if we ask *who* ate carrots or raised Lazarus, the answer must be, the eternal Son. We can say that "God suffered a terrible pain in his hands" at the crucifixion without imparting the human quality of suffering to God, because "his hands" have *become* the hands of the man Jesus.[32]

The "doctrine of the essential impassibility of the divine nature now seems . . . to be disappearing from the Christian doctrine of God."[33] Moltmann has been in the vanguard of the liberation theology, which believes that the God of the Exodus must be involved in our history, so much affected by its outcome that He will not be quite himself until the Eschaton.

Although one does not have to have been a youthful devotee of Wagner properly to conceive the pure energy of God's existence, one reason for the popularity of a suffering God within modern theology is that it failed to understand impassibility as the "pure vitality" of a wholly active nature.[34] That is, the protest of the passibilists is directed at a supra-worldly *Essence.* Since it is the supra-worldliness alone that constitutes the essence as "static," it seems appropriate to the divine passibilists to reposition the Essence within the suffering history of humanity. Whereas it was convivial to the

31. Hick, *Metaphor,* 27; McCabe, *God Matters,* 59, 47–48.
32. Gilson, "L'Esse du Verbe incarné," 88; Weinandy, *In the Likeness of Sinful Flesh,* 15; Weinandy, *Does God Suffer?* 205; Gilson, "L'Esse du Verbe incarné," 87; McCabe, *God Matters,* 47.
33. Moltmann, *Trinity and the Kingdom,* 32.
34. Weinandy, *Does God Suffer?* 124.

Baroque theologians who first conceived this Essence to place it *outside* the world, contemporary passibilists simply situates the same Essence *within* the world process. This suffering "divine" essence is "perilously like one of the gods."

On the other hand, "God the creator," that is, God with the peculiar "transcendence" of *Esse*, "is the liberator fundamentally *because* he is not a god." Transcendence has thus to be conceived analogously, not literally. It simply means that at "the heart of every creature is the source of *esse*, making it to be and to act." God cannot sympathize with human beings because He is not *other from* them; humans have to resort to sympathy and empathy, because they are outside of each other.[35]

We still seem to be left with the fact that an impassible God does not *share* our suffering, even in the crucifixion; but a God who suffers as God in the crucifixion does not engage in *human* suffering. Moltmann's crucified "God" suffers as a "God," not as a human being.[36] The Essence remains divine essence, though suffering.

God as *Esse* is the only God who can give us a *reason* to believe in Him, through the fact that He *causes* existent natures to be. The crucifixion cannot affect God as divine *Esse* because He would then cease to *be* Esse. Without the "impassibility of the Son of God" there is no "guarantee that it is . . . the divine Son of God . . . who truly suffers as man." Gilson could have said, not just that "the whole of Thomism," but Christianity itself was at stake in the single *Esse* in Christ. For the doctrine asserts that Christ is God as having "the same *esse* as the Father, as possessing the same being as the Father, the *essentia* of the Trinity itself." It follows from this that the Incarnation, and "the whole set of stories narrated in the Bible is . . . the interior life of the triune God visible (to the eyes of faith) in our history." "I don't," McCabe writes, "think you could have God more involved than that."[37] It would seem that "Saint Francis and Saint Dominic" can shepherd the Manichees home.

35. McCabe, *God Matters*, 42–43; ibid., referring to Thomas Aquinas, *Summa Theologiae* Ia, 8, 1 c; ibid., 44.

36. Weinandy, *Does God Suffer?* 204, 206.

37. Ibid., 205; Gilson, "L'Esse du Verbe incarné," 87; McCabe, *God Matters*, 51.

# Bibliography

## Manuscript Sources

### UNIVERSITY OF ST. MICHAEL'S COLLEGE ARCHIVES, TORONTO

Gilson, Étienne. Correspondence.
Gilson, Étienne. Papers.

### THE SAULCHOIR ARCHIVE, SAINT-JACQUES, PARIS

Chenu, Marie-Dominique. Papers.

## Primary Biographical Sources

Blondel, Maurice, et al. "La notion de philosophie chrétienne." *Bulletin de la société française de la philosophie* 31 (1931): 37–93. Transcript of the debate about Christian philosophy, March 21, 1931.

———. "La querelle de l'athéisme." *Bulletin de la Société française de la philosophie* 28 (1928): 45–95. Transcript of the meeting of March 24, 1928.

de Lubac, Henri, ed. *Letters of Étienne Gilson to Henri de Lubac.* Translated by Mary Emily Hamilton. San Francisco: Ignatius Press, 1988.

Dronke, Peter, ed. *Étienne Gilson's Letters to Bruno Nardi.* Sismel: Galluzzo, 1998.

Donneaud, Henry, ed. "Correspondance Étienne Gilson—Michel Labourdette." In "Autour d'Étienne Gilson: Études et documents." Special issue, *Revue Thomiste* 94, no. 3 (July–September 1994): 479–529.

Gilson, Étienne, and Jacques Maritain. *Deux approches de l'être: correspondance, 1923–1971.* Edited by Géry Prouvost. Paris: J. Vrin, 1991.

Gilson, Étienne. *Le philosophe et la théologie.* Paris: Librarie Arthème Fayard, 1960.

Kalinowski, Georges. *L'impossible métaphysique: En annexe trois lettres inédites de Étienne Gilson.* Paris: Beauchesne, 1981.

Lefèvre, Frédéric. *Une heure avec... Étienne Gilson*. Paris: Gallimard, 1925.

Prouvost, Géry, ed. "Lettres d'Étienne Gilson à Henri Gouhier." In "Autour d'Étienne Gilson: Études et documents." Special issue, *Revue Thomiste* 94, no. 3 (July–September 1994): 460–78.

Van Steenberghen, Fernand, ed. "Correspondance avec Étienne Gilson." *Revue philosophique de Louvain* 87 (November 1989): 612–25.


## Primary Sources: Works by Étienne Gilson

"1940–1950." *Le Monde,* January 14, 1950, 1.

"Action politique et action catholique." *Sept* 70 (June 28,1935): 4.

"Art et métaphysique." *Revue de métaphysique et de morale* 23 (1916): 243–67.

*The Arts of the Beautiful.* 1965. Reprint, Westport, CT: Greenwood Press, 1976. Originally published as *Introduction aux arts du beau* (Paris: J. Vrin, 1963).

*Autour de saint Thomas.* Edited by Jean-Francois Courtine. Paris: J. Vrin, 1983.

"Avon-nous des universités?" *Le Monde,* June 17, 1947, 1.

*Being and Some Philosophers.* 1949. Corrected and enlarged. Toronto: Pontifical Institute of Mediaeval Studies, 1952.

"Cajetan et l'humanisme théologique." *Archives d'histoire doctrinale et litteraire du moyen âge* 22 (1955): 113–36.

*Choir of Muses.* Translated by Maisie Ward. New York: Sheed and Ward, 1953. Originally published as *L'éclose des muses* (Paris: J. Vrin, 1951).

*The Christian Philosophy of St. Thomas Aquinas.* Translated by Laurence K. Shook, CSB. London: Victor Gollancz, 1961. Originally published as *Le Thomisme* (1948).

*Christianisme et philosophie.* 1936. Reprint, Paris: J. Vrin, 1949.

"Le Christianisme et la tradition philosophique." *Revue des sciences philosophiques et theologiques* 30 (1941): 249–66.

"Compagnons de route." In *Étienne Gilson: philosophe de la chrétienté,* 275–95. Paris: Éditions du Cerf, Paris, 1949.

*Constantes philosophiques de l'être.* Edited by Jean-Francoise Courtine. Paris: J. Vrin, 1983.

"La croisée des chemins." *Sept* 7 (April 14, 1934). Reprinted in *Pour un ordre catholique,* 53–57. Paris: Desclée de Brouwer, 1934.

*Dante et Béatrice: Études dantesques.* Paris: Vrin, 1974.

*Dante the Philosopher.* Translated by David Moore. 1948. Reprint, London: Sheed and Ward, 1952. Originally published as *Dante et la philosophie* (Paris: J. Vrin, 1939).

"De la Bible à François Villon." *Annuaire de l'École Practique des Hautes-Études. Section des sciences religieuses* (1923–1924). Reprinted as *De la Bible à François Villon Rabelais Françiscain.* Paris: J. Vrin, 1986.

"La démocratie en danger." *Sept* 2 (March 10, 1934): 3.

"Les deux ordres." *Sept* 22 (July 28, 1934). Reprinted in *Pour un ordre catholique,* 160–68. Paris: Desclée de Brouwer, 1934.

"L'éducation des Nations Unies." *Le Monde,* October 28–29, 1945, 1.

*The Elements of Christian Philosophy.* 1960. Reprint, New York: New American Library, 1963.

"En marge de l'Action Française." *Sept* 71 (July 5, 1935): 4.

"Erasme, citoyen du monde." *Nouvelles Litteraires,* May 6, 1939, 1–2.

"Essai sur la vie intérieure." *Revue philosophique de la France et de l'étranger* 89–90 (January–December 1920): 23–78.

"L'Esse du Verbe incarné selon saint Thomas d'Aquin." *Archives d'histoire doctrinale et litteraire du moyen âge* 35 (1968): 23–37. Reprinted in *Autour de Saint Thomas,* edited by Jean-Francois Courtine, 81–95. Paris: J. Vrin, Paris, 1983.

"L'état sans moral." *Sept* 6 (April 1934). Reprinted in *Pour un ordre catholique,* 49–53. Paris: Desclée de Brouwer, 1934.

"L'état sans religion." *Sept* 4 (March 1934). Reprinted in *Pour un ordre catholique,* 39–44. Paris: Desclée de Brouwer, 1934.

*L'être et l'essence.* Paris: J. Vrin, 1948.

*L'être et l'essence.* Revised and augmented. 1962. Reprint, Paris: J. Vrin, 1972.

"Le faux remède." *Sept* 8 (April 21, 1934). Reprinted in *Pour un ordre catholique,* 61–66. Paris: Desclée de Brouwer, 1934.

"Du fondement des jugements esthétiques." *Revue philosophique de la France et de l'étranger* 83 (1917): 524–46.

"The French View of the War." *America* 62 (1940): 452–56.

*From Aristotle to Darwin and Back Again: A Journey in Final Causality, Species, and Evolution.* Translated by John Lyon. London: Sheed and Ward, 1984. Originally published as *D'Aristote à Darwin et retour: essai sur quelques constantes de la biophilosophie* (Paris: J. Vrin, 1971).

"The Future of Augustinian Metaphysics." Translated by Edward Bullough. In *A Monument to St. Augustine: Essays on Some Aspects of His Thought Written in Commemoration of His Fifteenth Centenary,* by

M. C. D'Arcy et al., 289–315. 1930. Reprint, New York: Meridian Books, 1957.

*A Gilson Reader: Selected Writings of Etienne Gilson.* Edited by Anton Pegis. 1957. Reprint, New York: Doubleday, 1962.

"The Glory of Bergson." *Thought* 22, no. 87 (December 1947): 581–84.

*God and Philosophy.* 1941. Reprint, New Haven: Yale University Press, 1955.

*Héloise et Abélard.* Paris: J. Vrin, 1938.

"Historical Research and the Future of Scholasticism." *Modern Schoolman* 29, no. 1 (November 1951): 1–10.

"L'humanisme de saint Thomas d'Aquin." *Atti del V Congresso Internazionale di Filosofia* (Naples), 1925, 976–89.

"L'innéisme cartésien et la théologie." *Revue de métaphysique et de morale* 22 (1914): 456–99.

*Introduction à l'étude de Saint Augustin.* Paris: J. Vrin, 1929.

*Introduction au système de S. Thomas d'Aquin.* Strasbourg: A. Vix, 1919.

*La liberté chez Descartes et la théologie.* Paris: Librairie Félix Alcan, 1913.

*Linguistics and Philosophy: An Essay on the Philosophical Constants of Language.* Translated by John Lyon. Notre Dame: University of Notre Dame Press, 1988. Originally published as *Linguistique et philosophie: essai sur les constantes philosophiques de langage* (Paris: J. Vrin, 1969).

*Matières et formes: poiétiques particulières des arts majeurs.* Paris: J. Vrin, 1964.

"Mediaevalism in Toronto." *Commonweal* 9 (May 1, 1929): 738–40.

*Les métamorphoses de la cité de Dieu.* Louvain: Publications Universitaires de Louvain, 1952.

"Mon ami Lévy-Bruhl, philosophe, sociologue, analyste des mentalités." *Nouvelles littéraires,* March 18, 1939, 1.

"Le moyen âge et le naturalisme antique." Appendix to *Héloise et Abélard.* Paris: J. Vrin, 1938.

"Neutrality for France?" *Bulletin of the Atomic Scientists* 6 (1950): 203–5.

"De la notion d'être divin dans la philosophie de saint Thomas d'Aquin." *Doctor Communis* 18 (1965): 113–29.

"Note sur le *revelabile* selon Cajetan." *Medieval Studies* 15 (1953): 199–206.

"Note sur un texte de S. Thomas." *Revue Thomiste* 54 (1954): 148–152. Reprinted in *Autour de saint Thomas,* edited by Jean-Francois Courtine, 35–40. Paris: J. Vrin, Paris, 1983.

"Ordre catholique et unité national." *Sept* 47 (January 18, 1935): 3.

*Painting and Reality.* New York: Meridian Books, 1959.

"Par delà le Sillon et l'Action Française." *Sept* 69 (June 21, 1935): 4.

"Pierre Lombard et les théologies de l'essence." *Revue du moyen âge* 1 (1945): 61–64.

*La philosophie de saint Bonaventure.* Paris: J. Vrin, 1924.

"La Preuve du *De Ente et Essentia*." *Acta III Congressus Thomistici internationalis,* September 11–17, 1950, 257–60.

"Les principes et les causes." *Revue Thomiste* 52 (1952): 39–63.

"Le prix de la liberté." *Sept* 31 (September 28, 1934). Reprinted in *Pour un ordre catholique,* 141–52. Paris: Desclée de Brouwer, 1934.

"Pour une éducation nationale." *La vie intellectuelle* 6 (April 1945): 116–32.

*Pour un ordre catholique.* Paris: Desclée de Brouwer, 1934.

"Prolégomènes à la *Prima Via*." *Archives d'histoire doctrinale et littéraire du moyen âge* 35 (1963): 67–88. Reprinted in *Autour de Saint Thomas,* edited by Jean-Francois Courtine, 41–58. Paris: J. Vrin, 1983.

"Propos sur l'être et sa notion." In *San Tommaso e il pensiero moderno,* edited by Antonio Piolanti, 7–17. Pontificia Accademia Romana di S. Tommaso d'Aquino. Rome: Citta Nuova Editrice, 1975.

"Rabelais Françisain." *Revue d'histoire Françisain* (1924). Reprinted as *De la Bible à François Villon Rabelais Françiscain.* Paris: J. Vrin, 1986.

*Le réalisme méthodique.* Paris: Pierre Téqui, 1936.

*Reason and Revelation in the Middle Ages.* New York: Charles Scribner's Sons, 1939.

"Remarks on Experience in Metaphysics." In *Thomistic Papers V,* edited by Thomas A. Russman, OFM Cap, 40–48. Houston: Centre for Thomistic Studies, University of St. Thomas, 1990.

Review of *La discipline intellectuelle,* by Alfred Loisy. *Revue philosophique de la France et de l'étranger* 88 (1919): 129–31.

"Le rôle de la philosophie dans l'histoire de la civilization." *Revue de métaphysique et de morale* 34 (1927): 169–76.

*The Spirit of Mediaeval Philosophy.* The Gifford Lectures, 1931–1932. Translated by A. H. C. Downes. London: Sheed and Ward, 1936. Originally published as *L'esprit de la philosophie médiévale* (Paris: J. Vrin, 1932).

"Sur le positivisme absolu." *Revue philosophique de la France et de l'étranger* 68 (1909): 63–65.

"Sur la problématique thomiste de la vision béatifique." *Archives d'histoire doctrinale et littéraire du moyen âge* 21 (1964). Reprinted in *Autour de Saint Thomas,* edited by Jean-Francois Courtine, 59–80. Paris: J. Vrin, 1983.

"Terrain d'entente." *Sept* 9 (April 28, 1934). Reprinted in *Pour un ordre catholique,* 82–88. Paris: Desclée de Brouwer, 1934.

*Le Thomisme: introduction au système de saint Thomas d'Aquin,* 3rd ed. Paris: J. Vrin, 1927.

*Le Thomisme: introduction a la philosophie de saint Thomas d'Aquin,* 5th ed. Paris: J. Vrin, 1942–1944.

"Le thomisme et les philosophies existentielles." *La vie intellectuelle* 13 (June 1945): 144–55.

*Thomist Realism and the Critique of Knowledge.* Translated by Mark A Wauk. San Francisco: Ignatius Press, 1986. Originally published as *Réalisme thomiste et critique de la connaissance* (Paris: J. Vrin, 1939).

*Les tribulations de Sophie.* Paris: J. Vrin, 1967.

*The Unity of Philosophical Experience.* London: Sheed and Ward, 1938.

"Le Vatican et les nationalisations." *Le Monde,* August 8, 1946, 1–2.

## Secondary Sources

Amato, Joseph. *Mounier and Maritain: A French Catholic Understanding of the Modern World.* Tuscaloosa: University of Alabama Press, 1975.

Antliff, Mark. *Inventing Bergson: Cultural Politics and the Parisian Avant-Garde.* Princeton: Princeton University Press, 1993.

Aubert, Robert. *The Christian Centuries.* Vol. 5, *The Church in a Secularized Society.* Mahway, NJ: Paulist Press, 1987.

Balthasar, Hans Urs von. *The Glory of the Lord: A Theological Aesthetics.* Vol. 1, *Seeing the Form,* translated by Erasmo Leiva-Merikakis. San Francisco: Ignatius Press, 1982.

———. *The Glory of the Lord: A Theological Aesthetics.* Vol. 2, *Studies in Theological Style: Clerical Styles,* translated by Andrew Louth, Francis McDonagh, and Brian McNeil, CRV. Edinburgh: T&T Clark, 1984.

———. *The Glory of the Lord: A Theological Aesthetics.* Vol. 4, *The Realm of Metaphysics in Antiquity,* translated by Brian McNeil, CRV, Andrew Louth, John Saward, Rowan Williams, and Oliver Davies. Edinburgh: T&T Clark, 1989.

———. *The Glory of the Lord: A Theological Aesthetics.* Vol. 5, *The Realm of Metaphysics in the Modern Age,* translated by Oliver Davies, Andrew Louth, Brian McNeil, CRV, John Saward, and Rowan Williams. Edinburgh: T&T Clark, 1991.

———. *The Glory of the Lord: A Theological Aesthetics.* Vol. 7, *Theology, the New Covenant,* translated by Brian McNeil, CRV. Edinburgh: T&T Clark, 1989.

———. *The Office of Peter and the Structure of the Church.* Translated by Andrée Emery. San Francisco: Ignatius Press, 1986.

————. *The Theology of Henri de Lubac: An Overview.* Translated by Roxanne Mei Lum. San Francisco: Ignatius Press, 1991.

Barré, Jean-Luc. *Jacques et Raïssa Maritain: Les mendiants du ciel.* Paris: Stock, 1996.

Bars, Henry. "Gilson et Maritain." *Revue Thomiste* 7 (1979): 237–71.

Beach, John D. "Another Look at the Thomism of Étienne Gilson." *New Scholasticism* 50, no. 4 (Autumn 1976): 522–28.

Beaufret, Jean. "Sur la philosophie chrétienne." In *Étienne Gilson et nous: La philosophie et son histoire,* edited by Monique Couratier, 93–101. Paris: J. Vrin, 1980.

Beguin, Alfred. "L'affair Gilson." *Esprit* 19 (1951): 590–93.

Bergson, Henri. *Creative Evolution.* Translated by Arthur Mitchell. 1911. Reprint, Lanham: University Press of America, 1984. Originally published as *L'évolution créatrice* (Paris: Félix Alcan, 1908).

————. *An Introduction to Metaphysics.* Translated by T. E. Hulme. London: Macmillan, 1913. Originally published as *Introduction à la métaphysique* (Paris: E. Payen, [1903]).

————. *Time and Free Will: An Essay on the Immediate Data of Consciousness.* Translated by F. L. Pogson. London: S. Sonnenschein, 1910. Reprint, Montana: Kessinger Publishing Co., n.d. Originally published as *Essai sur les données immédiates de la conscience* (Paris: Félix Alcan, 1889).

Bonino, Serge-Thomas, OP. "Historiographie de l'école thomiste: le cas Gilson." In *Saint Thomas aux XXe siècle,* Actes du colloque du Centenaire de la *Revue Thomiste,* edited by Serge-Thomas Bonino, OP. Paris: Centre National de Livre-Saint Paul, 1994.

Bougerol, Jacques Guy. "Quand Étienne Gilson rencontre Saint Bonaventure." In *Étienne Gilson et nous: La philosophie et son histoire,* edited by Monique Couratier, 35–42. Paris: J. Vrin, 1980.

Bourke, Vernon J. "'Aeterni Patris,' Gilson, and Christian Philosophy." *Proceedings of the Catholic Philosophical Association* 53 (1979): 5–15.

Bury, J. P. T. *France, 1814–1940.* London: Methuen, 1949.

Chadwick, Owen. *A History of the Popes, 1830–1914.* Oxford: Clarendon Press, 1998.

Chenaux, Philippe. "La seconde vague thomiste." In *Intellectuels chrétiens et esprit des années 1920,* edited by Pierre Colin, 139–67. Paris: Cerf, 1997.

Chenu, Marie-Dominique, OP. *Une école de théologie: le Saulchoir.* Edited by Giuseppe Alberigo. 1937. Reprint, Paris: Éditions du Cerf, 1985.

————. "L'interprète de Saint Thomas d'Aquin." In *Étienne Gilson et nous: La philosophie et son histoire,* edited by Monique Couratier, 43–48. Paris: J. Vrin, 1980.

———. *Jacques Duquesne interroge le Père Chenu: un théologien en liberté.* Paris: Le Centurion, 1975.

———. "Les sens et les leçons d'une crise religieuse." *La vie intellectuelle* 13 (1931): 356–80.

———. "La théologie comme science au XIIIe siècle." *Archives d'histoire doctrinale et litteraire du moyen âge* 2 (1927): 31–71.

Cohn, Norman. *The Pursuit of the Millennium.* London: Secker and Warburg, 1957.

Cointet, Michèle. *L'église sous Vichy, 1940–1945: La repentence en question.* Paris: Librairie Académique Perrin, 1998.

Collins, James. *Three Paths in Philosophy.* Chicago: Henry Regnery, 1962.

Congar, Yves, OP. *Journal d'un théologien, 1946–1956.* Edited by Étienne Fouilloux. Paris: Cerf, 2000.

Conticello, Carmelo. "Métaphysique de l'être et théologie de la grâce dans le médiévalisme contemporain: É. Gilson et M.D. Chenu entre H. Bergson et A. Gardeil." In "Autour d'Étienne Gilson: Études et documents." Special issue, *Revue Thomiste* 94, no. 3 (July–September 1994): 431–59.

Courtine, Jean-Francois. "Gilson et Heidegger." In *Étienne Gilson et nous: La philosophie et son histoire,* edited by Monique Couratier, 103–16. Paris: J. Vrin, 1980.

Courtine-Denamy, Sylvie. *Three Women in Dark Times: Edith Stein, Hannah Arendt, Simone Weil.* Translated by G. M. Goshgarian. Ithaca: Cornell University Press, 2000.

D'Alverny, Marie-Thérèse. "Nécrologie Étienne Gilson (1884–1978)." *Cahiers de civilisation médièvale: X–XII siècles* 22 (1979): 425–30.

Daly, Gabriel, OSA. "Apologetics in the Modernist Period." In "Chesterton and the Modernist Crisis," edited by Aidan Nichols. Special issue, *Chesterton Review* 15 no. 1–2 (May 1989): 79–93.

Daniélou, Jean, SJ. "Étienne Gilson à l'Académie." *Études* 251 (April 1946): 263–64.

———. "Les orientations présentes de la pensée religieuse." *Études* 251 (April 1946): 5–21.

Del Noce, Augusto. "Thomism and the Critique of Rationalism: Gilson and Shestov." *Communio* 25, no. 4 (Winter 1998): 732–45.

de Lubac, Henri de. "Apologétique et théologie." *Nouvelle Revue Théologique* 57, no. 5 (May 1930): 361–78.

———. *At the Service of the Church: Henri de Lubac Reflects on the Circum-*

*stances that Occasioned His Writings.* Translated by Anne Elizabeth Englund. San Francisco: Ignatius Press, 1993.

———. "Causes internes de l'atténuation et de la disparition du sens du sacré." (1942). In de Lubac, *Théologie dans l'histoire II: Questions disputées et résistance au nazisme.* Paris: Desclée de Brouwer, 1990.

———. *Christian Resistance to Anti-Semitism: Memories from 1940–1944.* Translated by Sister Elizabeth Englund, OCD. San Francisco: Ignatius Press, 1990.

———. *The Mystery of the Supernatural.* Translated by Rosemary Sheed. London: Geoffrey Chapman, 1962.

———. *Surnaturel: études historiques.* Edited with an introduction by Michel Sales. 1946. Reprint, Paris: Desclée de Brouwer, 1991.

———. "Sur la philosophie chrétienne: Réflexions à la suite d'un débat." *Nouvelle revue théologique,* March 1936, 225–53.

Diodato, Roberto. "Note Sull' Ontologia dell' Arte di Étienne Gilson." *Rivista Filosofia Neoscholastica,* 78 (1986): 606–33.

Donneaud, Henry. "Note sur le *revelabile* selon Étienne Gilson." *Revue Thomiste* 96, no. 4 (1996): 633–52.

Dube, Wolf-Dieter. *The Expressionists.* Translated by Mary Whittall. London: Thames and Hudson, 1972.

Dunaway, John M., ed. *Exiles and Fugitives: The Letters of Jacques and Raissa Maritain, Allen Tate, and Caroline Gordon.* Baton Rouge: Louisiana State University Press, 1992.

Fessard, Gaston. *Au temps du prince-esclave: Écrits clandestins, 1940–1945.* Edited by Jacques Prévotat. Limoges: Critérion, 1989.

FitzGerald, Desmond J. "Étienne Gilson: From Historian to Philosopher." In *Thomistic Papers II,* edited by Leonard A. Kennedy, CSB, and Jack C. Marler, 29–55. Houston: Centre for Thomistic Studies, University of St. Thomas, 1986.

———. "Maritain and Gilson on the Challenge of Political Democracy." In *Reassessing the Liberal State: Reading Maritain's Man and the State,* edited by Timothy Fuller and John P. Hittinger, 61–72. Washington, DC.: American Maritain Association, distributed by Catholic University of America Press, 2001.

Floucat, Yves. "Gilson et la métaphysique thomiste de l'acte d'être." In "Autour d'Étienne Gilson: Études et documents." Special issue, *Revue Thomiste* 94, no. 3 (July–September 1994): 360–95.

Fouilloux, Étienne. *Une église en quête de liberté: La pensée catholique française entre modernisme et Vatican II, 1914–1926.* Paris: Desclée de Brouwer, 1988.

Frenay, Henri. *The Night Will End*. Translated by Dan Hofstadter. New York: McGraw-Hill, 1976.

Friedel, Helmut, and Annegret Hoberg. *The Blue Rider in the Lenbachhaus, Munich*. Munich: Prestel, 2000.

Gandillac, Maurice de. "Étienne Gilson: incomparable maître." In *Étienne Gilson et nous: la philosophie et son histoire,* edited by Monique Couratier, 9–11. Paris: J. Vrin, 1980.

Garrigou-Lagrange, Réginald, OP. "De intelligentia naturali et de primo objecto ab ipsa cognito." *Acta Pontificiae Academiae Romanae sancti Thomae Aquinatis et religionis catholicae* 6 (1939–1940): 137–54. Privately translated by Jason West.

———. *God: His Existence and His Nature; A Thomistic Solution of Certain Agnostic Antinomies*. 2 vols. Translated from the fifth French edition by Dom Bede Rose, OSB. St. Louis: B. Herder, 1939. Originally published as *Dieu, son existence et sa nature: solution thomiste des antinomies agnostiques* (Paris: G. Beauchense, 1914).

———. "La nouvelle théologie où va-t-elle?" *Angelicum* 23 (July–December 1946): 126–46.

———. Preface to *Du gouvernement royal,* by Thomas Aquinas. Translated by Claude Roguet and L'Abbé Poupon. Paris: Editions de la Gazette Francaise, 1926.

———. *Le sens commun: le philosophe de l'être et les formules dogmatiques,* 3rd ed. 1909. Reprint, Paris: Nouvelle Librairie Nationale, 1922.

Gleizes, A., and J. Metzinger. "Cubism." Translated by Robert L. Herbert. In *Modern Artists on Art: Ten Unabridged Essays,* edited by Robert L. Herbert, 1–18. Englewood Cliffs, NJ: Prentice-Hall, 1964. Essay originally published in 1912.

Golding, John. "Cubism." In *Concepts of Modern Art,* edited by Tony Richardson and Nikos Stangos, 53–81. New York: Harper and Row, 1974.

Gouhier, Henri. "De l'histoire de la philosophie à la philosophie." In *Étienne Gilson: philosophe de la chrétienté,* 53–69. Paris: Éditions du Cerf, 1949.

———. *Études sur l'histoire des idées en France depuis le XVIIe siècle*. Paris: J. Vrin, 1980.

———. "Post-Face: Etienne Gilson." In *Étienne Gilson et nous: la philosophie et son histoire,* edited by Monique Couratier, 145–57. Paris: J. Vrin, 1980.

Haight, Roger, SJ. *Jesus: Symbol of God*. New York: Orbis, 1999.

Hebblethwaite, Peter. "John XXIII." In *Modern Catholicism: Vatican II and After,* edited by Adrian Hastings, 27–34. New York: Oxford University Press, 1991.

Hellmann, John. "World War II and the Anti-Democratic Impulse in Catholicism." In *From Twilight to Dawn: The Cultural Vision of Jacques Maritain,* edited by Peter A. Redpath. Notre Dame: American Maritain Association, distributed by University of Notre Dame Press, 1990.

Hick, John. *The Metaphor of God Incarnate.* London: SCM, 1993.

Jaki, Stanley L. *Lord Gifford and His Lectures: A Centenary Retrospect.* Edinburgh: Scottish Academic Press, 1995.

Kandinsky, Wassily. *Concerning the Spiritual in Art.* Translated by M. T. H. Sadler. New York: Dover Publications, 1977. Originally published as *Über das Geistige in der Kunst* (1911).

———. "Reminiscences." Translated by Robert L. Herbert. In *Modern Artists on Art: Ten Unabridged Essays,* edited by Robert L. Herbert, 19–44. Englewood Cliffs, NJ: Prentice-Hall, 1964. Originally published 1913.

Kavanah, Aidan. "The Conciliar Documents (Sacrosanctum Concilium)." In *Modern Catholicism: Vatican II and After,* edited by Adrian Hastings, 68–73. Oxford University Press, 1991.

Kermode, Frank. "A Babylonish Dialect." In *T. S. Eliot: The Man and His Work,* edited by Allen Tate, 232–43. London: Penguin, 1966.

Knasas, John, FX. "Does Gilson Theologize Thomistic Metaphysics?" In *Thomistic Papers V,* edited by Thomas A. Russman, OFM Cap, 3–19. Houston: Centre for Thomistic Studies, University of St. Thomas, 1990.

———. "Gilson vs. Maritain: The Start of Thomistic Metaphysics." *Doctor Communis* 43 (1990): 250–65.

———. "A Heideggerian Critique of Aquinas and a Gilsonian Reply." *Thomist* 58, no. 3 (1994): 415–39.

Komonchak, Joseph. "A Hero of Vatican II: Yves Congar." *Commonweal* (December 1995).

———. "Theology and Culture at Mid-Century: The Example of Henri de Lubac." *Theological Studies* 51 (1990): 579–602.

Koninck, Charles de. "In Defence of Saint Thomas: A Reply to Father Eschmann's Attack on the Primacy of the Common Good." *Laval Théologique et Philosophique* 1, no. 2 (1945).

———. *De la primauté du bien commun contre les personnalistes: le principe de l'ordre nouveau.* Quebec: University of Laval, 1943.

Laberthonnière, L. *Le réalisme chrétien et l'idéalisme grec.* 1904. Reprint, Frankfurt: Minerva GMBH, 1975.

Lasserre, Pierre. *Le romanticisme française: essai sur la révolution dans les sentiments et dans les idées au XIX siècle.* 1907. Reprint, Paris: Librairie Garnier Frères, 1919.

Laudouze, André. *Dominicains Français et Action Française: 1899–1940.* Paris: Ouvrières, 1989.

Leo XIII (Pope). *Aeterni Patris.* Rome, 1879.

Lévy-Bruhl, Lucien. *Ethics and Moral Science.* Translated by Elizabeth Lee. London: Archibald Constable, 1905. Originally published as *La morale et la science des moeurs* (Paris: Félix Alcan, 1903).

Lewis, C. S. *The Pilgrim's Regress: An Allegorical Apology for Christianity, Reason, and Romanticism.* 1933. Reprint, Glasgow: William Collins Sons, 1977.

Loisy, Alfred. *L'évangile et l'église,* 4th ed. 1903. Reprint, Montier-en-De: Ceffonds, 1908.

———. *My Duel with the Vatican: The Autobiography of a Catholic Modernist.* Translated by Richard Wilson Boynton. 1924. Reprint, New York: Greenwood Press, 1968. Originally published as *Choses passées* (Paris: E. Nourry, 1913).

Lynton, Norbert. "Expressionism." In *Concepts of Modern Art,* edited by Tony Richardson and Nikos Stangos, 33–52. New York: Harper and Row, 1974.

Mandonnet, Pierre, OP. Review of *Le Thomisme: Introduction au système de S. Thomas d'Aquin* (*The Philosophy of Saint Thomas Aquinas,* translated by E. Bullough), by É. Gilson. Le Saulchoir, *Bulletin Thomiste* 1 (1924–1926): 132–36.

Marion, Jean-Luc. "L'instauration de la rupture: Gilson à la lecture de Descartes." In *Étienne Gilson et nous: La philosophie et son histoire,* edited by Monique Couratier, 13–34. Paris: J. Vrin, 1980.

Maritain, Jacques. *Art and Scholasticism and Other Essays.* Translated by J. F. Scanlan. 1930. Reprint, London: Sheed and Ward, 1943. Originally published as *Art et scolastique* (Paris: L'art catholique, 1920).

———. *Creative Intuition in Art and Poetry.* 1953. Reprint, Princeton: Princeton University Press, 1981.

———. *The Degrees of Knowledge.* Translated from the 2nd French edition by Bernard Wall. London: Geoffrey Bles, Centenary Press, 1937. Originally published as *Distinguer pour unir or Les Degrés du Savoir* (Paris: Desclée de Brouwer, 1932).

————. *Existence and the Existent.* Translated by Lewis Galantier and Gerald B. Phelan. 1948. Reprint Wesport, CT: Greenwood Press, 1964. Originally published as *Court traité de l'existence et de l'existant* (Paris: Hartmann, 1947).

————. *Man and the State.* Edited by Richard Sullivan. 1951. Reprint, London: Hollis and Carter, 1954.

————. "Réflexions sur la nature blessée." *Revue thomiste* 1 (1968): 5–40. Reprinted in *Approches sans entraves,* chapter 11, "Pour une épistémologie existentielle: Réflexions sur la nature blessée" (Paris: Librairie Arthème Fayard, 1973).

————. *The Rights of Man and Natural Law.* London: Geoffrey Bles, 1944. Originally published as *Les droits de l'homme et la loi naturelle* (New York: Éditions de la Maison française, 1942).

————. *Sept leçons sur l'être et les premiers principes de la raison spéculative.* Paris: Tequi, n.d.

————. *True Humanism.* Translated by M. R. Adamson. London: Geoffrey Bles, 1938. Originally published as *Humanisme intégral: problèmes temporels et spirituals d'une nouvelle chrétienté* (Paris: F. Aubier, 1936).

————. *Primauté du spirituel.* Paris: Librarie Plon, 1927.

Martindale, Charles. "Introduction: The Classic of All Europe." In *The Cambridge Companion to Virgil,* edited by Charles Martindale, 1–18. Cambridge: Cambridge University Press, 1997.

Massis, Henri. *Maurras et notre temps: Entretiens et souvenirs.* Paris: Librairie Plon, 1961.

Maurer, Armand, CSB. "Gilson on Linguistics and Philosophy of Art." *Doctor Communis* 38, no. 3 (September–December 1985): 335–44.

————. "Gilson's Use of History in Philosophy." In *Thomistic Papers V,* edited by Thomas A. Russman, OFM Cap, 25–36. Houston: Centre for Thomistic Studies, University of St. Thomas, 1990.

Maurras, Charles. "Le dilemme de Marc Sangnier: Essai sur la démocratie religieuse." In *La démocratie religieuse.* Paris: Nouvelle Librarie Nationale, Paris, 1921. First article in the series printed in *L'Action française,* July 1, 1904; second article, July 15, 1904. First published as a book in 1906.

Milbank, John, and Catherine Pickstock. *Truth in Aquinas.* London: Routledge, 2001.

McCabe, Herbert, OP. *God Matters.* London: Mowbray, 1987.

McCool, Gerald A., SJ. *From Unity to Pluralism: The Internal Evolution of Thomism.* New York: Fordham University Press, 1989.

McGrath, Margaret. *Étienne Gilson: A Bibliography/Une Bibliographie.* Toronto: Pontifical Institute of Mediaeval Studies, 1982.

McInerny, Ralph. "Gilson's Theory of Art." *Doctor Communis* 38, no. 3 (September–December 1985): 345–50.

———. "Maritain, Jacques (1882–1973)." *Routledge Encyclopedia of Philosophy,* edited by Edward Craig, 101–5. London: Routledge, 1998.

McLeod, Hugh. *Religion and the People of Western Europe, 1789–1970.* Oxford: Oxford University Press, 1981.

Nédoncelle, Maurice. *Is There a Christian Philosophy?* Translated by Illtyd Trethowan. London: Burns and Oates, 1960.

Noonan, John. "The Existentialism of Etienne Gilson." *New Scholasticism* 24 (1950): 417–38.

Orwell, George. "Inside the Whale." In *The Penguin Essays of George Orwell,* 107–39. London: Penguin, 1984.

Pegis, Anton. "Gilson and Thomism." *Thought* 21 (1946): 435–54.

Pezet, Ernest. *Chrétiens au service de la cité: de Léon XIII au Sillon et au MRP 1891–1965.* Paris: Nouvelles Editions Latines, 1965.

Pius X (Pope). *Pascendi Dominici Gregis.* Rome, September 8, 1907.

Pius XII (Pope). *Humani Generis.* Rome, August 1950.

Prévotat, Jacques. "Autour du parti de l'intelligence." In *Intellectuels chrétiens et esprit des années 1920,* edited by Pierre Colin, 169–93. Paris: Cerf, 1997.

Prouvost, Géry. "Avant-propos." In "Autour d'Étienne Gilson: Études et documents." Special issue, *Revue Thomiste* 94, no. 3 (July–September 1994): 355–59.

———. "Les relations entre philosophie et théologie chez É Gilson et les thomistes contemporains." In "Autour d'Étienne Gilson: Études et documents." Special issue, *Revue Thomiste* 94, no. 3 (July–September 1994): 413–30.

Radcliffe, Timothy, OP. "The Wellspring of Hope: Study and the Annunciation of the Good News." In *Sing a New Song: The Christian Vocation,* 54–81. Dublin: Dominican Publications, 1999.

Riet, Georges Van. *Thomistic Epistemology: Studies Concerning the Problem of Cognition in the Contemporary Thomistic School.* 2 vols. Translated by Gabriel Franks, Donald G. McCarthy, and George E. Hertrich. St. Louis: B. Herder, 1963–1964. Originally published as *L'epistémologie thomiste: recherches sur le problème de la connaissance dans l'école thomiste contemporaine* (Louvain: Bibliothèque Philosophique de Louvain, 1946).

Schmitz, Kenneth L. *What Has Clio to Do with Athena? Étienne Gilson: Historian and Philosopher.* Étienne Gilson Series no. 10. Toronto: Pontifical Institute of Medieval Studies, 1987.

Shook, Laurence K., CSB. *Étienne Gilson.* Toronto: Pontifical Institute of Mediaeval Studies, 1984.

———. "Maritain and Gilson: Early Relations." In *Thomistic Papers II,* edited by Leonard A. Kennedy, CSB, and Jack C. Marler, 7–27. Houston: Centre for Thomistic Studies, University of St. Thomas, 1986.

Simon, Yves R. *The Road to Vichy, 1918–1938,* rev. ed. Translated by James A. Corbett and George J. McMorrow. Lanham: University Press of America, 1988. Originally published as *La grande crise de la République française: observations sur le politique des Français de 1918 à 1938* (Montreal: Éditions de l'Arbre, 1942).

Smith, Gerard. "A Date in the History of Epistemology." *Thomist* 6 (1943): 246–55.

Sutton, Michael. *Nationalism, Positivism, and Catholicism: The Politics of Charles Maurras and French Catholics, 1890–1914.* Cambridge: Cambridge University Press, 1982.

Tate, Allen. "Religion and the Old South." [1930]. In *On the Limits of Poetry: Selected Essays, 1928–1948,* 305–22. New York: Swallow Press, 1948.

Van Steenberghen, Fernand. "Étienne Gilson et l'université de Louvain." *Revue philosophique de Louvain* 85 (1987): 5–21.

———. "Étienne Gilson, historien de la pensée médiévale." *Revue philosophique de Louvain* 77 (1979): 487–508.

———. "La II journée d'études de la société thomiste et la notion de 'philosophie chrétienne.'" *Revue néo-scholastique de philosophie* 35 (1933): 539–54.

———. "Les lettres d'Étienne Gilson au P. de Lubac." *Revue philosophique de Louvain* 87 (1989): 324–31.

———. "In Memoriam Étienne Gilson." *Revue philosophique de Louvain* 76 (1978): 538–45.

———. "Un incident révélateur au congrès thomiste de 1950." *Revue philosophique de Louvain* 86 (1988): 379–90.

Weber, Eugen. *Action Française: Royalism and Reaction in Twentieth-Century France.* California: Stanford University Press, 1962.

Weinandy, Thomas G., OFM Cap. *Does God Suffer?* Edinburgh: T &T Clark, 2000.

————. *In the Likeness of Sinful Flesh: An Essay on the Humanity of Christ.* Edinburgh: T&T Clark, 1993.

West, J. L. A. "The Thomistic Debate Concerning the Existence and Nature of Christian Philosophy: Toward a Synthesis." *The Modern Schoolman* 77 (November 1999): 49–72.

Wilhemsen, Frederick. "Existence and Esse." *New Scholasticism* 50 (1976): 20–45.

Wippel, John F. *Metaphysical Themes in Thomas Aquinas.* Washington, DC: Catholic University of America Press, 1984.

Zeldin, Theodore. *France, 1848–1945: Intellect and Pride.* Oxford: Oxford University Press, 1980.

# Index of Persons